# Spring Security 3.1

Secure your web applications from hackers with this step-by-step guide

**Robert Winch**

**Peter Mularien**

BIRMINGHAM - MUMBAI

# Spring Security 3.1

Copyright © 2012 Packt Publishing

All rights reserved. No part of this book may be reproduced, stored in a retrieval system, or transmitted in any form or by any means, without the prior written permission of the publisher, except in the case of brief quotations embedded in critical articles or reviews.

Every effort has been made in the preparation of this book to ensure the accuracy of the information presented. However, the information contained in this book is sold without warranty, either express or implied. Neither the author, nor Packt Publishing, and its dealers and distributors will be held liable for any damages caused or alleged to be caused directly or indirectly by this book.

Packt Publishing has endeavored to provide trademark information about all of the companies and products mentioned in this book by the appropriate use of capitals. However, Packt Publishing cannot guarantee the accuracy of this information.

First published: May 2010

Second published: December 2012

Production Reference: 1191212

Published by Packt Publishing Ltd.
Livery Place
35 Livery Street
Birmingham B3 2PB, UK.

ISBN 978-1-84951-826-0

www.packtpub.com

Cover Image by Asher Wishkerman (wishkerman@hotmail.com)

# Credits

**Authors**
Robert Winch
Peter Mularien

**Reviewers**
Marten Deinum
Brian Relph
Bryan Kelly

**Acquisition Editor**
Usha Iyer

**Lead Technical Editor**
Susmita Panda

**Technical Editors**
Lubna Shaikh
Worrell Lewis

**Copy Editors**
Brandt D'mello
Insiya Morbiwala
Alfida Paiva
Laxmi Subramanian

**Project Coordinator**
Michelle Quadros

**Proofreader**
Mario Cecere

**Indexers**
Monica Ajmera
Rekha Nair

**Graphics**
Aditi Gajjar

**Production Coordinator**
Arvindkumar Gupta

**Cover Work**
Arvindkumar Gupta

# About the Author

**Robert Winch** is currently a Senior Software Engineer at VMware and is the project lead of the Spring Security framework. In the past, he has worked as a Software Architect at Cerner, the largest provider of electronic medical systems in the U.S., securing health care applications. Throughout his career, he has developed hands on experience integrating Spring Security with an array of security standards (that is, LDAP, SAML, CAS, OAuth, and so on). Before he was employed at Cerner, he worked as an independent web contractor, in proteomics research at Loyola University Chicago, and on the Globus Toolkit at Argonne National Laboratory.

# Acknowledgement

Before we get started, I would like to extend my thanks to those who helped me make this book possible. First, I would like to thank Peter Mularien, for recommending me to Packt Publishing to write the second edition of his book *Spring Security 3, Packt Publishing*. It was very useful to have such a sound foundation to start Spring Security 3.1.

Writing a book is a very involved process and there were many that played a key part in the book's success. I would like to thank all the members of the team at Packt Publishing for making this possible. To Usha Iyer, for guiding me through the process; to Theresa Chettiar, for ensuring that I stayed focused and on time; and to Susmita Panda, for her diligence in reviewing the book. Thank you to my technical reviewers Peter Mularien, Marten Deinum, Brian Relph, and Bryan Kelly. Your feedback was critical in ensuring this book's success.

This book, the Spring Security Framework, and the Spring Framework are all made possible by the large and active community. Thank you to all of those who contribute to the Spring Framework through patches, JIRA submissions, and answering other user's questions. Thanks to Ben Alex for creating Spring Security. I'd like to extend my special thanks to Luke Taylor for his leadership of Spring Security. It was through his mentoring that I have grown into a leader in the Spring Security community.

Thank you to my friends and family for your continued support. Last, but certainly not least, I would like to thank my wife, Amanda. Without your love, patience, and encouragement, I would have never been able to finish this book. Thank you for taking such good care of me and reminding me to eat.

**Peter Mularien** is an experienced software architect and engineer, and the author of the book *Spring Security 3, Packt Publishing*. Peter currently works for a large financial services company and has over 12 years consulting and product experience in Java, Spring, Oracle, and many other enterprise technologies. He is also the reviewer of this book.

# About the Reviewers

**Marten Deinum** is a Java/software consultant working for Conspect. He has developed and architected software, primarily in Java, for small and large companies. He is an enthusiastic open source user and longtime fan, user, and advocate of the Spring Framework. He has held a number of positions including Software Engineer, Development Lead, Coach, and also as a Java and Spring Trainer. When not working or answering questions on the Spring Framework forums, he can be found in the water training for the triathlon or under the water diving or guiding other people around.

**Brian Relph** is currently a Software Engineer at Google, with a focus on web application development. In the past, he has worked as a Software Architect at Cerner, the largest provider of electronic medical systems in the U.S. Throughout his career, he has developed hands on experience in integrating Spring and Spring Security with an array of Java standards (that is, LDAP, CAS, OAuth, and so on), and other open source frameworks (Hibernate, Struts, and so on). He has also worked as an independent Web Contractor.

**Bryan Kelly** is currently a Software Architect at Cerner Corporation, the largest provider of electronic medical systems in the U.S. At Cerner, his primary responsibility is designing and implementing solutions that use the Spring Framework, Spring Security, and Hibernate for Web Applications and RESTful Web Services. Previously, he has worked as a Software Developer for CJK Software Consultants. Throughout his career, he has developed hands on experience in integrating Spring Security with an array of security standards (that is, LDAP, SAML v1 and v2, CAS, OAuth, OpenID, and so on).

> I would like to personally thank Rob Winch for the opportunity to be a technical reviewer of this book. I would like to thank my wife Melinda Kelly for her unwavering support while I used my personal time to review this book. I would also like to thank John Krzysztow of CJK Software Consultants for giving a high schooler a chance at professional software development.

# www.PacktPub.com

## Support files, eBooks, discount offers and more

You might want to visit www.PacktPub.com for support files and downloads related to your book.

Did you know that Packt offers eBook versions of every book published, with PDF and ePub files available? You can upgrade to the eBook version at www.PacktPub.com and as a print book customer, you are entitled to a discount on the eBook copy. Get in touch with us at service@packtpub.com for more details.

At www.PacktPub.com, you can also read a collection of free technical articles, sign up for a range of free newsletters and receive exclusive discounts and offers on Packt books and eBooks.

http://PacktLib.PacktPub.com

Do you need instant solutions to your IT questions? PacktLib is Packt's online digital book library. Here, you can access, read and search across Packt's entire library of books.

## Why Subscribe?

- Fully searchable across every book published by Packt
- Copy and paste, print and bookmark content
- On demand and accessible via web browser

## Free Access for Packt account holders

If you have an account with Packt at www.PacktPub.com, you can use this to access PacktLib today and view nine entirely free books. Simply use your login credentials for immediate access.

*To my wife for your love, patience, and support throughout this endeavor.*

# Table of Contents

| | |
|---|---|
| **Preface** | **1** |
| **Chapter 1: Anatomy of an Unsafe Application** | **7** |
|    Security audit | 8 |
|    About the sample application | 8 |
|    The JBCP calendar application architecture | 10 |
|    Application technology | 11 |
|    Reviewing the audit results | 12 |
|    Authentication | 14 |
|    Authorization | 16 |
|    Database credential security | 18 |
|    Sensitive information | 19 |
|    Transport-level protection | 19 |
|    Using Spring Security 3.1 to address security concerns | 19 |
|    Why Spring Security | 20 |
|    Summary | 20 |
| **Chapter 2: Getting Started with Spring Security** | **21** |
|    Hello Spring Security | 22 |
|       Importing the sample application | 22 |
|       Updating your dependencies | 22 |
|          Using Spring 3.1 and Spring Security 3.1 | 23 |
|       Implementing a Spring Security XML configuration file | 24 |
|       Updating your web.xml file | 27 |
|          ContextLoaderListener | 27 |
|          ContextLoaderListener versus DispatcherServlet | 28 |
|          springSecurityFilterChain | 29 |
|          DelegatingFilterProxy | 30 |
|          FilterChainProxy | 30 |
|       Running a secured application | 31 |
|       Common problems | 31 |

## A little bit of polish — 32
### Customizing login — 33
#### Configuring logout — 36
#### The page isn't redirecting properly — 38
#### Basic role-based authorization — 39
#### Expression-based authorization — 43
#### Conditionally displaying authentication information — 44
#### Customizing the behavior after login — 46
### Summary — 48
## Chapter 3: Custom Authentication — 49
### JBCP Calendar architecture — 49
#### CalendarUser — 50
#### Event — 50
#### CalendarService — 50
#### UserContext — 51
#### SpringSecurityUserContext — 52
### Logging in new users using SecurityContextHolder — 54
#### Managing users in Spring Security — 55
#### Logging in a new user to an application — 56
#### Updating SignupController — 57
### Creating a custom UserDetailsService object — 58
#### CalendarUserDetailsService — 58
#### Configuring UserDetailsService — 60
#### Removing references to UserDetailsManager — 60
#### CalendarUserDetails — 61
#### SpringSecurityUserContext simplifications — 62
##### Displaying custom user attributes — 63
### Creating a custom AuthenticationProvider object — 63
#### CalendarUserAuthenticationProvider — 64
#### Configuring CalendarUserAuthenticationProvider — 66
#### Authenticating with different parameters — 66
##### DomainUsernamePasswordAuthenticationToken — 67
##### Updating CalendarUserAuthenticationProvider — 67
##### Adding domain to the login page — 68
##### DomainUsernamePasswordAuthenticationFilter — 69
##### Updating our configuration — 70
### Which authentication method to use — 73
### Summary — 74
## Chapter 4: JDBC-based Authentication — 75
### Using Spring Security's default JDBC authentication — 75
#### Required dependencies — 76
#### Using the H2 database — 77

[ ii ]

| | |
|---|---|
| Provided JDBC scripts | 77 |
| Configuring the H2-embedded database | 77 |
| Configuring JDBC UserDetailsManager | 79 |
| Spring Security's default user schema | 79 |
| Defining users | 80 |
| Defining user authorities | 80 |
| **UserDetailsManager** | **81** |
| What other features does UserDetailsManager provide out of the box | 81 |
| **Group-based access control** | **82** |
| Configuring group-based access control | 83 |
| Configuring JdbcUserDetailsManager to use groups | 83 |
| Utilize the GBAC JDBC scripts | 84 |
| Group-based schema | 85 |
| Group authority mappings | 85 |
| **Support for a custom schema** | **86** |
| Determining the correct JDBC SQL queries | 87 |
| Updating the SQL scripts that are loaded | 87 |
| CalendarUser authority SQL | 88 |
| Insert custom authorities | 88 |
| Configuring the JdbcUserDetailsManager to use custom SQL queries | 89 |
| **Configuring secure passwords** | **91** |
| PasswordEncoder | 92 |
| Configuring password encoding | 94 |
| Configuring the PasswordEncoder | 94 |
| Making Spring Security aware of the PasswordEncoder | 94 |
| Hashing the stored passwords | 95 |
| Hashing a new user's passwords | 96 |
| Not quite secure | 97 |
| Would you like some salt with that password | 97 |
| Using salt in Spring Security | 98 |
| **Summary** | **102** |
| **Chapter 5: LDAP Directory Services** | **103** |
| **Understanding LDAP** | **104** |
| **LDAP** | **104** |
| **Common LDAP attribute names** | **105** |
| **Updating our dependencies** | **107** |
| **Configuring embedded LDAP integration** | **108** |
| **Configuring an LDAP server reference** | **109** |
| Enabling the LDAP AuthenticationProviderNext interface | 110 |
| **Troubleshooting embedded LDAP** | **110** |
| **Understanding how Spring LDAP authentication works** | **111** |

| | |
|---|---|
| **Authenticating user credentials** | **112** |
| Demonstrating authentication with Apache Directory Studio | 113 |
| **Binding anonymously to LDAP** | **113** |
| **Searching for the user** | **114** |
| **Binding as a user to LDAP** | **115** |
| **Determining user role membership** | **116** |
| Determining roles with Apache Directory Studio | 117 |
| **Mapping additional attributes of UserDetails** | **119** |
| **Advanced LDAP configuration** | **120** |
| **Sample JBCP LDAP users** | **120** |
| Password comparison versus bind authentication | 120 |
| **Configuring basic password comparison** | **121** |
| **LDAP password encoding and storage** | **122** |
| The drawbacks of a password comparison authenticator | 123 |
| **Configuring UserDetailsContextMapper** | **124** |
| Implicit configuration of UserDetailsContextMapper | 124 |
| **Viewing additional user details** | **125** |
| **Using an alternate password attribute** | **127** |
| **Using LDAP as UserDetailsService** | **128** |
| **Configuring LdapUserDetailsService** | **129** |
| Updating AccountController to use LdapUserDetailsService | 130 |
| **Integrating with an external LDAP server** | **131** |
| **Explicit LDAP bean configuration** | **132** |
| Configuring an external LDAP server reference | 132 |
| **Configuring LdapAuthenticationProvider** | **133** |
| Delegating role discovery to UserDetailsService | 135 |
| **Integrating with Microsoft Active Directory via LDAP** | **137** |
| Built-In Active Directory support in Spring Security 3.1 | 140 |
| **Summary** | **141** |
| **Chapter 6: Remember-me Services** | **143** |
| **What is remember-me** | **143** |
| **Dependencies** | **144** |
| **The token-based remember-me feature** | **145** |
| Configuring the token-based remember-me feature | 145 |
| How the token-based remember-me feature works | 146 |
| MD5 | 147 |
| Remember-me signature | 148 |
| Token-based remember-me configuration directives | 149 |
| **Is remember-me secure** | **150** |
| Authorization rules for remember-me | 151 |

*Table of Contents*

| | |
|---|---|
| **Persistent remember-me** | **152** |
| Using the persistent-based remember-me feature | 153 |
| Adding SQL to create the remember-me schema | 153 |
| Initializing the data source with the remember-me schema | 153 |
| Configuring the persistent-based remember-me feature | 154 |
| How does the persistent-based remember-me feature work | 154 |
| Are database-backed persistent tokens more secure | 155 |
| Cleaning up the expired remember-me sessions | 156 |
| **Remember-me architecture** | **158** |
| Remember-me and the user lifecycle | 159 |
| **Restricting the remember-me feature to an IP address** | **160** |
| Custom cookie and HTTP parameter names | 163 |
| **Summary** | **164** |
| **Chapter 7: Client Certificate Authentication** | **165** |
| **How client certificate authentication works** | **166** |
| **Setting up client certificate authentication infrastructure** | **168** |
| Understanding the purpose of a public key infrastructure | 168 |
| Creating a client certificate key pair | 169 |
| Configuring the Tomcat trust store | 170 |
| Importing the certificate key pair into a browser | 172 |
| Using Firefox | 172 |
| Using Chrome | 173 |
| Using Internet Explorer | 173 |
| Wrapping up testing | 174 |
| Troubleshooting client certificate authentication | 175 |
| **Configuring client certificate authentication in Spring Security** | **176** |
| Configuring client certificate authentication using the security namespace | 177 |
| How Spring Security uses certificate information | 178 |
| How Spring Security certificate authentication works | 178 |
| Handling unauthenticated requests with AuthenticationEntryPoint | 181 |
| Supporting dual-mode authentication | 182 |
| **Configuring client certificate authentication using Spring Beans** | **184** |
| Additional capabilities of bean-based configuration | 185 |
| **Considerations when implementing Client Certificate authentication** | **187** |
| **Summary** | **188** |
| **Chapter 8: Opening up to OpenID** | **189** |
| **The promising world of OpenID** | **189** |
| **Signing up for an OpenID** | **191** |
| **Enabling OpenID authentication with Spring Security** | **191** |
| **Additional required dependencies** | **192** |
| Configuring OpenID support in Spring Security | 193 |

[ v ]

Adding OpenID users — 195
CalendarUserDetailsService lookup by OpenID — 195
**The OpenID user registration problem** — **196**
How are OpenID identifiers resolved — 197
**Implementing user registration with OpenID** — **200**
Registering OpenIDAuthenticationUserDetailsService — 200
**Attribute Exchange** — **203**
Enabling AX in Spring Security OpenID — 204
Configuring different attributes for each OpenID Provider — 207
**Usability enhancements** — **208**
**Automatic redirection to the OpenID Provider** — **210**
Conditional automatic redirection — 211
**Is OpenID Secure** — **212**
**Summary** — **213**

## Chapter 9: Single Sign-on with Central Authentication Service — 215

**Introducing Central Authentication Service** — **216**
High-level CAS authentication flow — 216
Spring Security and CAS — 218
Required dependencies — 219
CAS installation and configuration — 220
**Configuring basic CAS integration** — **220**
Creating the CAS ServiceProperties object — 222
Adding the CasAuthenticationEntryPoint — 223
Enabling CAS ticket verification — 224
Proving authenticity with the CasAuthenticationProvider — 226
**Single logout** — **230**
Configuring single logout — 231
Clustered environments — 233
**Proxy ticket authentication for stateless services** — **234**
Configuring proxy ticket authentication — 235
Using proxy tickets — 237
Authenticating proxy tickets — 238
**Customizing the CAS Server** — **240**
CAS Maven WAR Overlay — 240
How CAS internal authentication works — 241
Configuring CAS to connect to our embedded LDAP server — 242
**Getting UserDetails from a CAS assertion** — **245**
Returning LDAP attributes in the CAS Response — 246
Mapping LDAP attributes to CAS attributes — 246
Authorizing CAS Services to access custom attributes — 247

| | |
|---|---|
| Getting UserDetails from a CAS assertion | 248 |
| GrantedAuthorityFromAssertionAttributesUser Details Service | 248 |
| Alternative ticket authentication using SAML 1.1 | 249 |
| How is attribute retrieval useful | 250 |
| **Additional CAS capabilities** | **250** |
| **Summary** | **251** |
| **Chapter 10: Fine-grained Access Control** | **253** |
| **Maven dependencies** | **254** |
| **Spring Expression Language (SpEL) integration** | **254** |
| WebSecurityExpressionRoot | 256 |
| Using the request attribute | 256 |
| Using hasIpAddress | 257 |
| MethodSecurityExpressionRoot | 258 |
| **Page-level authorization** | **258** |
| Conditional rendering with Spring Security tag library | 259 |
| Conditional rendering based on URL access rules | 259 |
| Conditional rendering using SpEL | 261 |
| Using controller logic to conditionally render content | 261 |
| WebInvocationPrivilegeEvaluator | 263 |
| What is the best way to configure in-page authorization | 264 |
| **Method-level security** | **265** |
| Why we secure in layers | 266 |
| Securing the business tier | 266 |
| Adding @PreAuthorize method annotation | 267 |
| Instructing Spring Security to use method annotations | 268 |
| Validating method security | 268 |
| Interface-based proxies | 269 |
| JSR-250 compliant standardized rules | 270 |
| Method security using Spring's @Secured annotation | 271 |
| Method security rules using aspect-oriented programming | 271 |
| Method security rules using bean decorators | 273 |
| Method security rules incorporating method parameters | 275 |
| Method security rules incorporating returned values | 277 |
| Securing method data through role-based filtering | 277 |
| Pre-filtering collections with @PreFilter | 279 |
| Comparing method authorization types | 279 |
| Practical considerations for annotation-based security | 280 |
| Method security on Spring MVC controllers | 280 |
| Class-based proxies | 282 |
| Class-based proxy limitations | 282 |
| **Summary** | **284** |
| **Chapter 11: Access Control Lists** | **285** |
| **Using access control lists for business object security** | **285** |
| Access control lists in Spring Security | 287 |

*Table of Contents*

| | |
|---|---|
| **Basic configuration of Spring Security ACL support** | **289** |
| Maven dependencies | 289 |
| Defining a simple target scenario | 289 |
| Adding ACL tables to the H2 database | 290 |
| Configuring SecurityExpressionHandler | 293 |
| AclPermissionCacheOptimizer | 294 |
| PermissionEvaluator | 295 |
| JdbcMutableAclService | 295 |
| BasicLookupStrategy | 296 |
| EhCacheBasedAclCache | 297 |
| ConsoleAuditLogger | 298 |
| AclAuthorizationStrategyImpl | 298 |
| Creating a simple ACL entry | 299 |
| **Advanced ACL topics** | **302** |
| How permissions work | 302 |
| **Custom ACL permission declaration** | **305** |
| Enabling your JSPs with the Spring Security JSP tag library through ACL | 307 |
| **Mutable ACLs and authorization** | **310** |
| Adding ACLs to newly created Events | 311 |
| **Considerations for a typical ACL deployment** | **312** |
| About ACL scalability and performance modelling | 313 |
| Do not discount custom development costs | 315 |
| **Should I use Spring Security ACL** | **316** |
| **Summary** | **317** |
| **Chapter 12: Custom Authorization** | **319** |
| **How requests are authorized** | **319** |
| Configuration of access decision aggregation | 323 |
| **Configuring to use a UnanimousBased access decision manager** | **323** |
| Expression-based request authorization | 325 |
| **Customizing request authorization** | **326** |
| Dynamically defining access control to URLs | 326 |
| JdbcRequestConfigMappingService | 326 |
| FilterInvocationServiceSecurityMetadataSource | 328 |
| BeanPostProcessor to extend namespace configuration | 330 |
| Removing our <intercept-url> elements | 331 |
| Creating a custom expression | 331 |
| CustomWebSecurityExpressionRoot | 331 |
| CustomWebSecurityExpressionHandler | 333 |
| Configuring and using CustomWebSecurityExpressionHandler | 334 |
| How does method security work | 334 |

| Creating a custom PermissionEvaluator | **338** |
|---|---|
| CalendarPermissionEvaluator | 338 |
| Configuring CalendarPermissionEvaluator | 340 |
| Securing our CalendarService | 340 |
| Benefits of a custom PermissionEvaluator | 341 |
| **Summary** | **342** |

## Chapter 13: Session Management — 343

| Configuring session fixation protection | **343** |
|---|---|
| Understanding session fixation attacks | 344 |
| Preventing session fixation attacks with Spring Security | 345 |
| Simulating a session fixation attack | 346 |
| Comparing session-fixation-protection options | 349 |
| **Restricting the number of concurrent sessions per user** | **349** |
| Configuring concurrent session control | 350 |
| Understanding concurrent session control | 351 |
| Testing concurrent session control | 352 |
| Configuring expired session redirect | 352 |
| Common problems with concurrency control | 353 |
| Preventing authentication instead of forcing logout | 354 |
| Other benefits of concurrent session control | 355 |
|     Displaying active sessions for a user | 357 |
| **How Spring Security uses the HttpSession** | **359** |
| HttpSessionSecurityContextRepository | 360 |
| Configuring how Spring Security uses HttpSession | 360 |
| Debugging with Spring Security's DebugFilter | 361 |
| **Summary** | **363** |

## Chapter 14: Integrating with Other Frameworks — 365

| Integrating with Java Server Faces (JSF) | **366** |
|---|---|
| Customizations to support AJAX | 366 |
|     DelegatingAuthenticationEntryPoint | 366 |
|     AjaxRequestMatcher | 367 |
|     Http401EntryPoint | 368 |
|     Configuration updates | 368 |
|     JavaScript updates | 370 |
| Proxy-based authorization with JSF | 371 |
| Custom login page in JSF | 371 |
| Spring Security Facelets tag library | 374 |
| **Google Web Toolkit (GWT) integration** | **377** |
| Spring Roo and GWT | 377 |
| Spring Security setup | 378 |
| GwtAuthenticationEntryPoint | 378 |

| | |
|---|---|
| GWT client updates | 379 |
| AuthRequestTransport | 379 |
| AuthRequiredEvent | 380 |
| LoginOnAuthRequired | 381 |
| Configuring GWT | 382 |
| Spring Security configuration | 383 |
| Method security | 384 |
| Method security with Spring Roo | 386 |
| Authorization with AspectJ | 386 |
| **Summary** | **388** |
| **Chapter 15: Migration to Spring Security 3.1** | **389** |
| Migrating from Spring Security 2 | 390 |
| Enhancements in Spring Security 3 | 390 |
| Changes to configuration in Spring Security 3 | 391 |
| Rearranged AuthenticationManager configuration | 391 |
| New configuration syntax for session management options | 393 |
| Changes to custom filter configuration | 393 |
| Changes to CustomAfterInvocationProvider | 395 |
| Minor configuration changes | 395 |
| Changes to packages and classes | 396 |
| Updates in Spring Security 3.1 | 398 |
| Summary | 399 |
| **Appendix: Additional Reference Material** | **401** |
| Getting started with the JBCP Calendar sample code | 401 |
| Creating a new workspace | 402 |
| Sample code structure | 402 |
| Importing the samples | 403 |
| Running the samples in Spring Tool Suite | 405 |
| Creating a Tomcat v7.0 server | 405 |
| Starting the samples within Spring Tool Suite | 407 |
| Shutting down the samples within Spring Tool Suite | 408 |
| Removing previous versions of the samples | 408 |
| Using HTTPS within Spring Tool Suite | 409 |
| Default URLs processed by Spring Security | 411 |
| Logical filter names migration reference | 412 |
| HTTPS setup in Tomcat | 413 |
| Generating a server certificate | 413 |
| Configuring Tomcat Connector to use SSL | 415 |
| Basic Tomcat SSL termination guide | 416 |
| Supplimentary materials | 417 |
| **Index** | **419** |

# Preface

Welcome to the world of Spring Security 3.1! We're certainly pleased that you have acquired the only published book, fully devoted to Spring Security 3.1. Before we get started with the book, we would like to give an overview of how the book is organized and how you can get the most out of it.

Once you have completed reading this book, you should be familiar with key security concepts and understand how to solve the majority of the real-world problems that you will need to solve with Spring Security. Through this discovery, you will gain an in-depth understanding of the Spring Security architecture, which will allow you to handle any unexpected use cases the book does not cover.

The book is divided into four main sections. The first section (Chapters 1 and 2) provides an introduction to Spring Security and allows you to get started with Spring Security quickly. The second section (Chapters 3 to 9) provides in-depth instructions for integrating with a number of different authentication technologies. The next section (Chapters 10 to 12) explains how Spring Security's authorization support works. Finally, the last section (Chapters 13 to 15) provides specialized topics and guides that help you perform very specific tasks.

Security is a very interwoven concept and as such so are many of the topics in the book. However, once you have read through Chapters 1 to 3, each chapter in the book is fairly independent of another. This means that you can easily skip from chapter to chapter and still understand what is happening. The goal was to provide a cookbook style guide that when read in its entirety still gave a clear understanding of Spring Security.

Preface

The book uses a simple Spring Web MVC-based application to illustrate how to solve real-world problems. The application is intended to be very simple and straightforward, and purposely contains very little functionality—the goal of this application is to encourage you to focus on the Spring Security concepts, and not get tied up in the complexities of application development. You will have a much easier time following the book if you take the time to review the sample application source code, and try to follow along with the exercises. Some tips on getting started are found in the *Getting started with the JBCP Calendar sample code* section in *Appendix, Additional Reference Material*.

## What this book covers

*Chapter 1, Anatomy of an Unsafe Application*, covers a hypothetical security audit of our `Calendar` application, illustrating common issues that can be resolved through proper application of Spring Security. You will learn about some basic security terminology and review some prerequisites for getting the sample application up and running.

*Chapter 2, Getting Started with Spring Security*, demonstrates the "Hello World" installation of Spring Security. Afterwards, this chapter walks the reader through some of the most common customizations of Spring Security.

*Chapter 3, Custom Authentication*, incrementally explains the Spring Security authentication architecture by customizing key pieces of the authentication infrastructure to address real-world problems. Through these customizations you will gain an understanding of how Spring Security authentication works and how you can integrate with existing and new authentication mechanisms.

*Chapter 4, JDBC-based Authentication*, covers authenticating against a database using Spring Security's built-in JDBC support. We then discuss how we can secure our passwords using Spring Security's new cryptography module.

*Chapter 5, LDAP Directory Services*, provides a guide to application integration with an LDAP directory server.

*Chapter 6, Remember-me Authentication*, discusses several built-in strategies for how to securely allow a user to select to be remembered after the browser has been closed. Then, the chapter compares each of the approaches and demonstrates how to create your own custom implementation.

*Chapter 7, Client Certificate Authentication*, makes X.509 certificate-based authentication a clear alternative for certain business scenarios where managed certificates can add an additional layer of security to our application.

*Chapter 8, Opening up To OpenID*, covers OpenID-enabled login and user attribute exchange, as well as a high-level overview of the logical flow of the OpenID protocol.

*Chapter 9, Single Sign-on with Central Authentication Service*, shows how integrating with Central Authentication Service (CAS) can provide single sign-on and single logout support to your Spring Security-enabled applications. It also demonstrates how you can use CAS proxy ticket support for use with stateless services.

*Chapter 10, Fine-grained Access Control*, covers in-page authorization checking (partial page rendering), and business-layer security using Spring Security's method security capabilities.

*Chapter 11, Access Control Lists*, teaches you the concepts and basic implementation of business object-level security using the Spring Security Access Control Lists module—a powerful module with very flexible applicability to challenging business security problems.

*Chapter 12, Custom Authorization*, explains how Spring Security's authorization works by writing custom implementations of key parts of Spring Security's authorization infrastructure.

*Chapter 13, Session Management*, discusses how Spring Security manages and secures user sessions. The chapter starts by explaining session fixation attacks and how Spring Security defends against them. It then discusses how you can manage the logged-in users and restrict the number of concurrent sessions a single user has. Finally, we describe how Spring Security associates a user to `HttpSession` and how to customize this behavior.

*Chapter 14, Integrating with other Frameworks*, is a reference for how to integrate Spring Security with a number of other technologies including Java Server Faces (JSF), AJAX, Google Widget Toolkit (GTW), Spring Roo, and AspectJ.

*Chapter 15, Migration to Spring Security 3.1*, provides a migration path from Spring Security 2 and Spring Security 3, including notable configuration changes, class and package migrations, and important new features. It also highlights the new features that can be found in Spring Security 3.1 and provides references to examples of the features in the book.

*Appendix, Additional Reference Material*, contains some reference material that is not directly related to Spring Security, but is still relevant to the topics covered in the book. Most importantly, it contains a section that assists in running the sample code included with the book.

# What you need for this book

The following list provides the required software in order to run the sample applications included with the book. Some chapters have additional requirements that are outlined within the chapter itself.

- Java Development Kit 1.6+ can be downloaded from Oracle's website `http://www.oracle.com/technetwork/java/javase/downloads/index.html`
- Spring Tool Suite 3.1.0.RELEASE+ can be downloaded from `http://www.springsource.org/sts`
- Apache Tomcat 7 can be downloaded from `http://tomcat.apache.org/download-70.cgi`

# Who this book is for

This book is intended for Java web developers and assumes a basic understanding of creating Java web applications, XML, and the Spring Framework. You are not expected to have any previous experience with Spring Security.

# Conventions

In this book, you will find a number of styles of text that distinguish between different kinds of information. Here are some examples of these styles, and an explanation of their meaning.

Code words in text are shown as follows: " We encourage you to import the `chapter02.00-calendar` project into your IDE."

A block of code is set as follows:

```
<dependency>
  <groupId>org.springframework.security</groupId>
  <artifactId>spring-security-config</artifactId>
  <version>3.1.0.RELEASE</version>
</dependency>
```

# Preface

When we wish to draw your attention to a particular part of a code block, the relevant lines or items are set in bold:

```
</listener>

<filter>
  <filter-name>springSecurityFilterChain</filter-name>
  <filter-class>
     org.springframework.web.filter.DelegatingFilterProxy
  </filter-class>
</filter>
<filter-mapping>
  <filter-name>springSecurityFilterChain</filter-name>
  <url-pattern>/*</url-pattern>
</filter-mapping>

<servlet>
```

**New terms** and **important words** are shown in bold. Words that you see on the screen, in menus or dialog boxes for example, appear in the text like this: "It would be nice to display a greeting similar to **Welcome user1@example.com**".

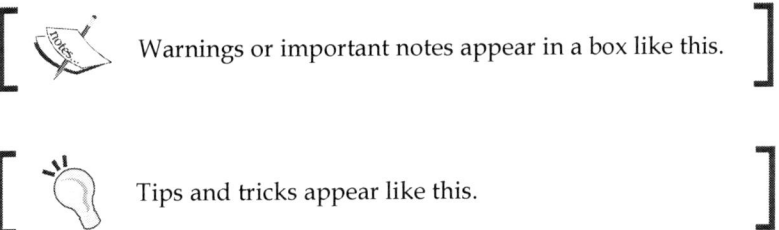

> Warnings or important notes appear in a box like this.

> Tips and tricks appear like this.

## Reader feedback

Feedback from our readers is always welcome. Let us know what you think about this book—what you liked or may have disliked. Reader feedback is important for us to develop titles that you really get the most out of.

To send us general feedback, simply send an e-mail to feedback@packtpub.com, and mention the book title via the subject of your message.

If there is a book that you need and would like to see us publish, please send us a note in the **SUGGEST A TITLE** form on www.packtpub.com or e-mail suggest@packtpub.com.

If there is a topic that you have expertise in and you are interested in either writing or contributing to a book, see our author guide on www.packtpub.com/authors.

# Customer support

Now that you are the proud owner of a Packt book, we have a number of things to help you to get the most from your purchase.

## Downloading the example code

You can download the example code files for all Packt books you have purchased from your account at http://www.PacktPub.com. If you purchased this book elsewhere, you can visit http://www.PacktPub.com/support and register to have the files e-mailed directly to you.

## Errata

Although we have taken every care to ensure the accuracy of our content, mistakes do happen. If you find a mistake in one of our books—maybe a mistake in the text or the code—we would be grateful if you would report this to us. By doing so, you can save other readers from frustration and help us improve subsequent versions of this book. If you find any errata, please report them by visiting http://www.packtpub.com/support, selecting your book, clicking on the **errata submission form** link, and entering the details of your errata. Once your errata are verified, your submission will be accepted and the errata will be uploaded on our website, or added to any list of existing errata, under the Errata section of that title. Any existing errata can be viewed by selecting your title from http://www.packtpub.com/support.

## Piracy

Piracy of copyright material on the Internet is an ongoing problem across all media. At Packt, we take the protection of our copyright and licenses very seriously. If you come across any illegal copies of our works, in any form, on the Internet, please provide us with the location address or website name immediately so that we can pursue a remedy.

Please contact us at copyright@packtpub.com with a link to the suspected pirated material.

We appreciate your help in protecting our authors, and our ability to bring you valuable content.

## Questions

You can contact us at questions@packtpub.com if you are having a problem with any aspect of the book, and we will do our best to address it.

# Anatomy of an Unsafe Application

Security is arguably one of the most critical architectural components of any web-based application written in the 21st century. In an era where malware, criminals, and rogue employees are always present and actively testing software for exploits, smart and comprehensive use of security is a key element to any project for which you'll be responsible.

This book is written to follow a pattern of development that, we feel, provides a useful premise for tackling a complex subject—taking a web-based application with a Spring 3.1 foundation, and understanding the core concepts and strategies for securing it with Spring Security 3.1. We compliment this approach by providing sample code for each chapter in the form of complete web applications.

Whether you're already using Spring Security or are interested in taking your basic use of the software to the next level of complexity, you'll find something to help you in this book.

During the course of this chapter, we will:

- Review the results of a fictional security audit
- Discuss some common security problems of web-based applications
- Learn several core software security terms and concepts

If you are already familiar with basic security terminology, you may skip to *Chapter 2, Getting Started with Spring Security*, where we start using the basic functionality of the framework.

# Security audit

It's early in the morning at your job as a software developer for the **Jim Bob Circle Pants Online Calendar** (`JBCPCalendar.com`), and you're halfway through your first cup of coffee when you get the following e-mail from your supervisor:

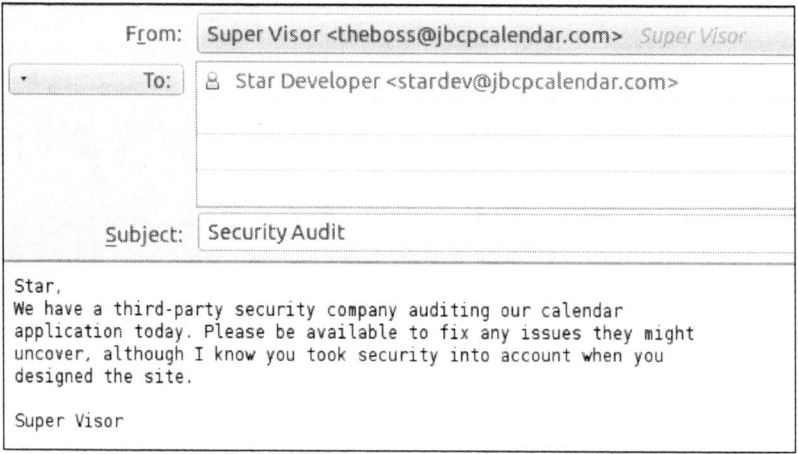

What? You didn't think a lot about security when you designed the application? In fact, at this point, you are not even sure what a security audit is. Sounds like you'll have a lot to learn from the security auditors! Later in this chapter, we will review what an audit is, along with the results of the audit. First, let's spend a bit of time examining the application that's under review.

# About the sample application

Although we'll be working through a contrived scenario, as we progress through this book, the design of the application and the changes that we'll make to it are drawn from real-world usage of Spring-based applications. The `Calendar` application allows users to create and view events.

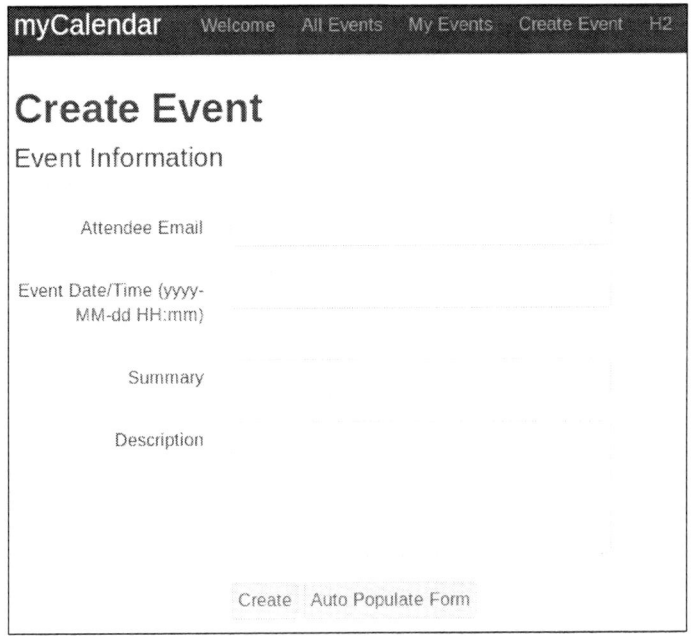

After entering the details for a new event, you will be presented with the following screenshot:

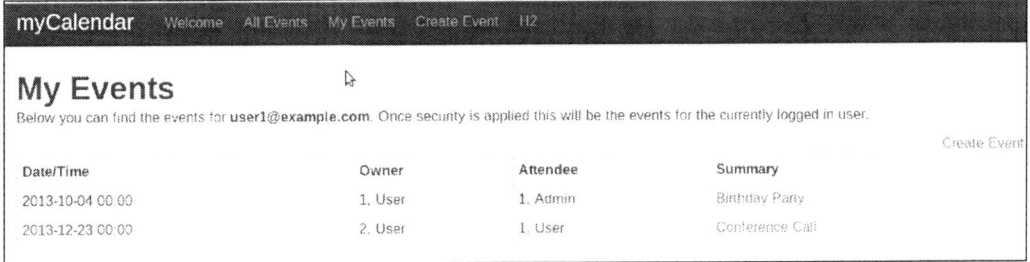

The application is designed to be simplistic, to allow us to focus on the important aspects of security and not get tied up in the details of **Object Relational Mapping (ORM)** and complex UI techniques. We expect you to refer to other supplementary material in the *Supplementary Materials* section in *Appendix, Additional Reference Material* of this book to cover some of the baseline functionality that is provided as part of the sample code.

The code is written in Spring and Spring Security 3.1, but it would be relatively easy to adapt many of the examples to other versions of Spring Security. Refer to the discussion about the detailed changes between Spring Security 2 and 3.1 in *Chapter 15, Migration to Spring Security 3.1*, for assistance in translating the examples to the Spring Security 2 syntax. There should be no effort in translating the examples from Spring Security 3.1 to 3.0 since, other than the new features we leverage; the transition should be completely passive.

Please don't use this application as a baseline to build a real online calendar application. It has been purposely structured to be simple and to focus on the concepts and configuration that we illustrate in the book.

# The JBCP calendar application architecture

The web application follows a standard three-tier architecture, consisting of a web, service, and data access layer, as indicated in the following diagram:

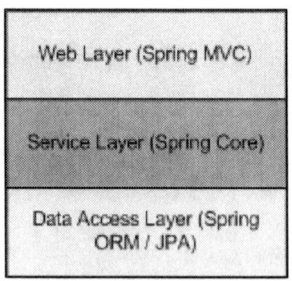

You can find additional material about MVC architectures in the *Appendix, Additional Reference Material*.

The web layer encapsulates MVC code and functionality. In this sample application, we use the Spring MVC framework, but we could just as easily use Spring Web Flow, Struts, or even a Spring-friendly web stack, such as Apache Wicket.

In a typical web application leveraging Spring Security, the web layer is where much of the configuration and augmentation of code takes place. For example, the EventsController is used to transform an HTTP request into persisting an event into the database. If you haven't had a lot of experience with web applications and Spring MVC specifically, it would be wise to review the baseline code closely and make sure you understand it before we move on to more complex subjects. Again, we've tried to make the website as simple as possible, and the construct of a calendar application is used just to give a sensible title and light structure to the site.

>  You can find detailed instructions on setting up the sample application within the *Appendix, Additional Reference Material*.

The service layer encapsulates the business logic for the application. In our sample application, we use `DefaultCalendarService` as a very light facade over the data access layer, to illustrate particular points around securing application service methods. The service layer is also used to operate on both Spring Security APIs and our Calendar APIs within a single method call. We will discuss this in greater detail in *Chapter 3, Custom Authentication*.

In a typical web application, this layer would incorporate business rules validation, composition and decomposition of business objects, and cross-cutting concerns, such as auditing.

The data access layer encapsulates the code responsible for manipulating contents of database tables. In many Spring applications, this is where you would see the use of an **Object Relational Mapping** (**ORM**), such as Hibernate or JPA. It exposes an object-based API to the service layer. In our sample application, we use a basic JDBC functionality to achieve persistence to the in-memory H2 database. For example, our `JdbcEventDao` is used to save `Event` objects to the database.

In a typical web application, a more comprehensive data access solution would be utilized. As ORM, and more generally data access, tends to be confusing for some developers, this is an area we have chosen to simplify, as much as possible, for the purposes of clarity.

# Application technology

We have endeavored to make the application as easy to run as possible, by focusing on some basic tools and technologies that almost every Spring developer would have on their development machine. Nevertheless, we provide the supplementary "getting started" information in *Getting started with JBCP Calendar sample code* section in *Appendix, Additional Reference Material*.

The primary method for integrating with the sample code is by providing Maven 3 compatible projects. Since many IDEs have rich integration with Maven, users should be able to import the code into any IDE that supports Maven. As many developers use Maven, we felt this was the most straightforward method of packaging the examples. Whatever development environment you are familiar with, hopefully you will find a way to work through the examples while you read the book.

Many IDEs provide Maven tooling that can automatically download the Spring and Spring Security 3.1 Javadoc and source code for you. However, there may be times when this is not possible. In such cases, you'll want to download the full releases of both Spring 3.1 and Spring Security 3.1. The Javadoc and source code are at the top notch, if you get confused or want more information, and the samples can provide an additional level of support or reassurance in your learning. Visit the *Appendix*, *Additional Reference Material*, to find additional information about Maven, which gives information about running the samples, obtaining the source code and Javadoc, and alternatives to building your projects without Maven.

# Reviewing the audit results

Let's return to our e-mail and see how the audit is progressing. Uh-oh, the results don't look good:

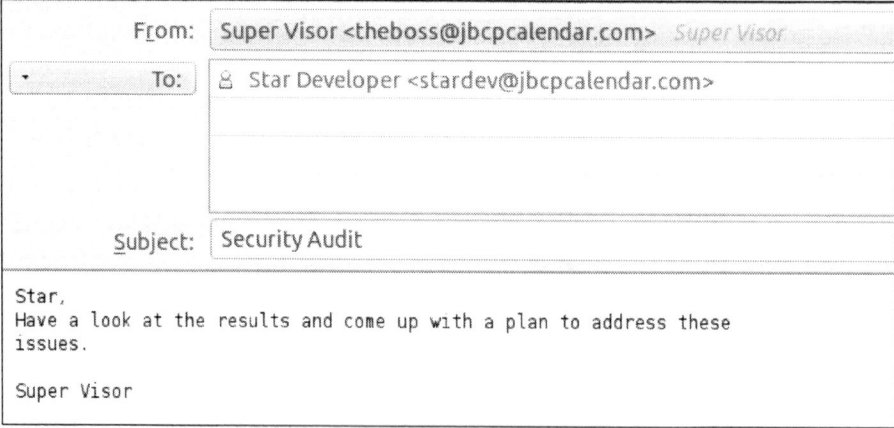

APPLICATION AUDIT RESULTS

This application exhibits the following insecure behavior:

- Inadvertent privilege escalation due to lack of URL protection and general authentication
- Inappropriate or non-existent use of authorization
- Missing database credential security
- Personally-identifiable or sensitive information is easily accessible or unencrypted
- Insecure transport-level protection due to lack of SSL encryption
- Risk level is high

We recommend that this application be taken offline until these issues can be resolved.

Ouch! This result looks bad for our company. We'd better work to resolve these issues as quickly as possible.

Third-party security specialists are often hired by companies (or their partners or customers) to audit the effectiveness of their software security, through a combination of white hat hacking, source code review, and formal or informal conversations with application developers and architects.

White hat hacking or ethical hacking is done by professionals who are hired to instruct companies on how to protect themselves better rather than with the intent to be malicious.

Typically, the goal of security audits is to provide management or clients with an assurance that basic secure development practices have been followed to ensure integrity and safety of the customer's data and system function. Depending on the industry the software is targeted for, the auditor may also test using industry-specific standards or compliance metrics.

> Two specific security standards that you're likely to run into at some point in your career are the **Payment Card Industry Data Security Standard (PCI DSS)** and the **Health Insurance Privacy and Accountability Act (HIPAA)** privacy rules. Both the standards are intended to ensure safety of specific sensitive information (credit card and medical information, respectively) through a combination of process and software controls. Many other industries and countries have similar rules around sensitive or **Personally Identifiable Information (PII)**. Failure to follow these standards is not only a bad practice, but something that could expose you or your company to significant liability (not to mention bad press) in the event of a security breach.

Receiving the results of a security audit can be an eye-opening experience. However, following through with the required software improvements can be a perfect opportunity for self-education and software improvement, and can allow you to implement practices and policies that lead to a secure software.

Let's review the auditor's findings, and come up with a plan to address them in detail.

# Authentication

Inadvertent privilege escalation due to lack of URL protection and general authentication.

Authentication is one of the two key security concepts that you must internalize when developing secure applications (the other being authorization). **Authentication** identifies who is attempting to request a resource. You may be familiar with authentication in your daily online and offline life, in very different contexts:

- **Credential-based authentication**: When you log in to your web-based e-mail account, you most likely provide your username and password. The e-mail provider matches your username with a known user in its database, and verifies that your password matches with what they have on record. These credentials are what the e-mail system uses to validate that you are a valid user of the system. First, we'll use this type of authentication to secure sensitive areas of the JBCP calendar application. Technically speaking, the e-mail system can check credentials not only in the database but anywhere, for example, a corporate directory server, such as Microsoft Active Directory. A number of these types of integrations are covered throughout this book.

- **Two-factor authentication**: When you withdraw money from your bank's automated teller machine, you swipe your ID card and enter your personal identification number before you are allowed to retrieve cash or conduct other transactions. This type of authentication is similar to the username and password authentication, except that the username is encoded on the card's magnetic strip. The combination of the physical card and user-entered PIN allows the bank to ensure that you should have access to the account. The combination of a password and a physical device (your plastic ATM card) is an ubiquitous form of two-factor authentication. In a professional, security-conscious environment, it's common to see these types of devices in regular use for access to highly secure systems, especially dealing with finance or personally identifiable information. A hardware device, such as RSA's SecurID, combines a time-based hardware device with server-based authentication software, making the environment extremely difficult to compromise.

- **Hardware authentication**: When you start your car in the morning, you slip your metal key into the ignition and turn it to get the car started. Although it may not feel similar to the other two examples, the correct match of the bumps on the key and the tumblers in the ignition switch function as a form of hardware authentication.

There are literally dozens of forms of authentication that can be applied to the problem of software and hardware security, each with their own pros and cons. We'll review some of these methods as they apply to Spring Security throughout the first half of this book. Our application lacks any type of authentication, which is why the audit included the risk of inadvertent privilege escalation.

Typically, a software system will be divided into two high-level realms, such as unauthenticated (or anonymous) and authenticated, as shown in the following screenshot:

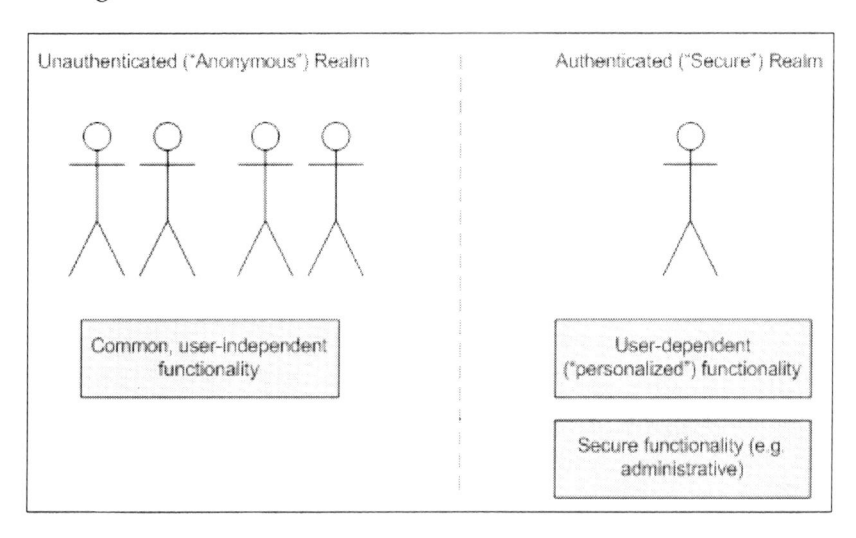

Application functionality in the anonymous realm is the functionality that is independent of a user's identity (think of a welcome page for an online application).

Anonymous areas do not:

- Require a user to log into the system or otherwise identify themselves to be usable
- Display sensitive information, such as names, addresses, credit cards, and orders
- Provide functionality to manipulate the overall state of the system or its data

Unauthenticated areas of the system are intended for use by everyone, even by users who we haven't specifically identified yet. However, it may be that, additional functionality appears to identified users in these areas (for example, the ubiquitous `Welcome {First Name}` text). Selective display of content to authenticated users is fully supported through use of the Spring Security tag library, and is covered in *Chapter 10, Fine-grained Access Control*.

We'll resolve this finding and implement form-based authentication using Spring Security's automatic configuration capability in *Chapter 2, Getting Started with Spring Security*. Afterwards, we will explore various other means of performing authentication (which usually revolve around systems integration with enterprise or other external authentication stores).

# Authorization

Inappropriate or non-existent use of authorization.

Authorization is the second of two core security concepts that is crucial in implementing and understanding application security. **Authorization** uses the information that was validated during authentication to determine if access should be granted to a particular resource. Built around the authorization model for the application, authorization partitions the application functionality and data, such that availability of these items can be controlled by matching the combination of privileges, functionality, and data with users. Our application's failure at this point of the audit indicates that the application's functionality isn't restricted by the user role. Imagine if you were running an e-commerce site and the ability to view, cancel, or modify order and customer information was available to any user of the site!

Authorization typically involves two separate aspects that combine to describe the accessibility of the secured system.

The first is the mapping of an authenticated principal to one or more authorities (often called **roles**). For example, a casual user of your website might be viewed as having visitor authority, while a site administrator might be assigned administrative authority.

The second is the assignment of authority checks to secured resources of the system. This is typically done at the time a system is developed, either through an explicit declaration in code or through configuration parameters. For example, the screen that allows viewing of other users' events should be made available only to those users having administrative authority.

> A secured resource may be any aspect of the system that should be conditionally available based on the authority of the user.

Secured resources of a web-based application could be individual web pages, entire portions of the website, or portions of individual pages. Conversely, secured business resources might be method calls on classes or individual business objects.

You might imagine an authority check that would examine the principal, look up its user account, and determine if the principal is in fact an administrator. If this authority check determines that the principal who is attempting to access the secured area is, in fact, an administrator, then the request will succeed. If, however, the principal does not have sufficient authority, the request should be denied.

Let's take a closer look at the example of a particular secured resource, the **All Events** page. The **All Events** page requires administrative access (after all, we don't want regular users viewing other users' events), and, as such, looks for a certain level of authority in the principal accessing it.

If we think about how a decision might be made when a site administrator attempts to access the protected resource, we'd imagine that the examination of actual authority versus required authority might be expressed concisely in terms of the set theory. We might then choose to represent this decision as a Venn diagram for the administrative user:

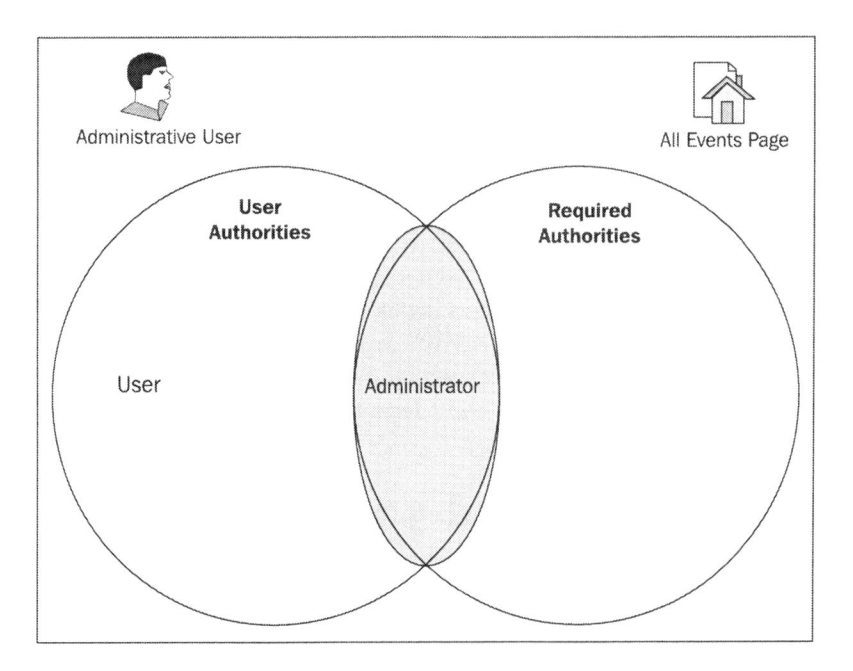

There is an intersection between **User Authorities** (**User** and **Administrator**) and **Required Authorities** (**Administrator**) for the page, so the user is provided with access.

Contrast this with an unauthorized user:

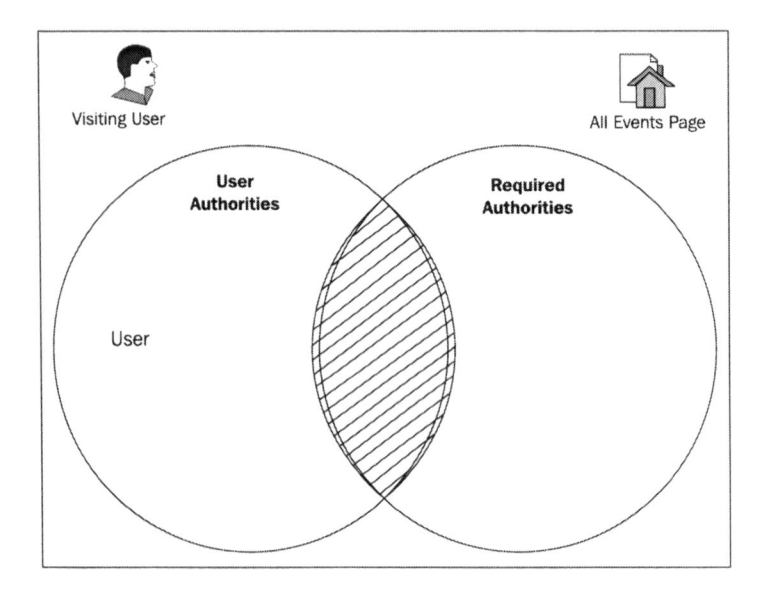

The sets of authorities are disjoint, and have no common elements. So, the user is denied access to the page. Thus, we have demonstrated the basic principle of authorization of access to resources.

In reality, there's real code making this decision with the consequence of the user being granted or denied access to the requested protected resource. We'll address the basic authorization problem with Spring Security's authorization infrastructure in *Chapter 2, Getting Started with Spring Security* followed by more advanced authorization in *Chapter 10, Fine-grained Access Control* and *Chapter 11, Access Control Lists*.

# Database credential security

Database credentials not secured and easily accessible.

Through the examination of the application source code and configuration files, the auditors noted that user passwords were stored in plain text in the configuration files, making it very easy for a malicious user with access to the server to gain access to the application.

As the application contains personal and financial data, a rogue user being able to access any data could expose the company to identity theft or tampering. Protecting access to the credentials used to access the application should be a top priority for us, and an important first step is ensuring that one point of failure in security does not compromise the entire system.

We'll examine the configuration of Spring Security's database access layer for credential storage, which uses JDBC connectivity, in *Chapter 4, JDBC-based Authentication*. In the same chapter, we'll also look at built-in techniques to increase the security of passwords stored in the database.

# Sensitive information

Personally identifiable or sensitive information is easily accessible or unencrypted.

The auditors noted that some significant and sensitive pieces of data were completely unencrypted or masked anywhere in the system. Fortunately, there are some simple design patterns and tools that allow us to protect this information securely with Spring Security's annotation-based AOP support.

# Transport-level protection

Insecure transport-level protection due to lack of SSL encryption.

While in the real world, it's unthinkable that an online application containing private information would operate without SSL protection; unfortunately JBCP calendar is in just this situation. SSL protection ensures that communication between the browser client and the web application server are secure against many kinds of tampering and snooping.

In the *HTTPS setup in Tomcat* section in *Appendix, Additional Reference Material*, we'll review the basic options for using transport-level security as part of the definition of the secured structure of the application.

# Using Spring Security 3.1 to address security concerns

Spring Security 3.1 provides a wealth of resources that allow for many common security practices to be declared or configured in a straightforward manner. In the coming chapters, we'll apply a combination of source code and application configuration changes to address all of the concerns raised by the security auditors (and more), and give ourselves the confidence that our calendar application is secure.

With Spring Security 3.1, we'll be able to make the following changes to increase our application security:

- Segment users of the system into user classes
- Assign levels of authorization to user roles
- Assign user roles to user classes
- Apply authentication rules globally across application resources
- Apply authorization rules at all levels of the application architecture
- Prevent common types of attacks intended to manipulate or steal a user's session

# Why Spring Security

Spring Security exists to fill a gap in the universe of Java third-party libraries, much as the Spring Framework originally did when it was first introduced. Standards such as **Java Authentication and Authorization Service (JAAS)** or **Java EE Security** do offer some ways of performing some of the same authentication and authorization functions, but Spring Security is a winner because it packages up everything you need to implement a top-to-bottom application security solution in a concise and sensible way.

Additionally, Spring Security appeals to many, because it offers out-of-the-box integration with many common enterprise authentication systems; so it's adaptable to most situations with little effort (beyond configuration) on the part of the developer.

It's in wide use, because there's really no other mainstream framework quite like it!

# Summary

In this chapter, we have:

- Reviewed common points of risk in an unsecured web application
- Reviewed the basic architecture of the sample application
- Discussed the strategies for securing the application

In the next chapter, we'll explore how to get Spring Security set up quickly and get a basic understanding of how it works.

# 2
# Getting Started with Spring Security

In this chapter, we'll apply a minimal Spring Security configuration to start addressing our first finding—inadvertent privilege escalation due to lack of URL protection and general authentication—from the security audit discussed in *Chapter 1, Anatomy of an Unsafe Application*. We will then build on the basic configuration to provide a customized experience for our users. This chapter is intended to get you up and running with Spring Security and to provide a foundation for any other security-related tasks you will need to perform.

During the course of this chapter, we will:

- Implement a basic level of security on the JBCP Calendar application, using Spring Security's automatic configuration option
- Learn how to customize both the login and logout experience
- Configure Spring Security to restrict access differently, depending upon the URL
- Leverage Spring Security's expression-based access control
- Conditionally display basic information about the logged-in user using Spring Security's JSP library
- Determine the user's default location after login, based upon role

# Hello Spring Security

Although Spring Security can be extremely difficult to configure, the creators of the product have been thoughtful and have provided us with a very simple mechanism to enable much of the software's functionality with a strong baseline. From this baseline, additional configuration will allow a fine level of detailed control over the security behavior of our application.

We'll start with our unsecured calendar application from *Chapter 1, Anatomy of an Unsafe Application*, and turn it into a site that's secured with rudimentary username and password authentication. This authentication serves merely to illustrate the steps involved in enabling Spring Security for our web application; you'll see that there are some obvious flaws in this approach that will lead us to make further configuration refinements.

## Importing the sample application

We encourage you to import the `chapter02.00-calendar` project into your IDE, and follow along by obtaining the source code for *Chapter 2*, as described in the *Getting started with JBCP Calendar sample code* section in *Appendix, Additional Reference Material*.

For each chapter, you will find multiple revisions of the code that represent checkpoints within the book. This makes it easy to compare your work with the "correct answers" as you go. At the beginning of each chapter, we will import the first revision of that chapter as a starting point. For example, in this chapter, we start with `chapter02.00-calendar`, and the first checkpoint will be `chapter02.01-calendar`. In *Chapter 3, Custom Authentication*, we will start with `chapter03.00-calendar`, and the first checkpoint will be `chapter03.01-calendar`. There are additional details in *Appendix, Getting started with JBCP Calendar sample code*, so be sure to refer to it for details.

## Updating your dependencies

The first step is to update the project's dependencies to include the necessary Spring Security `.jar` files. Update the Maven `pom.xml` file from the sample application you imported previously, to include the Spring Security `.jar` files that we will use in the following few sections.

> Throughout the book, we will be demonstrating how to provide the required dependencies using Maven. The pom.xml file is located in the root of the project and represents all that is needed to build the project (including the project's dependencies). Remember that Maven will download the transitive dependencies for each listed dependency. So, if you are using another mechanism to manage dependencies, ensure that you also include the transitive dependencies. When managing the dependencies manually, it is useful to know that the Spring Security reference includes a list of its transitive dependencies. A link to the Spring Security reference can be found in *Appendix, Additional Reference Material*.

pom.xml

```xml
<dependency>
    <groupId>org.springframework.security</groupId>
    <artifactId>spring-security-config</artifactId>
    <version>3.1.0.RELEASE</version>
</dependency>
<dependency>
    <groupId>org.springframework.security</groupId>
    <artifactId>spring-security-core</artifactId>
    <version>3.1.0.RELEASE</version>
</dependency>
<dependency>
    <groupId>org.springframework.security</groupId>
    <artifactId>spring-security-web</artifactId>
    <version>3.1.0.RELEASE</version>
</dependency>
```

> **Downloading the example code**
> You can download the example code files for all Packt books you have purchased from your account at http://www.PacktPub.com. If you purchased this book elsewhere, you can visit http://www.PacktPub.com/support and register to have the files e-mailed directly to you.

# Using Spring 3.1 and Spring Security 3.1

It is important to ensure that all of the Spring dependency versions match and all the Spring Security versions match; this includes transitive versions. Since Spring Security 3.1 builds with Spring 3.0, Maven will attempt to bring in Spring 3.0 dependencies. This means, in order to use Spring 3.1, you must ensure to explicitly list the Spring 3.1 dependencies or use Maven's dependency management features, to ensure that Spring 3.1 is used consistently. Our sample applications provide an example of the former option, which means that no additional work is required by you.

In the following code, we present an example fragment of what is added to the Maven pom.xml file to utilize Maven's dependency management feature, to ensure that Spring 3.1 is used throughout the entire application:

```xml
<project ...>

...
<dependencyManagement>
  <dependencies>
    <dependency>
      <groupId>org.springframework</groupId>
      <artifactId>spring-aop</artifactId>
      <version>3.1.0.RELEASE</version>
    </dependency>
    … list all Spring dependencies (a list can be found in our
      sample application's pom.xml ...
    <dependency>
      <groupId>org.springframework</groupId>
      <artifactId>spring-web</artifactId>
      <version>3.1.0.RELEASE</version>
    </dependency>
  </dependencies>
</dependencyManagement>
</project>
```

> If you are using Spring Tool Suite, any time you update the pom.xml file, ensure you right-click on the project and navigate to **Maven | Update Project...**, and select **OK**, to update all the dependencies.

*[handwritten note: STS: UPDATE MAVEN DEPENDENCIES]*

For more information about how Maven handles transitive dependencies, refer to the Maven documentation, which is listed in *Appendix, Additional Reference Material*.

# Implementing a Spring Security XML configuration file

The next step in the configuration process is to create an XML configuration file, representing all Spring Security components required to cover standard web requests.

Create a new XML file in the `src/main/webapp/WEB-INF/spring/` directory with the name `security.xml` and the following contents. Among other things, the following file demonstrates how to require a user to log in for every page in our application, provide a login page, authenticate the user, and require the logged-in user to be associated to `ROLE_USER` for every `URL:URL` element:

src/main/webapp/WEB-INF/spring/security.xml

```xml
<?xml version="1.0" encoding="UTF-8"?>
<bean:beans
  xmlns:bean="http://www.springframework.org/schema/beans"
  xmlns:xsi="http://www.w3.org/2001/XMLSchema-instance"
  xmlns="http://www.springframework.org/schema/security"
  xsi:schemaLocation="http://www.springframework.org/schema/beans
  http://www.springframework.org/schema/beans/spring-beans-3.1.xsd
  http://www.springframework.org/schema/security
  http://www.springframework.org/schema/security/spring-security-
  3.1.xsd">
  <http auto-config="true">
    <intercept-url pattern="/**" access="ROLE_USER"/>
  </http>
  <authentication-manager>
    <authentication-provider>
      <user-service>
        <user name="user1@example.com"
          password="user1"
          authorities="ROLE_USER"/>
      </user-service>
    </authentication-provider>
  </authentication-manager>
</bean:beans>
```

> If you are using Spring Tool Suite, you can easily create Spring configuration files by using **File | New Spring Bean Configuration File**. This wizard allows you to select the XML namespaces you wish to use, making configuration easier by not requiring the developer to remember the namespace locations and helping prevent typographical errors. You will need to manually change the schema definitions as illustrated in the preceding code. Remember that the next checkpoint (`chapter02.01-calendar`) has a working solution, so the file can be copied from there as well.

This is the only Spring Security configuration required to get our web application secured with a minimal standard configuration. This style of configuration, using a Spring Security-specific XML dialect, is known as the **security namespace style**, named after the XML namespace (http://www.springframework.org/schema/security) associated with the XML configuration elements.

Let's take a minute to break this configuration apart, so we can get a high-level idea of what is happening. The `<http>` element creates a servlet filter, which ensures that the currently logged-in user is associated to the appropriate role. In this instance, the filter will ensure that the user is associated with ROLE_USER. It is important to understand that the name of the role is arbitrary. Later, we will create a user with ROLE_ADMIN and will allow this user to have access to additional URLs that our current user does not have access to.

The `<authentication-manager>` element is how Spring Security authenticates the user. In this instance, we utilize an in-memory data store to compare a username and password.

Our example and explanation of what is happening are a bit contrived. An in-memory authentication store would not work for a production environment. However, it allows us to get up and running quickly. We will incrementally improve our understanding of Spring Security as we update our application to use production quality security throughout the book.

> Users who dislike Spring's XML configuration will be disappointed to learn that there isn't an alternative annotation-based or Java-based configuration mechanism for Spring Security, as there is with Spring Framework.
>
> There is an experimental approach that uses Scala to configure Spring Security, but at the time of this writing, there are no known plans to release it. If you like, you can learn more about it at https://github.com/tekul/scalasec/. Still, perhaps in the future, we'll see the ability to easily configure Spring Security in other ways.

Although annotations are not prevalent in Spring Security, certain aspects of Spring Security that apply security elements to classes or methods are, as you'd expect, available via annotations. We'll cover these in *Chapter 10, Fine-grained Access Control*.

# Updating your web.xml file

The next steps involve a series of updates to the `web.xml` file. Some of the steps have already been performed because the application was already using Spring MVC. However, we will go over these requirements to ensure that these more fundamental Spring requirements are understood, in the event that you are using Spring Security in an application that is not Spring-enabled.

## ContextLoaderListener

The first step of updating the `web.xml` file is to ensure that it contains the `o.s.w.context.ContextLoaderListener` listener, which is in charge of starting and stopping the Spring root `ApplicationContext` interface. `ContextLoaderListener` determines which configurations are to be used, by looking at the `<context-param>` tag for `contextConfigLocation`. It is also important to specify where to read the Spring configurations from. Our application already has `ContextLoaderListener` added, so we only need to add the newly created `security.xml` configuration file, as shown in the following code snippet:

src/main/webapp/WEB-INF/web.xml

```
    <context-param>
      <param-name>contextConfigLocation</param-name>
      <param-value>
        /WEB-INF/spring/services.xml
        /WEB-INF/spring/i18n.xml
        /WEB-INF/spring/security.xml
      </param-value>
    </context-param>
    <listener>
      <listener-class>
        org.springframework.web.context.ContextLoaderListener
      </listener-class>
    </listener>
```

The updated configuration will now load the `security.xml` file from the `/WEB-INF/spring/` directory of the WAR. As an alternative, we could have used `/WEB-INF/spring/*.xml` to load all the XML files found in `/WEB-INF/spring/`. We choose not to use the `*.xml` notation to have more control over which files are loaded. This is necessary, since in subsequent chapters, we provide additional files that will not be used until later in the chapter.

## ContextLoaderListener versus DispatcherServlet

You may have noticed that `o.s.web.servlet.DispatcherServlet` specifies a `contextConfigLocation` component of its own.

src/main/webapp/WEB-INF/web.xml

```
<servlet>
  <servlet-name>Spring MVC Dispatcher Servlet</servlet-name>
  <servlet-class>
    org.springframework.web.servlet.DispatcherServlet
  </servlet-class>
  <init-param>
    <param-name>contextConfigLocation</param-name>
    <param-value>
      /WEB-INF/mvc-config.xml
    </param-value>
  </init-param>
  <load-on-startup>1</load-on-startup>
</servlet>
```

`DispatcherServlet` creates `o.s.context.ApplicationContext`, which is a child of the root `ApplicationContext` interface. Typically, Spring MVC-specific components are initialized in the `ApplicationContext` interface of `DispatcherServlet`, while the rest are loaded by `ContextLoaderListener`. It is important to know that beans in a child `ApplicationContext` (such as those created by `DispatcherServlet`) can reference beans of its parent `ApplicationContext` (such as those created by `ContextLoaderListener`). However, the parent `ApplicationContext` cannot refer to beans of the child `ApplicationContext`. This is illustrated in the following diagram where `childBean` can refer to `rootBean`, but `rootBean` cannot refer to `childBean`.

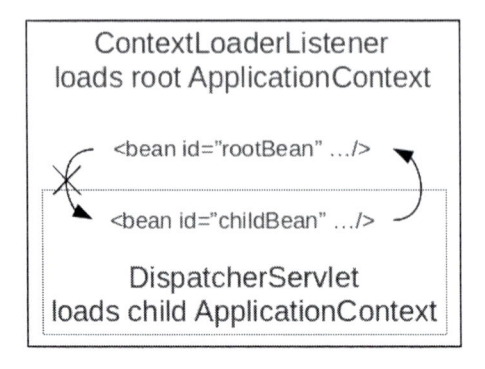

ContextLoaderListener
loads root ApplicationContext

&lt;bean id="rootBean" .../&gt;

&lt;bean id="childBean" .../&gt;

DispatcherServlet
loads child ApplicationContext

As with most usage of Spring Security, we do not need Spring Security to refer to any of the MVC-declared beans. Therefore, we have decided to have `ContextLoaderListener` initialize all of Spring Security's configuration.

## springSecurityFilterChain

The next step is to configure `springSecurityFilterChain` to intercept all requests by updating `web.xml`. Servlet `<filter-mapping>` elements are considered in the order that they are declared. Therefore, ==it is critical for `springSecurityFilterChain` to be declared first, to ensure the request is secured prior to any other logic being invoked==. Update your `web.xml` file with the following configuration:

src/main/webapp/WEB-INF/web.xml

```xml
    </listener>

    <filter>
        <filter-name>springSecurityFilterChain</filter-name>
        <filter-class>
            org.springframework.web.filter.DelegatingFilterProxy
        </filter-class>
    </filter>
    <filter-mapping>
        <filter-name>springSecurityFilterChain</filter-name>
        <url-pattern>/*</url-pattern>
    </filter-mapping>

    <servlet>
```

Not only is it important for Spring Security to be declared as the first `<filter-mapping>` element, but we should also be aware that, with the example configuration, Spring Security will not intercept forwards, includes, or errors. Often, it is not necessary to intercept other types of requests, but if you need to do this, the dispatcher element for each type of request should be included in `<filter-mapping>`. We will not perform these steps for our application, but you can see an example, as shown in the following code snippet:

src/main/webapp/WEB-INF/web.xml

```xml
    <filter-mapping>
        <filter-name>springSecurityFilterChain</filter-name>
        <url-pattern>/*</url-pattern>
        <dispatcher>REQUEST</dispatcher>
        <dispatcher>ERROR</dispatcher>
        ...
    </filter-mapping>
```

*Getting Started with Spring Security*

## DelegatingFilterProxy

The `o.s.web.filter.DelegatingFilterProxy` class is a servlet filter provided by Spring Web that will delegate all work to a Spring bean from the root `ApplicationContext` that must implement `javax.servlet.Filter`. Since, by default, the bean is looked up by name, using the value of `<filter-name>`, we must ensure we use `springSecurityFilterChain` as the value of `<filter-name>`. Pseudo-code for how `o.s.web.filter.DelegatingFilterProxy` works for our `web.xml` file can be found in the following code snippet:

```
public class DelegatingFilterProxy implements Filter {
  void doFilter(request, response, filterChain) {
    Filter delegate =
      applicationContet.getBean("springSecurityFilterChain")
      delegate.doFilter(request,response,filterChain);
  }
}
```

## FilterChainProxy

When working in conjunction with Spring Security, `o.s.web.filter.DelegatingFilterProxy` will delegate to Spring Security's `o.s.s.web.FilterChainProxy`, which was created in our minimal `security.xml` file. `FilterChainProxy` allows Spring Security to conditionally apply any number of servlet filters to the servlet request. We will learn more about each of the Spring Security filters and their role in ensuring that our application is properly secured, throughout the rest of the book. The pseudo-code for how `FilterChainProxy` works is as follows:

```
public class FilterChainProxy implements Filter {
  void doFilter(request, response, filterChain) {
    // lookup all the Filters for this request
    List<Filter> delegates =
      lookupDelegates(request,response)
    // invoke each filter unless the delegate decided to stop
    for delegate in delegates {
      if continue processing
        delegate.doFilter(request,response,filterChain)
    }
    // if all the filters decide it is ok allow the
    // rest of the application to run
    if continue processing
      filterChain.doFilter(request,response)
  }
}
```

[ 30 ]

> Due to the fact that both `DelegatingFilterProxy` and `FilterChainProxy` are the front door to Spring Security, when used in a web application, it is here that you would add a debug point when trying to figure out what is happening.

## Running a secured application

If you have not already done so, restart the application and visit `http://localhost:8080/calendar/`, and you will be presented with the following screen:

Great job! We've implemented a basic layer of security in our application, using Spring Security. At this point, you should be able to log in using `user1@example.com` as the **User** and `user1` as the **Password** (`user1@example.com`/`user1`). You'll see the calendar welcome page, which describes at a high level what to expect from the application in terms of security.

> Your code should now look like `chapter02.01-calendar`.

## Common problems

Many users have trouble with the initial implementation of Spring Security in their application. A few common issues and suggestions are listed next. We want to ensure that you can run the example application and follow along!

- Make sure you can build and deploy the application before putting Spring Security in place.
- Review some introductory samples and documentation on your servlet container if needed.

- It's usually easiest to use an IDE, such as Eclipse, to run your servlet container. Not only is deployment typically seamless, but the console log is also readily available to review for errors. You can also set breakpoints at strategic locations, to be triggered on exceptions to better diagnose errors.

- If your XML configuration file is incorrect, you will get this (or something similar to this): `org.xml.sax.SAXParseException: cvc-elt.1: Cannot find the declaration of element 'beans'`. It's quite common for users to get confused with the various XML namespace references required to properly configure Spring Security. Review the samples again, paying attention to avoid line wrapping in the schema declarations, and use an XML validator to verify that you don't have any malformed XML. Better yet, use Spring Tool Suite to create your bean definitions and XML namespace declarations as we discussed earlier in this chapter.

- If you get an error stating `"BeanDefinitionParsingException: Configuration problem: Unable to locate Spring NamespaceHandler for XML schema namespace [http://www.springframework.org/schema/security] ..."`, ensure that the `spring-security-config-3.1.0.RELEASE.jar` file is on your classpath. Also ensure the version matches the other Spring Security JARs and the XML declaration in your Spring configuration file.

- Make sure the versions of Spring and Spring Security that you're using match and that there aren't any unexpected Spring JARs remaining as part of your application. As previously mentioned, when using Maven, it can be a good idea to declare the Spring dependencies in the dependency management section.

# A little bit of polish

Stop at this point and think about what we've just built. You may have noticed some obvious issues that will require some additional work and knowledge of the Spring Security product before we are production-ready. Try to make a list of the changes that you think are required, before this security implementation is ready to roll out to the public-facing website.

Applying the "Hello World" Spring Security implementation was blindingly fast and has provided us with a login page, username, and password-based authentication, as well as automatic interception of URLs in our calendar application. However, there are gaps between what the automatic configuration setup provides and what our end goal is, which are listed as follows:

- While the login page is helpful, it's completely generic and doesn't look like the rest of our JBCP Calendar application. We should add a login form that's integrated with our application's look and feel.

- There is no obvious way for a user to log out.
- We've locked down all pages in the application, including the **Welcome** page, which a potential user may want to browse anonymously. We'll need to refine the roles required to accommodate anonymous, authenticated, and administrative users.
- We do not display any contextual information to indicate to the user that they are authenticated. It would be nice to display a greeting similar to **Welcome user1@example.com**.
- We've had to hardcode the username, password, and role information of the user in the XML configuration file. Recall this section of XML we added:

```xml
<user-service>
  <user name="user1@example.com"
    password="user1"
    authorities="ROLE_USER"/>
</user-service>
```

You can see that the username and password are right there in the file. It would be unlikely that we'd want to add a new XML declaration to the file for every user of the system! To address this, we'll need to update the configuration with another type of authentication. We'll explore different authentication options throughout the first half of the book.

# Customizing login

We've seen how Spring Security makes it very easy to get started. Now let's see how we can customize the login experience. In the following code snippet, we demonstrate the usage of some of the more common ways to customize login, but we encourage you to refer to Spring Security's reference documentation, which includes an Appendix with all of the supported attributes. First, update your `security.xml` file as follows:

src/main/webapp/WEB-INF/spring/security.xml

```xml
    <http ...>
        ...
        <form-login login-page="/login/form"
            login-processing-url="/login"
            username-parameter="username"
            password-parameter="password"
            authentication-failure-url="/login/form?error"/>
    </http>
```

The `login-page attribute` specifies where Spring Security will redirect the browser if a protected page is accessed and the user is not authenticated. If a login page is not specified, Spring Security will redirect the user to `/spring_security_login`. Then `o.s.s.web.filter.FilterChainProxy` will choose `o.s.s.web.authentication.ui.DefaultLoginPageGeneratingFilter`, which renders the default login page, as one of the delegates since `DefaultLoginPageGeneratingFilter` is configured to process `/spring_security_login` by default. Since we have chosen to override the default URL, we are in charge of rendering the login page when the URL `/login/form` is requested.

The `login-processing-url` attribute defaults to `/j_spring_security_check`, and specifies the URL that the login form (which should include the username and password) should be submitted to, using an HTTP post. When Spring Security processes this request, it will attempt to authenticate the user.

The `username-parameter` and the `password-parameter` attributes default to `j_username` and `j_password` respectively and specify the HTTP parameters that Spring Security will use to authenticate the user when processing `login-processing-url`.

The `authentication-failure-url` attribute specifies the page that Spring Security will redirect to if the username and password submitted to `login-processing-url` are invalid.

> It may be obvious, but if we only wanted to add a custom login page, we would only need to specify the `login-page` attribute. We would then create our login form using the default values for the remaining attributes. However, it is often a good practice to override the values of anything visible to users, to prevent exposing that we are using Spring Security. Revealing what frameworks we are using is a type of "information leakage", making it easier for attackers to determine potential holes in our security.

The next step is to create a login page. We can use any technology we want to render the login page, as long as the login form produces the HTTP request that we specified with our Spring Security configuration, when submitted. By ensuring the HTTP request conforms to our configuration, Spring Security can authenticate the request for us. Create the following `login.jsp` file:

> Remember that if you are having problems typing anything in the book, you can refer to the solution in the next checkpoint (`chapter02.02-calendar`).

src/main/webapp/WEB-INF/views/login.jsp

```jsp
<?xml version="1.0" encoding="ISO-8859-1" ?>
<%@ page language="java" contentType="text/html; charset=ISO-8859-1"
    pageEncoding="ISO-8859-1"%>
<%@ taglib prefix="c" uri="http://java.sun.com/jsp/jstl/core" %>

<c:set var="pageTitle" value="Please Login" scope="request"/>
<jsp:include page="./includes/header.jsp"/>

<c:url value="/login" var="loginUrl"/>
<form action="${loginUrl}" method="post">
    <c:if test="${param.error != null}">
        <div class="alert alert-error">
            Failed to login.
            <c:if test="${SPRING_SECURITY_LAST_EXCEPTION != null}">
              Reason: <c:out value="${SPRING_SECURITY_LAST_EXCEPTION.
              message}" />
            </c:if>
        </div>
    </c:if>
    <c:if test="${param.logout != null}">
        <div class="alert alert-success">
            You have been logged out.
        </div>
    </c:if>
    <label for="username">Username</label>
    <input type="text" id="username" name="username"/>
    <label for="password">Password</label>
    <input type="password" id="password" name="password"/>
    <div class="form-actions">
        <input id="submit" class="btn" name="submit" type="submit"
        value="Login"/>
    </div>
</form>
<jsp:include page="./includes/footer.jsp"/>
```

There are a number of items that are worth highlighting in `login.jsp`.

- The form action should be `/login`, to match the value provided for the `login-processing-url` attribute we specified.
- For security reasons, Spring Security only attempts to authenticate when using `post`, by default.

# Getting Started with Spring Security

- We can use `param.error` to see if there was a problem logging in, since the value of our `authentication-failure-url` attribute, `/login/form?error`, contains the HTTP parameter error.
- The session attribute, `SPRING_SECURITY_LAST_EXCEPTION`, contains the last `o.s.s.core.AuthenticationException` exception, which can be used to display the reason for a failed login. The error messages can be customized by leveraging Spring's internationalization support.
- The input names for the username and password inputs are chosen to correspond to the values we specified for the `username-parameter` and `password-parameter` attributes in our `security.xml` configuration.

The last step is to make Spring MVC aware of our new URL. This can be done by adding the following method to `WebMvcConfig`:

src/main/java/com/packtpub/springsecurity/web/config/WebMvcConfig.java

```
import org.springframework.web.servlet.config.annotation.ViewControllerRegistry;
...
public class WebMvcConfig extends WebMvcConfigurationSupport {
  public void addViewControllers(ViewControllerRegistry registry){
    registry.addViewController("/login/form")
        .setViewName("login");
  }
  ...
}
```

## Configuring logout

Spring Security's `<http>` configuration automatically adds support for logging the user out. All that is needed is to create a link that points to `/j_spring_security_logout`. However, we will demonstrate how to customize the URL used to log the user out. The first step is to update the Spring Security configuration.

*[handwritten: SECURITY.XML]*
src/main/webapp/WEB-INF/spring/security.xml

```
<http ...>
  ...
  <logout logout-url="/logout"
          logout-success-url="/login/form?logout"/>
</http>
```

The next step is to provide a link for the user to click that will log them out. We will update `header.jsp`, so that the **Logout** link appears on every page.

src/main/webapp/WEB-INF/views/includes/header.jsp   *HEADER.JSP*

```jsp
<div id="nav-account" ..>
    <ul class="nav">
        <c:url var="logoutUrl" value="/logout"/>
        <li>
            <a
                    href="${logoutUrl}">Logout</a>
        </li>
    </ul>
</div>
```

The last step is to update `login.jsp` to display a message indicating logout was successful when the parameter `logout` is present.

src/main/webapp/WEB-INF/views/login.jsp   *LOGIN.JSP*

```jsp
</c:if>
<c:if test="${param.logout != null}">
    <div class="alert alert-success">
        You have been logged out.
    </div>
</c:if>
<p>
    <label for="username">Username</label>
...
```

> Your code should now look like `chapter02.02-calendar`.

[ 37 ]

## The page isn't redirecting properly

If you have not already, restart the application and visit `http://localhost:8080/calendar/` in FireFox; you will see an error similar to the following:

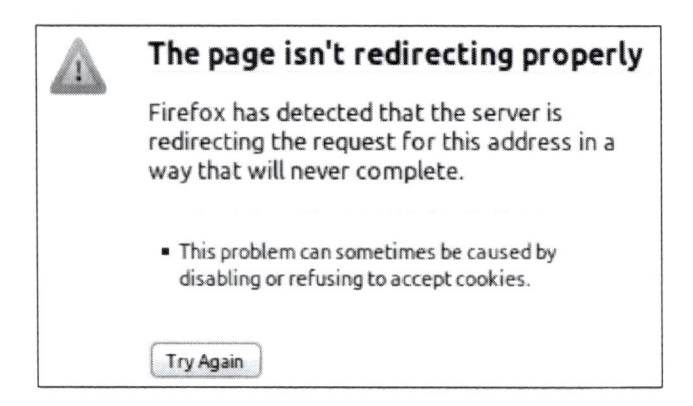

> **The page isn't redirecting properly**
>
> Firefox has detected that the server is redirecting the request for this address in a way that will never complete.
>
> - This problem can sometimes be caused by disabling or refusing to accept cookies.
>
> [ Try Again ]

What went wrong? The problem is that, since Spring Security is no longer rendering the login page, we must allow everyone (not just `ROLE_USER`) access to the login page. Without granting access to the login page, the following happens:

1. We request the **Welcome** page in the browser.
2. Spring Security sees that the **Welcome** page requires `ROLE_USER` and that we are not authenticated, so it redirects the browser to the **Login** page.
3. The browser requests the **Login** page.
4. Spring Security sees that the **Login** page requires `ROLE_USER` and that we are still not authenticated, so it redirects the browser to the **Login** page again.
5. The browser requests the **Login** page again.
6. Spring Security sees that the **Login** page requires `ROLE_USER`.

The process could just keep repeating indefinitely. Fortunately for us, Firefox realizes that there are too many redirects occurring, stops performing the redirect, and displays a very informative error message. In the next section, we will learn how to fix this error by configuring URLs differently, depending on the access that they require.

## Basic role-based authorization

We can expand on the Spring Security configuration from Hello Spring Security to vary the access control by URL. In this section, you will find a configuration that allows more granular control over how resources can be accessed. In the following configuration, Spring Security will:

- Completely ignore any request that starts with `/resources/`. This is beneficial, since our images, CSS, and JavaScript do not need to use Spring Security.
- Allow anonymous users to access the **Welcome**, **Login**, and **Logout** pages.
- Only allow administrators access to the **All Events** page.
- Add an administrator that can access the **All Events** page.

src/main/webapp/WEB-INF/spring/security.xml    *SECURITY.XML*

```xml
    <http pattern="/resources/**" security="none"/>
    <http auto-config="true">
        <intercept-url pattern="/"
                access="ROLE_ANONYMOUS,ROLE_USER"/>
        <intercept-url pattern="/login/*"
                access="ROLE_ANONYMOUS,ROLE_USER"/>
        <intercept-url pattern="/logout"
                access="ROLE_ANONYMOUS,ROLE_USER"/>
        <intercept-url pattern="/events/" access="ROLE_ADMIN"/>
        <intercept-url pattern="/**" access="ROLE_USER"/>
        ...
    </http>
    <authentication-manager>
        <authentication-provider>
            <user-service>
                <user name="user1@example.com"
                      password="user1"
                      authorities="ROLE_USER"/>
                <user name="admin1@example.com"
                      password="admin1"
                      authorities="ROLE_USER,ROLE_ADMIN"/>
            </user-service>
        </authentication-provider>
    </authentication-manager>
```

*Getting Started with Spring Security*

> Note that we do not include /calendar, the application's context root, in the Spring Security configuration, because Spring Security takes care of the context root transparently for us. In this way, we will not need to update our configuration if we decide to deploy to a different context root.

In Spring Security 3.1, you can specify multiple <http> elements that allow you to have greater control over how security is applied to different portions of your application. The first <http> element states that Spring Security should ignore any URL that starts with /resources/, and the second <http> element states that any other request will be processed by it. There are a few important things to note about using multiple <http> elements:

- If no path attribute is specified, it is the equivalent of using a path of /**, which matches all requests.

- Each <http> element is considered in order, and only the first match is applied. So, the order in which they appear in your configuration file is important. The implication is that only the last <http> tag can use a path that matches every request. If you do not follow this rule, Spring Security will produce an error. The following example illustrates the error:

  ```
  <!-- matches every request -->
  <http auto-config="true">
      ...
  </http>
  <!-- never considered since previous http matches everything.
       Spring Security will report an error to prevent this.
       To fix add path attribute to first http element -->
  <http auto-config="true">
      ...
  </http>
  ```

- The default pattern is backed by o.s.s.web.util.AntPathRequestMatcher, which will compare the specified pattern as an Ant pattern to determine wheter it matches the servletPath and pathInfo of the HttpServletRequest. Note that query strings are ignored when determining whether a request is a match. Internally, Spring Security uses o.s.u.AntPathMatcher to do all the work. A summary of the rules is listed as follows:
  - ? matches a single character.
  - * matches zero or more characters, excluding /.
  - ** matches zero or more directories in a path.

- The pattern `"/events/**"` matches `"/events"`, `"/events/"`, `"/events/1"`, and `"/events/1/form?test=1"`; it does not match `"/events123"`.
- The pattern `"/events*"` matches `"/events"`, and `"/events123"`; it does not match `"/events/"` or `"/events/1"`.
- The pattern `"/events*/**"` matches `"/events"`, `"/events/"`, `"/events/1"`, `"/events123"`, `"/events123/456"`, and `"/events/1/form?test=1"`.

- A more advanced option is to use the optional `request-matcher-ref` attribute. This method provides the ultimate flexibility in how a request maps to an `<http>` element by using the `o.s.s.web.util.RequestMatcher` interface.

The `path` attribute on the `<intercept-url>` elements further refines the filtering on the request and allows access control to be applied. You can see that the updated configuration allows different types of access, depending on the URL pattern. ROLE_ANONYMOUS is of particular interest since we have not defined it anywhere in `security.xml`. This is the default authority assigned to a user that is not logged in. The following line from the updates to our `security.xml` file is what allows anonymous (unauthenticated) users and users with the ROLE_USER authority to access the **Login** page. We will cover more detail about access control options in the second half of the book.

```
<intercept-url pattern="/login/*"
       access="ROLE_ANONYMOUS,ROLE_USER"/>
```

When defining `<intercept-url>` elements, there are a number of things to keep in mind:

- Just as each `<http>` element is considered from top to bottom, so are `<intercept-url>` elements. This means it is important to specify the most specific elements first. The following example illustrates a configuration that does not specify the more specific pattern first, which will result in warnings from Spring Security at startup:

```
<http ...>
  <!-- matches every request, so it will not continue -->
  <intercept-url pattern="/**"
    access="ROLE_USER"/>
  <!-- below will never match -->
  <intercept-url pattern="/login/form"
    access="ROLE_ANONYMOUS,ROLE_USER"/>
    ...
</http>
```

*Getting Started with Spring Security*

- It is important to note that if `<http>` is marked as `security="none"`, there can be no child `<intercept-url>` elements defined. This is because `security="none"` states that Spring Security should ignore all requests that match this `<http>` tag. Defining a child `<intercept-url>` element with `security="none"` contradicts any `<intercept-url>` declaration. An example is as follows:

  ```
  <http pattern="/http/**" security="none">
      <!-- below will produce an error since
           it would never be executed -->
      <intercept-url pattern="/**"
              access="ROLE_USER"/>
      ...
  </http>
  ```

- The `path` attribute of the `<intercept-url>` element is independent and is not aware of the path attribute of the `<http>` element. For example, the following would never match a request since a request cannot start with both `/http` and `/intercept-url` at the same time (these two patterns are mutually exclusive):

  ```
  <http pattern="/http/**" ...>
      <!-- below will never match -->
      <intercept-url pattern="/intercept-url/**"
              access="ROLE_USER"/>
      ...
  </http>
  ```

If you have not done so already, restart the application and visit `http://localhost:8080/calendar/`. Experiment with the application to see all the updates you have made.

1. Select a link that requires authentication and observe the new login page.
2. Try typing an invalid username/password and view the error message.
3. Try logging in as an admin (`admin1@example.com`/`admin1`), and view all of the events. Note that we are able to view all the events.
4. Try logging out and view our logout success message.
5. Try logging in as a regular user (`user1@example.com`/`user1`), and view all of the events. Note that we get an access denied page.

> Your code should now look like `chapter02.03-calendar`.

[ 42 ]

## Expression-based authorization

You may have noticed that granting access to everyone was not nearly as concise as we may have liked. Fortunately, Spring Security can leverage **Spring Expression Language** (SpEL) to determine whether a user has authorization. In the following code snippet, you can see the updates when using SpEL with Spring Security:

src/main/webapp/WEB-INF/spring/security.xml

```
<http auto-config="true"
      use-expressions="true">
    <intercept-url pattern="/"
        access="permitAll"/>
    <intercept-url pattern="/login/*"
        access="permitAll"/>
    <intercept-url pattern="/logout"
        access="permitAll"/>
    <intercept-url pattern="/events/"
        access="hasRole('ROLE_ADMIN')"/>
    <intercept-url pattern="/**"
        access="hasRole('ROLE_USER')"/>
    <form-login ../>
    ...
</http>
```

> You may notice that the /events/ security constraint is brittle. For example, the URL /events is not protected by Spring Security to restrict ROLE_ADMIN. This demonstrates the need to ensure that we provide multiple layers of security. We will exploit this sort of weakness in *Chapter 10, Fine-grained Access Control*.

Changing the access attribute from ROLE_ANONYMOUS, ROLE_USER to permitAll might not seem like much, but this only scratches the surface of the power of Spring Security's expressions. We will go into much greater detail about access control and Spring Expressions in the second half of the book. Go ahead and verify that the updates work by running the application.

> You code should now look like chapter02.04-calendar.

[ 43 ]

## Conditionally displaying authentication information

Currently, our application has no indication whether we are logged in or not. In fact, it appears as though we are always logged in, since the **Logout** link is always displayed. In this section, we will demonstrate how to display the authenticated user's username and conditionally display portions of the page using Spring Security's JSP tag library.

The first step is to update your dependencies to include the `spring-security-taglibs-3.1.0.RELEASE.jar` file. Since we are using Maven, we will add a new dependency declaration in our `pom.xml` file, as follows:

pom.xml

```xml
    <dependencies>
      ...
      <dependency>
        <groupId>org.springframework.security</groupId>
        <artifactId>spring-security-taglibs</artifactId>
        <version>3.1.0.RELEASE</version>
      </dependency>
    </dependencies>
```

The next step is to update `header.jsp` to leverage the Spring Security tag library. You can find the updates as follows:

src/main/webapp/WEB-INF/views/includes/header.jsp

```jsp
    <%@ taglib prefix="c" uri="http://java.sun.com/jsp/jstl/core" %>
    <%@ taglib prefix="sec" uri="http://www.springframework.org/security/tags" %>
    <!DOCTYPE html>
    ...
      <div id="nav-account" class="nav-collapse pull-right">
        <ul class="nav">
          <sec:authorize
              access="authenticated"
              var="authenticated"/>
          <c:choose>
            <c:when test="${authenticated}">
              <li id="greeting">
                <div>
                  Welcome
                  <sec:authentication property="name" />
                </div>
              </li>
```

```
              <c:url var="logoutUrl" value="/logout"/>
              <li>
                <a id="navLogoutLink" href="${logoutUrl}">Logout</a>
              </li>
          </c:when>
          <c:otherwise>
              <c:url var="loginUrl" value="/login/form"/>
              <li>
                <a id="navLoginLink" href="${loginUrl}">Login</a>
              </li>
          </c:otherwise>
        </c:choose>
      </ul>
    </div>
    ...
```

The `<sec:authorize />` tag determines whether the user is authenticated or not and assigns it to the variable `authenticated`. The `access` attribute should be rather familiar from the `<intercept-url />` element. In fact, both components leverage the same SpEL support. In order for the tag to be able to use SpEL support, ensure that you specify `<http use-expressions="true">` in your Spring Security configuration as we have already done, otherwise Spring Security will throw an exception stating it cannot find `o.s.s.web.access.expression.WebSecurityExpressionHandler`. If you choose, there are attributes on the JSP tag libraries that do not use expressions. However, using SpEL is typically the preferred method since it is more powerful.

The `<sec:authentication />` tag will look up the current `o.s.s.core.Authentication` object. The `property` attribute will find the `principal` attribute on `o.s.s.core.Authentication`, which in this case is `o.s.s.core.userdetails.UserDetails`. It then obtains the `UserDetails` username property and renders it to the page. Don't worry if the details of this are confusing. We are going to go over this in more detail in *Chapter 3, Custom Authentication*.

If you haven't done so already, restart the application to see the updates we have made. At this point, you may realize that we are still displaying links we do not have access to. For example, `user1@example.com` should not see a link to the **All Events** page. Rest assured, we'll fix this when we cover the JSP tags in greater detail in *Chapter 10, Fine-grained Access Control*.

Your code should now look like `chapter02.05-calendar`.

# Customizing the behavior after login

We have already discussed how to customize a user's experience during login, but sometimes it is necessary to customize the behavior after login. In this section, we will discuss how Spring Security behaves after login and will provide a simple mechanism to customize this behavior.

In the default configuration, Spring Security has two different flows after successful authentication. The first scenario occurs if a user never visits a resource that requires authentication. In this instance, after a successful login attempt, the user will be sent to the `default-target-url` attribute of the `<form-login>` element. If left undefined, `default-target-url` will be the context root of the application.

If a user requests a protected page before being authenticated, Spring Security will remember the last protected page that was accessed prior to authenticating using `o.s.s.web.savedrequest.RequestCache`. Upon successful authentication, Spring Security will send the user to the last protected page that was accessed prior to authentication. For example, if an unauthenticated user requests the **My Events** page, they will be sent to the login page.

After successfully authenticating, they will be sent to the previously requested **My Events** page.

A common requirement is to customize Spring Security to send the user to a different `default-target-url` attribute, depending on the user's role. Let's take a look at how this can be accomplished.

The first step is to configure the `default-target-url` attribute of the `<form-login>` element. Go ahead and update `security.xml` to use `/default` instead of the context root.

src/main/webapp/WEB-INF/spring/security.xml

```
<http ...>
    ...
    <form-login login-page="/login/form"
            login-processing-url="/login"
            username-parameter="username"
            password-parameter="password"
            authentication-failure-url="/login/form?error"
            default-target-url="/default"/>
    ...
</http>
```

The next step is to create a controller that processes /default. In the following code, you will find a sample Spring MVC controller, DefaultController, which demonstrates how to redirect administrators to the **All Events** page and other users to the **Welcome** page. Create a new file in the following location:

src/main/java/com/packtpub/springsecurity/web/controllers/DefaultController.java

```java
// imports omitted
@Controller
public class DefaultController {
    @RequestMapping("/default")
    public String defaultAfterLogin(HttpServletRequest request) {
        if (request.isUserInRole("ROLE_ADMIN")) {
            return "redirect:/events/";
        }
        return "redirect:/";
    }
}
```

> In Spring Tool Suite you can use *Shift* + *CTRL* + *O* to automatically add the missing imports.

There are a few things to point out about DefaultController and how it works. The first is that Spring Security makes the HttpServletRequest parameter aware of the currently logged-in user. In this instance, we are able to inspect which role the user belongs to, without relying on any of Spring Security's APIs. This is good because if Spring Security's APIs change or we decide we want to switch our security implementation, we have less code that needs to be updated. It should also be noted that while we implement this controller with a Spring MVC controller, our default-target-url attribute could be handled by any controller implementation (for example, Struts, a standard Servlet, and so on) we desire.

If you wish to always go to default-target-url, you can leverage the always-use-default-target attribute. We will not do this in our configuration, but you can see an example of this, as follows:

```xml
<form-login ...
        always-use-default-target="true"/>
```

You are now ready to give it a try. Restart the application and go directly to the **My Events** page, then log in; you will see that you are at the **My Events** page. Next, log out and try logging in as `user1@example.com`. You should go to the **Welcome** page. Log out and log in as `admin1@example.com`, and you will be sent to the **All Events** page.

> Your code should now look like `chapter02.06-calendar`.

# Summary

In this chapter we have applied a very basic Spring Security configuration, shown how to customize the user's login and logout experience, and demonstrated how to display basic information such as a username in our web application

In the next chapter, we will discuss how authentication in Spring Security works and how we can customize it to our needs.

# 3
# Custom Authentication

In *Chapter 2*, *Getting Started with Spring Security*, we demonstrated how to use an in-memory data store to authenticate the user. In this chapter, we'll explore how to solve some common, real-world problems by extending Spring Security's authentication support to use our existing set of APIs. Through this exploration, we'll get an understanding of each of the building blocks that Spring Security uses in order to authenticate users.

During the course of this chapter we will:

- Discover how to obtain the details of the currently logged-in user
- Add the ability to log in after creating a new account
- Learn the simplest method for indicating to Spring Security that a user is authenticated
- Create custom `UserDetailsService` and `AuthenticationProvider` implementations that properly decouple the rest of the application from Spring Security
- Add domain-based authentication to demonstrate how to authenticate with more than just a username and password

## JBCP Calendar architecture

Since this chapter is about integrating Spring Security with custom users and APIs, we will start with a quick introduction to the domain model within the JBCP Calendar application.

## CalendarUser

Our calendar application uses a domain object named `CalendarUser`, which contains information about our users.

src/main/java/com/packtpub/springsecurity/domain/CalendarUser.java

```java
public class CalendarUser implements Serializable {
    private Integer id;
    private String firstName;
    private String lastName;
    private String email;
    private String password;

    ... accessor methods omitted ..
}
```

## Event

Our application has an Event object that contains information about each event.

src/main/java/com/packtpub/springsecurity/domain/Event.java

```java
public class Event {
    private Integer id;
    private String summary;
    private String description;
    private Calendar when;
    private CalendarUser owner;
    private CalendarUser attendee;

    ... accessor methods omitted ..
}
```

## CalendarService

Our application contains a `CalendarService` interface that can be used for accessing and storing our domain objects. The code for `CalendarService` is as follows:

src/main/java/com/packtpub/springsecurity/service/CalendarService.java

```java
public interface CalendarService {
    CalendarUser getUser(int id);
    CalendarUser findUserByEmail(String email);
    List<CalendarUser> findUsersByEmail(String partialEmail);
```

```
    int createUser(CalendarUser user);
    Event getEvent(int eventId);
    int createEvent(Event event);
    List<Event> findForUser(int userId);
    List<Event> getEvents();
}
```

We won't go over the methods in `CalendarService`, but they should be fairly straightforward. If you would like details about what each method does, please consult the Javadoc in the sample code.

## UserContext

Like most applications, our application requires us to interact with the currently logged-in user. We have created a very simple interface called `UserContext`, to manage the currently logged-in user.

src/main/java/com/packtpub/springsecurity/service/UserContext.java

```
public interface UserContext {
    CalendarUser getCurrentUser();
    void setCurrentUser(CalendarUser user);
}
```

This means that our application can call `UserContext.getCurrentUser()` to obtain the details of the currently logged-in user. It can also call `UserContext.setCurrentUser(CalendarUser)` to specify which user is logged in. Later in this chapter, we will explore how we can write an implementation of this interface that uses Spring Security to access our current user. Obtaining the details of the current user using `SecurityContextHolder`.

Spring Security provides quite a few different methods for authenticating a user. However, the net result is that Spring Security will populate `o.s.s.core.context.SecurityContext` with an `o.s.s.core.Authentication`. The `Authentication` object represents all the information we gathered at the time of authentication (username, password, roles, and so on). The `SecurityContext` is then set on the `o.s.s.core.context.SecurityContextHolder`. This means that Spring Security and developers can use `SecurityContextHolder` to obtain information about the currently logged-in user. An example of obtaining the current username is illustrated below:

```
String username = SecurityContextHolder.getContext()
    .getAuthentication()
    .getName();
```

Custom Authentication

**NB:** > It should be noted that null checks should always be done on the `Authentication` object, as it could be `null` if the user is not logged in.

## SpringSecurityUserContext

The current `UserContext` implementation, `UserContextStub`, is a stub that always returns the same user. This means that the **My Events** page will always display the same user no matter who is logged in. Let's update our application to utilize the current Spring Security user's username to determine which events to display on the **My Events** page.

> You should be starting with the sample code in `chapter03.00-calendar`.

The first step is to comment out the `@Component` attribute on `UserContextStub`, so that our application no longer uses our canned results.

> The `@Component` annotation is used in conjunction with the `<context:component-scan />` element found in `src/main/webapp/WEB-INF/spring/services.xml`, to automatically create a Spring Bean rather than creating explicit XML configuration for each bean. You can learn more about Spring's classpath scanning in the Spring Reference the link `http://static.springsource.org/spring/docs/current/spring-framework-reference/html/`.

`src/main/java/com/packtpub/springsecurity/service/UserContextStub.java`

```
...
//@Component
public class UserContextStub implements UserContext {
...
```

[ 52 ]

Chapter 3

The next step is to utilize `SecurityContext` to obtain the currently logged-in user. We have included `SpringSecurityUserContext` within this chapter's code, which is wired up with the necessary dependencies but contains no actual functionality. Open `SpringSecurityUserContext` and add the `@Component` annotation. Next, replace the `getCurrentUser` implementation as follows:

src/main/java/com/packtpub/springsecurity/service/SpringSecurityUserContext.java

```java
@Component
public class SpringSecurityUserContext implements UserContext {
    private final CalendarService calendarService;
    private final UserDetailsService userDetailsService;

    @Autowired
    public SpringSecurityUserContext(CalendarService
      calendarService,UserDetailsService userDetailsService) {
        this.calendarService = calendarService;
        this.userDetailsService = userDetailsService;
    }

    public CalendarUser getCurrentUser() {
        SecurityContext context = SecurityContextHolder.getContext();
        Authentication authentication = context.getAuthentication();
        if (authentication == null) {
            return null;
        }

        String email = authentication.getName();
        return calendarService.findUserByEmail(email);
    }

    public void setCurrentUser(CalendarUser user) {
        throw new UnsupportedOperationException();
    }
}
```

*[Handwritten annotation: IMPORTANT CODE FOR OBTAINING THE AUTHENTICATED USER]*

[ 53 ]

### Custom Authentication

*[THE ESSENCE]* Our code obtains the username from the current Spring Security `Authentication` object and utilizes that to look up the current `CalendarUser` object by the e-mail address. Since our Spring Security username is an e-mail address, we are able to use the e-mail address to link `CalendarUser` with the Spring Security user. Note that if we were to link accounts, we would normally want to do this with a key that we generated rather than something that may change (that is, an e-mail address). We follow the good practice of returning only our domain object to the application. This ensures that our application is only aware of our `CalendarUser` object and thus is not coupled to Spring Security.

This code may seem eerily similar to when we used the `<sec:authentication />` tag in *Chapter 2*, *Getting Started with Spring Security*, to display the current user's username. In fact, the Spring Security tag library uses `SecurityContextHolder` in the same manner as we have done here. We could use our `UserContext` interface to place the current user on `HttpServletRequest` and thus remove our dependency on the Spring Security tag library.

Start up the application, visit `http://localhost:8080/calendar/`, and log in with `admin1@example.com` as the username and `admin1` as the password. Visit the **My Events** page, and you will see that only the events for that current user who is the owner or the attendee are displayed. Try creating a new event; you will observe that the owner of the event is now associated with the logged-in user. Log out of the application and repeat these steps with `user1@example.com` as the username and `user1` as the password.

[ 💡 Your code should now look like `chapter03.01-calendar`. ]

*[03.02]*
## Logging in new users using SecurityContextHolder

A common requirement is to allow users to create a new account and then automatically log them into the application. In this section, we'll describe the simplest method for indicating that a user is authenticated, by utilizing `SecurityContexHolder`.

[ 54 ]

# Managing users in Spring Security

The application provided in *Chapter 1, Anatomy of an Unsafe Application*, provides a mechanism for creating a new `CalendarUser` object, so it should be fairly trivial to create our `CalendarUser` object after a user signs up. However, Spring Security has no knowledge of `CalendarUser`. This means that we will need to add a new user in Spring Security too. Don't worry, we will remove the need for the dual maintenance of users later in this chapter.

Spring Security provides an `o.s.s.provisioning.UserDetailsManager` interface for managing users. Remember our in-memory Spring Security configuration?

```
<user-service>
    <user name="user1@example.com"
        password="user1"
        authorities="ROLE_USER"/>
    ...
</user-service>
```

The `<user-service>` element creates an in-memory implementation of `UserDetailsManager`, named `o.s.s.provisioning.InMemoryUserDetailsManager`, which can be used to create a new Spring Security user. Since we have already defined `UserDetailsManager` in our Spring configuration, all we need to do is update our existing `CalendarService` implementation, `DefaultCalendarService`, to add a user in Spring Security. Make the following updates to `DefaultCalendarService`:

src/main/java/com/packtpub/springsecurity/service/DefaultCalendarService.java

```java
public int createUser(CalendarUser user) {
    List<GrantedAuthority> authorities =
            AuthorityUtils.createAuthorityList("ROLE_USER");
    UserDetails userDetails = new User(user.getEmail(), user.getPassword(),
            authorities);
    // create a Spring Security user
    userDetailsManager.createUser(userDetails);
    // create a CalendarUser
    return userDao.createUser(user);
}
```

# Custom Authentication

In order to leverage `UserDetailsManager`, **we first convert `CalendarUser` into Spring Security's `UserDetails` object.** Later, we use `UserDetailsManager` to save the `UserDetails` object. The conversion is necessary, because Spring Security has no understanding of how to save our custom `CalendarUser` object, so we must map `CalendarUser` to an object Spring Security understands. You will notice that the `GrantedAuthority` object corresponds to the `authorities` attribute of our `security.xml` file. We hard code this for simplicity and due to the fact that there is no concept of roles in our existing system.

## Logging in a new user to an application

Now that we are able to add new users to the system, we need to indicate that the user is authenticated. Update `SpringSecurityUserContext` to set the current user on Spring Security's `SecurityContextHolder` object, as follows:

src/main/java/com/packtpub/springsecurity/service/SpringSecurityUserContext.java

```java
public void setCurrentUser(CalendarUser user) {
    UserDetails userDetails =
        userDetailsService.loadUserByUsername(user.getEmail());
    Authentication authentication = new
        UsernamePasswordAuthenticationToken(userDetails,
        user.getPassword(),userDetails.getAuthorities());
    SecurityContextHolder.getContext().
        setAuthentication(authentication);
}
```

The first step we perform is to convert our `CalendarUser` object into Spring Security's `UserDetails`. This is necessary, because just as Spring Security didn't know how to save our custom `CalendarUser` object, Spring Security does not understand how to make security decisions with our custom `CalendarUser` object. We use Spring Security's `o.s.s.core.userdetails.UserDetailsService` interface to obtain the same `UserDetails` object we saved with `UserDetailsManager`. `UserDetailsService` provides a subset, lookup by username, of the functionality provided by Spring Security's `UserDetailsManager` object that we have already seen.

Next, we create a `UsernamePasswordAuthenticationToken` object and place `UserDetails`, the password, and `GrantedAuthority` in it. Lastly, we set the authentication on `SecurityContextHolder`. In a web application, Spring Security will automatically associate the `SecurityContext` object in `SecurityContextHolder` to our HTTP session for us.

[ 56 ]

> It is important that Spring Security not be instructed to ignore a URL (that is, using security="none", as discussed in *Chapter 2, Getting Started with Spring Security*) in which SecurityContextHolder is accessed or set. This is because Spring Security will ignore the request and thus not persist SecurityContext for subsequent requests. The proper method to allow access to the URL in which SecurityContextHolder is used is to specify the access attribute of the <intercept-url> element (that is, <intercept-url ... access="permitAll"/>).

It is worth mentioning that we could have converted CalendarUser by creating a new User object directly, instead of looking it up in UserDetailsService. For example, the following code would also authenticate the user:

```
List<GrantedAuthority> authorities =
   AuthorityUtils.createAuthorityList("ROLE_USER");
UserDetails userDetails = new
   User("username","password",authorities);
Authentication authentication = new
   UsernamePasswordAuthenticationToken(
   userDetails,userDetails.getPassword(),userDetails
   .getAuthorities());
SecurityContextHolder.getContext()
   .setAuthentication(authentication);
```

The advantage of this approach is that there is no need for hitting the data store again. In our case, the data store is an in-memory data store, but this could be backed by a database, which could have some security implications. The disadvantage of this approach is that we do not get much code reuse. Since this method is invoked infrequently, we opt for code reuse. In general, it is best to evaluate each situation separately to determine which approach makes the most sense.

## Updating SignupController

The application has a SignupController object, which is what processes the HTTP request to create a new CalendarUser object. The last step is to update SignupController to create our user and then indicate that they are logged in. Make the following updates to SignupController:

src/main/java/com/packtpub/springsecurity/web/controllers/SignupController.java

```
@RequestMapping(value="/signup/new",method=RequestMethod.POST)
public String signup(@Valid SignupForm signupForm,
   BindingResult result, RedirectAttributes redirectAttributes) {
```

## Custom Authentication

```
    ... existing validation …
    user.setPassword(signupForm.getPassword());
    int id = calendarService.createUser(user);
    user.setId(id);
    userContext.setCurrentUser(user);
    redirectAttributes.addFlashAttribute("message", "Success");
    return "redirect:/";
}
```

If you have not done so already, restart the application, visit http://localhost:8080/calendar/, create a new user, and see that the new user is automatically logged in.

> Your code should now look like chapter03.02-calendar.

# Creating a custom UserDetailsService object

While we are able to link our domain model (CalendarUser) with Spring Security's domain model (UserDetails), we have to maintain multiple representations of the user. To resolve this dual maintenance, we can implement a custom UserDetailsService object to translate our existing CalendarUser domain model into an implementation of Spring Security's UserDetails interface. By translating our CalendarUser object into UserDetails, Spring Security can make security decisions using our custom domain model. This means that we will no longer need to manage two different representations of a user.

## CalendarUserDetailsService

Up to this point, we have needed two different representations of users. One for Spring Security to make security decisions and one for our application to associate our domain objects to. Create a new class named CalendarUserDetailsService that will make Spring Security aware of our CalendarUser object. This will ensure that Spring Security can make decisions based upon our domain model. Create a new file named CalendarUserDetailsService.java, as follows:

src/main/java/com/packtpub/springsecurity/core/userdetails/
CalendarUserDetailsService.java

```
    // imports and package declaration omitted
    @Component
    public class CalendarUserDetailsService implements
```

```
    UserDetailsService {
    private final CalendarUserDao calendarUserDao;

    @Autowired
    public CalendarUserDetailsService(CalendarUserDao
      calendarUserDao) {
      this.calendarUserDao = calendarUserDao;
    }

    public UserDetails loadUserByUsername(String username) throws
      UsernameNotFoundException {
      CalendarUser user = calendarUserDao.findUserByEmail(username);
      if (user == null) {
        throw new UsernameNotFoundException("Invalid
          username/password.");
      }
      Collection<? extends GrantedAuthority> authorities =
        CalendarUserAuthorityUtils.createAuthorities(user);
      return new User(user.getEmail(), user.getPassword(),
        authorities);
    }
}
```

> Within Spring Tool Suite you can use *Shift+Ctrl+O* to easily add the missing imports. Alternatively, you can copy the code from the next checkpoint (chapter03.03-calendar).

Here we utilize `CalendarUserDao` to obtain `CalendarUser` by using the e-mail address. We take care not to return a `null` value; instead, a `UsernameNotFoundException` exception should be thrown, as returning `null` breaks the `UserDetailsService` interface. We then convert `CalendarUser` into `UserDetails`, implemented by the user, as we did in the previous sections.

We now utilize a utility class named `CalendarUserAuthorityUtils` that we provided in the sample code. This will create `GrantedAuthority` based upon the e-mail address, so that we can support users and administrators. If the e-mail starts with admin, the user is treated as ROLE_ADMIN, ROLE_USER. Otherwise, the user is treated as ROLE_USER. Of course, we would not do this in a real application, but it's this simplicity that allows us to focus on this lesson.

# Configuring UserDetailsService

Now that we have a new `UserDetailsService` object, let's update the Spring Security configuration to utilize it. Update the `security.xml` file as follows:

src/main/webapp/WEB-INF/spring/security.xml

```
<authentication-manager>
  <authentication-provider
    user-service-ref="calendarUserDetailsService"/>
</authentication-manager>
```

`CalendarUserDetailsService` is added to our Spring configuration automatically, since we leverage classpath scanning and the `@Component` annotation. This means we only need to update Spring Security to refer to the `CalendarUserDetailsService` we just created. We are also able to remove the `<user-service>` element, Spring Security's in-memory implementation of `UserDetailsService`, since we are now providing our own `UserDetailsService` implementation.

# Removing references to UserDetailsManager

We need to remove the code we added in the `DefaultCalendarService` that used `UserDetailsManager` to synchronize the Spring Security users and `CalendarUsers`. First, the code is not necessary, since Spring Security now refers to our `CalendarUserDetailsService`. Second, since we removed the `<user-service>` element, there is no `UserDetailsManager` object defined in our Spring configuration. Go ahead and remove all references to `UserDetailsManager` found in `DefaultCalendarSerivce`. The updates will look similar to the following sample snippets:

src/main/java/com/packtpub/springsecurity/service/
DefaultCalendarService.java

```
public class DefaultCalendarService implements CalendarService {
    private final EventDao eventDao;
    private final CalendarUserDao userDao;

    @Autowired
    public DefaultCalendarService(EventDao eventDao, CalendarUserDao userDao) {
        this.eventDao = eventDao;
        this.userDao = userDao;
    }
    ...
    public int createUser(CalendarUser user) {
        return userDao.createUser(user);
    }
}
```

Chapter 3

Start up the application and see that Spring Security's in-memory `UserDetailsManager` object is no longer necessary (we removed it from our `security.xml` file).

> Your code should now look like chapter03.03-calendar.

## CalendarUserDetails

We have successfully eliminated the need to manage both Spring Security users and our `CalendarUser` objects. However, it is still cumbersome for us to continually need to translate between the two objects. Instead, we will create a `CalendarUserDetails` object, which can be referred to as both `UserDetails` and `CalendarUser`. Update `CalendarUserDetailsService` to use `CalendarUserDetails`, as follows:

src/main/java/com/packtpub/springsecurity/core/userdetails/
CalendarUserDetailsService.java

```java
    public UserDetails loadUserByUsername(String username) throws
      UsernameNotFoundException {
      ...
      return new CalendarUserDetails(user);
    }

    private final class CalendarUserDetails extends
      CalendarUser implements UserDetails {
      CalendarUserDetails(CalendarUser user) {
        setId(user.getId());
        setEmail(user.getEmail());
        setFirstName(user.getFirstName());
        setLastName(user.getLastName());
        setPassword(user.getPassword());
      }
      public Collection<? extends GrantedAuthority>
        getAuthorities() {
        return CalendarUserAuthorityUtils.createAuthorities(this);
      }

      public String getUsername() {
        return getEmail();
      }
      public boolean isAccountNonExpired() { return true; }
      public boolean isAccountNonLocked() { return true; }
      public boolean isCredentialsNonExpired() { return true; }
      public boolean isEnabled() { return true; }
    }
```

# Custom Authentication

In the next section, we will see that our application can now refer to the principal authentication on the current `CalendarUser` object. However, Spring Security can continue to treat `CalendarUserDetails` as a `UserDetails` object.

## SpringSecurityUserContext simplifications

We have updated `CalendarUserDetailsService` to return a `UserDetails` object that extends `CalendarUser` and implements `UserDetails`. This means that, rather than having to translate between the two objects, we can simply refer to a `CalendarUser` object. Update `SpringSecurityUserContext` as follows:

```
public class SpringSecurityUserContext implements UserContext {
  public CalendarUser getCurrentUser() {
    SecurityContext context = SecurityContextHolder.getContext();
    Authentication authentication = context.getAuthentication();
    if(authentication == null) {
    return null;
    }
    return (CalendarUser) authentication.getPrincipal();
  }

  public void setCurrentUser(CalendarUser user) {
    Collection authorities =
      CalendarUserAuthorityUtils.createAuthorities(user);
    Authentication authentication = new
      UsernamePasswordAuthenticationToken(user,
    user.getPassword(),authorities);
    SecurityContextHolder.getContext()
      .setAuthentication(authentication);
  }
}
```

The updates no longer require the use of `CalendarUserDao` or Spring Security's `UserDetailsService` interface. Remember our loadUserByUsername method from the previous section? The result of this method call becomes the principal of the authentication. Since our updated `loadUserByUsername` method returns an object that extends `CalendarUser`, we can safely cast the principal of the `Authentication` object to `CalendarUser`. We can pass a `CalendarUser` object as the principal into the constructor for `UsernamePasswordAuthenticationToken` when invoking `setCurrentUser`. This allows us to still cast the principal to a `CalendarUser` object when invoking `getCurrentUser`.

## Displaying custom user attributes

Now that `CalendarUser` is populated into the Spring Security's authentication, we can update our UI to display the name of the current user rather than the e-mail address. Update the `header.jsp` file with the following code:

src/main/webapp/WEB-INF/views/includes/header.jsp

```
<c:when test="${authenticated}">
    <li id="greeting">
        <div>
            Welcome <sec:authentication property="principal.name" />
        </div>
    </li>
    ...
</c:when>
```

Internally, the `<sec:authentication property="principal.name"/>` tag executes the following code. Observe that the highlighted values correlate to the property attribute of the authentication tag we specified in `header.jsp`.

```
SecurityContext context = SecurityContextHolder.getContext();
Authentication authentication = context.getAuthentication();
CalendarUser user = (CalendarUser) authentication.getPrincipal();
String firstAndLastName = user.getName();
```

Restart the application, visit `http://localhost:8080/calendar/`, and log in to view the updates. Instead of seeing the current user's e-mail, you should now see their first and last names.

> Your code should now look like `chapter03.04-calendar`.

# Creating a custom AuthenticationProvider object

Spring Security delegates to an `AuthenticationProvider` object to determine whether a user is authenticated or not. This means we can write custom `AuthenticationProvider` implementations to inform Spring Security how to authenticate in different ways. The good news is that Spring Security provides quite a few `AuthenticationProvider` objects so more often than not you will not need to create one. In fact, up until this point, we have been utilizing Spring Security's `o.s.s.authentication.dao.DaoAuthenticationProvider` object, which compares the username and password returned by `UserDetailsService`.

*Custom Authentication*

# CalendarUserAuthenticationProvider

Throughout the rest of this section, we are going to create a custom `AuthenticationProvider` object named `CalendarUserAuthenticationProvider` that will replace `CalendarUserDetailsService`. Then, we will use `CalendarUserAuthenticationProvider` to consider an additional parameter to support authenticating users from multiple domains. Create a new class named `CalendarUserAuthenticationProvider`, as follows:

> We must use an `AuthenticationProvider` object rather than `UserDetailsService`, because the `UserDetails` interface has no notion for a domain parameter.

src/main/java/com/packtpub/springsecurity/authentication/CalendarUserAuthenticationProvider.java

```java
// … imports omitted ...
@Component
public class CalendarUserAuthenticationProvider implements
  AuthenticationProvider {
  private final CalendarService calendarService;

  @Autowired
  public CalendarUserAuthenticationProvider(CalendarService
    calendarService) {
    this.calendarService = calendarService;
  }

  public Authentication authenticate(Authentication
    authentication) throws AuthenticationException {
    UsernamePasswordAuthenticationToken token =
      (UsernamePasswordAuthenticationToken) authentication;
    String email = token.getName();
    CalendarUser user = null;
    if(email != null) {
      user = calendarService.findUserByEmail(email);
    }
    if(user == null) {
      throw new UsernameNotFoundException("Invalid
        username/password");
    }
    String password = user.getPassword();
    if(!password.equals(token.getCredentials())) {
      throw new BadCredentialsException("Invalid
```

*Chapter 3*

```
            username/password");
    }
    Collection<? extends GrantedAuthority> authorities =
        CalendarUserAuthorityUtils.createAuthorities(user);
    return new UsernamePasswordAuthenticationToken(user, password,
        authorities);
}

public boolean supports(Class<?> authentication) {
    return UsernamePasswordAuthenticationToken
        .class.equals(authentication);
    }
}
```

> Remember that you can use *Shift+Ctrl+O* within Eclipse to easily add the missing imports. Alternativey, you can copy the implementation from chapter03.05-calendar.

Before Spring Security can invoke the authenticate method, the supports method must return true for the Authentication class that will be passed in. In this case, AuthenticationProvider can authenticate a username and password. We do not accept subclasses of UsernamePasswordAuthenticationToken, since there may be additional fields that we do not know how to validate.

The authenticate method accepts an Authentication object as an argument that represents an authentication request. In practical terms, it is the input from the user that we need to attempt to validate. If authentication fails, the method should throw an o.s.s.core.AuthenticationException exception. If authentication succeeds, it should return an Authentication object that contains the proper GrantedAuthority objects for the user. The returned Authentication object will be set on SecurityContextHolder. If authentication cannot be determined, the method should return null.

The first step in authenticating the request is to extract the information from the Authentication object that we need to authenticate the user. In our case, we extract the username and look up CalendarUser by the e-mail address, just as CalendarUserDetailsService did. If the provided username and password match CalendarUser, we will return a UsernamePasswordAuthenticationToken object with proper GrantedAuthority. Otherwise, we will throw an AuthenticationException exception.

Custom Authentication

Remember how the login page leveraged SPRING_SECURITY_LAST_EXCEPTION to explain why login failed? The message for the AuthenticationException exception thrown in AuthenticationProvider is the last AuthenticationException and will be displayed by our login page in the event of a failed login.

# Configuring CalendarUserAuthenticationProvider

Next, update the security.xml file to refer to our newly created CalendarUserAuthenticationProvider object, and remove the reference to CalendarUserDetailsService.

src/main/webapp/WEB-INF/spring/security.xml

```
<authentication-manager>
    <authentication-provider
            ref="calendarUserAuthenticationProvider"/>
</authentication-manager>
```

Restart the application and ensure everything is still working. As a user, we do not notice anything different. However, as a developer, we know that CalendarUserDetails is no longer required; we are still able to display the current user's first and last names, and Spring Security is still able to leverage CalendarUser for authentication.

> Your code should now look like chapter03.05-calendar.

# Authenticating with different parameters

One of the strengths of AuthenticationProvider is that it can authenticate with any parameters you wish. For example, maybe your application uses a random identifier for authentication, or perhaps it is a multi-tenant application and requires a username, password, and a domain. In the following section, we will update CalendarUserAuthenticationProvider to support multiple domains.

> A domain is a way to scope our users. For example, if we deploy our application once but have multiple clients using the same deployment, each client may want a user with the username admin. By adding a domain to our user object, we can ensure that each user is distinct and still supports this requirement.

[ 66 ]

## DomainUsernamePasswordAuthenticationToken

When a user authenticates, Spring Security submits an `Authentication` object to `AuthenticationProvider` with the information provided by the user. The current `UsernamePasswordAuthentication` object only contains a username and password field. Create a `DomainUsernamePasswordAuthenticationToken` object that contains a `domain` field.

src/main/java/com/packtpub/springsecurity/authentication/
DomainUsernamePasswordAuthenticationToken.java

```
public final class DomainUsernamePasswordAuthenticationToken
  extends UsernamePasswordAuthenticationToken {
  private final String domain;

  // used for attempting authentication
  public DomainUsernamePasswordAuthenticationToken(String
    principal, String credentials, String domain) {
    super(principal, credentials);
    this.domain = domain;
  }
  // used for returning to Spring Security after being
  //authenticated
  public DomainUsernamePasswordAuthenticationToken(CalendarUser
    principal, String credentials, String domain,
    Collection<? extends GrantedAuthority> authorities) {
    super(principal, credentials, authorities);
    this.domain = domain;
  }

  public String getDomain() {
    return domain;
  }
}
```

## Updating CalendarUserAuthenticationProvider

Now, we need to update `CalendarUserAuthenticationProvider` to utilize the `domain` field.

src/main/java/com/packtpub/springsecurity/authentication/
CalendarUserAuthenticationProvider.java

```
public Authentication authenticate(Authentication authentication)
  throws AuthenticationException {
  DomainUsernamePasswordAuthenticationToken token =
    (DomainUsernamePasswordAuthenticationToken) authentication;
  String userName = token.getName();
  String domain = token.getDomain();
```

# Custom Authentication

```
    String email = userName + "@" + domain;
    ... previous validation of the user and password ...
    return new DomainUsernamePasswordAuthenticationToken(user,
      password, domain, authorities);
}

public boolean supports(Class<?> authentication) {
  return DomainUsernamePasswordAuthenticationToken
    .class.equals(authentication);
}
```

We first update the `supports` method so that Spring Security will pass `DomainUsernamePasswordAuthenticationToken` into our `authenticate` method. We then use the domain information to create our e-mail address and authenticate, as we had previously done. Admittedly, this example is contrived. However, the example is able to illustrate how to authenticate with an additional parameter.

`CalendarUserAuthenticationProvider` can now use the new `domain` field. However, there is no way for a user to specify the domain. For this, we must update our `login.jsp` file.

## Adding domain to the login page

Open up the `login.jsp` file, and add a new input named `domain`, as follows:

src/main/webapp/WEB-INF/views/login.jsp

```
...
<input type="text" id="username" name="username"/>
<label for="domain">Domain</label>
<input type="text" id="domain" name="domain"/>
<label for="password">Password</label>
 <input type="text" id="username" name="username"/>
   <label for="domain">Domain</label> <input type="text" id="domain"
name="domain"/>
   <label for="password">Password</label>
...
```

Now, a domain will be submitted when users attempt to log in. However, Spring Security is unaware of how to use that domain to create a `DomainUsernamePasswordAuthenticationToken` and pass it into `AuthenticationProvider`. To fix this, we will need to create `DomainUsernamePasswordAuthenticationFilter`.

[ 68 ]

# DomainUsernamePasswordAuthenticationFilter

Spring Security provides a number of servlet filters that act as controllers for authenticating users. The filters are invoked as one of the delegates of the `FilterChainProxy` object that we discussed in *Chapter 2, Getting Started with Spring Security*. Previously, the `<form-login />` element instructed Spring Security to use `o.s.s.web.authentication.UsernamePasswordAuthenticationFilter`, to act as a login controller. The filter's job is to do the following:

- Obtain a username and password from the HTTP request
- Create a `UsernamePasswordAuthenticationToken` object with the information obtained from the HTTP request
- Request that Spring Security validate `UsernamePasswordAuthenticationToken`
- If the token is validated, it will set the authentication returned to it on `SecurityContextHolder`, just as we did when a new user signed up for an account.
- We will need to extend `UsernamePasswordAuthenticationFilter` to leverage our newly created `DoainUsernamePasswordAuthenticationToken` object. Create a `DomainUsernamePasswordAuthenticationFilter` object as follows:

src/main/java/com/packtpub/springsecurity/web/authentication/DomainUsernamePasswordAuthenticationFilter.java

```java
public final class
  DomainUsernamePasswordAuthenticationFilter
  extends UsernamePasswordAuthenticationFilter {

  public Authentication
    attemptAuthentication(HttpServletRequest request,
    HttpServletResponse response) throws
    AuthenticationException {
    if (!request.getMethod().equals("POST")) {
      throw new AuthenticationServiceException(
        "Authentication method not supported: " +
        request.getMethod());
    }
    String username = obtainUsername(request);
    String password = obtainPassword(request);
    String domain = request.getParameter("domain");

    // authRequest.isAuthenticated() = false since no
    //authorities are specified
```

```
        DomainUsernamePasswordAuthenticationToken authRequest
          = new DomainUsernamePasswordAuthenticationToken(
          username, password, domain);

        setDetails(request, authRequest);
        return this.getAuthenticationManager()
          .authenticate(authRequest);
    }
}
```

The new `DomainUsernamePasswordAuthenticationFilter` object will do the following:

- Obtain a username, password, and domain from the `HTTP` request.
- Create our `DomainUsernamePasswordAuthenticationToken` object with information obtained from the `HTTP` request.
- Request that Spring Security validate `DomainUsernamePasswordAuthenticationToken`. The work is delegated to `CalendarUserAuthenticationProvider`.
- If the token is validated, its superclass will set the authentication returned by `CalendarUserAuthenticationProvider` on `SecurityContextHolder`, just as we did to authenticate a user after they created a new account.

## Updating our configuration

Now that we have created all the code required for an additional parameter, we need to configure Spring Security to be aware of it. The following code snippet includes the required updates to our `security.xml` file to support our additional parameter:

`src/main/webapp/WEB-INF/spring/security.xml`

```
<http use-expressions="true"
  auto-config="true"
  entry-point-ref="loginEntryPoint">
  <custom-filter ref="domainFormLoginFilter"
    position="FORM_LOGIN_FILTER"/>
    ...
    ...
  <form-login login-page="/login/form"
    login-processing-url="/login"
    username-parameter="username"
    password-parameter="password"
    authentication-failure-url="/login/form?error"
    default-target-url="/default"/>
    ...
```

```xml
</http>
<authentication-manager alias="authenticationManager">
   ...
</authentication-manager>

<bean:bean xmlns="http://www.springframework.org/schema/beans"
  id="domainFormLoginFilter"
  class="com.packtpub.springsecurity.web.authentication
  .DomainUsernamePasswordAuthenticationFilter">
  <property name="filterProcessesUrl" value="/login"/>
  <property name="authenticationManager"
    ref="authenticationManager"/>
  <property name="usernameParameter" value="username"/>
  <property name="passwordParameter" value="password"/>
  <property name="authenticationSuccessHandler">
    <bean class="org.springframework.security.web.authentication
      .SavedRequestAwareAuthenticationSuccessHandler">
      <property name="defaultTargetUrl" value="/default"/>
    </bean>
  </property>
  <property name="authenticationFailureHandler">
    <bean class="org.springframework.security.web.authentication
      .SimpleUrlAuthenticationFailureHandler">
      <property name="defaultFailureUrl" value=
        "/login/form?error"/>
    </bean>
  </property>
</bean:bean>
<bean:bean xmlns="http://www.springframework.org/schema/beans"
  id="loginEntryPoint" class="org.springframework.security.web.
  authentication.LoginUrlAuthenticationEntryPoint">
  <bean:constructor-arg value="/login/form"/>
</bean:bean>
```

> The preceding code configures standard beans in our Spring Security configuration. We do this to demonstrate that it can be done. However, throughout much of the rest of the book we include standard bean configuration in its own file as this makes the configuration less verbose.
>
> If you are having trouble or prefer not to type all of this, you may copy it from chapter03.06-cvalendar.

## Custom Authentication

You can see that deviating from using the Spring Security namespace has made our configuration much more verbose. The following are a few highlights from the configuration updates:

- We removed `auto-config` and added a reference to `o.s.s.web.AuthenticationEntryPoint`, which determines what happens when a request for a protected resource occurs and the user is not authenticated. In our case, we are redirected to a login page.
- We remove `<form-login/>` and use a `<custom-filter />` element to insert our custom filter into `FilterChainProxy`. The position indicates the order in which the delegates of `FilterChain` are considered and cannot overlap with another filter.
- We added the configuration for our custom filter, which refers to the authentication manager created by the `<authentication-manager/>` element.

> If we do not remove `auto-config` or `<form-login/>`, and try to use `<custom-filter position="FORM_LOGIN"/>`, Spring Security will report an error similar to the following:
>
> ```
> "Filter beans '<domainFormLoginFilter>' and '<org.
> springframework.security.web.authentication.UsernamePass
> wordAuthenticationFilter#chapter03.00-calendar#src/main/
> webapp/WEB-INF/spring/security.xml#34>' have the same
> 'order'"
> ```

You can now restart the application and try the following steps, following along with our diagram to understand how all the pieces fit together:

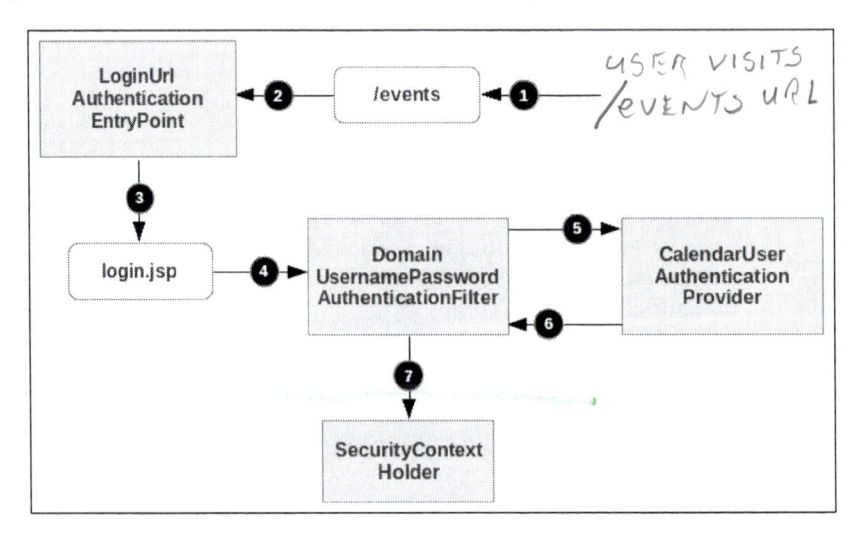

[ 72 ]

1. Visit `http://localhost:8080/calendar/events`.
2. Spring Security will intercept the secured URL and use `LoginUrlAuthenticationEntryPoint` to process it.
3. `LoginUrlAuthenticationEntryPoint` will send the user to the login page. Enter `admin1` as the username, `example.com` as the domain, and `admin1` as the password.
4. `DomainUsernamePasswordAuthenticationFilter` will intercept the process of the login request. It will then obtain the username, domain, and password from the `HTTP` request and create a `DomainUsernamePasswordAuthenticationToken` object.
5. `DomainUsernamePasswordAuthenticationFilter` submits `DomainUsernamePasswordAuthenticationToken` to `CalendarUserAuthenticationProvider`.
6. `CalendarUserAuthenticationProvider` validates `DomainUsernamePasswordAuthenticationToken` and then returns an authenticated `DomainUsernamePasswordAuthenticationToken` object (that is, `isAuthenticated()` returns `true`).
7. `DomainUserPasswordAuthenticationFilter` updates `SecurityContext` with `DomainUsernamePasswordAuthenticationToken` and places it on `SecurityContextHolder`.

> Your code should look like `chapter03.06-calendar`.

# Which authentication method to use

We have covered the three main methods of authenticating, so which one is the best? Like all solutions, each comes with its pros and cons. You can find a summary of when to use a specific type of authentication by referring to the following list:

- `SecurityContextHolder`: Interacting directly with `SecurityContextHolder` is certainly the easiest way of authenticating a user. It works well when you are authenticating a newly created user or authenticating in an unconventional way. By using `SecurityContextHolder` directly, we do not have to interact with so many Spring Security layers. The downside is that we do not get some of the more advanced features Spring Security provides automatically. For example, if we want to send the user to the previously requested page after login, we would have to manually integrate that into our controller.

2. `UserDetailsService`: Creating a custom `UserDetailsService` object is an easy mechanism for Spring Security to make security decisions based on our custom domain model. It also provides a mechanism to hook into other Spring Security features. For example, Spring Security requires `UserDetailsService` in order to use the built-in **Remember Me** support covered in *Chapter 6, Remember-me Services*. `UserDetailsService` does not work when authentication is not based upon a username and password.

3. `AuthenticationProvider`: This is the most flexible method for extending Spring Security. It allows a user to authenticate with any parameters that we wish. However, if we wish to leverage features such as Spring Security's Remember Me, we will still need `UserDetailsService`.

# Summary

This chapter has used real-world problems to introduce the basic building blocks used in Spring Security. It also demonstrates to us how we can make Spring Security authenticate against our custom domain objects by extending the basic building blocks. In short, we have learned the following:

- `SecurityContextHolder` is the central location for determining the current user. Not only can it be used by developers to get the current user but also to set the currently logged-in user.
- How to create custom `UserDetailsService` and `AuthenticationProvider` objects.
- How to perform authentication with more than just a username and password.

In the next chapter, we will explore some of the built-in support for JDBC-based authentication.

# 4
# JDBC-based Authentication

In the previous chapter, we saw how we can extend Spring Security to utilize our `CalendarDao` interface and our existing domain model to authenticate users. In this chapter, we will see how we can use Spring Security's built-in JDBC support. To keep things simple, this chapter's sample code is based on our Spring Security setup from *Chapter 2, Getting Started with Spring Security*. In this chapter we will:

- Use Spring Security's built-in JDBC-based authentication support
- Utilize Spring Security's group-based authorization to make administering users easier
- Learn how to use Spring Security's `UserDetailsManager` interface
- Configure Spring Security to utilize our existing `CalendarUser` schema to authenticate users
- Learn how we can secure passwords using Spring Security's new cryptography module

## Using Spring Security's default JDBC authentication

If your application has not yet implemented security or your security infrastructure is using a database, Spring Security provides an out-of-the-box support that can simplify solving your security needs. Spring Security provides a default schema for users, authorities, and groups. If that does not meet your needs, it allows for the querying and managing the users to be customized. In the next section, we are going to go through the basic steps for setting up JDBC Authentication with Spring Security.

# Required dependencies

Our application has already defined all the necessary dependencies required for this chapter. However, if you are using Spring Security's JDBC support, you are likely going to want the following dependencies listed in your pom.xml file. It is important to highlight that the JDBC driver that you will use will depend on which database you are using. Consult your database vendor's documentation for details on which driver is needed for your database.

> Remember that all the Spring versions need to match, and Spring Security versions need to match (this includes transitive dependency versions). If you are having difficulty getting this to work in your own application, you may want to define the dependency management section in pom.xml to enforce this, as shown in *Chapter 2, Getting Started with Spring Security*. As previously mentioned, you will not need to worry about this when using the sample code, since we have already set up the necessary dependencies for you.

pom.xml

```xml
<!-- matching JDBC driver -->
<dependency>
  <groupId>com.h2database</groupId>
  <artifactId>h2</artifactId>
  <version>1.3.163</version>
  <scope>runtime</scope>
</dependency>
<dependency>
  <groupId>org.springframework.security</groupId>
  <artifactId>spring-security-config</artifactId>
  <version>3.1.0.RELEASE</version>
  <scope>runtime</scope>
</dependency>
<dependency>
  <groupId>org.springframework.security</groupId>
  <artifactId>spring-security-core</artifactId>
  <version>3.1.0.RELEASE</version>
</dependency>
<dependency>
  <groupId>org.springframework</groupId>
  <artifactId>spring-jdbc</artifactId>
  <version>3.1.0.RELEASE</version>
</dependency>
<dependency>
  <groupId>org.springframework</groupId>
  <artifactId>spring-tx</artifactId>
  <version>3.1.0.RELEASE</version>
</dependency>
```

# Using the H2 database

The first portion of this exercise involves setting up an instance of the Java-based H2 relational database, populated with the Spring Security default schema. We'll configure H2 to run in memory using Spring 3.1's embedded database configuration feature—a significantly simpler method of configuration than setting up the database by hand. You can find additional information on the H2 website (http://www.h2database.com/).

Keep in mind that in our sample application, we'll use H2, primarily, due to its ease of setup. Spring Security will work with any database that supports ANSI SQL out of the box. We encourage you to tweak the configuration and use the database of your preference, if you're following along with the examples. As we didn't want this portion of the book to focus on the complexities of database setup, we chose convenience over realism for the purposes of the exercises.

# Provided JDBC scripts

We've supplied all the SQL files that are used for creating the schema and data in an H2 database for this chapter in the src/main/resouces/database/h2/ folder. Any files prefixed with security- are to support Spring Security's default JDBC implementation. Any SQL files prefixed with calendar- are custom SQL files for our JBCP Calendar application. Hopefully, this will make running the samples a little easier. If you're following along with your own database instance, you may have to adjust the schema definition syntax to fit your particular database. Additional database schemas can be found in the Spring Security reference. You can find a link to the Spring Security reference in the book's *Appendix*.

# Configuring the H2-embedded database

To configure the H2 embedded database, we need to create a DataSource and run SQL to create the Spring Security table structure. In our application, we do not need to configure a DataSource since our services.xml file already declares one using Spring's <jdbc:embedded-database /> element. We will need to update the SQL that is loaded at startup to include Spring Security's basic schema definition, Spring Security user definitions, and the authority mappings for those users. You can find the DataSource definition and the relevant updates in the following code snippet:

src/main/webapp/WEB-INF/spring/services.xml

```
<?xml version="1.0" encoding="UTF-8"?>
<beans xmlns="http://www.springframework.org/schema/beans"
  xmlns:xsi="http://www.w3.org/2001/XMLSchema-instance"
```

## JDBC-based Authentication

```
    xmlns:jdbc="http://www.springframework.org/schema/jdbc"
    xmlns:p="http://www.springframework.org/schema/p"
    xsi:schemaLocation="http://www.springframework.org/schema/jdbc
    http://www.springframework.org/schema/jdbc/spring-jdbc-3.1.xsd
    http://www.springframework.org/schema/beans
    http://www.springframework.org/schema/beans/spring-beans-3.1.xsd
    ... >
...
    <jdbc:embedded-database id="dataSource" type="H2">
      <jdbc:script location="classpath:/database/h2/calendar-
        schema.sql"/>
      <jdbc:script location="classpath:/database/h2/calendar-
        data.sql"/>
      <jdbc:script location="classpath:/database/h2/security-
        schema.sql"/>
      <jdbc:script location="classpath:/database/h2/security-
        users.sql"/>
      <jdbc:script location="classpath:/database/h2/security-user-
        authorities.sql"/>
    </jdbc:embedded-database>
</beans>
```

> You will notice we are using the Spring jdbc namespace in this example. If you were creating a new file, you would need to ensure that you add the declaration at the top. You can use the **Spring Tool Suite** to add the xmlns:jdbc declaration to your Spring configuration just as we did in the previous chapter with the Spring Security namespace. If you are unfamiliar with XML declarations, you can also copy-paste from the sample code when integrating with your own application.

Remember that the <jdbc:embedded-database> declaration creates this database only in memory, so you won't see anything on the disk, and you won't be able to use standard tools to query it. However, you can use the H2 console that is embedded into the application to interact with the database. See the instructions on the **Welcome Page** of our application to learn how to use it.

## Configuring JDBC UserDetailsManager

We'll modify the `security.xml` file to declare that we're using a JDBC `UserDetailsManager` implementation, instead of the Spring Security in-memory `UserDetailsService` implementation that we configured in *Chapter 2, Getting Started with Spring Security*. This is done with a simple change to the `<authentication-manager>` declaration:

src/main/webapp/WEB-INF/spring/security.xml

```
...
<authentication-manager>
  <authentication-provider>
    <jdbc-user-service id="userDetailsService"
        data-source-ref="dataSource"/>
  </authentication-provider>
</authentication-manager>
...
```

We replace the previous `<user-service>` tag along with all of the child elements with `<jdbc-user-service>`, as shown in the preceding code snippet. The value of `data-source-ref` matches the `id` of the `<jdbc:embedded-database>` declaration that we updated in the previous step.

## Spring Security's default user schema

Let's take a look at each of the SQL files used to initialize the database. The first script we added contains the default Spring Security schema definition for users and their authorities. The following script has been adapted from Spring Security's appendix to have explicitly named constraints, to make troubleshooting easier:

src/main/resources/database/h2/security-schema.sql

```
create table users(
    username varchar(256) not null primary key,
    password varchar(256) not null,
    enabled boolean not null
);
create table authorities (
    username varchar(256) not null,
    authority varchar(256) not null,
    constraint fk_authorities_users
        foreign key(username) references users(username)
);
create unique index ix_auth_username on authorities
(username,authority);
```

## Defining users

The next script is in charge of defining the users in our application. The included SQL creates the same users that we have used throughout the entire book so far. The file also adds an additional user disabled1@example.com, which will not be able to log in since we indicate it as disabled.

src/main/resources/database/h2/security-users.sql

```
insert into users (username,password,enabled)
    values ('user1@example.com','user1',1);
insert into users (username,password,enabled)
    values ('admin1@example.com','admin1',1);
insert into users (username,password,enabled)
    values ('user2@example.com','admin1',1);
insert into users (username,password,enabled)
    values ('disabled1@example.com','disabled1',0);
```

## Defining user authorities

You may have noticed that there is no indication if a user is an administrator or a regular user. The next file specifies a direct mapping of the user to their corresponding authorities. If a user did not have an authority mapped to it, Spring Security would not allow that user to be logged in.

src/main/resources/database/h2/security-user-authorities.sql

```
insert into authorities(username,authority)
    values ('user1@example.com','ROLE_USER');
insert into authorities(username,authority)
    values ('admin1@example.com','ROLE_ADMIN');
insert into authorities(username,authority)
    values ('admin1@example.com','ROLE_USER');
insert into authorities(username,authority)
    values ('user2@example.com','ROLE_USER');
insert into authorities(username,authority)
    values ('disabled1@example.com','ROLE_USER');
```

After the SQL is added to the embedded database configuration, we should be able to start the application and log in. Try logging in with our new user using disabled1@example.com as the username and disabled1 as the password. Notice that Spring Security does not allow the user to log in and provides the error message Reason: User is disabled.

> Your code should look like calendar04.01-calendar now.

# UserDetailsManager

We have already leveraged the use of Spring Security's `InMemoryUserDetailsManager` class in *Chapter 3, Custom Authentication*, to look up the current `CalendarUser` application in our `SpringSecurityUserContext` implementation of `UserContext`. This allowed us to determine which `CalendarUser` should be used when looking up the events for the **My Events** page. *Chapter 3, Custom Authentication*, also demonstrated how to update `DefaultCalendarService` to utilize `InMemoryUserDetailsManager`, to ensure that we created a new Spring Security user when we created `CalendarUser`. This chapter re-uses exactly the same code. The only difference is now the `UserDetailsManager` implementation is backed by Spring Security's `JdbcUserDetailsManager` class, which uses a database instead of an in-memory data store.

## What other features does UserDetailsManager provide out of the box

Although these types of functions are relatively easy to write with additional JDBC statements, Spring Security actually provides an out-of-the-box functionality to support many common `Create`, `Read`, `Update`, and `Delete` (**CRUD**) operations on users in JDBC databases. This can be convenient for simple systems, and a good base to build on for any custom requirements that a user may have.

| Method | Description |
| --- | --- |
| void createUser(UserDetails user) | Creates a new user with the given UserDetails information, including any declared GrantedAuthority authorities. |
| void updateUser(final UserDetails user) | Updates a user with the given UserDetails information. Updates GrantedAuthority and removes the user from the user cache. |
| void deleteUser(String username) | Deletes the user with the given username, and removes the user from the user cache. |
| boolean userExists(String username) | Indicates whether or not a user (whether active or inactive) exists with the given username. |
| void changePassword(String oldPassword, String newPassword) | Changes the password of the currently logged-in user. The user must supply the correct current password in order for the operation to succeed. |

## JDBC-based Authentication

If `UserDetailsManager` does not provide all the methods that are necessary for your application, you can extend the interface to provide these custom requirements. For example, if you needed the ability to list all the possible users in an administrative view, you could write your own interface with this method and provide an implementation that points at the same data store as `UserDetailsManager` that you are currently using.

# Group-based access control

`JdbcUserDetailsManager` supports the ability to add a level of indirection between the users and the `GrantedAuthority` declarations, by grouping `GrantedAuthority` into logical sets called **groups**. Users are then assigned one or more groups, whose membership confers a set of `GrantedAuthority` declarations.

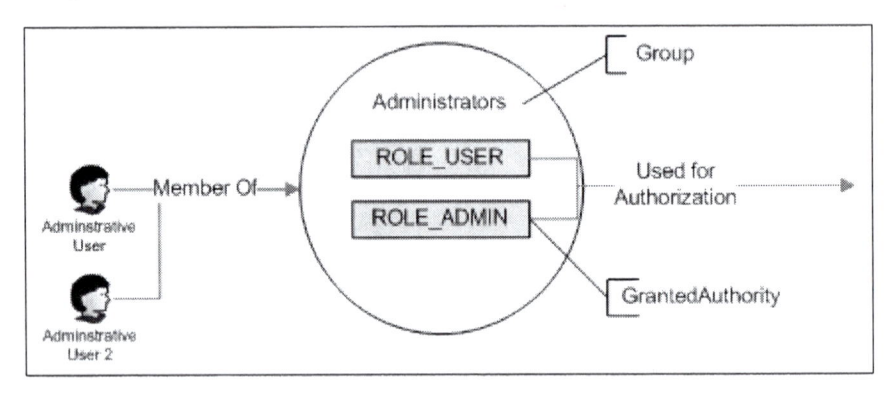

As you see in the diagram, this indirection allows the assignment of the same set of roles to multiple users, by simply assigning any new users to existing groups. Compare this with the behavior we've seen so far, where we assigned `GrantedAuthority` directly to individual users.

This bundling of common sets of authorities can be helpful in the following scenarios:

- You need to segregate users into communities, with some overlapping roles between groups.
- You want to globally change the authorization for a class of user. For example, if you have a "supplier" group, you might want to enable or disable their access to particular portions of the application.
- You have a large number of users, and you don't need a user-level authority configuration.

Unless your application has a very small user base, there is a very high likelihood that you'll be using group-based access control. While group-based access control is slightly more complex than other strategies, the flexibility and simplicity in managing a user's access makes this complexity worthwhile. This indirect technique of aggregating user privileges by group is commonly referred to as **Group-Based Access Control** (**GBAC**).

Group-based access control is an approach common to almost every secured operating system or software package in the market. Microsoft **Active Directory** (**AD**) is one of the most visible implementations of large-scale GBAC, due to its design of slotting AD users into groups and assignment of privileges to those groups. Management of privileges in large AD-based organizations is made exponentially simpler through the use of GBAC.

Try to think of the security models of the software you use—how are the users, groups, and privileges managed? What are the pros and cons of the way the security model is written?

Let's add a level of abstraction to the JBCP Calendar application and apply the concept of group-based authorization to the site.

# Configuring group-based access control

We'll add two groups to the application—regular users, which we'll call **Users**, and administrative users, which we'll call **Administrators**. Our existing accounts will be associated to the appropriate groups through an additional SQL script.

# Configuring JdbcUserDetailsManager to use groups

By default, Spring Security does not use GBAC. Therefore, we must instruct Spring Security to enable the use of groups. Modify the `security.xml` file to use `group-authorities-by-username-query`, as follows:

src/main/webapp/WEB-INF/spring/security.xml

```
    ...
    <authentication-manager>
      <authentication-provider>
        <jdbc-user-service id="userDetailsService"
          data-source-ref="dataSource"
          group-authorities-by-username-query=
          "select
          g.id, g.group_name, ga.authority
```

```
        from
        groups g, group_members gm, group_authorities ga
        where
        gm.username = ? and
        g.id = ga.group_id and
        g.id = gm.group_id"
      />
    </authentication-provider>
  </authentication-manager>
  ...
```

## Utilize the GBAC JDBC scripts

Next, we need to update the scripts that are being loaded at startup. We need to remove the `security-user-authorities.sql` mapping, so that our users no longer obtain their authorities with a direct mapping. We then need to add two additional SQL scripts. Update `DataSource` to load the SQL required for GBAC, as follows:

src/main/webapp/WEB-INF/spring/services.xml

```
    ...
    <jdbc:embedded-database id="dataSource" type="H2">
      <jdbc:script location="classpath:/database/h2/calendar-
        schema.sql"/>
      <jdbc:script location="classpath:/database/h2/calendar-
        data.sql"/>
      <jdbc:script location="classpath:/database/h2/security-
        schema.sql"/>
      <jdbc:script location="classpath:/database/h2/security-
        users.sql"/>
      <jdbc:script
        location="classpath:/database/h2/security-groups-
        schema.sql"/>
      <jdbc:script
        location="classpath:/database/h2/security-groups-
        mappings.sql"/>
    </jdbc:embedded-database>
    ...
```

## Group-based schema

It may be obvious, but the first SQL file we added contains updates to the schema to support group-based authorization. You can find the contents of the file, in the following code snippet:

src/main/resources/database/h2/security-groups-schema.sql

```sql
create table groups (
  id bigint generated by default as identity(start with 0) primary key,
  group_name varchar(256) not null
);
create table group_authorities (
  group_id bigint not null,
  authority varchar(256) not null,
  constraint fk_group_authorities_group
  foreign key(group_id) references groups(id)
);
create table group_members (
  id bigint generated by default as identity(start with 0) primary key,
  username varchar(256) not null,
  group_id bigint not null,
  constraint fk_group_members_group
  foreign key(group_id) references groups(id)
);
```

## Group authority mappings

Now, we need to map our existing users to groups, and the groups to authorities. This is done in the `security-groups-mappings.sql` file. Mapping based upon groups can be convenient, because many times organizations already have a logical group of users for other reasons. By utilizing the existing groupings of users, it can drastically simplify our configuration. This is how our layer of indirection helps us. We have included the group definitions, group to authority mappings, and a few users to the following group mappings:

src/main/resources/database/h2/security-groups-mappings.sql

```sql
    -- Create the Groups
    insert into groups(group_name) values ('Users');
    insert into groups(group_name) values ('Administrators');
    -- Map the Groups to Roles
    insert into group_authorities(group_id, authority)
      select id,'ROLE_USER' from groups where group_name='Users';
```

# JDBC-based Authentication

```
    insert into group_authorities(group_id, authority)
      select id,'ROLE_USER' from groups where
      group_name='Administrators';
    insert into group_authorities(group_id, authority)
      select id,'ROLE_ADMIN' from groups where
      group_name='Administrators';
    -- Map the users to Groups
    insert into group_members(group_id, username)
      select id,'user1@example.com' from groups where
      group_name='Users';
    insert into group_members(group_id, username)
      select id,'admin1@example.com' from groups where
      group_name='Administrators';
    ...
```

Go ahead and start the application, and it will behave just as before; however, the additional layer of abstraction between the users and roles simplifies managing large groups of users.

> Your code should look like `calendar04.02-calendar` now.

## Support for a custom schema

It's common for new users of Spring Security to begin their experience by adapting the JDBC user, group, or role mapping to an existing schema. Even though a legacy database doesn't conform to the expected Spring Security schema, we can still configure `JdbcDaoImpl` to map to it.

We will now update Spring Security's JDBC support to use our existing `CalendarUser` database along with a new `calendar_authorities` table.

We can easily change the configuration of `JdbcUserDetailsManager` to utilize this schema, and override Spring Security's expected table definitions and columns that we're using for the JBCP Calendar application.

# Determining the correct JDBC SQL queries

`JdbcUserDetailsManager` has three SQL queries that have a well-defined parameter and set of returned columns. We must determine the SQL that we'll assign to each of these queries, based on its intended functionality. Each SQL query used by `JdbcUserDetailsManager` takes the username presented at login as its one and only parameter.

| Namespace query attribute name | Description | Expected SQL columns |
|---|---|---|
| users-by-username-query | Returns one or more users matching the username; only the first user is used. | Username (string) <br> Password (string) <br> Enabled (Boolean) |
| authorities-by-username-query | Returns one or more granted authorities directly provided to the user; typically used when GBAC is disabled. | Username (string) <br> Granted Authority (string) |
| group-authorities-by-username-query | Returns granted authorities and group details provided to the user through group membership; used when GBAC is enabled. | Group Primary Key (any) <br> Group Name (any) <br> Granted Authority (string) |

Be aware that in some cases, the return columns are not used by the default `JdbcUserDetailsManager` implementation, but they must be returned anyway.

# Updating the SQL scripts that are loaded

We need to initialize `DataSource` with our custom schema rather than the Spring Security's default schema. Update the `services.xml` file, as follows:

src/main/webapp/WEB-INF/spring/services.xml

```
...
<jdbc:embedded-database id="dataSource" type="H2">
  <jdbc:script location="classpath:/database/h2/calendar-
  schema.sql"/>
  <jdbc:script location="classpath:/database/h2/calendar-data.sql"/>
  <jdbc:script
    location="classpath:/database/h2/calendar-authorities.sql"/>
</jdbc:embedded-database>
...
```

*JDBC-based Authentication*

Notice that we have removed all of the scripts that start with `security-`, and replaced them with `calendar-authorities.sql`.

## CalendarUser authority SQL

You can view the `CalendarUser` authority mappings in the following code snippet. Notice that we use the ID as the foreign key, which is better than utilizing the username as a foreign key (as Spring Security does). By using the ID as the foreign key, we can allow users to easily change their username.

src/main/resources/database/h2/calendar-authorities.sql

```
create table calendar_user_authorities (
    id bigint identity,
    calendar_user bigint not null,
    authority varchar(256) not null,
);
-- user1@example.com
insert into calendar_user_authorities(calendar_user, authority)
    select id,'ROLE_USER' from calendar_users where
    email='user1@example.com';
-- admin1@example.com
insert into calendar_user_authorities(calendar_user, authority)
    select id,'ROLE_ADMIN' from calendar_users where
        email='admin1@example.com';
insert into calendar_user_authorities(calendar_user, authority)
    select id,'ROLE_USER' from calendar_users where
    email='admin1@example.com';
-- user2@example.com
insert into calendar_user_authorities(calendar_user, authority)
    select id,'ROLE_USER' from calendar_users where
    email='user2@example.com';
```

## Insert custom authorities

We need to update `DefaultCalendarService` to insert the authorities for the user using our custom schema when we add a new `CalendarUser` class. This is because, while we reused the schema for the user definition, we did not define custom authorities in our existing application. Update `DefaultCalendarService`, as follows:

src/main/java/com/packtpub/springsecurity/service/DefaultCalendarService.java

```
import org.springframework.jdbc.core.JdbcOperations;
...
```

```java
public class DefaultCalendarService implements CalendarService {
    ...
    private final JdbcOperations jdbcOperations;

    @Autowired
    public DefaultCalendarService(EventDao eventDao, CalendarUserDao userDao,
JdbcOperations jdbcOperations) {
        ...
        this.jdbcOperations = jdbcOperations;
    }
    ...
    public int createUser(CalendarUser user) {
        int userId = userDao.createUser(user);
        jdbcOperations.update(
          "insert into calendar_user_authorities(calendar_user,authority) values (?,?)",
            userId, "ROLE_USER");
        return userId;
    }
}
```

> You may have noticed the JdbcOperations interface that is used for inserting our user. This is a convenient template provided by Spring that helps manage boilerplate code, such as connection and transaction handling. For more details, refer to the *Appendix* of this book to find the Spring Reference.

# Configuring the JdbcUserDetailsManager to use custom SQL queries

In order to use the custom SQL queries for our non-standard schema, we'll simply update our <jdbc-user-details-service> tag to include new queries. This is quite similar to how we enabled support for GBAC, except instead of using the default SQL we will use our modified SQL. Notice that we remove our old group-authorities-by-username-query attribute, since we will not be using it in this example in order to keep things simple.

src/main/webapp/WEB-INF/spring/security.xml

```
...
<authentication-manager>
  <authentication-provider>
    <jdbc-user-service id="userDetailsService"
```

## JDBC-based Authentication

```
      data-source-ref="dataSource"
      users-by-username-query="
      select
        email,password,true
      from
        calendar_users
      where
        email = ?"
      authorities-by-username-query="
      select
        cua.id, cua.authority
      from
        calendar_users cu, calendar_user_authorities cua
      where
        cu.email = ? and  cu.id = cua.calendar_user"
    />
  </authentication-provider>
</authentication-manager>
...
```

This is the only configuration required to use Spring Security, to read settings from an existing, non-default schema! Start up the application and ensure that everything is working properly.

> Your code should look like `calendar04.03-calendar` now.

Keep in mind that the utilization of an existing schema commonly requires an extension of `JdbcUserDetailsManager` to support changing of passwords, renaming of user accounts, and other user-management functions.

If you are using `JdbcUserDetailsManager` to perform user management tasks, then there are over twenty SQL queries utilized by the class that are accessible through the configuration. However, only the three covered are available through the namespace configuration. Please refer to the Javadoc or source code to review the defaults for the queries used by `JdbcUserDetailsManager`.

# Configuring secure passwords

We recall from the security audit in *Chapter 1, Anatomy of an Unsafe Application* that the security of passwords stored in cleartext was a top priority of the auditors. In fact, in any secured system, password security is a critical aspect of trust and authoritativeness of an authenticated principal. Designers of a fully secured system must ensure that passwords are stored in a way in which malicious users would have an impractically difficult time compromising them.

The following general rules should be applied to passwords stored in a database:

- Passwords must not be stored in cleartext (plain text)
- Passwords supplied by the user must be compared to the recorded passwords in the database
- A user's password should not be supplied to the user upon demand (even if the user forgets it)

For the purposes of most applications, the best fit for these requirements involves one-way encoding, known as **hashing**, of the passwords. Using a cryptographic hash provides properties such as security and uniqueness that are important to properly authenticate users with the added bonus that once it is hashed, the password cannot be extracted from the value that is stored.

In most secure application designs, it is neither required nor desirable to ever retrieve the user's actual password upon request, as providing the user's password to them without proper additional credentials could present a major security risk. Instead, most applications provide the user the ability to reset their password, either by presenting additional credentials (such as their social security number, date of birth, tax ID, or other personal information), or through an email-based system.

> **Storing other types of sensitive information**
>
> Many of the guidelines listed that apply to passwords apply equally to other types of sensitive information, including social security numbers and credit card information (although, depending on the application, some of these may require the ability to decrypt).
>
> It's quite common for databases storing this type of information to represent it in multiple ways, for example, a customer's full 16-digit credit card number would be stored in a highly encrypted form, but the last four digits might be stored in cleartext (for reference, think of any Internet commerce site that displays XXXX XXXX XXXX 1234 to help you identify your stored credit cards).

*JDBC-based Authentication*

You may already be thinking ahead and wondering, given our (admittedly unrealistic) approach of using SQL to populate our H2 database with users, how do we encode the passwords? H2, or most other databases, for that matter, don't offer encryption methods as built-in database functions.

Typically, the **bootstrap** process (populating a system with initial users and data) is handled through some combination of SQL loads and Java code. Depending on the complexity of your application, this process can get very complicated.

For the JBCP Calendar application, we'll retain the `<jdbc:embedded-database/>` declaration and the corresponding SQL, and then add some SQL that will modify the passwords to their hashed values.

## PasswordEncoder

Password hashing in Spring Security is encapsulated and defined by implementations of the `o.s.s.authentication.encoding.PasswordEncoder` interface. Simple configuration of a password encoder is possible through the `<password-encoder>` declaration within the `<authentication-provider>` element, as follows:

```
<authentication-manager>
  <authentication-provider user-service-ref="jdbcUserService">
    <password-encoder hash="sha-256"/>
  </authentication-provider>
</authentication-manager>
```

You'll be happy to learn that Spring Security ships with a number of implementations of `PasswordEncoder`, which are applicable for different needs and security requirements. The implementation used can be specified using the hash attribute of the `<password-encoder>` declaration.

The following table provides a list of the out-of-the-box implementation classes and their benefits. Note that all implementations reside in the `o.s.s.authentication.encoding` package.

| Implementation class | Description | Hash value |
| --- | --- | --- |
| PlaintextPasswordEncoder | Encodes the password as plaintext; this is the default. | plaintext |
| Md4PasswordEncoderPasswordEncoder | Encoder utilizing the MD4 hash algorithm. MD4 is not a secure algorithm—use of this encoder is not recommended. | md4 |
| Md5PasswordEncoderPassword | Encoder utilizing the MD5 one-way encoding algorithm. | |
| ShaPasswordEncoderPasswordEncoder | Encoder utilizing the SHA one-way encoding algorithm. This encoder can support configurable levels of encoding strength. | sha<br><br>sha-256 |
| LdapShaPasswordEncoder | Implementation of LDAP SHA and LDAP SSHA algorithms used in integration with LDAP authentication stores. We'll learn more about this algorithm in Chapter 5, *LDAP Directory Services*, where we cover LDAP. | {sha}<br><br>{ssha} |

As with many other areas of Spring Security, it's also possible to reference a bean definition implementing `PasswordEncoder` to provide more precise configuration and allow `PasswordEncoder` to be wired into other beans through the dependency injection. For the JBCP Calendar application, we'll need to use this bean reference method in order to hash the passwords of the newly created users.

Let's walk through the process of configuring basic password encoding for the JBCP Calendar application.

# Configuring password encoding

Configuring basic password encoding involves two pieces: hashing the passwords we load into the database after the SQL script executes, and ensuring that the Spring Security is configured to work with `PasswordEncoder`.

## Configuring the PasswordEncoder

First, we'll declare an instance of a PasswordEncoder as a normal Spring bean:

src/main/webapp/WEB-INF/spring/security.xml

```
...
</authentication-manager>

<bean:bean id="passwordEncoder"
  xmlns="http://www.springframework.org/schema/beans"
  class="org.springframework.security.authentication
  .encoding.ShaPasswordEncoder">
  <constructor-arg value="256"/>
</bean:bean>
```

You'll note that we're using the `SHA-256 PasswordEncoder` implementation. This is an efficient one-way encryption algorithm, commonly used for password storage.

## Making Spring Security aware of the PasswordEncoder

We'll need to configure Spring Security to have a reference to `PasswordEncoder`, so that it can encode and compare the presented password during user login. Simply add a `<password-encoder>` declaration and refer to the bean ID we defined in the previous step:

src/main/webapp/WEB-INF/spring/security.xml

```
...
<authentication-manager>
    <authentication-provider>
        <jdbc-user-service ... />
        <password-encoder ref="passwordEncoder"/>
    </authentication-provider>
</authentication-manager>
...
```

If you were to try the application at this point, you'd notice that what were previously valid login credentials would now be rejected. This is because the passwords stored in the database (loaded with the `calendar-users.sql` script) are not stored as a hash that matches the password encoder. We'll need to update the stored passwords to be a hashed value.

## Hashing the stored passwords

As illustrated in the following diagram, when a user submits a password, Spring Security hashes the submitted password and then compares that against the unhashed password in the database:

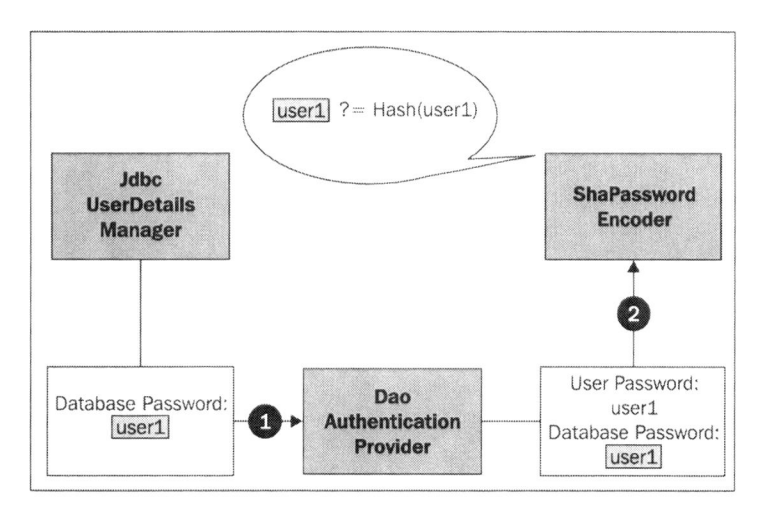

This means that users cannot log into our application. To fix this, we will update the SQL that is loaded at startup time to update the passwords to be the hashed values. Update the `services.xml` file, as follows:

src/main/webapp/WEB-INF/spring/services.xml

```
...
<jdbc:embedded-database id="dataSource" type="H2">
  <jdbc:script location="classpath:/database/h2/calendar-
    schema.sql"/>
  <jdbc:script location="classpath:/database/h2/calendar-
    data.sql"/>
  <jdbc:script location="classpath:/database/h2/calendar-
    authorities.sql"/>
  <jdbc:script location="classpath:/database/h2/calendar-
    sha256.sql"/>
</jdbc:embedded-database>
...
```

# JDBC-based Authentication

`calendar-sha256.sql` simply updates the existing passwords to their expected hashed value, as follows:

```
update calendar_users set password =
'0a041b9462caa4a31bac3567e0b6e6fd9100787db2ab433d96f6d178cabfce90'
where email = 'user1@example.com';
```

How did we know what value to update the password to? We have provided `o.s.s.authentication.encoding.Sha256PasswordEncoderMain` to demonstrate how to use the configured `PasswordEncoder` interface to hash the existing passwords. The relevant code is as follows:

```
ShaPasswordEncoder encoder = new ShaPasswordEncoder(256);
String encodedPassword = encoder.encodePassword(password, null);
```

## Hashing a new user's passwords

If we tried running the application and creating a new user, we would not be able to log in. This is because the newly-created user's password would not be hashed. We need to update `DefaultCalendarService` to hash the password. Make the following updates to ensure that newly-created users' passwords are hashed:

src/main/java/com/packtpub/springsecurity/service/
DefaultCalendarService.java

```
import org.springframework.security.authentication.encoding.
PasswordEncoder;
// other imports omitted
public class DefaultCalendarService implements CalendarService {
...
    private final PasswordEncoder passwordEncoder;

    @Autowired
    public DefaultCalendarService(EventDao eventDao,
      CalendarUserDao userDao, JdbcOperations jdbcOperations,
      PasswordEncoder passwordEncoder) {
        ...
        this.passwordEncoder = passwordEncoder;
    }
    ...
    public int createUser(CalendarUser user) {
        String encodedPassword =
          passwordEncoder.encodePassword(user.getPassword(),
          null);
```

[ 96 ]

```
            user.setPassword(encodedPassword);
            ...
            return userId;
        }
    }
```

## Not quite secure

Go ahead and start the application. Try creating a new user with `user1` as the password. Log out of the application, then use the instructions on the `Welcome` page to open the H2 console, and view all the users' passwords. Did you notice that the hashed values for the newly created user and `user1@example.com` are the same value? The fact that we have now figured out another user's password is a little disturbing. We will solve this with a technique known as **salting**.

> Your code should look like `calendar04.04-calendar` now.

## Would you like some salt with that password

If the security auditor were to examine the encoded passwords in the database, he'd find something that would still make him concerned about the website's security. Let's examine the stored username and password values for a few of our users:

| Username | Plaintext password | Hashed password |
| --- | --- | --- |
| admin1@example.com | admin1 | 25f43b1486ad95a1398e3eeb3d83bc4010015fcc9bedb35b432e00298d5021f7 |
| user1@example.com | user1 | 0a041b9462caa4a31bac3567e0b6e6fd9100787db2ab433d96f6d178cabfce90 |

This looks very secure—the encrypted passwords obviously bear no resemblance to the original passwords. What could the auditor be concerned about? What if we add a new user who happens to have the same password as our `user1@example.com` user?

| Username | Plain-text password | Hashed password |
| --- | --- | --- |
| hacker@example.com | user1 | 0a041b9462caa4a31bac3567e0b6e6fd9100787db2ab433d96f6d178cabfce90 |

[ 97 ]

Now, note that the encrypted password of the `hacker@example.com` user is exactly the same as the real user! Thus, a hacker who had somehow gained the ability to read the encrypted passwords in the database could compare their known password's encrypted representation with the unknown one for the user account, and see they are the same! If the hacker had access to an automated tool to perform this analysis, they could likely compromise the user's account within a matter of hours.

While it is difficult to guess a single password, hackers can calculate all the hashes ahead of time and store a mapping of the hash to the original password. Then figuring out the original password is a matter of looking up the password by its hashed value in constant time. This is a hacking technique known as **rainbow tables**.

One common and effective method of adding another layer of security to encrypted passwords is to incorporate a salt. A **salt** is a second plaintext component, which is concatenated with the plaintext password prior to performing the hash in order to ensure that two factors must be used to generate (and thus compare) the hashed password values. Properly selected salts can guarantee that no two passwords will ever have the same hashed value, thus preventing the scenario that concerned our auditor, and avoiding many common types of brute force password cracking techniques.

Best practice salts generally fall into one of the two categories:

- They are algorithmically generated from some piece of data associated with the user; for example, the timestamp that the user created
- They are randomly generated and stored in some form
- They are plaintext or two-way encrypted along with the user's password record

Remember that because the salt is added to the plaintext password, it can't be one-way encrypted—the application needs to be able to look up or derive the appropriate salt value for a given user's record in order to calculate the hash of the password, to compare with the stored hash of the user when performing authentication.

## Using salt in Spring Security

Spring Security 3.1 provides a new cryptography module that is included in the `spring-security-core` module or available separately in `spring-security-crypto`. The `crypto` module contains its own `o.s.s.crypto.password.PasswordEncoder`. In fact, using this interface is the preferred method for encoding passwords, because it will salt passwords using a random salt. At the time of this writing, there are three implementations of `o.s.s.crypto.password.PasswordEncoder`.

| Class | Description |
|---|---|
| o.s.s.crypto.bcrypt.BCryptPasswordEncoder | Uses the bcrypt hashing function. It supports salt and the ability to become slower to perform over time as technology improves. This helps protect against brute-force search attacks. |
| o.s.s.crypto.password.NoOpPasswordEncoder | Does no encoding (returns the password in its plaintext form). |
| o.s.s.crypto.password.StandardPasswordEncoder | Uses SHA-256 with multiple iterations and a random salt value. |

> For those who are familiar with Spring Security 3.0, salt used to be provided using `o.s.s.authentication.dao.SaltSource`. While still supported, this mechanism is not demonstrated in this book, since it is not the preferred mechanism for providing salt.

## Updating the Spring Security configuration

The first step is to update our Spring Security configuration. Remove our old ShaPasswordEncoder and add the new StandardPasswordEncoder as follows:

src/main/webapp/WEB-INF/spring/security.xml...

```
</authentication-manager>
<bean:bean id="passwordEncoder"
  class="org.springframework.security.crypto
  .password.StandardPasswordEncoder"/>
...
```

## Migrating existing passwords

We need to update our existing passwords to use the values produced by the new `PasswordEncoder` class. If you would like to generate your own passwords, you can use the following code:

```
StandardPasswordEncoder encoder = new StandardPasswordEncoder();

String encodedPassword = encoder.encode("password");
```

Remove the previously used `calendar-sha256.sql` file, and add the provided `saltedsha256.sql` file.

src/main/webapp/WEB-INF/spring/services.xml

```
...
<jdbc:embedded-database id="dataSource" type="H2">
  <jdbc:script location="classpath:/database/h2/calendar-
    schema.sql"/>
  <jdbc:script location="classpath:/database/h2/calendar-
    data.sql"/>
  <jdbc:script location="classpath:/database/h2/calendar-
    authorities.sql"/>
  <jdbc:script location="classpath:/database/h2/calendar-
    saltedsha256.sql"/>
</jdbc:embedded-database>
...
```

## Updating DefaultCalendarUserService

The `<password-encoder>` element we defined previously is smart enough to handle the new password encoder interface. However, `DefaultCalendarUserService` needs to update to the new interface. Make the following updates to `DefaultCalendarUserService`:

src/main/java/com/packtpub/springsecurity/service/DefaultCalendarService.java

```
import org.springframework.security.authentication.encoding.
PasswordEncoder;
import org.springframework.security.crypto.password.PasswordEncoder;
// other imports omitted
public class DefaultCalendarService implements CalendarService {
  ...
  public int createUser(CalendarUser user) {
    String encodedPassword =
      passwordEncoder.encode(user.getPassword());
    user.setPassword(encodedPassword);
    ...
    return userId;
  }
}
```

## Trying out the salted passwords

Start up the application and try creating another user with the password `user1`. Use the H2 console to compare the new user's password to `user1@example.com`, and observe that they are different.

> Your code should look like `calendar04.05-calendar` now.

Spring Security now generates a random salt and combines this with the password before hashing our password. It then adds the random salt to the beginning of the password in plaintext, so that passwords can be checked. The stored password can be summarized as follows:

```
salt = randomsalt()
hash = hash(salt+originalPassword)
storedPassword = salt + hash
```

This is the pseudo code for hashing a newly created password.

To authenticate a user, `salt` and `hash` can be extracted from the stored password, since both `salt` and `hash` are fixed lengths. Then, the extracted `hash` can be compared against a new `hash`, computed with extracted `salt` and the inputted password.

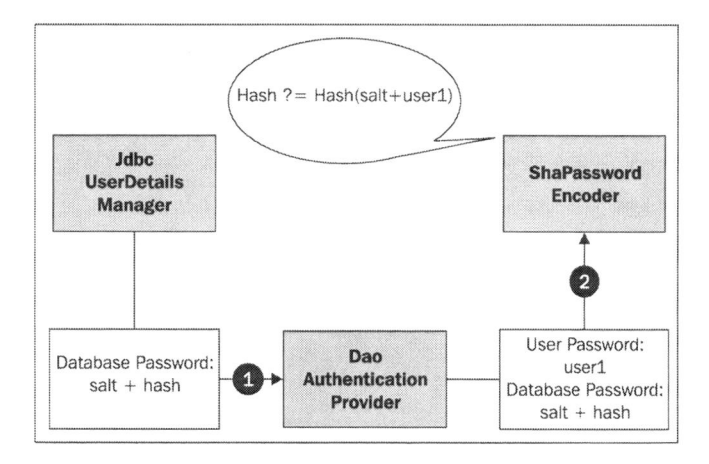

Following is the pseudo code for validating a salted password:

```
storedPassword = datasource.lookupPassword(username)
salt, expectedHash = extractSaltAndHash(storedPassword)
actualHash = hash(salt+inputedPassword)
authenticated = (expectedHash == actualHash)
```

# Summary

In this chapter, we learned how to use Spring Security's built-in JDBC support. Specifically we have:

- Learned that Spring Security provides a default schema for new applications
- Learned how to implement group-based access control and how it can make managing users easier
- Demonstrated how to integrate Spring Security's JDBC support with an existing database
- Learned to secure our passwords by hashing them and using a randomly-generated salt

In the next chapter, we will explore Spring Security's built-in support for LDAP-based authentication.

# 5
# LDAP Directory Services

In this chapter, we will review the **Lightweight Directory Access Protocol** (LDAP) and learn how it can be integrated into a Spring Security-enabled application to provide authentication, authorization, and user information services to interested constituents.

During the course of this chapter we will:

- Learn some of the basic concepts related to the LDAP protocol and server implementations
- Configure a self-contained LDAP server within Spring Security
- Enable LDAP authentication and authorization
- Understand the model behind LDAP search and user matching
- Retrieve additional user details from standard LDAP structures
- Differentiate between LDAP authentication methods and evaluate the pros and cons of each type
- Explicitly configure Spring Security LDAP using Spring Bean declarations
- Connect to external LDAP directories
- Explore the built-in support for Microsoft Active Directory

We will also explore how to customize Spring Security for more flexibility when dealing with custom Active Directory deployments.

## Understanding LDAP

LDAP has its roots in logical directory models dating back over thirty years—conceptually akin to a combination of an organizational chart and an address book. Today, LDAP is used more and more as a way to centralize corporate user information, partition thousands of users into logical groups, and allow unified sharing of user information between many disparate systems.

For security purposes, LDAP is quite commonly used to facilitate centralized username and password authentication—users' credentials are stored in the LDAP directory, and authentication requests can be made against the directory, on the user's behalf. This eases management for administrators, as user credentials—login ID, password, and other details—are stored in a single location in the LDAP directory. Additionally, organizational information, such as group or team assignments, geographic location, and corporate hierarchy membership, are defined based on the user's location in the directory.

## LDAP

At this point, if you have never used LDAP before, you may be wondering what it is. We'll illustrate a sample LDAP schema with a screenshot, from the Apache Directory Server 1.5 example directory.

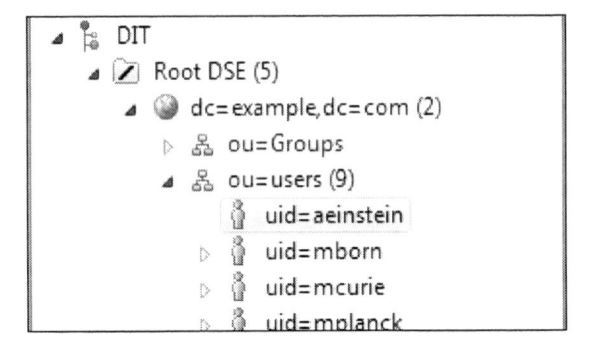

```
▲ DIT
   ▲ Root DSE (5)
      ▲ dc=example,dc=com (2)
         ▷ ou=Groups
         ▲ ou=users (9)
              uid=aeinstein
           ▷ uid=mborn
           ▷ uid=mcurie
           ▷ uid=mplanck
```

Starting at a particular user entry for Albert Einstein (highlighted in the screenshot), we can infer Mr. Einstein's organizational membership by starting at his node in the tree and moving upward. We can see that the user **aeinstein** is a member of the organizational unit (**ou**) **users**, which itself is a part of the domain example.com (the abbreviation **dc** shown in the screenshot stands for **domain component**). Preceding this are organizational elements (**DIT** and **Root DSE**) of the LDAP tree itself, which don't concern us in the context of Spring Security The position of user aeinstein in the LDAP hierarchy is semantically and definitively meaningful—you can imagine a much more complex hierarchy easily illustrating the organizational and departmental boundaries of a huge organization.

The complete top-to-bottom path formed by walking the tree down to an individual leaf node forms a string composed of all intervening nodes along the way, as with Mr. Einstein's node path:

```
uid=aeinstein,ou=users,dc=example,dc=com
```

This node path is unique, and is known as a node's **distinguished name** (**DN**). The distinguished name is akin to a database primary key, allowing a node to be uniquely identified and located in a complex tree structure. We'll see a node's DN used extensively throughout the authentication and searching process with Spring Security LDAP integration.

We note that there are several other users listed at the same level of the organization as Mr. Einstein. All of these users are assumed to be within the same organizational position as Mr. Einstein. Although this example organization is relatively simple and flat, the structure of LDAP is arbitrarily flexible, with many levels of nesting and logical organization possible.

Spring Security LDAP support is assisted by the **Spring LDAP module** (http://www.springsource.org/ldap), which is actually a separate project from the core Spring Framework and Spring Security projects. It's considered to be stable and provides a helpful set of wrappers around the standard Java LDAP functionality.

# Common LDAP attribute names

Each actual entry in the tree is defined by one or more object classes. An object class is a logical unit of organization, grouping a set of semantically-related attributes. By declaring an entry in the tree as an instance of a particular object class, such as person, the organizer of the LDAP directory is able to provide users of the directory with a clear indication of what each element of the directory represents.

LDAP has a rich set of standard schemas covering the available LDAP object classes and their applicable attributes (along with gobs of other information). If you are planning on doing extensive work with LDAP, it's highly advised that you review a good reference guide, such as the appendix of the book *Zytrax OpenLDAP* (`http://www.zytrax.com/books/ldap/ape/`), or *Internet2 Consortium's Guide to Person-related Schemas* (`http://middleware.internet2.edu/eduperson/`).

In the previous section, we were introduced to the fact that each entry in an LDAP tree has a distinguished name, which uniquely identifies it in the tree. The DN is composed of a series of attributes, one (or more) of which is used to uniquely identify the path down the tree of the entry represented by the DN. As each segment of the path described by the DN represents an LDAP attribute, you could refer to the available, well-defined LDAP schemas and object classes to determine what each of the attributes in any given DN means.

We've included some of the common attributes and their meanings in the following table. These attributes tend to be organizing attributes—meaning that they are typically used to define the organizational structure of the LDAP tree—and are ordered from top to bottom in the structure that you're likely to see in a typical LDAP install.

| Attribute Name | Description | Example |
| --- | --- | --- |
| dc | Domain Component—generally the highest level of organization in an LDAP hierarchy. | `dc=jbcpcalendar,dc=com` |
| c | Country—some LDAP hierarchies are structured at a high level by country. | `c=US` |
| o | Organization name—a parent business organization used for classifying LDAP resources. | `o=Oracle Corporation` |
| ou | Organizational unit—a divisional business organization, generally within an organization. | `ou=Product Development` |
| cn | Common name—the common name or unique or human-readable name for the object. For humans, this is usually the person's full name, while for other resources in LDAP (computers, and so on) it's typically the hostname. | `cn=Super Visor`<br>`cn=Jim Bob` |

| Attribute Name | Description | Example |
|---|---|---|
| uid | User ID—although not organizational in nature, the uid is generally what Spring looks for in user authentication and search. | uid=svisor |
| userPassword | User password—stores the password for the person object to which this attribute is associated. It is typically one-way hashed using SHA or something similar. | userPassword=plaintext<br>userPassword={SHA}cryptval |

Remember that there are hundreds of standard LDAP attributes—these represent a very small fraction of those you are likely to see when integrating with a fully-populated LDAP server. The attributes in the table do, however, tend to be organizing attributes on the directory tree, and as such, will probably form various search expressions or mappings that you will use to configure Spring Security to interact with the LDAP server.

## Updating our dependencies

We have already included all the dependencies you need for this chapter, so you will not need to make any updates to your pom.xml file. However, if you were just adding LDAP support to your own application, you would need to add spring-security-ldap as a dependency in pom.xml, as follows:

pom.xml

```
<dependency>
  <groupId>org.springframework.security</groupId>
  <artifactId>spring-security-ldap</artifactId>
  <version>3.1.0.RELEASE</version>
</dependency>
```

As mentioned previously, Spring Security's LDAP support is built on top of Spring LDAP. Maven will automatically bring this dependency in as a transitive dependency, so there is no need to explicitly list it.

If you were using ApacheDS to run an LDAP Server within your web application, as we are doing in our `Calendar` application, you would need to add dependencies on the relevant Apache DS jars. There is no need to make these updates to our sample application since we have already included them. Note that these dependencies are not necessary if you are connecting to an external LDAP server.

pom.xml

```xml
<dependency>
    <groupId>org.apache.directory.server</groupId>
    <artifactId>apacheds-core</artifactId>
    <version>1.5.5</version>
    <scope>runtime</scope>
</dependency>
<dependency>
    <groupId>org.apache.directory.server</groupId>
    <artifactId>apacheds-protocol-ldap</artifactId>
    <version>1.5.5</version>
    <scope>runtime</scope>
</dependency>
<dependency>
    <groupId>org.apache.directory.shared</groupId>
    <artifactId>shared-ldap</artifactId>
    <version>0.9.15</version>
    <scope>runtime</scope>
</dependency>
```

## Configuring embedded LDAP integration

Let's now enable the JBCP Calendar application to support LDAP-based authentication. Fortunately, this is a relatively simple exercise, using the embedded LDAP server and a sample LDIF file. For this exercise, we will be using an LDIF file created for this book, intended to capture many of the common configuration scenarios with LDAP and Spring Security. We have included several more sample LDIF files, some from Apache DS 1.5, and one from the Spring Security unit tests, which you may choose to experiment with as well.

# Configuring an LDAP server reference

The first step is to declare the embedded LDAP server reference in the `security.xml` file. The LDAP server declaration occurs outside of the `<http>` element at the same level as `<authentication-manager>`. Make the following updates to your `security.xml` file:

src/main/webapp/WEB-INF/spring/security.xml

```
<http …>
    …
</http>
<ldap-server id="ldapServer"
        ldif="classpath:/ldif/calendar.ldif"
        root="dc=jbcpcalendar,dc=com"/>
<authentication-manager>
```

> You should be starting with the source from chapter05.00-calendar.

We are loading the `calendar.ldif` file from `classpath`, and using it to populate the LDAP server. The `root` attribute declares the root of the LDAP directory using the specified DN. This should correspond to the logical root DN in the LDIF file we're using.

> Be aware that for embedded LDAP servers, the root is required, even though the XML schema does not indicate as such. If it is not specified, or is specified incorrectly, you may receive several odd errors upon initialization of the Apache DS server. Also be aware that the `ldif` resource should only load a single `ldif`, otherwise the server will fail to start up. Spring Security requires a single resource, since using something such as `classpath*:calendar.ldif` does not provide the deterministic ordering that is required.

We'll reuse the bean ID defined here, later in the Spring Security configuration files, when we declare the LDAP user service and other configuration elements. All other attributes on the `<ldap-server>` declaration are optional when using the embedded LDAP mode.

# Enabling the LDAP AuthenticationProviderNext interface

Next, we'll need to configure another `AuthenticationProvider` that checks user credentials against the LDAP provider. Simply update the Spring Security configuration to use an `o.s.s.ldap.authentication.LdapAuthenticationProvider` reference, as follows:

src/main/webapp/WEB-INF/spring/security.xml

```
    <authentication-manager>
        <ldap-authentication-provider server-ref="ldapServer"
            user-search-filter="(uid={0})"
            group-search-base="ou=Groups">
        </ldap-authentication-provider>
    </authentication-manager>
```

We'll discuss these attributes a bit more, later. For now, get the application back up and running, and try logging in with `admin1@example.com` as the username and `admin1` as the password. You should be logged in!

> Your source code should look like `chapter05.01-calendar`.

# Troubleshooting embedded LDAP

It is quite possible that you will run into hard-to-debug problems with embedded LDAP. Apache DS is not usually very friendly with its error messages, doubly so in Spring Security embedded mode. If you are getting a `404` error when trying to access the application in your browser, there is a good chance that things did not start up properly. Some things to double-check if you can't get this simple example running are:

- Ensure the `root` attribute is set on the `<ldap-server>` declaration in your configuration file, and make sure it matches the root defined in the LDIF file that's loaded at startup. If you get errors referencing missing partitions, it's likely that either the `root` attribute was missed or doesn't match your LDIF file.

- Be aware that a failure starting up the embedded LDAP server is not a fatal failure. In order to diagnose errors loading LDIF files, you will need to ensure that the appropriate log settings, including logging for the Apache DS server, are enabled, at least at ERROR level. The LDIF loader is under the `org.apache.directory.server.protocol.shared.store` package, and this should be used to enable logging of LDIF load errors.

- If the application server shuts down non-gracefully, you may be required to delete some files in your temporary directory (`%TEMP%` on Windows systems or `/tmp` in Linux-based systems) in order to start the server again. The error messages regarding this are (fortunately) fairly clear. Unfortunately, embedded LDAP isn't as seamless and easy to use as the embedded H2 database, but it is still quite a bit easier than trying to download and configure many of the freely-available external LDAP servers.

An excellent tool for troubleshooting or accessing LDAP servers in general is the **Apache Directory Studio** project, which offers standalone and Eclipse plugin versions. The free download is available at `http://directory.apache.org/studio/`. If you want to follow along with the book, you may want to download Apache Directory Studio 1.5 now.

# Understanding how Spring LDAP authentication works

We saw that we were able to log in using a user defined in the LDAP directory. But what exactly happens when a user issues a login request for a user in LDAP? There are three basic steps to the LDAP authentication process:

1. Authenticate the credentials supplied by the user against the LDAP directory.

2. Determine the `GrantedAuthority` object that the user has, based on their information in LDAP.

3. Pre-load information from the LDAP entry for the user into a custom `UserDetails` object, for further use by the application.

# Authenticating user credentials

For the first step, authentication against the LDAP directory, a custom authentication provider is wired into AuthenticationManager. o.s.s.ldap.authentication. LdapAuthenticationProvider takes the user's provided credentials and verifies them against the LDAP directory, as illustrated in the following diagram:

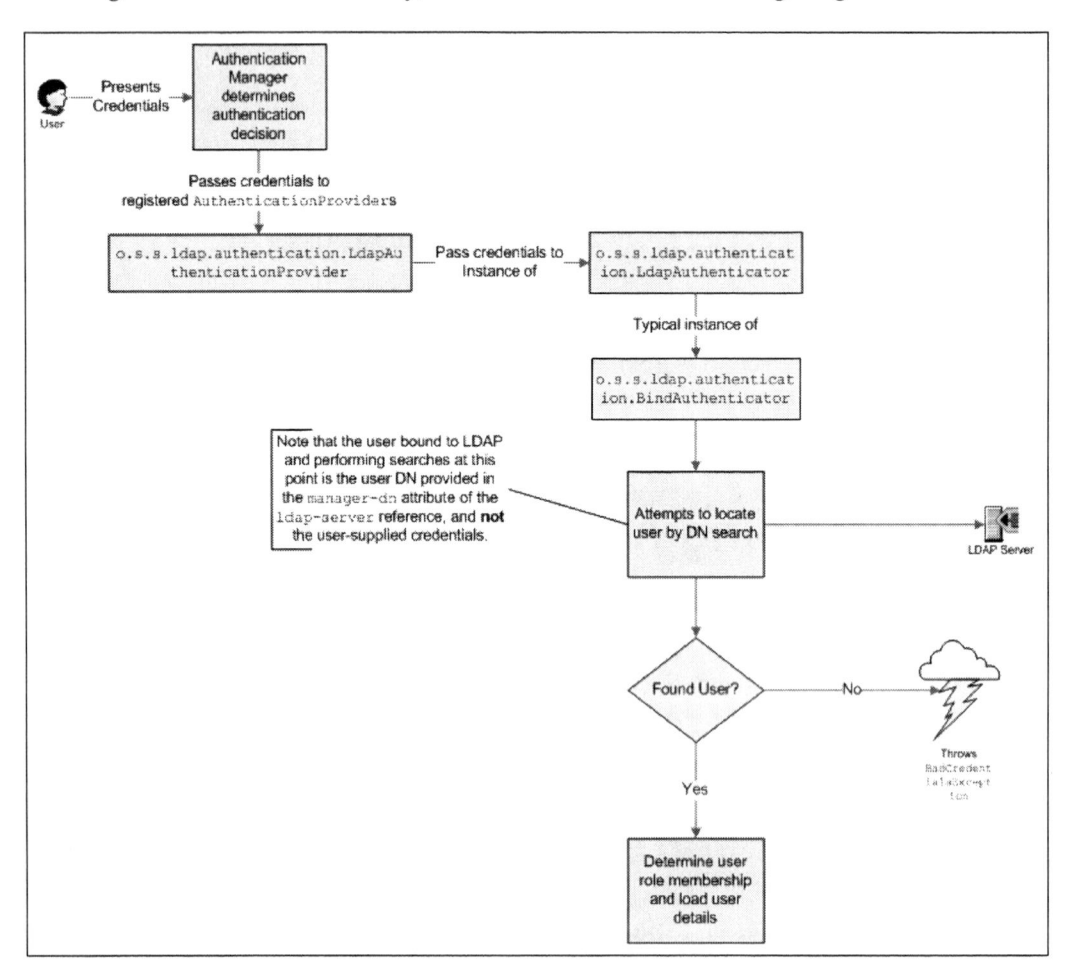

We can see that the `o.s.s.ldap.authentication.LdapAuthenticator` defines a delegate to allow the provider to make the authentication request in a customizable way. The implementation that we've implicitly configured to this point, `o.s.s.ldap.authentication.BindAuthenticator`, attempts to use the user's credentials to bind (log in) to the LDAP server as if it were the user themselves making a connection. For an embedded server, this is sufficient for our authentication needs; however, external LDAP servers may be stricter, and in these, users may not be allowed to bind to the LDAP directory. Fortunately, an alternative method of authentication exists, which we will explore later in this chapter.

As noted in the diagram, keep in mind that the search is performed under an LDAP context created by the credentials specified in the `<ldap-server>` reference's `manager-dn` attribute. With an embedded server, we don't use this information, but with an external server reference, unless `manager-dn` is supplied, anonymous binding is used. To retain some control over the public availability of information in the directory, is very common for organizations to require valid credentials to search an LDAP directory, and as such, `manager-dn` will be almost always required in real-world scenarios. The `manager-dn` attribute represents the full DN of a user with valid access to bind the directory and perform searches.

# Demonstrating authentication with Apache Directory Studio

We are going to demonstrate how the authentication process works by using Apache Directory Studio 1.5 to connect to our embedded LDAP instance and performing the same steps that Spring Security is performing. We will use `user1@example.com` throughout the simulation. These steps will help to ensure a firm grasp of what is happening behind the scenes and will help in the event that you are having difficulty figuring out the correct configuration.

Ensure that the `calendar` application is started up and working. Next, start Apache Directory Studio 1.5 and close the **Welcome** screen.

# Binding anonymously to LDAP

The first step is to bind anonymously to LDAP. The bind is done anonymously because we did not specify the `manager-dn` and `manager-password` attributes on our `<ldap-server>` element. Within Apache Directory Studio, create a connection using the following steps:

1. Click on **File** | **New** | **LDAP Browser** | **LDAP Connection**.
2. Click on **Next**.

3. Enter the following information, and then click on **Next**:
   - **Connection name**: `calendar-anonymous`
   - **Hostname**: `localhost`
   - **Port**: `33389`
4. We did not specify `manager-dn`, so select **No Authentication** for **Authentication Method**.
5. Click on **Finish**.

You can safely ignore the message indicating no default schema information is present. You should now see that you are connected to the embedded LDAP instance.

## Searching for the user

Now that we have a connection, we can use it to look up the user's DN that we wish to bind to.

1. Right-click on **DIT**, and select **New | New Search**.
2. Enter a search base of `dc=jbcpcalendar,dc=com`. This corresponds to the root element of our `<ldap-server/>` tag that we specified.
3. Enter a filter of `uid=user1@example.com`. This corresponds to the value we specified for the `user-search-filter` attribute of our `<ldap-authentication-provider/>` tag. Note that we included the parentheses and have substituted the username we are attempting to log in with, for the `{0}` value.
4. Click on **Search**.
5. Click on the DN of the single result returned by our search. You can now see our LDAP user being displayed. Note that this DN matches the value we searched for. Remember this DN as it will be used in our next step.

# Binding as a user to LDAP

Now that we have found the full DN of our user, we need to try to bind to LDAP as that user, to validate the submitted password. These steps are the same as our anonymous bind we already did, except that we will specify credentials of the user that we are authenticating.

Within ApacheDS, create a connection using the following steps:

1. Select **File | New | LDAP Browser | LDAP Connection**.
2. Click on **Next**
3. Enter the following information and click on **Next**.
   - **Connection name**: `calendar-user1`
   - **Hostname**: `localhost`
   - **Port**: `33389`
4. Leave **Authentication Method** as **Simple Authentication**.
5. Enter the DN from our search result as **Bind DN**. The value should be `uid=admin1@example.com,ou=Users,dc=jbcpcalendar,dc=com`.

   The Bind password should be the password that was submitted at the time of login. In our case, we want to use `admin1` to successfully authenticate. If the wrong password was entered, we would fail to connect and Spring Security would report an error.

6. Click on **Finish**.

Spring Security will determine that the username and password were correct for this user, when it is able to successfully bind with the provided username and password (similar to how we were able to create a connection). Spring Security will then proceed with determining the user's role membership.

## Determining user role membership

After the user has been successfully authenticated against the LDAP server, authorization information must be determined next. Authorization is defined by a principal's list of roles, and an LDAP-authenticated user's role membership is determined as illustrated in the following diagram:

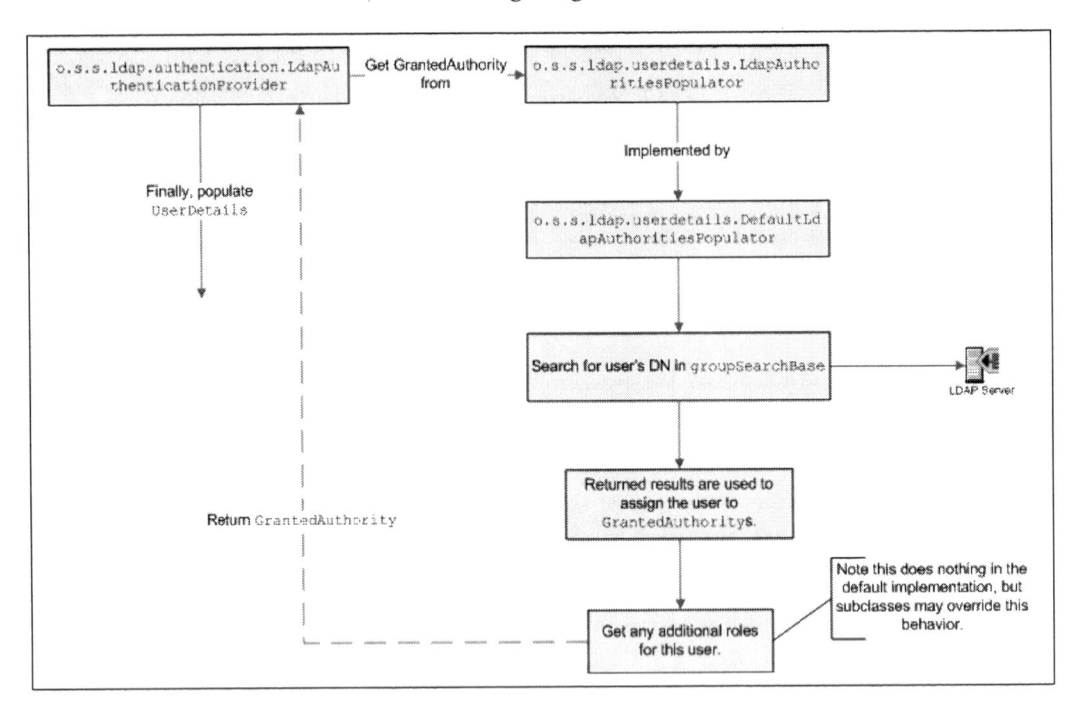

We can see that after authenticating the user against LDAP, `LdapAuthenticationProvider` delegates to `LdapAuthoritiesPopulator`. `DefaultLdapAuthoritiesPopulator` will attempt to locate the authenticated user's DN in an attribute located at or below another entry in the LDAP hierarchy. The DN of the location searched for user role assignments is defined in the `group-search-base` attribute; in our sample, we set this to `group-search-base="ou=Groups"`. When the user's DN is located within an LDAP entry below the DN of `group-search-base`, an attribute on the entry in which their DN is found is used to confer a role to them.

> You'll notice that we mix the case of these attributes—`groupSearchBase` in the class flow diagram versus `group-search-base` referred to in the text. This is intentional—the text refers to the XML configuration attributes, while the diagram refers to the members of the relevant classes. They are similarly named, but appropriately adjusted for the context (XML and Java) in which they occur.

How Spring Security roles are associated with LDAP users can be a little confusing, so let's look at the JBCP Calendar LDAP repository and see how the association of a user to a role works. `DefaultLdapAuthoritiesPopulator` uses several attributes of the `<ldap-authentication-provider>` declaration to govern the searching of roles for the user. These attributes are used approximately in the following order:

1. `group-search-base`: It defines the base DN under which the LDAP integration should look for one or more matches for the user's DN. The default value performs a search from the LDAP root, which may be expensive.

2. `group-search-filter`: It defines the LDAP search filter used to match the user's DN to an attribute of an entry located under `group-search-base`. This search filter is parameterized with two parameters—the first (`{0}`) being the user's DN, and the second (`{1}`) being the user's username. The default value is `uniqueMember={0}`.

3. `group-role-attribute`: It defines the attribute of the matching entries, which will be used to compose the user's `GrantedAuthority` object. The default value is `cn`.

4. `role-prefix`: It is the prefix that will be prepended to the value found in `group-role-attribute`, to make a Spring Security `GrantedAuthority` object. The default value is `ROLE_`.

This can be a little abstract and hard for new developers to follow, because it's very different from anything we've seen so far with our JDBC-based `UserDetailsService` implementations. Let's continue walking through the login process with our `user1@example.com` user in the JBCP Calendar LDAP directory.

# Determining roles with Apache Directory Studio

We will now try to determine the roles for our user with Apache Directory Studio. Using the `calendar-user1` connection we created previously, perform the following steps:

1. Right-click on `DIT` and select **New | New Search**.
2. Enter a search base of `ou=Groups,dc=jbcpcalendar,dc=com`. This corresponds to the `root` element of the `<ldap-server/>` tag we specified, plus the `group-search-base` attribute we specified for the `<ldap-authentication-provider/>` tag.

## LDAP Directory Services

3. Enter a filter of (uniqueMember=uid=user1@example.com,ou=Users,dc=jbcpcalendar,dc=com). This corresponds to the default group-search-filter attribute of (uniqueMember={0}). Notice that we have substituted the full DN of the user we found in our previous exercise for the the {0} value.

4. Click on **Search**.

5. You will observe that the User group is the only group returned in our search results. Click on the DN of the single result returned by our search. You can now see the User group displayed in Apache DS. Note that the group has a uniqueMember attribute with the full DN of our user and other users.

6. Spring Security now creates the GrantedAuthority object for each result by forcing the name of the group that was found to uppercase and prepending ROLE_ to the group name. The pseudo-code would look similar to the following code snippet:

```
foreach group in groups:
  authority = ("ROLE_"+group).upperCase()
  grantedAuthority = new GrantedAuthority(authority)
```

> **Spring LDAP is as flexible as your gray matter**
>
> Keep in mind that although this is one way to organize an LDAP directory to be compatible with Spring Security, typical usage scenarios are exactly the opposite—an LDAP directory already exists that Spring Security needs to be wired into. In many cases, you will be able to reconfigure Spring Security to deal with the hierarchy of the LDAP server; however, it's key that you plan effectively and understand how Spring works with LDAP when it's querying. Use your brain, map out the user search and group search, and come up with the most optimal plan you can think of—keep the scope of searches as minimal and as precise as possible.

Can you describe how the results of the login process would differ for our admin1@example.com user? If you are confused at this point, we'd suggest that you take a breather and try using Apache Directory Studio to work through browsing the embedded LDAP server configured by the running an application. It can be easier to grasp the flow of Spring Security's LDAP configuration, if you can attempt to search the directory yourself by following the algorithm described previously.

# Mapping additional attributes of UserDetails

Finally, once the LDAP lookup has assigned the user a set of `GrantedAuthority` objects, `o.s.s.ldap.userdetails.LdapUserDetailsMapper` will consult `o.s.s.ldap.userdetails.UserDetailsContextMapper` to retrieve any additional details to populate the `UserDetails` object for application use.

With `<ldap-authentication-provider>`, we've configured to this point that `LdapUserDetailsMapper` will be used to populate a `UserDetails` object with information gleaned from the user's entry in the LDAP directory.

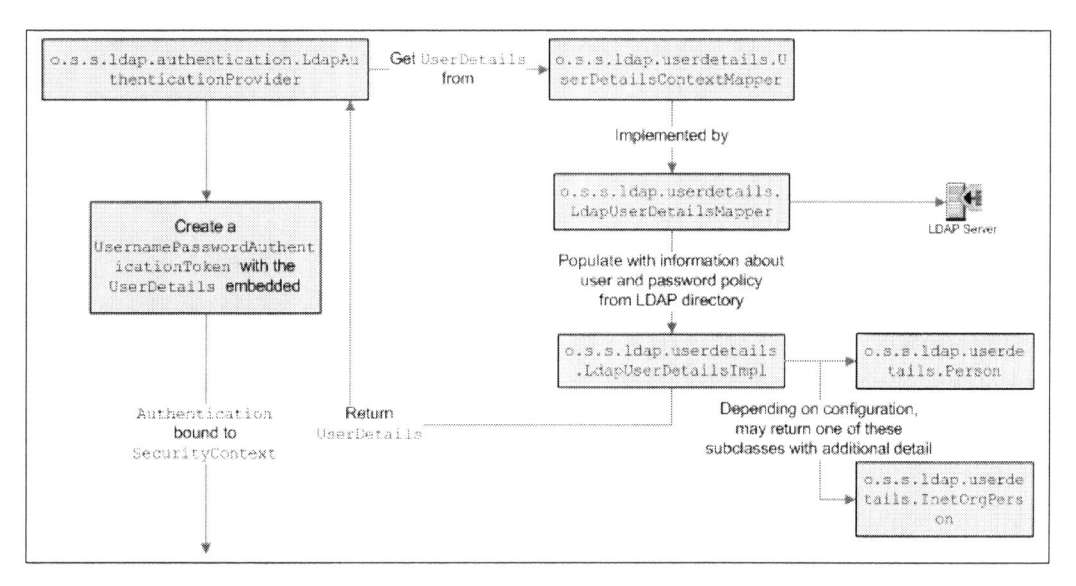

We'll see in a moment how `UserDetailsContextMapper` can be configured to pull a wealth of information from the standard LDAP `person` and `inetOrgPerson` objects. With the baseline `LdapUserDetailsMapper`, little more than username, password, and `GrantedAuthority` is stored.

Although there is more machinery involved behind the scenes in LDAP user authentication and detail retrieval, you'll notice that the overall process seems somewhat similar (authenticating the user and populating `GrantedAuthority`) to the JDBC authentication that we've studied in *Chapter 4, JDBC-based Authentication*. As with JDBC authentication, there is an ability to perform advanced configuration of LDAP integration. Let's dive deeper and see what's possible!

## Advanced LDAP configuration

Once we get beyond the basics of LDAP integration, there's a plethora of additional configuration capability in the Spring Security LDAP module, that is still within the security XML namespace style of configuration. These include retrieval of user personal information, additional options for user authentication, and the use of LDAP as the `UserDetailsService` interface in conjunction with a standard `DaoAuthenticationProvider` class.

## Sample JBCP LDAP users

We've supplied a number of different users in the JBCP Calendar LDIF file. The following quick reference chart may help you with the advanced configuration exercises or in self-exploration:

| Username/Password | Role(s) | Password encoding |
|---|---|---|
| admin1@example.com/admin1 | ROLE_ADMIN, ROLE_USER | Plaintext |
| user1@example.com/user1 | ROLE_USER | Plaintext |
| shauser@example.com/shauser | ROLE_USER | {sha} |
| sshauser@example.com/sshauser | ROLE_USER | {ssha} |
| hasphone@example.com/hasphone | ROLE_USER | Plaintext (in `telephoneNumber` attribute) |

We'll explain why password encoding matters, in the next section.

## Password comparison versus bind authentication

Some LDAP servers will be configured so that certain individual users are not allowed to bind directly to the server, or so that anonymous binding (what we have been using for user search to this point) is disabled. This tends to occur in very large organizations, which want a restricted set of users to be able to read information from the directory. In these cases, the standard Spring Security LDAP authentication strategy will not work, and an alternative strategy must be used, implemented by `o.s.s.ldap.authentication.PasswordComparisonAuthenticator` (a sibling class of `BindAuthenticator`).

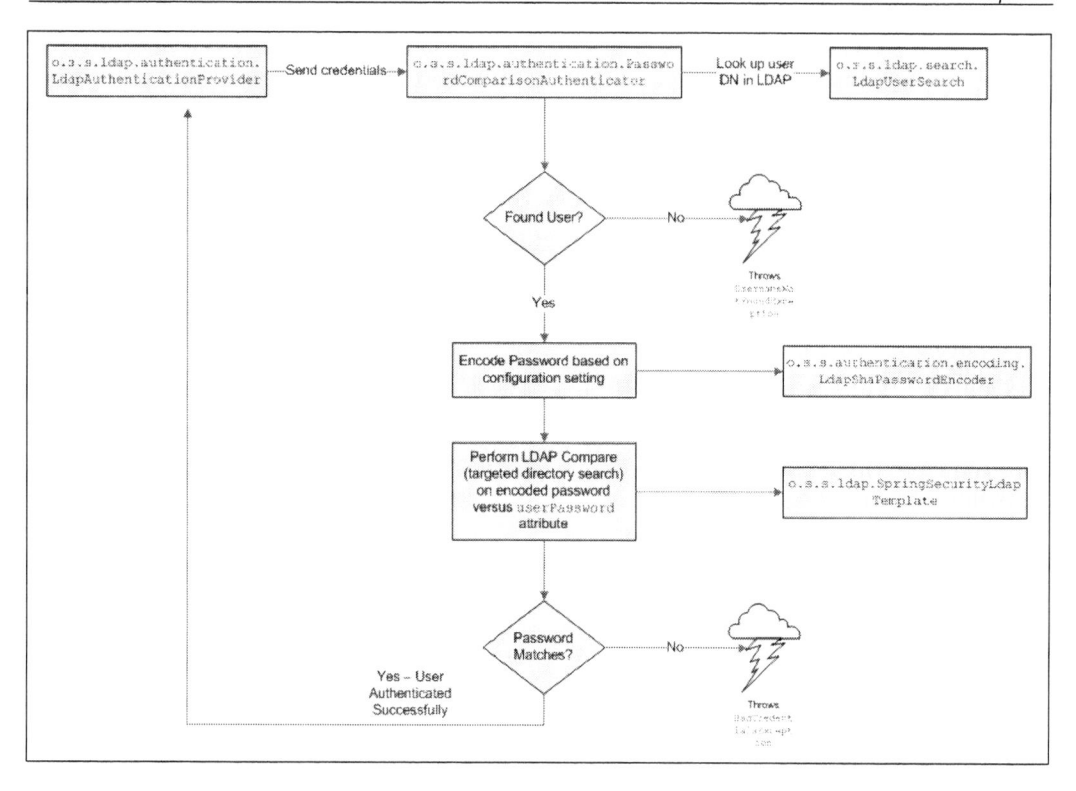

`PasswordComparisonAuthenticator` binds to LDAP and searches for the DN matching the username provided by the user. It then compares the user-supplied password with the `userPassword` attribute stored on the matching LDAP entry. If the encoded password matches, the user is authenticated, and the flow proceeds as with `BindAuthenticator`.

## Configuring basic password comparison

Configuring password comparison authentication instead of bind authentication is as simple as adding a sub-element to the `<ldap-authentication-provider>` declaration. Update the `security.xml` file as follows:

src/main/webapp/WEB-INF/spring/security.xml

```
    <ldap-authentication-provider server-ref="ldapServer"
            user-search-filter="(uid={0})"
            group-search-base="ou=Groups">
        <password-compare/>
    </ldap-authentication-provider>
```

The default `PasswordComparisonAuthenticator` class uses the LDAP password encoding algorithm of SHA (recall that we discussed the SHA-1 password algorithm extensively in the previous chapter). After restarting the server, you can attempt to log in using `shauser@example.com` as the username and `shauser` as the password.

> Your code should look like `chapter05.02-calendar`.

## LDAP password encoding and storage

LDAP has general support for a variety of password encoding algorithms, ranging from plain text to one-way hash algorithms, similar to those we explored in the previous chapter, with database-backed authentication. The most common storage formats for LDAP passwords are **SHA** (SHA-1 one-way hashed), and **SSHA** (SHA-1 one-way hashed, with a salt value). Other password formats often supported by many LDAP implementations are thoroughly documented in *RFC 2307, An Approach to Using LDAP as a Network Information Service* (http://tools.ietf.org/html/rfc2307).The designers of RFC 2307 did a very clever thing with regards to password storage. Passwords retained in the directory are, of course, encoded with whatever algorithm is appropriate (SHA, and so on), but then they are prefixed with the algorithm used to encode the password. This makes it very easy for the LDAP server to support multiple algorithms for password encoding. For example, an SHA-encoded password is stored in the directory as `{SHA}5baa61e4c9b93f3f06822 50b6cf8331b7ee68fd8`.

We can see that the password storage algorithm is very clearly indicated (with the `{SHA}` notation) and stored along with the password.

SSHA is an attempt to combine the strong SHA-1 hash algorithm with password salting to prevent dictionary attacks. As with password salting, which we reviewed in the previous chapter, the salt is added to the password prior to calculating the hash. When the hashed password is stored in the directory, the salt value is appended to the hashed password. The password is prepended with `{SSHA}`, so that the LDAP directory knows that the user-supplied password needs to be compared differently. The majority of modern LDAP servers utilize SSHA as the default password storage algorithm.

# The drawbacks of a password comparison authenticator

Now that you know a bit about how LDAP uses passwords and we have `PasswordComparisonAuthenticator` set up, what do you think will happen if you log in using our `sshauser@example.com` user with their password stored in the SSHA format? Go ahead, put the book aside and try it, and then come back.

Your login was denied, right? And yet you were still able to log in as the user with the SHA-encoded password. Why? The password encoding and storage didn't matter to us when we were using bind authentication. Why do you think that is?

The reason it didn't matter with bind authentication was because the LDAP server was taking care of authentication and validation of the user's password. With password compare authentication, Spring Security LDAP is responsible for encoding the password in the format expected by the directory and then matching it against the directory to validate the authentication.

For security purposes, password comparison authentication can't actually read the password from the directory (reading directory passwords is often denied by security policy). Instead, `PasswordComparisonAuthenticator` performs an LDAP search, rooted at the user's directory entry, attempting to match with a password attribute and value as determined by the password that's been encoded by Spring Security. So, when we try to log in with `sshauser@example.com`, `PasswordComparisonAuthenticator` is encoding the password using the configured SHA algorithm and attempting to do a simple match, which fails as the directory password for this user is stored in the SSHA format.

What happens if we change the hash algorithm for `PasswordComparisonAuthenticator` to use SSHA? Update the `security.xml` as follows:

src/main/webapp/WEB-INF/spring/security.xml

```
<password-compare hash="{ssha}"/>
```

> Your code should look like `chapter05.03-calendar`.

Restart and try it out—it still doesn't work. Let's think why that might be. Remember that SSHA uses a salted password, with the salt value stored in the LDAP directory along with the password. However, `PasswordComparisonAuthenticator` is coded so that it cannot read anything from the LDAP server (this typically violates the security policy at companies that don't allow binding). Thus, when `PasswordComparisonAuthenticator` computes the hashed password, it has no way to determine what salt value to use.

In conclusion, `PasswordComparisonAuthenticator` is valuable in certain limited circumstances where security of the directory itself is a concern, but it will never be as flexible as straight bind authentication.

# Configuring UserDetailsContextMapper

As we noted earlier, an instance of `o.s.s.ldap.userdetails.UserDetailsContextMapper` is used to map a user's entry into the LDAP server to a `UserDetails` object in memory. The default `UserDetailsContextMapper` object behaves similarly to `JdbcDaoImpl` in the level of detail that is populated on the returned `UserDetails` object—that is to say, not a lot of information is returned besides the username and password.

However, an LDAP directory potentially contains many more details about individual users than usernames, passwords, and roles. Spring Security ships with two additional methods of pulling more user data from two of the standard LDAP object schemas—`person` and `inetOrgPerson`.

# Implicit configuration of UserDetailsContextMapper

In order to configure a different `UserDetailsContextMapper` implementation than the default, we simply need to declare what `LdapUserDetails` class we want `LdapAuthenticationProvider` to return. The security namespace parser will be smart enough to instantiate the correct `UserDetailsContextMapper` implementation based on the type of `LdapUserDetails` interface requested.

Let's reconfigure our `security.xml` file to use the `inetOrgPerson` version of the mapper. Update the `security.xml` as illustrated below:

src/main/webapp/WEB-INF/spring/security.xml

```
    <ldap-authentication-provider server-ref="ldapServer"
            user-search-filter="(uid={0})"
            group-search-base="ou=Groups"
            user-details-class="inetOrgPerson">

    </ldap-authentication-provider>
```

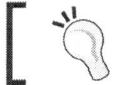

> Make sure to remove the `<password-encoder />` tag as we did in the previous sample.

If you were to restart the application and attempt to log in as an LDAP user, you would see that nothing changed. In fact, `UserDetailsContextMapper` has changed behind the scenes to read additional detail in the case where attributes from the `inetOrgPerson` schema are available in the user's directory entry. Try authenticating with `admin1@example.com` as the username and `admin1` as the password.

# Viewing additional user details

To assist in this area, we'll add the ability to view the current account to the JBCP Calendar application. We'll use this page to illustrate how the richer `person` and `inetOrgPerson` LDAP schemas can provide additional (optional) information to your LDAP-enabled application.

You may have noticed that this chapter came with an additional controller named `AccountController`. You can see the relevant code as follows:

src/main/java/com/packtpub/springsecurity/web/controllers/AccountController.java

```
...
@RequestMapping("/accounts/my")
public String view(Model model) {
  Authentication authentication =
    SecurityContextHolder.getContext().getAuthentication();
  // null check on authentication omitted
  Object principal = authentication.getPrincipal();
  model.addAttribute("user", principal);
  model.addAttribute("isLdapUserDetails", principal instanceof
    LdapUserDetails);
  model.addAttribute("isLdapPerson", principal instanceof Person);
  model.addAttribute("isLdapInetOrgPerson", principal instanceof
    InetOrgPerson);
  return "accounts/show";
}
...
```

This code will retrieve the `UserDetails` object (principal) stored in the `Authentication` object by `LdapAuthenticationProvider` and determine what type of `LdapUserDetailsImpl` interface it is. The page code itself will then display various details, depending on the type of `UserDetails` object that has been bound to the user's authentication information, as we see in the following JSP code. We have already included JSP as well.

`src/main/webapp/WEB-INF/views/accounts/show.jsp`

```jsp
<dl>
  <dt>Username</dt>
  <dd><c:out value="${user.username}"/></dd>
  <dt>DN</dt>
  <dd><c:out value="${user.dn}"/></dd>
  <c:if test="${isLdapPerson}">
    <dt>Description</dt>
    <dd><c:out value="${user.description}"/></dd>
    <dt>Telephone</dt>
    <dd id="phone"><c:out value="${user.telephoneNumber}"/></dd>
    <dt>Full Name(s)</dt>
    <c:forEach items="${user.cn}" var="cn">
      <dd><c:out value="${cn}"/></dd>
    </c:forEach>
  </c:if>
  <c:if test="${isLdapInetOrgPerson}">
    <dt>Email</dt>
    <dd><c:out value="${user.mail}"/></dd>
    <dt>Street</dt>
    <dd><c:out value="${user.street}"/></dd>
  </c:if>
</dl>
```

The only work that actually needs to be done is to add a link in our `header.jsp` file, as shown in the following code snippet:

```jsp
<li id="greeting">
  <div>
    Welcome
    <c:url var="accountUrl" value="/accounts/my"/>
    <a id="navMyAccount" href="${accountUrl}">
       <sec:authentication property="name" />
    </a>
  </div>
</li>
```

We've added two more users that you can use to examine the differences in the available data elements.

| Username | Password | Type |
|---|---|---|
| shainet@example.com | shainet | inetOrgPerson |
| shaperson@example.com | shaperson | person |

> Your code should look like chapter05.04-calendar.

Restart the server and examine the Account Details page for each of the types of users by clicking on the username in the upper-right corner. You'll note that, when user-details-class is configured to use inetOrgPerson, although o.s.s.ldap.userdetails.InetOrgPerson is what is returned, the fields may or may not be populated, depending on the available attributes in the directory entry.

In fact, inetOrgPerson has many more attributes than we've illustrated on this simple page. You can review the full list in *RFC 2798, Definition of the inetOrgPerson LDAP Object Class* (http://tools.ietf.org/html/rfc2798).

One thing you may notice is that there is no facility to support additional attributes that may be specified on an entry but don't fall into a standard schema. The standard UserDetailsContextMapper interfaces don't support arbitrary lists of attributes, but it is possible nonetheless to customize it with a reference to your own UserDetailsContextMapper interface through the use of the user-context-mapper-ref attribute.

# Using an alternate password attribute

In some cases, it may be necessary to use an alternate LDAP attribute instead of userPassword, for authentication purposes. This can happen on occasions when companies have deployed custom LDAP schemas or don't have a requirement for strong password management (arguably, this is never a good idea, but it definitely does occur in the real world).

`PasswordComparisonAuthenticator` also supports the ability to verify the user's password against an alternate LDAP entry attribute instead of the standard `userPassword` attribute. This is very easy to configure, and we can demonstrate a simple example using the plaintext `telephoneNumber` attribute. Update the `security.xml` as follows:

src/main/webapp/WEB-INF/spring/security.xml

```
<ldap-authentication-provider server-ref="ldapServer"
  user-search-filter="(uid={0})"
  group-search-base="ou=Groups"
  user-details-class="inetOrgPerson">
    <password-compare
      hash="plaintext"
      password-attribute="telephoneNumber"/>
</ldap-authentication-provider>
```

We can restart the server and attempt to log in with `hasphone@example.com` as the username and `0123456789` as the password (telephone number).

Of course, this type of authentication has all the perils we discussed earlier about authentication based on `PasswordComparisonAuthenticator`; however, it's good to be aware of it on the off chance that it comes up with an LDAP implementation.

# Using LDAP as UserDetailsService

One thing to note is that LDAP may also be used as `UserDetailsService`. As we will discuss later in the book, `UserDetailsService` is required to enable various other bits of functionality in the Spring Security infrastructure, including the **remember me** and **OpenID authentication** features.

We will modify our `AccountController` object to use the `LdapUserDetailsService` interface, to obtain the user. Before doing this, make sure to remove the `<password-compare>` element, as shown in the following code snippet:

src/main/webapp/WEB-INF/spring/security.xml

```
<authentication-manager>
    <ldap-authentication-provider server-ref="ldapServer"
        user-search-filter="(uid={0})"
        group-search-base="ou=Groups"
        user-details-class="inetOrgPerson"/>
</authentication-manager>
```

# Configuring LdapUserDetailsService

Configuration of LDAP as a `UserDetailsService` functions very similarly to the configuration of an LDAP `AuthenticationProvider`. Like a JDBC `UserDetailsService`, an LDAP `UserDetailsService` is configured as a sibling to the `<http>` declaration. Make the following updates to `security.xml`:

src/main/webapp/WEB-INF/spring/security.xml

```
...
<ldap-server .../>
<ldap-user-service id="ldapUserService"
        server-ref="ldapServer"
        user-search-filter="(uid={0})"
        group-search-base="ou=Groups"
        user-details-class="inetOrgPerson"/>
<authentication-manager>
...
```

Functionally, `o.s.s.ldap.userdetails.LdapUserDetailsService` is configured in almost exactly the same way as `LdapAuthenticationProvider`, with the exception that there is no attempt to use the principal's username to bind to LDAP. Instead, the credentials supplied by the `<ldap-server>` reference itself are used to perform the user lookup.

> Do not make the very common mistake of configuring `<authentication-provider>` with `user-details-service-ref` referring to `LdapUserDetailsService`, if you intend to authenticate the user against LDAP itself! As discussed previously, the `password` attribute often cannot be retrieved from LDAP due to security reasons, which makes `UserDetailsService` useless for authenticating. As noted previously, `LdapUserDetailsService` uses the `manager-dn` attribute supplied with the `<ldap-server>` declaration to get its information—this means that it does not attempt to bind the user to LDAP and as such may not behave as you expect.

# Updating AccountController to use LdapUserDetailsService

We will now update the `AccountController` object to use the `LdapDetailsUserDetailsService` interface, to look up the user that it displays.

src/main/java/com/packtpub/springsecurity/web/controllers/AccountController.java

```
@Controller
public class AccountController {
  private final UserDetailsService userDetailsService;

  @Autowired
  public AccountController(UserDetailsService userDetailsService) {
    this.userDetailsService = userDetailsService;
  }

  @RequestMapping("/accounts/my")
  public String view(Model model) {
    Authentication authentication =
      SecurityContextHolder.getContext().getAuthentication();
    // null check omitted
    String principalName = authentication.getName();
    Object principal =
      userDetailsService.loadUserByUsername(principalName);
    ...
  }
}
```

Obviously, this example is a bit silly, but it demonstrates the usage of `LdapUserDetailsService`. Go ahead and restart the application and give this a try with the username admin1@example.com and the password admin1. Can you figure out how to modify the controller to display an arbitrary user's information? Can you figure out how you should modify the security settings to restrict access to an administrator?

> Your code should look like chapter05.06-calendar.

# Integrating with an external LDAP server

It is likely that once you test the basic integration with the embedded LDAP server, you will want to interact with an external LDAP server. Fortunately, this is very straightforward and can be done using a slightly different syntax along with the same `<ldap-server>` instruction we provided to set up the embedded LDAP server.

Update the Spring Security configuration to connect to an external LDAP server on port 33389, as follows:

src/main/webapp/WEB-INF/spring/security.xml

```
    <ldap-server id="ldapServer"
            url="ldap://localhost:33389/dc=jbcpcalendar,dc=com"
            manager-dn="uid=admin,ou=system"
            manager-password="secret"/>
    <ldap-user-service id="ldapUserService"
```

The notable differences here (aside from the LDAP URL) are that the DN and password for an account are provided. The account (which is actually optional) should be allowed to bind to the directory and perform searches across all relevant DNs for user and group information. The binding resulting from the application of these credentials against the LDAP server URL is used for the remaining LDAP operations across the LDAP-secured system.

Be aware that many LDAP servers also support SSL-encrypted LDAP (LDAPS)—this is, of course, preferred for security purposes and is supported by the Spring LDAP stack. Simply use `ldaps://` at the beginning of the LDAP server URL. LDAPS typically runs on TCP port 636. Note that there are many commercial and non-commercial implementations of LDAP. The exact configuration parameters that you will use for connectivity, user binding, and population of `GrantedAuthoritys` will wholly depend on both the vendor and the structure of the directory. We will cover one very common LDAP implementation, **Microsoft Active Directory**, in the next section.

If you do not have an LDAP server handy and would like to give this a try, go ahead and add the following code to your `security.xml` file, which starts up the embedded LDAP server we have been using:

src/main/webapp/WEB-INF/spring/security.xml

```
    <ldap-server id="ldapServer"
            url="ldap://localhost:33389/dc=jbcpcalendar,dc=com"
            manager-dn="uid=admin,ou=system"
```

```
            manager-password="secret"/>
<ldap-server ldif="classpath:/ldif/calendar.ldif"
        root="dc=jbcpcalendar,dc=com"/>
<ldap-user-service id="ldapUserService"
```

If this isn't convincing, start up an LDAP server using Apache Directory Studio and import `calendar.ldif` into it. You can then connect to the external LDAP server.

> Your code should look like `chapter05.07-calendar`.

## Explicit LDAP bean configuration

In this section, we'll lead you through the set of bean configurations required to explicitly configure both a connection to an external LDAP server and the `LdapAuthenticationProvider` interface required to support authentication against an external server. As with other explicit bean-based configurations, you really want to avoid doing this, unless you find yourself in a situation where the capabilities of the security namespace style of configuration will not support your business or technical requirements, in which case, read on!

## Configuring an external LDAP server reference

To implement this configuration, we'll assume that we have a local LDAP server running on port `33389`, with the same configuration corresponding to the `<ldap-server>` example provided in the previous section. The required bean definition is already provided in `security-explicitly-ldap.xml`. In fact, to keep things simple, we have provided the entire `security-ldap-explicitly.xml` file. Review the LDAP server reference in the following code snippet:

src/main/webapp/WEB-INF/spring/security-ldap-explicitly.xml

```
<bean id="ldapServer"
  class="org.springframework.security.ldap
  .DefaultSpringSecurityContextSource">
  <constructor-arg
```

```
        value="ldap://localhost:33389/dc=jbcpcalendar,dc=com"/>

    <property name="userDn" value="uid=admin,ou=system"/>
    <property name="password" value="secret"/>
</bean>
```

Next, we'll need to configure `LdapAuthenticationProvider`, which is a bit more complex.

## Configuring LdapAuthenticationProvider

If you've read and understood the explanations throughout this chapter, describing how Spring Security LDAP authentication works behind the scenes, this bean configuration will be perfectly understandable, albeit a bit complex. We'll configure `LdapAuthenticationProvider` with the following characteristics:

- User credential binding authentication (not password compare)
- Use of the `InetOrgPerson` in `UserDetailsContextMapper`

Let's get to it—we'll explore the already configured `LdapAuthenticationProvider` first:

src/main/webapp/WEB-INF/spring/security-ldap-explicitly.xml

```
<bean id="ldapAuthenticationProvider"
  class="org.springframework.security.ldap.authentication
    .LdapAuthenticationProvider">
  <constructor-arg ref="ldapBindAuthenticator"/>
  <constructor-arg ref="ldapAuthoritiesPopulator"/>
  <property name="userDetailsContextMapper"
    ref="ldapUserDetailsContextMapper"/>
</bean>
```

The next bean provided for us is `BindAuthenticator`, and the supporting `FilterBasedLdapUserSearch` bean is used to locate the user's DN in the LDAP directory prior to binding:

src/main/webapp/WEB-INF/spring/security-ldap-explicitly.xml

```
<bean id="ldapBindAuthenticator"
  class="org.springframework.security.ldap.authentication
    .BindAuthenticator">
  <constructor-arg ref="ldapServer"/>
  <property name="userSearch" ref="ldapSearch"/>
</bean>
```

```xml
<bean id="ldapSearch"
  class="org.springframework.security.ldap.search
    .FilterBasedLdapUserSearch">
  <constructor-arg value=""/> <!-- user-search-base -->
  <constructor-arg value="(uid={0})"/> <!-- user-search-filter -->
  <constructor-arg ref="ldapServer"/>
</bean>
```

Finally, `LdapAuthoritiesPopulator` and `UserDetailsContextMapper` perform the roles we've examined earlier in the chapter:

src/main/webapp/WEB-INF/spring/security-ldap-explicitly.xml

```xml
<bean id="ldapAuthoritiesPopulator"
  class="org.springframework.security.ldap.userdetails
    .DefaultLdapAuthoritiesPopulator">
  <constructor-arg ref="ldapServer"/>
  <constructor-arg value="ou=Groups"/>
  <property name="groupSearchFilter" value="(uniqueMember={0})"/>
</bean>

<bean id="ldapUserDetailsContextMapper"
  class="org.springframework.security.ldap.userdetails
    .InetOrgPersonContextMapper"/>
```

In the next step, we must update Spring Security to utilize our explicitly configured `LdapAuthenticationProvider`. Update the `security.xml` file to use our new configuration, ensuring to remove the old `<authentication-provider>` element.

src/main/webapp/WEB-INF/spring/security.xml

```xml
<authentication-manager>
    <authentication-provider ref="ldapAuthenticationProvider"/>
</authentication-manager>
```

Finally, update `web.xml` to use the already provided `security-explicitly-ldap.xml` configuration.

src/main/webapp/WEB-INF/web.xml

```xml
<param-value>
    ...
    /WEB-INF/spring/security.xml
    /WEB-INF/spring/security-ldap-explicitly.xml
</param-value>
```

At this point, we have fully configured LDAP authentication with explicit Spring Bean notation. Employing this technique in the LDAP integration is useful in a few cases where the security namespace does not expose certain configuration attributes, or where custom implementation classes are required to provide functionality tailored to a particular business scenario. We'll explore one such scenario later in this chapter, when we examine how to connect to Microsoft Active Directory via LDAP.

Go ahead and start the application and give the configuration a try. Assuming you have an external LDAP server running or you have kept the configured in-memory `<ldap-server>` element, everything should still be working.

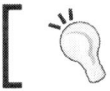

> Your code should look like `chapter05.08-calendar`.

# Delegating role discovery to UserDetailsService

One technique for populating user roles that are available to use with explicit bean configuration is the support for looking up a user by username in the `UserDetailsService`, and getting the `GrantedAuthority` objects from this source. Configuration is as simple as replacing the bean with the id ldapAuthoritiesPopulator bean with an updated UserDetailsServiceLdapAuthoritiesPopulator with a reference to `UserDetailsService`. Make the following updates to our security-ldap-explicitly.xml ensuring to remove the previous ldapAuthoritiesPopulator bean definition:

src/main/webapp/WEB-INF/spring/security-ldap-explicitly.xml

```xml
    <bean class="org.springframework.security.ldap.userdetails.
    DefaultLdapAuthoritiesPopulator"
            id="ldapAuthoritiesPopulator">
        <constructor-arg ref="ldapServer"/>
        <constructor-arg value="ou=Groups"/>
        <property name="groupSearchFilter" value="(uniqueMember={0})"/>
    </bean>
    <bean class="org.springframework.security.ldap.authentication.
    UserDetailsServiceLdapAuthoritiesPopulator"
            id="ldapAuthoritiesPopulator">
        <constructor-arg ref="userDetailsService"/>
    </bean>
```

## LDAP Directory Services

We will also need to ensure that we have defined `userDetailsService`. To keep things simple, add an in-memory `UserDetailsService`, as follows:

src/main/webapp/WEB-INF/spring/security.xml

```
...
    </authentication-manager>
    <user-service id="userDetailsService">
        <user name="user1@example.com"
            password="user1"
            authorities="ROLE_USER"/>
        <user name="admin1@example.com"
            password="admin1"
            authorities="ROLE_USER,ROLE_ADMIN"/>
    </user-service>
</bean:beans>
```

You should now be able to authenticate with `admin1@example.com` as the username and `admin1` as the password. Naturally, we could also substitute this in-memory `UserDetailsService` interface for the JDBC-based one we discussed in the previous chapter.

> Your code should look like `chapter05.09-calendar`.

The logistical and managerial problem you may foresee with this is that the usernames and roles must be managed both in the LDAP server and the repository used by `UserDetailsService` — this is probably not a scalable model with a large user base.

The more common use of this scenario is when LDAP authentication is required to ensure that users of the secured application are valid corporate users but the application itself wants to store authorization information. This keeps potentially application-specific data out of the LDAP directory, which can be a beneficial separation of concerns.

# Integrating with Microsoft Active Directory via LDAP

One of the convenient features of Microsoft Active Directory is not only its seamless integration with Microsoft Windows-based network architectures, but also that it can be configured to expose the contents of Active Directory using the LDAP protocol. If you are a Windows shop, it is probable that any LDAP integration you do will be against your Active Directory instance.

Depending on your configuration of Microsoft Active Directory (and the directory administrator's willingness to configure it to support Spring Security LDAP), you may have a difficult time not with the authentication and binding process, but with the mapping of Active Directory information to the user's `GrantedAuthority` objects within the Spring Security system.

The sample Active Directory LDAP tree for JBCP Calendar corporate, within our LDAP browser, looks similar to the one in the following screenshot:

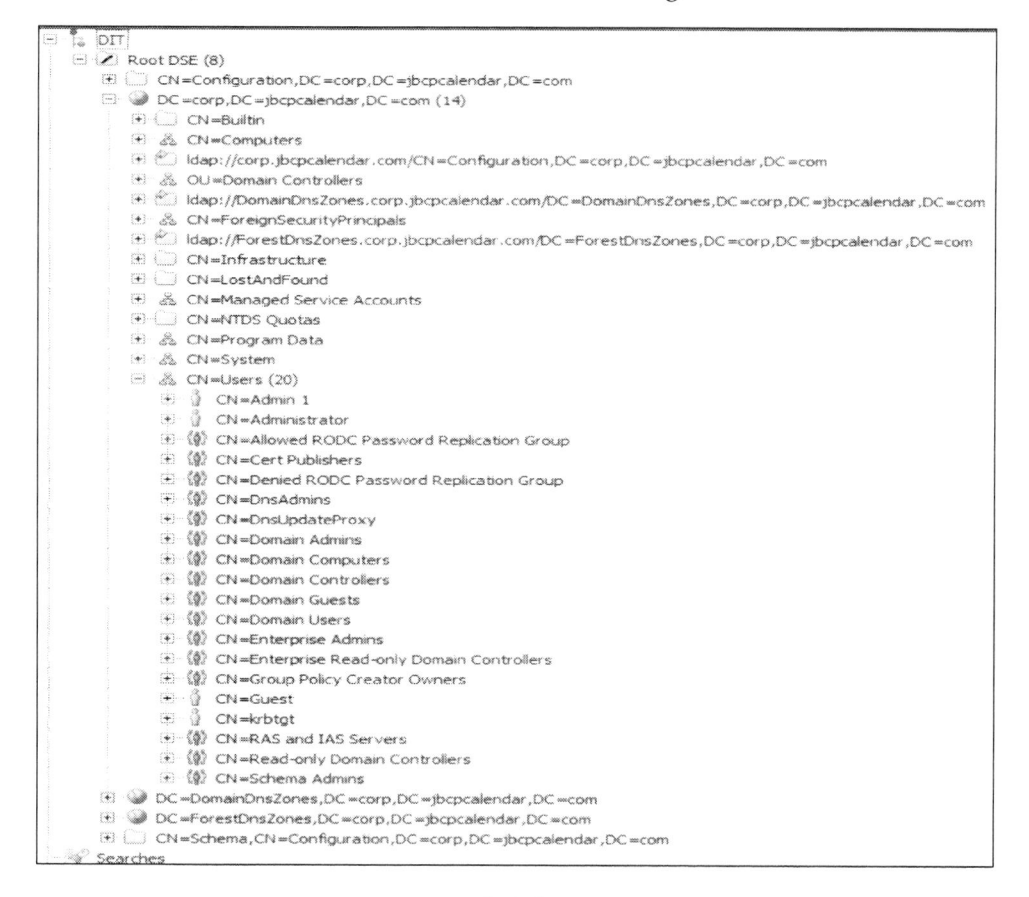

# LDAP Directory Services

What you do not see here is `ou=Groups`, as we saw in our sample LDAP structure earlier; this is because Active Directory stores group membership as attributes on the LDAP entries of users themselves.

Let's use our recently acquired knowledge of explicit bean configuration to write an `LdapAuthoritiesPopulator` implementation that obtains `GrantedAuthority` from the user's `memberOf` attribute. In the following section, you will find the `ActiveDirectoryLdapAuthoritiesPopulator` that is provided in this chapter's sample code:

src/main/java/com/packtpub/springsecurity/ldap/userdetails/ad/ActiveDirectoryLdapAuthoritiesPopulator.java

```java
    public final class ActiveDirectoryLdapAuthoritiesPopulator
      implements LdapAuthoritiesPopulator {

        public Collection<? extends GrantedAuthority>
          getGrantedAuthorities(DirContextOperations userData, String
            username) {
          String[] groups =
            userData.getStringAttributes("memberOf");
          List<GrantedAuthority> authorities = new
            ArrayList<GrantedAuthority>();

          for (String group : groups) {
            LdapRdn authority = new
              DistinguishedName(group).removeLast();
            authorities.add(new
              SimpleGrantedAuthority(authority.getValue()));
          }
          return authorities;
        }
    }
```

Now, we need to alter our configuration to support our Active Directory structure. Assuming we are starting with the bean configuration detailed in the previous section, make the following updates:

src/main/webapp/WEB-INF/spring/security-explicitly-ldap.xml

```xml
    <bean id="ldapServer"
      class="org.springframework.security.ldap
        .DefaultSpringSecurityContextSource">
      <constructor-arg value="ldap://corp.jbcpcalendar.com
```

```xml
        /dc=corp,dc=jbcpcalendar,dc=com"/>

    <property name="userDn" value="CN=Administrator,CN=Users,
      DC=corp,DC=jbcpcalendar,DC=com"/>
    <property name="password" value="admin123!"/>
</bean>

<bean id="ldapAuthenticationProvider"
    class="org.springframework.security.ldap
    .authentication.LdapAuthenticationProvider">
    <constructor-arg ref="ldapBindAuthenticator"/>
    <constructor-arg ref="ldapAuthoritiesPopulator"/>
    <!-- removed userDetailsContextMapper -->
</bean>

...

<bean id="ldapSearch"
    class="org.springframework.security.ldap.search
    .FilterBasedLdapUserSearch">
    <constructor-arg value="CN=Users"/> <!-- use-search-base -->
    <constructor-arg value="(sAMAccountName={0})"/> <!-- user-
      search-filter -->
    <constructor-arg ref="ldapServer"/>
</bean>

<bean id="ldapAuthoritiesPopulator"
    class="com.packtpub.springsecurity.ldap.userdetails
    .ad.ActiveDirectoryLdapAuthoritiesPopulator"/>
<!-- removed ldapUserDetailsContextMapper -->
```

If you have it defined, you will want to remove `<ldap-server>` and `<ldap-user-service>` in `security.xml`. Finally, you will want to remove the references to `UserDetailsService` from `AccountController`.

The `sAMAccountName` attribute is the Active Directory equivalent of the `uid` attribute we used in a standard LDAP entry. Although most Active Directory LDAP integrations are likely to be more complex than this example, this should give you a starting point to jump off and explore from with your conceptual understanding of the inner workings of Spring Security LDAP integration; supporting even a complex integration will be much easier.

> If you want to run this sample, you will need an instance of Active Directory up and running that matches the schema displayed in the screenshot. The alternative is to adjust the configuration to match your Active Directory's schema. A simple way to play around with Active Directory is to install Active Directory Lightweight Directory Services, which can be found at http://www.microsoft.com/download/en/details.aspx?id=14683.

## Built-In Active Directory support in Spring Security 3.1

Spring Security added Active Directory support in Spring Security 3.1. In fact, the `ActiveDirectoryLdapAuthoritiesPopulator` from the previous section is based on the newly-added support. To utilize the built-in support in Spring Security 3.1, we can replace our entire `security-explicitly-ldap.xml` file with the following configuration:

src/main/webapp/WEB-INF/spring/security-explicitly-ldap.xml

```xml
<bean id="ldapAuthenticationProvider"
  class="org.springframework.security.ldap.authentication
  .ad.ActiveDirectoryLdapAuthenticationProvider">
  <constructor-arg value="corp.jbcpcalendar.com"/>
  <constructor-arg value="ldap://corp.jbcpcalendar.com/"/>
  <property name="convertSubErrorCodesToExceptions" value="true"/>
</bean>
```

Of course, if you are going to use it, you need to ensure that you wire it to `AuthenticationManager`. We have already done this, but a reminder of what the configuration looks like can be found in the following code snippet:

```xml
<authentication-manager>
    <authentication-provider ref="ldapAuthenticationProvider"/>
</authentication-manager>
```

There are a few things that should be noted about the provided `ActiveDirectoryLdapAuthenticationProvider` class:

1. The users that need to be authenticated must be able to bind to Active Directory (there is no manager user).
2. The default method for populating users' authorities is to search the users' `memberOf` attributes.
3. Users must contain an attribute named `userPrincipalName`, which is in the `username@<domain>` format. Here, `<domain>` is the first constructor argument to `ActiveDirectoryLdapAuthenticationProvider`. This is due to the fact that, after the bind occurs, this is how the context for the `memberOf` lookup is found.

Due to the complex LDAP deployments that occur in the real world, the built in support will more likely than not provide a guide to as how you can integrate with your custom LDAP schema.

# Summary

We have seen that LDAP servers can be relied upon to provide authentication and authorization information as well as rich user profile information, when requested. In this chapter, we covered:

- LDAP terminology and concepts, and how LDAP directories might be commonly organized to work with Spring Security
- Configuration of both standalone (embedded) and external LDAP servers from a Spring Security configuration file
- Authentication and authorization of users against LDAP repositories, and subsequent mapping to Spring Security actors
- Differences in authentication schemes and password storage and security mechanisms in LDAP, and how they are treated in Spring Security
- Mapping user detail attributes from the LDAP directory to the `UserDetails` object for rich information exchange between LDAP and the Spring-enabled application
- Explicit bean configuration for LDAP, and the pros and cons of this approach
- Integration with Active Directory

In the next chapter, we will discuss Spring Security's **Remember Me** feature, which allows a user's session to securely persist even after closing the browser.

# 6
# Remember-me Services

In this chapter, we'll add the ability for an application to remember a user even after their session has expired and the browser is closed. The following topics will be covered in this chapter:

- Discuss what remember-me is
- Learn how to use the token-based remember-me feature
- Discuss how secure remember-me is, and various ways of making it more secure
- Enable the persistent-based remember-me feature, and how to handle additional considerations for using it
- Present the overall remember-me architecture
- Learn how to create a custom remember-me implementation that is restricted to the user's IP address

## What is remember-me

A convenient feature to offer frequent users of the website is the remember-me feature. This feature allows a user to elect to be remembered even after their browser is closed. In Spring Security, this is implemented through the use of a remember-me cookie that is stored in the user's browser. If Spring Security recognizes that the user is presenting a remember-me cookie, then the user will be automatically logged in to the application, and will not need to enter a username or password.

> **What is a cookie?**
> A cookie is a way for a client (that is, a web browser) to persist the state. For more information about cookies, refer to additional online resources, such as Wikipedia (http://en.wikipedia.org/wiki/HTTP_cookie).

Spring Security provides two different strategies that we will discuss in this chapter. The first is **Token-based** remember-me feature, which relies on a cryptographic signature. The second method, **Persistent-based** remember-me feature, requires a data store (a database). As we previously mentioned, we will discuss these strategies in much greater detail throughout this chapter. The remember-me feature must be explicitly configured in order to enable it. Let's start off by trying the token-based remember-me feature and see how it affects the flow of the login experience.

# Dependencies

The token-based remember-me section does not need any additional dependencies other than the basic setup from *Chapter 2, Getting Started with Spring Security*. However, you will want to ensure to include the following additional dependencies in your pom.xml file, if you are leveraging the persistent-based remember-me feature. We have already included these dependencies in the chapter's sample, so there is no need to update the sample application.

pom.xml

```xml
<!-- matching JDBC driver (depends on which database you use) -->
<dependency>
  <groupId>com.h2database</groupId>
  <artifactId>h2</artifactId>
  <version>1.3.163</version>
  <scope>runtime</scope>
</dependency>
<dependency>
  <groupId>org.springframework</groupId>
  <artifactId>spring-jdbc</artifactId>
  <version>3.1.0.RELEASE</version>
</dependency>
<dependency>
  <groupId>org.springframework</groupId>
  <artifactId>spring-tx</artifactId>
  <version>3.1.0.RELEASE</version>
</dependency>
```

# The token-based remember-me feature

Spring Security provides two different implementations of the remember-me feature. We will start off by exploring how to set up the token-based remember-me services.

## Configuring the token-based remember-me feature

Completing this exercise will allow us to provide a simple and secure method to keep users logged in for extended periods of time. To start, modify the `security.xml` configuration file to add the `<remember-me>` declaration.

> You should start with chapter06.00-calendar.

src/main/webapp/WEB-INF/spring/security.xml

```xml
<http auto-config="true" use-expressions="true">
    ...
    <remember-me key="jbcpCalendar"/>
    <logout logout-url="/logout"
            logout-success-url="/login/form?logout"/>
</http>
```

If we try running the application now, we'll see nothing different in the flow. This is because we also need to add a field to the login form that allows the user to opt in to this functionality. Edit the `login.jsp` file to add a checkbox similar to the following:

src/main/webapp/WEB-INF/views/login.jsp

```jsp
...
<p>
<input type="password" id="password" name="password"/>
<label for="remember">Remember Me?</label>
<input type="checkbox" id="remember"
        name="_spring_security_remember_me"
        value="true"/>
<div class="form-actions">
</p>
<p>
    <input id="submit" name="submit" type="submit" value="Login"/>
</p>
```

> Your code should look like `chapter06.01-calendar`.

When we next log in, if the **Remember Me** box is selected, a remember-me cookie is set in the user's browser. Spring Security understands that it should remember the user by inspecting the HTTP parameter `_spring_security_remember_me`.

If the user then closes his/her browser and reopens it to an authenticated page on the JBCP Calendar website, he/she won't be presented with the login page a second time. Try it yourself now—log in with the **Remember Me** option selected, bookmark the home page, then restart the browser, and access the home page. You'll see that you're immediately logged in successfully without needing to supply your login credentials again.

If this appears to be happening to you, it means that your browser or a browser plugin is restoring the session. One tip is to try closing the tab first and then close the browser. One more effective solution is to use a browser plugin, such as **Firecookie** (https://addons.mozilla.org/en-US/firefox/addon/firecookie/), to remove the `JSESSIONID` cookie. This can often save time and annoyance during the development and verification of this type of a feature on your site.

# How the token-based remember-me feature works

The remember-me feature sets a cookie on the user's browser containing a **Base64-encoded** string with the following pieces:

- The username
- An expiration date/time
- An MD5 hash value of the expiration date/time, username, password, and the key attribute of the `<remember-me>` element
- These bits are combined into a single cookie value that is stored on the browser for later use

# MD5

MD5 is one of the several well-known cryptographic hash algorithms. **Cryptographic hash algorithms** compute a compact and unique text representation of input data with arbitrary length, called a digest. This **digest** can be used to determine if an untrusted input should be trusted, by comparing the digest of the untrusted input to a known valid digest of the expected input. The following diagram illustrates how this works:

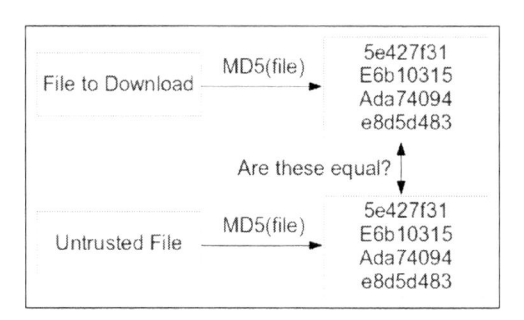

For example, many open source software sites allow mirrors to distribute their software to help increase download speeds. However, as a user of the software, we would want to be sure that the software is authentic and doesn't include any viruses. The software distributor will calculate and publish the expected MD5 checksum on their website with their known good version of the software. Then, we can download the file from any location. Before we install the software, we calculate the untrusted MD5 checksum on the file we downloaded. We then compare the untrusted MD5 checksum to the expected MD5 checksum. If the two values match, we know that we can safely install the file we downloaded. If the two values do not match, we should not trust the downloaded file and delete it.

Although it is impossible to obtain the original data from the hash value, MD5 is vulnerable to several types of attack, including the exploitation of weaknesses in the algorithm itself and rainbow table attacks. **Rainbow tables** typically contain the pre-computed hash values of millions of input values. This allows attackers to look for the hash value in the rainbow table and determine the actual (unhashed) value. Spring Security combats this by including the expiration date, the user's password, and the `<remember-me>` key in the hashed value.

## Remember-me signature

We can see how MD5 can ensure that we have downloaded the correct file, but how does this apply to Spring Security's remember-me service? Much like the file we downloaded, the cookie is untrusted, but we can trust it if we can validate the signature that originated from our application. When a request comes in with the remember-me cookie, its contents are extracted and the expected signature is compared to the signature found in the cookie. The steps in calculating the expected signature are illustrated in the following diagram:

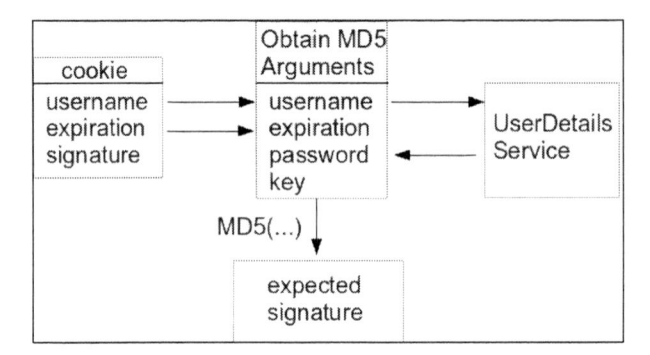

The remember-me cookie contains the username, expiration, and a signature. Spring Security will extract the username and expiration from the cookie. It will then utilize the username from the cookie to look up the password using `UserDetailsService`. The key is already known because it was provided using the `<remember-me>` element. Now that all the arguments are known, Spring Security can calculate the expected signature using the username, expiration date, password, and key. It then compares the expected signature against the cookie's signature.

If the two signatures match, we can trust that the username and expiration date are valid. Forging a signature is next to impossible without knowing the remember-me key (which only the application knows) and the user's password (which only this user knows). This means if the signatures match and if the token is not expired, the user can be logged in.

> You have anticipated that if the user changes their username or password, any remember-me token set will no longer be valid. Make sure that you provide appropriate messaging to users if you allow them to change these bits of their account. Later in this chapter, we will look at an alternative remember-me implementation that is reliant only on the username and not on the password.

Note that it is still possible to differentiate between users who have been authenticated with a remember-me cookie and users who have presented the username and password (or equivalent) credentials. We'll experiment with this shortly when we investigate the security of the remember-me feature.

## Token-based remember-me configuration directives

Two configuration changes are commonly made to alter the default behavior of the `<remember-me>` functionality:

| Attribute | Description |
| --- | --- |
| `key` | Defines a unique key used when producing the remember-me cookie's signature. |
| `token-validity-seconds` | Defines the length of time (in seconds). The remember-me cookie will be considered valid for authentication. It is also used to set the cookie expiration timestamp. |

As you may infer from the discussion of how the cookie contents are hashed, the `key` attribute is critical for security of the remember-me feature. Make sure that the key you choose is likely to be unique to your application, and long enough so that it can't be easily guessed.

Keeping in mind the purpose of this book, we've kept the key values relatively simple, but if you're using remember-me in your own application, it's suggested that your key contains the unique name of your application and is at least 36 random characters long. Password generator tools (search Google for "online password generator") are a great way to get a pseudo-random mix of alphanumeric and special characters to compose your remember-me key. For applications that exist in multiple environments (such as development, test, and production), the remember-me cookie value should include this fact as well. This will prevent remember-me cookies from inadvertently being used in the wrong environment during testing!

An example key value in a production application might be similar to the following:

```
prodJbcpCalendar-rmkey-paLLwApsifs24THosE62scabWow78PEaCh99Jus
```

The `token-validity-seconds` attribute is used to set the number of seconds after which the remember-me token will not be accepted for the automatic login function, even if it is otherwise a valid token. The same attribute is also used to set the maximum lifetime of the remember-me cookie on the user's browser.

*Remember-me Services*

> **Configuration of the remember-me session cookies**
>
> If `token-validity-seconds` is set to -1, the login cookie will be set to a session cookie, which does not persist after the browser is closed by the user. The token will be valid (assuming the user doesn't close the browser) for a non-configurable length of two weeks. Don't confuse this with the cookie that stores your user's session ID—they're two different things with similar names!

You may have noticed that we listed very few of the attributes. Don't worry, we will spend time covering some of the other configuration attributes throughout this chapter.

## Is remember-me secure

Any feature related to security, which has been added for user convenience, has the potential to expose a security risk to our carefully-protected site. The remember-me feature, in its default form, runs the risk of the user's cookie from being intercepted and re-used by a malicious user. The following diagram illustrates how this might happen:

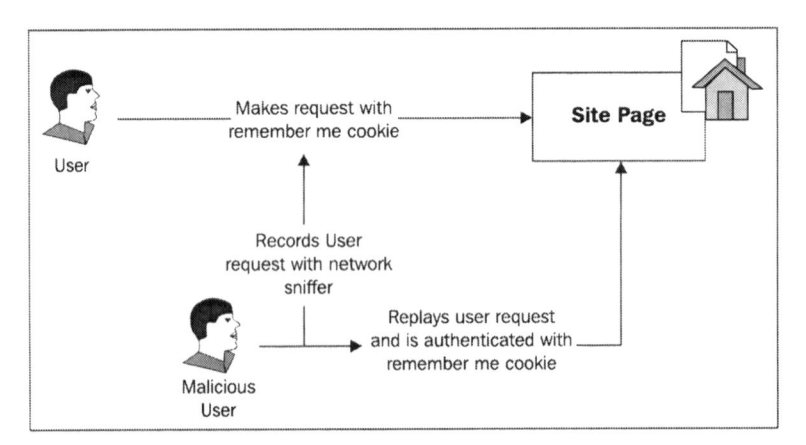

Use of SSL (covered in the *Appendix*) and other network security techniques can mitigate this type of attack, but be aware that there are other techniques, such as **cross-site scripting (XSS)** that could steal or compromise a remembered user session. While convenient for the user, we don't want to risk financial or other personal information from being inadvertently changed or possibly stolen if the remembered session is misused.

> Although we don't cover the malicious user behavior in detail in this book, when implementing any secured system it is important to understand the techniques employed by users who may be trying to hack your customers or employees. XSS is one such technique, but many others exist. It's highly recommended that you review the **OWASP Top Ten** article (http://www.owasp.org/index.php/Category:OWASP_Top_Ten_Project) for a good starting list, and also pick up a web application security reference book, where many of the techniques demonstrated are illustrated to apply to any technology.

One common approach for maintaining the balance between convenience and security is identifying the functional locations in the site where personal or sensitive information could be present. You can then use the `fullyAuthenticated` expression to ensure these locations are protected using authorization that checks not just the user's role, but that they have been authenticated with a full username and password. We will explore this feature in greater detail in the next section.

# Authorization rules for remember-me

We'll fully explore the advanced authorization techniques later in *Chapter 10, Fine-grained Access Control*, however, it's important to realize that it's possible to differentiate access rules based on whether an authenticated session was remembered.

Let's assume we want to limit users trying to access the H2 admin console to administrators who have authenticated using a username and password. This is similar to the behavior found in other major consumer-focused commerce sites, which restrict access to the elevated portions of the site until a password is entered. Keep in mind that every site is different, so don't blindly apply such rules to your secure site. For our sample application, we'll concentrate on protecting the H2 database console. Update the `security.xml` file to use the keyword `fullyAuthenticated`, which ensures that remembered users who try to access the H2 database are denied access. This is shown in the following code snippet:

src/main/webapp/WEB-INF/spring/security.xml

```
<http auto-config="true" use-expressions="true">
  ...
  <intercept-url pattern="/admin/**"
    access="hasRole('ROLE_ADMIN') and fullyAuthenticated"/>
  ...
</http>
```

The existing rules remain unchanged. We've added a rule that requires requests for account information to have the appropriate `GrantedAuthority` of `ROLE_USER`, and that the user is fully authenticated; that is, during this authenticated session, they have actually presented a username and password or other suitable credentials. Note the syntax of the **SpEL** logical operators here—`and`, `or`, and `not` are used for logical operators in SpEL. This was thoughtful of the SpEL designers, as the `&&` operator would be awkward to represent in XML!

> Your code should look like `chapter06.02-calendar`.

Go ahead and log in with the username `admin1@example.com` and the password `admin1` ensuring to select the **Remember Me** feature. Access the H2 database console and see that the access is granted. Now, delete the `JSESSIONID` cookie (or close the tab and then all the browser instances), and ensure that access is still granted to the **All Events** page. Now, navigate to the H2 console and observe that the access is denied.

> **Checking Full Authentication without Expressions**
> If your application does not use SpEL expressions for access declarations, you can still check if the user is fully authenticated, by using the `IS_AUTHENTICATED_FULLY` access rule (For example, `access=" IS_AUTHENTICATED_FULLY"`). Be aware, however, that standard role access declarations aren't as expressive as SpEL ones, so you will have trouble handling complex Boolean expressions.

This approach combines the usability enhancements of the remember-me feature with additional level of security, by requiring a user to present a full set of credentials to access sensitive information. Throughout the rest of the chapter, we will explore other ways of making the remember-me feature more secure.

# Persistent remember-me

Spring Security provides the capability to alter the method for validating the remember-me cookie by leveraging different implementations of the `RememberMeServices` interface. In this section, we will discuss how we can use the persistent remember-me tokens using a database, and how this can increase the security of our application.

# Using the persistent-based remember-me feature

Modifying our remember-me configuration at this point to persist to the database is surprisingly trivial. The Spring Security configuration parser will recognize a new `data-source-ref` attribute on the `<remember-me>` declaration, and simply switch implementation classes for `RememberMeServices`. Let's now review the steps required to accomplish this.

## Adding SQL to create the remember-me schema

We have placed the SQL file containing the expected schema in our `resources` folder in the same place we did for *Chapter 3, Custom Authentication*. You can view the schema definition in the following code snippet:

src/main/resources/database/h2/security-rememberme-schema.sql

```sql
create table persistent_logins (
    username varchar_ignorecase(100) not null,
    series varchar(64) primary key,
    token varchar(64) not null,
    last_used timestamp not null
);
```

## Initializing the data source with the remember-me schema

You will need to ensure the database is initialized with the schema. We will do this by adding another script element to our embedded database declaration. Update the `services.xml` file shown as follows:

src/main/webapp/WEB-INF/spring/services.xml

```xml
<jdbc:embedded-database id="dataSource" type="H2">
    ...
    <jdbc:script location=
      "classpath:/database/h2/security-rememberme-schema.sql"/>
</jdbc:embedded-database>
```

# Configuring the persistent-based remember-me feature

Finally, we'll need to make some brief configuration changes to the `<remember-me>` declaration to point it to the data source we're using:

```
<http auto-config="true" use-expressions="true">
    ...
    <remember-me key="jbcpCalendar"
            data-source-ref="dataSource"/>
    ...
</http>
```

This is all we need to do to switch over to using the persistent-based remember-me authentication. As you can see, the namespace configuration makes this quite simple. Go ahead and start up the application, and give it a try. From a user's standpoint, we do not notice any difference, but we know that the implementation backing this feature has changed.

> Your code should look like `chapter06.03-calendar`.

# How does the persistent-based remember-me feature work

Instead of validating a signature present in the cookie, the persistent-based remember-me service validates if the token exists in a database. Each persistent remember-me cookie consists of the following:

- **Series identifier**: Identifies the initial login of a user. This remains consistent each time the user is automatically logged in from the original session.

- **Token value**: A unique value that changes each time a user is authenticated using the remember-me feature.

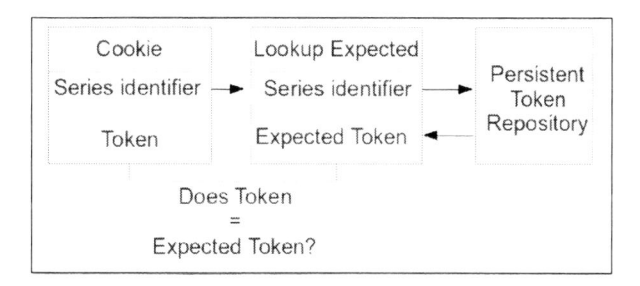

```
┌─────────────────────────────────────────────────────┐
│    Cookie             Lookup Expected               │
│                                          Persistent │
│  Series identifier ──▶ Series identifier ──▶ Token  │
│                                          Repository │
│    Token              Expected Token   ◀─           │
│                                                     │
│                  Does Token                         │
│                       =                             │
│                  Expected Token?                    │
└─────────────────────────────────────────────────────┘
```

When the remember-me cookie is submitted, Spring Security will use a `o.s.s.web.authentication.rememberme.PersistentTokenRepository` implementation to look up the expected token value and an expiration using the submitted series identifier. It will then compare the token value in the cookie to the expected token value. If the token is not expired and the two tokens match, the user is considered authenticated. A new remember-me cookie with the same series identifier, a new token value, and an updated expiration date will be generated.

If the series token submitted is found in the database, but the tokens do not match, it can be assumed that someone stole the remember-me cookie. In this case, Spring Security will terminate this series of remember-me tokens and warn the user that their login has been compromised.

# Are database-backed persistent tokens more secure

Just like `TokenBasedRememberMeServices`, persistent tokens may be compromised by cookie theft or other man-in-the-middle techniques. The use of SSL, as covered in the *Appendix*, can circumvent man-in-the-middle techniques. If you are using a Servlet 3.0 environment (that is, Tomcat 7), Spring Security will mark the cookie as `HttpOnly`, which will help to mitigate against the cookie being stolen in the event of an XSS vulnerability in the application. To learn more about the `HttpOnly` attribute, refer to the external resource on cookies provided earlier in the chapter.

One of the advantages of using the persistent-based remember-me feature is that we can detect if the cookie is compromised. If the correct series token and an incorrect token is presented, we know that any remember-me feature using that series token should be considered compromised, and we should terminate any sessions associated with it. Since the validation is stateful, we can also terminate the specific remember-me feature without needing to change the user's password.

# Cleaning up the expired remember-me sessions

The downside of using the persistent-based remember-me feature is that there is no built-in support for cleaning up the expired sessions. In order to do this, we need to implement a background process that cleans up the expired sessions. We have included code within the chapter's sample code to perform the cleanup. For conciseness, we display a version that does not do validation or error handling, in the following code snippet below. You can view the full version in the sample code of this chapter.

src/main/java/com/packtpub/springsecurity/web/authentication/rememberme/JdbcTokenRepositoryImplCleaner.java

```java
public final class JdbcTokenRepositoryImplCleaner implements
   Runnable {
   private final JdbcOperations jdbcOperations;
   private final long tokenValidityInMs;

   public JdbcTokenRepositoryImplCleaner(JdbcOperations
      jdbcOperations,
      long tokenValidityInMs) {
      this.jdbcOperations = jdbcOperations;
      this.tokenValidityInMs = tokenValidityInMs;
   }

   public void run() {
      long expiredInMs = System.currentTimeMillis() -
         tokenValidityInMs;
      jdbcOperations.update(
         "delete from persistent_logins where last_used <= ?",
         new Date(expiredInMs)
      );
   }
}
```

The sample code for this chapter also includes a simple Spring configuration that will execute the cleaner every ten minutes. If you are unfamiliar with Spring's task abstraction and want to learn it, then you may want to read more about it in the Spring reference at http://static.springsource.org/spring/docs/3.1.x/spring-framework-reference/html/scheduling.html. You can find the relevant configuration in the following code snippet. Remember that jdbcTemplate is already configured in our services.xml file.

*Chapter 6*

src/main/webapp/WEB-INF/spring/cleaner.xml

```xml
<bean id="tokenRepositoryCleaner"
    class="com.packtpub.springsecurity.web.authentication
      .rememberme.JdbcTokenRepositoryImplCleaner">
  <constructor-arg ref="jdbcTemplate"/>
  <constructor-arg value="600000"/>
</bean>
<task:scheduled-tasks>
  <task:scheduled ref="tokenRepositoryCleaner"
    method="run"
    fixed-delay="600000"/>
</task:scheduled-tasks>
```

> Keep in mind that this configuration is not cluster-aware. Therefore, if this is deployed to a cluster, the cleaner will execute once for every JVM that the application is deployed to.

The only thing that needs to be done in our application is to add the cleaner.xml to the web.xml file, so that it gets loaded. Go ahead and update web.xml, as follows:

src/main/webapp/WEB-INF/web.xml

```xml
<param-value>
    ...
    /WEB-INF/spring/security.xml
    /WEB-INF/spring/cleaner.xml
</param-value>
```

Start up the application and give the updates a try. The configuration that was provided will ensure that the cleaner is executed every ten minutes. You may want to change the cleaner task to run more frequently and to clean up the more recently used remember-me tokens by modifying cleaner.xml. You can then create a few remember-me tokens and see that they get deleted, by querying for them in the H2 database console.

> Your code should look like chapter06.04-calendar.

# Remember-me architecture

We have gone over the basic architecture of both `TokenBasedRememberMeServices` and `PersistentTokenBasedRememberMeServices`, but we have not described the overall architecture. Let's see how all the remember-me pieces fit together.

The following diagram illustrates the different components involved in the process of validating a token-based remember-me token:

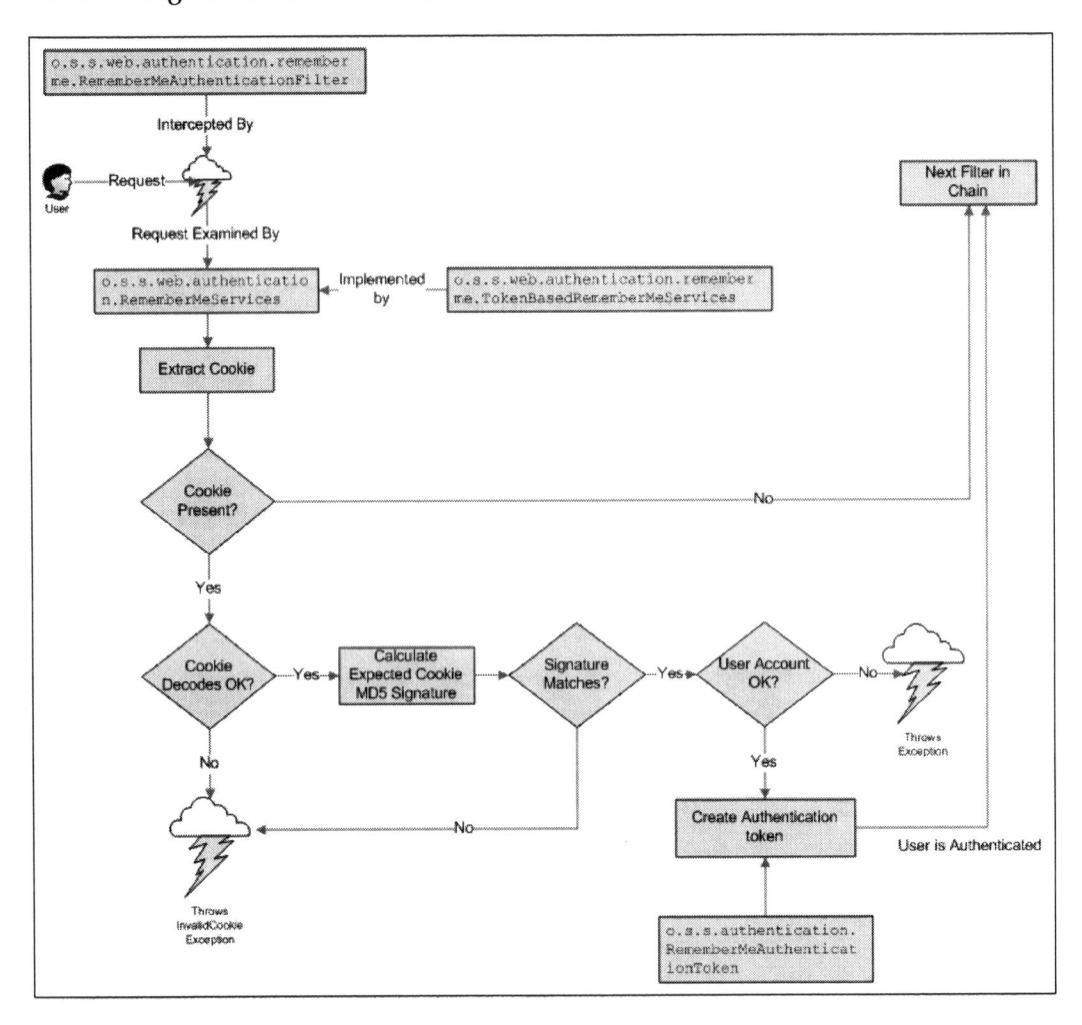

As with any of the Spring Security filters, `RememberMeAuthenticationFilter` is invoked from within `FilterChainProxy`. The job of `RememberMeAuthenticationFilter` is to inspect the request, and if it is of interest, action is taken.

`RememberMeAuthenticationFilter` will use the `RememberMeServices` implementation to determine if the user is already logged in. `RememberMeServices` does this by inspecting the HTTP request for a remember-me cookie that is then validated using either the token-based validation or the persistent-based validation we previously discussed. If the token checks out, the user will be logged in.

## Remember-me and the user lifecycle

The implementation of `RememberMeServices` is invoked at several points in the user lifecycle (the lifecycle of an authenticated user's session). To assist in your understanding of the remember-me functionality, it can be helpful to be aware of the points in time when remember-me services are informed of lifecycle functions:

| Action | What should happen? | RememberMeServices method invoked |
| --- | --- | --- |
| Successful login | Implementation sets a remember-me cookie (if the `form` parameter has been sent) | `loginSuccess` |
| Failed login | Implementation should cancel the cookie, if it's present | `loginFailed` |
| User logout | Implementation should cancel the cookie, if it's present | `logout*` |

> The `logout` method is not present on the `RememberMeServices` interface. Instead, each `RememberMeServices` implementation also implements the `LogoutHandler` interface, which contains the `logout` method. By implementing the `LogoutHandler` interface, each `RememberMeServices` implementation can perform the necessary cleanup when the user logs out.

Knowing where and how `RememberMeServices` ties in to the user's lifecycle will be important when we begin to create custom authentication handlers, because we need to ensure that any authentication processor treats `RememberMeServices` consistently, to preserve the usefulness and security of this functionality.

# Restricting the remember-me feature to an IP address

Let's put our understanding of the remember-me architecture to use. A common requirement is that any remember-me token should be tied to the IP address of the user that created it. This adds additional security to the remember-me feature. To do this, we only need to implement a custom `PersistentTokenRepository` interface. The configuration changes that we will make will illustrate how to configure a custom `RememberMeServices`. Throughout this section, we will take a look at `IpAwarePersistentTokenRepository`, which is included in the chapter's source code. `IpAwarePersistenTokenRepository` ensures that the series identifier is internally combined with the current user's IP address, and the series identifier includes only the identifier externally. This means, whenever a token is looked up or saved, the current IP address is used to lookup or persist the token. In the following code snippets, you can see `IpAwarePersistentTokenRepository` works. If you want to dig in even deeper, we encourage you to view the source included with the chapter.

The trick to looking up the IP address is using Spring's `RequestContextHolder`. The relevant code is as follows:

> It should be noted that in order to use `RequestContextHolder`, you need to ensure you have set up your web.xml file to use `RequestContextListener`. We have already performed this setup for our sample code. However, this can be useful when utilizing the example code in an external application. Refer to the Javadoc of `IpAwarePersistentTokenRepository` for details on how to set this up.

src/main/java/com/packtpub/springsecurity/web/authentication/rememberme/IpAwarePersistentTokenRepository.java

```
private String ipSeries(String series) {
  ServletRequestAttributes attributes =
    (ServletRequestAttributes)
    RequestContextHolder.getRequestAttributes();
  return series + attributes.getRequest().getRemoteAddr();
}
```

We can build on this method to force tokens that are saved to include the IP address in the series identifier:

```
public void createNewToken(PersistentRememberMeToken token) {
  String ipSeries = ipSeries(token.getSeries());
  PersistentRememberMeToken ipToken = tokenWithSeries(token,
    ipSeries);
  this.delegateRepository.createNewToken(ipToken);
}
```

You can see that we first created a new series with the IP address concatenated to it. The `tokenWithSeries` method is just a helper that creates a new token with all the same values except a new series. We then submit the new token with a series identifier that includes the IP address to `delegateRepsository`, which is the original implementation of `PersistentTokenRepository`.

Whenever the tokens are looked up, we require that the current user's IP address is appended to the series identifier. This means that there is no way for a user to obtain a token for a user with a different IP address.

```
public PersistentRememberMeToken getTokenForSeries(String seriesId) {
    String ipSeries = ipSeries(seriesId);
    PersistentRememberMeToken ipToken =
            delegateRepository.getTokenForSeries(ipSeries);
    return tokenWithSeries(ipToken, seriesId);
}
```

The remainder of the code is quite similar. Internally, we treat the series identifier to include the IP address, and externally we present only the original series identifier. By doing this, we enforce the constraint that only the user who created the remember-me token can use it.

Let's review the Spring configuration included in this chapter's sample code for `IpAwarePersistentTokenRepository`. In the following code snippet, we first create `RememberMeServices` needed. We then create `PersistentTokenRepository`:

src/main/webapp/WEB-INF/spring/ipTokenRepository.xml

```
<bean id="remembermeServices"
  class="org.springframework.security.web.authentication
    .rememberme.PersistentTokenBasedRememberMeServices">
  <!-- must match remember-me's key attribute -->
  <constructor-arg value="jbcpCalendar"/>
  <constructor-arg ref="userDetailsService"/>
  <constructor-arg ref="tokenRepository"/>
</bean>
```

## Remember-me Services

```xml
<bean id="tokenRepository" class="com.packtpub.springsecurity.web
  .authentication.rememberme.IpAwarePersistentTokenRepository">
  <constructor-arg>
    <bean class="org.springframework.security.web
      .authentication.rememberme.JdbcTokenRepositoryImpl">
    <property name="dataSource" ref="dataSource"/>
    </bean>
  </constructor-arg>
</bean>
```

In order for Spring security to utilize our custom `RememberMeServices`, we need to update our security configuration to point to it. Go ahead and make the following updates to `security.xml`.

src/main/webapp/WEB-INF/spring/security.xml

```xml
<http ...>
    ...
    <remember-me key="jbcpCalendar"
            services-ref="remembermeServices"/>
    <logout logout-url="/logout"
            logout-success-url="/login/form?logout"/>
</http>
```

We also need to update `web.xml` to pick up the new Spring bean configuration file that includes our custom `RememberMeServices` interface. Add `ipTokenRepository.xml` to the list of configurations in `web.xml`.

src/main/webapp/WEB-INF/web.xml

```xml
<param-value>
    ...
    /WEB-INF/spring/cleaner.xml
    /WEB-INF/spring/ipTokenRepository.xml
</param-value>
```

Now, go ahead and start up the application. You can use a second computer along with a plugin, such as Firecookie, to manipulate your remember-me cookie. If you try to use the remember-me cookie from one computer on another computer, Spring security will now ignore the remember-me request and delete the associated cookie.

> Your code should look like `chapter06.05-calendar`.

Note that the IP-based remember-me tokens may behave unexpectedly, if the user is behind a shared or load balanced network infrastructure, such as a multi-WAN corporate environment. In most scenarios, however, the addition of an IP address to the remember-me function provides an additional, welcome layer of security to a helpful user feature.

## Custom cookie and HTTP parameter names

Curious users may wonder if the expected value of the remember-me form field checkbox, `_spring_security_remember_me`, or the cookie name, `SPRING_SECURITY_REMEMBER_ME_COOKIE`, can be changed, to obscure the use of Spring Security. While the `<remember-me>` declaration does not allow this flexibility, now that we've declared our own `RememberMeServices` implementation as a Spring Bean, we can simply define more properties to change the checkbox and cookie names:

src/main/webapp/WEB-INF/spring/ipTokenRepository.xml

```
<bean id="remembermeServices"
  class="org.springframework.security.web.authentication
  .rememberme.PersistentTokenBasedRememberMeServices">
  ...
  <property name="parameter" value="rememberme"/>
  <property name="cookieName" value="rememberme"/>
</bean>
```

Don't forget to change the `login.jsp` page to set the name of the checkbox form field, to match the parameter value we declared. Go ahead and make the updates to `login.jsp`.

src/main/webapp/WEB-INF/views/login.jsp

```
<input type="checkbox" id="remember"
        name="rememberme"
        value="true"/>
```

We'd encourage you to do some experimentation here, to ensure you understand how these settings are related. Go ahead and start up the application and give it a try.

> Your code should look like `chapter06.06-calendar`.

[ 163 ]

# Summary

This chapter explained and demonstrated the use of Spring Security's remember-me feature. We started with the most basic setup and learned how to gradually make the feature more secure. Specifically, we learned the following:

- What token-based remember-me services was and how to configure it
- How persistent-based remember-me services could provide additional security, how it works, and the additional considerations necessary when using it.
- How to create a custom remember-me implementation that restricted the remember-me token to a specific IP address
- Various other ways to make the remember-me feature more secure

Up next is certificate-based authentication, where we will discuss how to use trusted client-side certificates to perform authentication.

# 7
# Client Certificate Authentication

Although username and password authentication is extremely common, as we discussed in *Chapter 1, Anatomy of an Unsafe Application*, and *Chapter 2, Getting Started with Spring Security*, forms of authentication exist that allow users to present different types of credentials. Spring Security caters to these requirements as well. In this chapter, we'll move beyond form-based authentication to explore authentication using trusted client-side certificates.

During the course of this chapter we will:

- Learn how client certificate authentication is negotiated between the user's browser and a compliant server
- Configure Spring Security to authenticate users with client certificates
- Understand the architecture of client certificate authentication in Spring Security
- Explore advanced configuration options related to client certificate authentication
- Review pros, cons, and common troubleshooting steps when dealing with client certificate authentication

# How client certificate authentication works

Client certificate authentication requires a request for information from the server and a response from the browser, to negotiate a trusted authentication relationship between the client (that is, a user's browser) and the server application. This trusted relationship is built through the use of the exchange of trusted and verifiable credentials, known as **certificates**.

Unlike much of what we have seen to this point, with client certificate authentication, the servlet container or application server itself is typically responsible for negotiating the trust relationship between the browser and server, by requesting a certificate, evaluating it, and accepting it as valid.

Client certificate authentication is also known as mutual authentication and is part of the **Secure Sockets Layer** (**SSL**) protocol and its successor, **Transport Layer Security** (**TLS**). As mutual authentication is part of the SSL and TLS protocols, it follows that an HTTPS connection (secured with SSL or TLS) is required in order to make use of client certificate authentication. For more details on SSL/TLS support in Spring Security, please refer to our discussion and implementation of SSL/TLS in the *Appendix*. Setting up SSL/TLS in Tomcat (or the application server you have been using to follow along with the examples) is required, to implement client certificate authentication. As in the *Appendix*, we will refer to SSL/TLS as SSL for the remainder of this chapter.

The following sequence diagram illustrates the interaction between the client browser and the web server, when negotiating an SSL connection and validating the trust of a client certificate used for mutual authentication:

*Chapter 7*

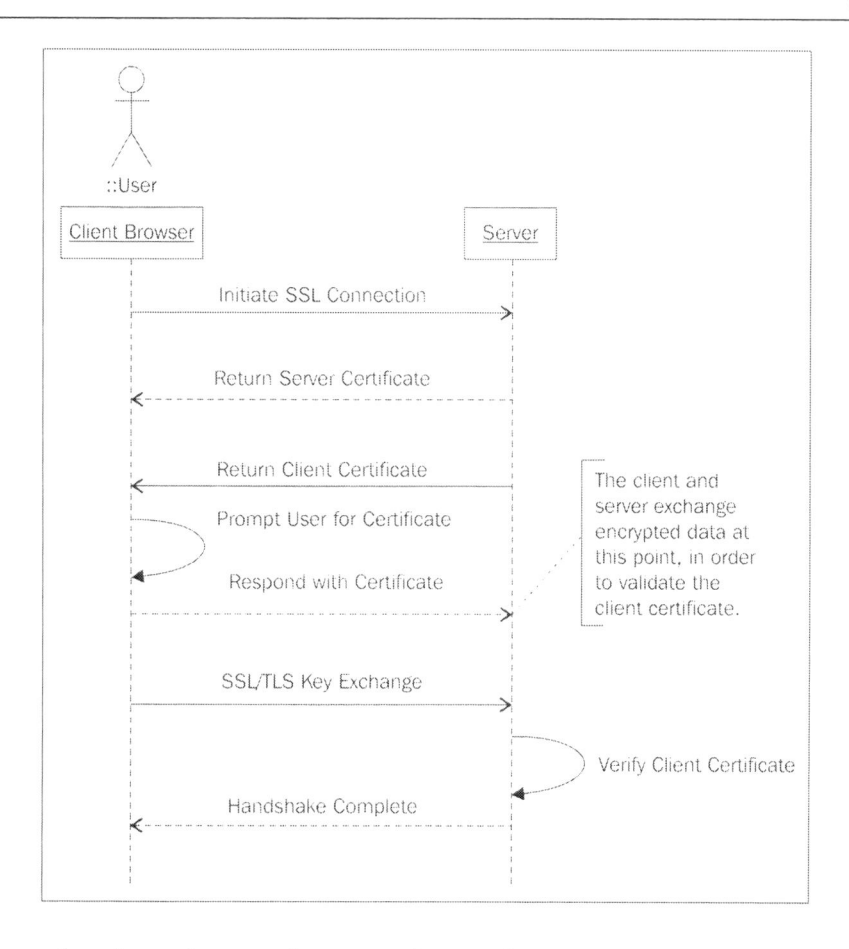

```
                    O
                   /|\
                   / \
                  ::User
    ┌──────────────┐                        ┌──────────┐
    │Client Browser│                        │  Server  │
    └──────┬───────┘                        └─────┬────┘
           │       Initiate SSL Connection        │
           ├─────────────────────────────────────>│
           │                                      │
           │       Return Server Certificate      │
           │<─────────────────────────────────────┤
           │                                      │
           │       Return Client Certificate      │
           │<─────────────────────────────────────┤      ┌────────────────────┐
           │  Prompt User for Certificate         │      │ The client and     │
           │──┐                                   │      │ server exchange    │
           │  │                                   │      │ encrypted data at  │
           │<─┘                                   │      │ this point, in order│
           │     Respond with Certificate         │      │ to validate the    │
           ├─────────────────────────────────────>│      │ client certificate.│
           │                                      │      └────────────────────┘
           │       SSL/TLS Key Exchange           │
           ├─────────────────────────────────────>│
           │                                      │──┐
           │                                      │  │ Verify Client Certificate
           │                                      │<─┘
           │       Handshake Complete             │
           │<─────────────────────────────────────┤
```

We can see that the exchange of two certificates, the server and client certificates, provides authentication that both parties are known and can be trusted to continue their conversation securely. In the interest of clarity, we omit some details of the SSL handshake and trust checking of the certificates themselves; however, you are encouraged to do further reading in the area of the SSL and TLS protocols, and certificates in general, as many good reference guides on these subjects exist. *RFC 5246, The Transport Layer Security (TLS) Protocol V1.2* (`http://tools.ietf.org/html/rfc5246`), is a good place to begin reading about client certificate presentation, and if you'd like to get into more detail, *SL and TLS: Designing and Building Secure Systems*, Eric Rescorla, Addison-Wesley, is an incredibly detailed review of the protocol and its implementation.

An alternative name for client certificate-based authentication is X.509 authentication. The term X.509 is derived from the X.509 standard, originally published by the ITU-T organization for use in directories based on the X.500 standard (the origins of LDAP, as you may recall from *Chapter 5, LDAP Directory Services*). Later, this standard was adapted for use in securing internet communications.

We mention this here because many of the classes in Spring Security related to this subject refer to X.509. Remember that X.509 doesn't define the mutual authentication protocol itself, but defines the format and structure of the certificates and the encompassing trusted certificate authorities instead.

# Setting up client certificate authentication infrastructure

Unfortunately for you as an individual developer, being able to experiment with client certificate authentication requires some non-trivial configuration and setup prior to the relatively easy integration with Spring Security. As these setup steps tend to cause a lot of problems for first-time developers, we felt it was important to walk you through them.

We assume that you are using a local, self-signed server certificate and self-signed client certificates as well as Apache Tomcat. This is typical of most development environments; however, it's possible that you may have access to a valid server certificate, a **certificate authority** (**CA**), or another application server. If this is the case, you may use these setup instructions as guidelines and configure your environment in an analogous manner. Please refer to the SSL setup instructions in the *Appendix* for assistance with configuring Tomcat and Spring Security to work with SSL in a standalone environment.

# Understanding the purpose of a public key infrastructure

This chapter focuses on setting up a self-contained development environment for the purposes of learning and education. However, in most cases where you are integrating Spring Security into an existing client certificate-secured environment, there will be a significant amount of infrastructure (usually a combination of hardware and software) in place to provide functionality, such as certificate granting and management, user self-service, and revocation. Environments of this type define a public key infrastructure—a combination of hardware, software, and security policies that result in a highly secure authentication-driven network ecosystem.

In addition to being used for web application authentication, certificates or hardware devices in these environments can be used for secure, non-repudiated e-mail (using S/MIME), network authentication, and even physical building access (using PKCS 11-based hardware devices).

While the management overhead of such an environment can be high (and requires both IT and process excellence to implement well), it is arguably one of the most secure possible operating environments for technology professionals.

# Creating a client certificate key pair

The self-signed client certificate is created in the same way as the self-signed server certificate is created, by generating a key pair using the `keytool` command. A client certificate key pair differs, in that it requires the key store to be available to the web browser and requires the client's public key to be loaded into the server's trust store (we'll explain what this is in a moment).

If you do not wish to generate your own key right now, you may skip to the next section and use the sample certificates in the `src/etc/keys` folder in the sample chapter. Otherwise, create the client key pair as follows:

```
keytool -genkeypair -alias jbcpclient -keyalg RSA -validity 365
-keystore jbcp_clientauth.p12 -storetype PKCS12
```

> You can find additional information about `keytool`, along with all the configuration options, on Oracle's site at http://docs.oracle.com/javase/6/docs/technotes/tools/solaris/keytool.html.

Most of the arguments to `keytool` are fairly arbitrary for this use case. However, when prompted to set up the first and last name (the common name, or CN, portion of the owner's **Distinguished Name** or **DN**) for the client certificate, ensure that the answer to the first prompt matches a user that we have set up in our Spring Security JDBC store. For example, `admin1@example.com` is an appropriate value since we have the `admin1@example.com` user set up with Spring Security. An example of the command-line interaction is as follows:

```
What is your first and last name?
  [Unknown]:  admin1@example.com
... etc
Is CN=admin1@example.com, OU=JBCP Calendar, O=JBCP, L=Chicago, ST=IL, C=US correct?
  [no]:  yes
```

*Client Certificate Authentication*

We'll see why this is important, when we configure Spring Security to access the information from the certificate-authenticated user. We have one final step before we can set up certificate authentication within Tomcat, which is explained in the following section.

## Configuring the Tomcat trust store

Recall that the definition of a key pair includes both a private and public key. Much as with SSL certificates verifying and securing server communication, the validity of the client certificate needs to be verified against the certifying authority that created it.

As we have created our own self-signed client certificate using the `keytool` command, the Java VM will not implicitly trust it as having been assigned by a trusted certificate authority.

As such, we will need to force Tomcat to recognize the certificate as a trusted certificate. We do this by exporting the public key from the key pair and adding it to the Tomcat trust store. Again, if you do not wish to perform this step now, you can use the existing trust store in `src/etc/keys` and skip to where we configure `server.xml`, later in this section.

First, we'll export the public key to a standard certificate file named `jbcp_clientauth.cer`, as follows:

```
keytool -exportcert -alias jbcpclient -keystore jbcp_clientauth.p12
-storetype PKCS12 -storepass changeit -file jbcp_clientauth.cer
```

Next, we'll import the certificate into the trust store (this will create the trust store, but in a typical deployment scenario, you'd probably already have some other certificates in the trust store).

```
keytool -importcert -alias jbcpclient -keystore tomcat.truststore
-file jbcp_clientauth.cer
```

The preceding command will create the trust store called `tomcat.truststore` and prompt you for a password (we chose the password `changeit`). You'll also see some information about the certificate and will finally be asked to confirm that you do trust the certificate:

```
Owner: CN=admin1@example.com, OU=JBCP Calendar, O=JBCP, L=Chicago,
ST=IL, C=US
Issuer: CN=admin1@example.com, OU=JBCP Calendar, O=JBCP, L=Chicago,
ST=IL, C=US
Serial number: 4f5be716
```

```
Valid from: Sat Mar 10 17:43:18 CST 2012 until: Sun Feb 26 17:43:18
CST 2062
Certificate fingerprints:
    MD5:  A3:91:8C:2C:B4:6A:71:E4:18:B7:28:DE:0A:49:8E:B6
    SHA1: BB:4E:42:BE:F2:B4:3A:A6:31:21:70:43:FE:D3:51:A6:EC:4F:16:F5
    Signature algorithm name: SHA1withRSA
    Version: 3
Trust this certificate? [no]:  yes
```

Remember the location of the new `tomcat.truststore` file, as we will need to reference it in our Tomcat configuration.

> **What's the difference between a key store and a trust store?**
>
> The **Java Secure Socket Extension** (**JSSE**) documentation defines a key store as a storage mechanism for private keys and their corresponding public keys. The key store (containing key pairs) is used to encrypt or decrypt secure messages and so on. The trust store is intended to store only public keys for trusted communication partners when verifying identity (similar to how the trust store is used in certificate authentication). In many common administration scenarios, however, the key store and trust store are combined into a single file (in Tomcat, this would be done through the use of the `keystoreFile` and `truststoreFile` attributes of the **connector**). The format of the files themselves can be exactly the same (really, each file can be any JSSE-supported keystore format, including **Java Key Store** (**JKS**), PKCS 12, and so on).

As previously mentioned, we assume you have already configured the SSL Connector as outlined in the *Appendix*. If you do not see the `keystoreFile` or `keystorePass` attributes in `server.xml`, it means you should visit the *Appendix* to get SSL set up.

Finally, we'll need to point Tomcat at the trust store and enable client certificate authentication. This is done by adding three additional attributes to the SSL Connector in the Tomcat `server.xml` file, as follows:

sever.xml

```
<Connector port="8443" protocol="HTTP/1.1" SSLEnabled="true"
  maxThreads="150" scheme="https" secure="true"
  sslProtocol="TLS"
  keystoreFile="<KEYSTORE_PATH>/tomcat.keystore"
  keystorePass="changeit"
  truststoreFile="<CERT_PATH>/tomcat.truststore"
  truststorePass="changeit"
  clientAuth="true"
  />
```

> The `server.xml` file can be found at `TOMCAT_HOME/conf/server.xml`. If you are interacting with Tomcat using Eclipse or Spring Tool Suite, you will find a project named `Servers` that contains `server.xml`. For example, if you are using Tomcat 7, the path in your Eclipse workspace might look something similar to `/Servers/Tomcat v7.0 Server at localhost-config/server.xml`.

This should be the remaining configuration required to trigger Tomcat to request a client certificate when any SSL connection is made. Of course, you will want to ensure you replace both `<CERT_PATH>` and `<KEYSTORE_PATH>` with the full paths. For example, on a Unix-based operating system, the path might look like `/home/rwinch/packt/chapter7/keys/tomcat.keystore`. Go ahead and try to start up Tomcat to ensure that the server starts up without any errors in the logs.

> There's also a way to configure Tomcat to optionally use client certificate authentication—we'll enable this later in the chapter. For now, we require the use of client certificates to even connect to the Tomcat server in the first place. This makes it easier to diagnose whether or not you have set this up correctly!

The final step is to import the certificate into the client browser.

# Importing the certificate key pair into a browser

Depending on what browser you are using, the process of importing a certificate may differ. We will provide instructions for installations of Firefox, Chrome, and Internet Explorer, here, but if you are using another browser, please consult its help section or your favorite search engine for assistance.

## Using Firefox

Follow these steps to import the key store containing the client certificate key pair in FireFox:

1. Click on **Edit | Preferences**.
2. Click on the **Advanced** button.
3. Click on the **Encryption** tab.
4. Click on the **View Certificates** button. The **Certificate Manager** window should open up.

5. Click on the **Your Certificates** tab.
6. Click on the **Import...** button.
7. Browse to the location where you saved the `jbcp_clientauth.p12` file and select it.
8. You will need to enter the password (that is, `changeit`) that you used when you created the file.

The client certificate should be imported, and you should see it in the list.

## Using Chrome

Follow these steps to import the key store containing the client certificate key pair in Chrome:

1. Click on the wrench icon on the browser toolbar.
2. Select **Settings**.
3. Click on **Show advanced settings...**.
4. In the **HTTPS/SSL** section, click on the **Manage certificates...** button.
5. In the **Your Certificates** tab, click on the **Import...** button.
6. Browse to the location where you saved the `jbcp_clientauth.p12` file and select it.
7. You will need to enter the password (that is, `changeit`) that you used when you created the file.
8. Click on **OK**.

## Using Internet Explorer

As Internet Explorer is tightly integrated into the Windows OS, it's a bit easier to import the key store.

1. Double-click on the `jbcp_clientauth.p12` file in Windows Explorer. The **Certificate Import Wizard** window should open.
2. Click on **Next** and accept the default values until you are prompted for the certificate password.
3. Enter the certificate password (that is, `changeit`) and click on **Next**.
4. Accept the default **Automatically select the certificate store** option and click on **Next**.
5. Click on **Finish**.

To verify that the certificate was installed correctly, you will need to follow another series of steps.

1. Open the **Tools** menu (*ALT+X*) in Internet Explorer.
2. Click on the **Internet Options** menu item.
3. Click on the **Content** tab.
4. Click on the **Certificates** button.
5. Click on the **Personal** tab, if it is not already selected. You should see the certificate listed here.

## Wrapping up testing

You should now be able to connect to the JBCP Calendar site using the client certificate. Navigate to `https://localhost:8443/calendar/`, taking care to use HTTPS and 8443. If all is set up correctly, you should be prompted for a certificate when you attempt to access the site—in Firefox, the certificate is displayed as follows:

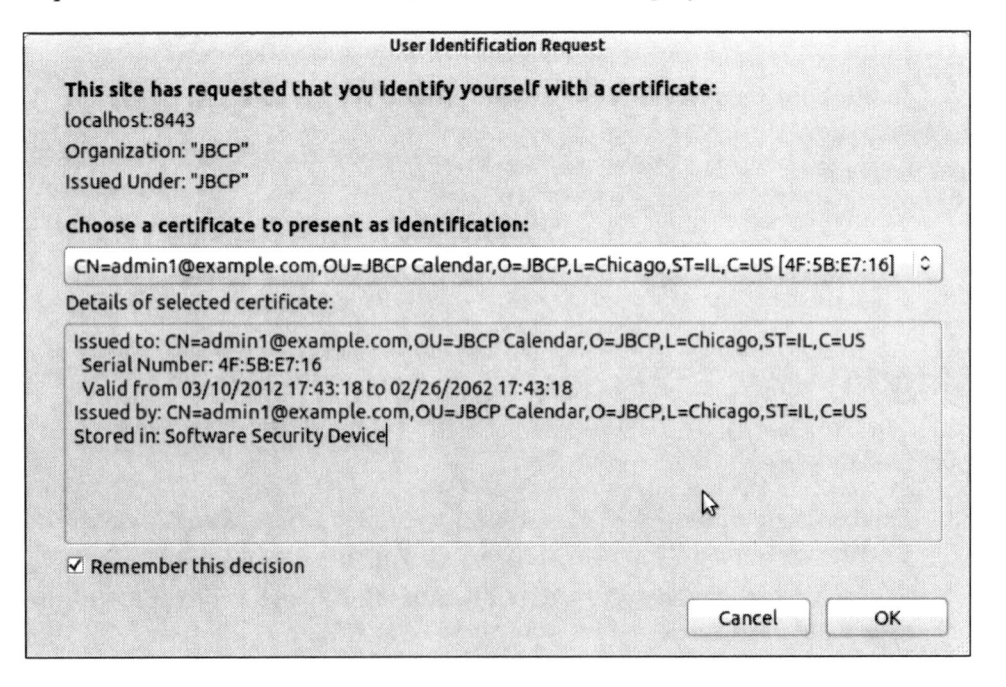

**User Identification Request**

**This site has requested that you identify yourself with a certificate:**
localhost:8443
Organization: "JBCP"
Issued Under: "JBCP"

**Choose a certificate to present as identification:**

CN=admin1@example.com,OU=JBCP Calendar,O=JBCP,L=Chicago,ST=IL,C=US [4F:5B:E7:16]

Details of selected certificate:

Issued to: CN=admin1@example.com,OU=JBCP Calendar,O=JBCP,L=Chicago,ST=IL,C=US
 Serial Number: 4F:5B:E7:16
 Valid from 03/10/2012 17:43:18 to 02/26/2062 17:43:18
Issued by: CN=admin1@example.com,OU=JBCP Calendar,O=JBCP,L=Chicago,ST=IL,C=US
Stored in: Software Security Device

☑ Remember this decision

[ Cancel ] [ OK ]

You'll notice, however, that if you attempt to access a protected section of the site, such as the **My Events** section, you'll be redirected to the login page. This is because we haven't yet configured Spring Security to recognize the information in the certificate—at this point, all the negotiation between the client and server has stopped at the Tomcat server itself.

> You should start with the code from `chapter07.00-calendar`.

# Troubleshooting client certificate authentication

Unfortunately, if we said that getting client certificate authentication configured correctly for the first time, without anything going wrong, was easy, we'd be lying to you. The fact is, although this is a great and very powerful security apparatus, it is poorly documented by both the browser and web server manufacturers, and the error messages, when present, can be confusing at best and misleading at worst.

Remember that, at this point, we have not involved Spring Security in the equation at all, so a debugger will most probably not help you (unless you have the Tomcat source code handy). Some common errors and things to check are as follows:

- You aren't prompted for a certificate when you access the site. There are many possible causes for this, and this can be the most puzzling problem to try to solve. Here are some things to check:
    - Ensure that the certificate has been installed in the browser client you are using. Sometimes, you need to restart the whole browser (close all windows), if you attempted to access the site previously and were rejected.
    - Ensure you are accessing the SSL port for the server (typically `8443` in a development setup), and have selected the `https` protocol in your URL. Client certificates are not presented for insecure browser connections. Make sure the browser also trusts the server SSL certificate, even if you have to force it to trust a self-signed certificate.
    - Ensure you have added the `clientAuth` directive to your Tomcat configuration (or equivalent for whatever application server you are using).

- If all else fails, use a network analyzer or packet sniffer, such as **Wireshark** (http://www.wireshark.org/) or **Fiddler2** (http://www.fiddler2.com/) to review the traffic and SSL key exchange over the wire (check with your IT department first—many companies do not allow tools of this kind on their networks).

- If you are using a self-signed client certificate, make sure the public key has been imported into the server's trust store. If you are using a CA-assigned certificate, make sure the CA is trusted by the JVM or that the CA certificate is imported into the server's trust store.

- Internet Explorer, in particular, does not report details of client certificate failures at all (it simply reports a generic **Page Cannot be Displayed** error). Use Firefox for diagnosing whether an issue you are seeing is related to client certificates or not.

# Configuring client certificate authentication in Spring Security

Unlike authentication mechanisms that we have utilized thus far, the use of client certificate authentication results in the user's request having been pre-authenticated by the server. As the server (Tomcat) has already established that the user has provided a valid and trustworthy certificate, Spring Security can simply trust this assertion of validity.

An important component of the secure login process is still missing, that is, authorization of the authenticated user. This is where our configuration of Spring Security comes in—we must add a component to Spring Security that will recognize the certificate authentication information from the user's HTTP session (populated by Tomcat), and then validate the presented credentials against the Spring Security UserDetailsService invocation. The invocation of UserDetailsService will result in the determination of whether the user declared in the certificate is known to Spring Security at all, and then it will assign GrantedAuthority as per usual login rules.

# Configuring client certificate authentication using the security namespace

With all the complexity of LDAP configuration, configuring client certificate authentication is a welcome reprieve. If we are using the security namespace style of configuration, the addition of client certificate authentication is a simple one-line configuration change, added within the `<http>` declaration. Go ahead and make the following changes to the provided `security.xml` configuration.

src/main/webapp/WEB-INF/spring/security.xml

```
<http ...>
    ...
    <x509 user-service-ref="userDetailsService"/>
</http>
<authentication-manager>
    <authentication-provider>
        <user-service id="userDetailsService">
            <user name="user1@example.com"
                  password="user1"
                  authorities="ROLE_USER"/>
            <user name="admin1@example.com"
                  password="admin1"
                  authorities="ROLE_USER,ROLE_ADMIN"/>
        </user-service>
    </authentication-provider>
</authentication-manager>
```

> Observe that the `<x509>` element references our existing `userDetailsService` configuration. For simplicity, we use the in-memory implementation. However, we could easily swap this out with any other implementation (i.e., the JDBC implementation covered in *Chapter 4, JDBC-based Authentication*).

After restarting the application, you'll again be prompted for a client certificate, but this time you should be able to access areas of the site requiring authorization. You can see from the logs (if you have them enabled) that you have been logged in as the `admin1@example.com` user.

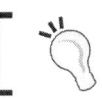

> Your code should look like `chapter07.01-calendar`.

# How Spring Security uses certificate information

As previously discussed, Spring Security's involvement in certificate exchange is to pick up information from the presented certificate and map the user's credentials to a user service. What we did not see in the use of the `<x509>` declaration was the magic that makes this happen. Recall that, when we had set the client certificate up, a DN similar to an LDAP DN was associated with the certificate:

```
Owner: CN=admin@example.com, OU=JBCP Calendar, O=JBCP, L=Chicago, ST=IL, C=US
```

Spring Security uses the information in this DN to determine the actual username of the principal and it will look for this information in `UserDetailsService`. In particular, it allows for the specification of a regular expression, which is used to match a portion of the DN established with the certificate, and utilize this portion of the DN as the principal name. The implicit, default configuration for the `<x509>` declaration would be as follows:

```
<x509 user-service-ref="userDetailsService"
        subject-principal-regex="CN=(.*?),"/>
```

We can see that this regular expression would match the `admin1@example.com` value as the principal's name. This regular expression must contain a single matching group, but it can be configured to support the username and DN issuance requirements of your application, for example, if the DNs for your organization's certificates include the `email` or `userid` fields, the regular expression can be modified to use these values as the authenticated principal's name.

# How Spring Security certificate authentication works

Let's review the various actors involved in the review and evaluation of the client certificates and translation into a Spring Security-authenticated session, with the help of the following diagram:

*Chapter 7*

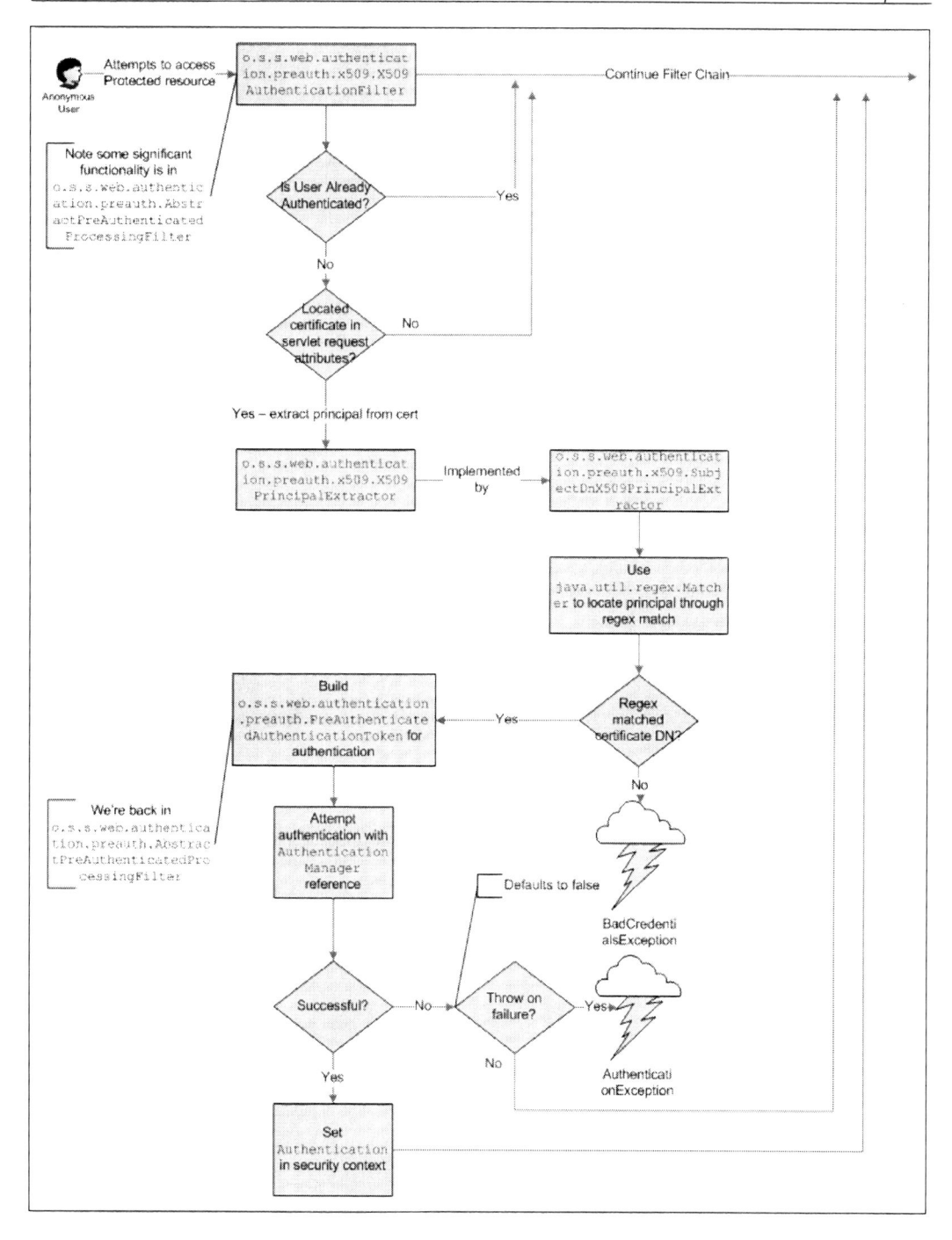

## Client Certificate Authentication

We can see that `o.s.s.web.authentication.preauth.x509.X509AuthenticationFilter` is responsible for examining the request of an unauthenticated user for the presentation of client certificates. If it sees that the request includes a valid client certificate, it will extract the principal using `o.s.s.web.authentication.preauth.x509.SubjectDnX509PrincipalExtractor`, using regular expression matching on the certificate owner's DN, as previously described.

> Be aware that although the diagram indicates that examination of the certificate occurs for unauthenticated users, a check can also be performed when the presented certificate identifies a different user than the one which was previously authenticated. This would result in a new authentication request using the newly provided credentials. The reason for this should be clear—any time a user presents a new set of credentials, the application must be aware of this and react in a responsible fashion by ensuring that the user is still able to access it.

Once the certificate has been accepted (or rejected/ignored), as with other authentication mechanisms, an `Authentication` token is built and passed along to `AuthenticationManager` for authentication. We can now review the very brief illustration of the `o.s.s.web.authentication.preauth.PreAuthenticatedAuthenticationProvider` handling of the authentication token:

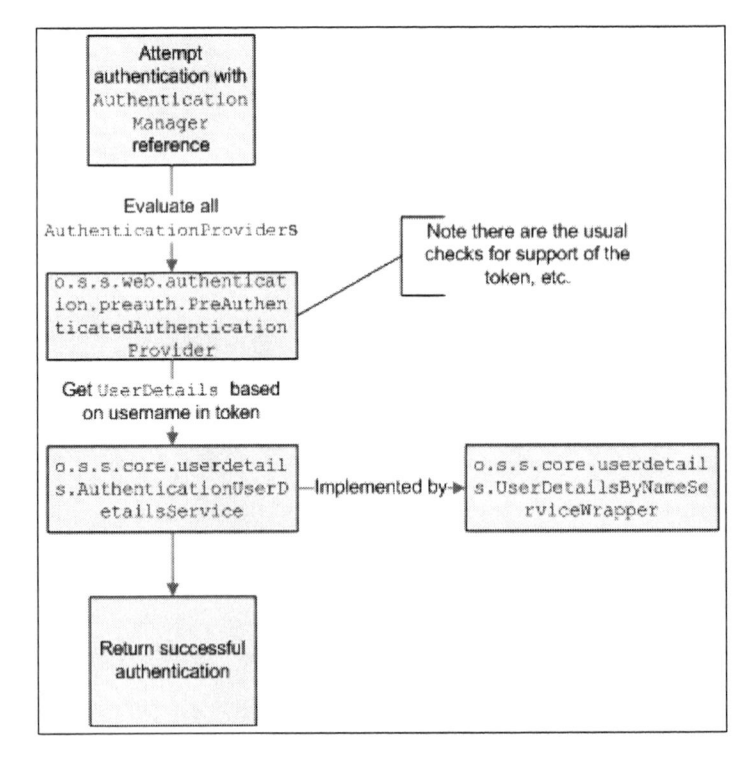

```
Attempt authentication with AuthenticationManager reference
        |
        v
Evaluate all AuthenticationProviders
        |
o.s.s.web.authentication.preauth.PreAuthenticatedAuthenticationProvider  ----  Note there are the usual checks for support of the token, etc.
        |
Get UserDetails based on username in token
        |
        v
o.s.s.core.userdetails.AuthenticationUserDetailsService  --Implemented by-->  o.s.s.core.userdetails.UserDetailsByNameServiceWrapper
        |
        v
Return successful authentication
```

Though we will not go over them in detail, there are a number of other preauthenticated mechanisms supported by Spring Security. Some examples include **Java EE role mapping** (J2eePreAuthenticatedProcessingFilter), **WebSphere integration** (WebSpherePreAuthenticatedProcessingFilter), and **Site Minder-style authentication** (RequestHeaderAuthenticationFilter). If you understand the process flow of client certificate authentication, understanding these other authentication types is significantly easier.

## Handling unauthenticated requests with AuthenticationEntryPoint

Since X509AuthenticationFilter will continue processing the request if authentication fails, we'll need to handle situations where the user does not authenticate successfully and has requested a protected resource. The way that Spring Security allows developers to customize this is by plugging in a custom o.s.s.web.AuthenticationEntryPoint implementation. In a default form login scenario, LoginUrlAuthenticationEntryPoint is used to redirect the user to a login page if they have been denied access to a protected resource and are not authenticated.

In contrast, in typical client certificate authentication environments, alternative methods of authentication are simply not supported (remember that Tomcat expects the certificate well before the Spring Security form login will take place anyway). As such, it doesn't make sense to retain the default behavior of redirection to a form login page. Instead, we'll modify the entry point to simply return an **HTTP 403 Forbidden** message, using o.s.s.web.authentication.Http403ForbiddenEntryPoint. Go ahead and make the following updates in your security.xml file.

src/main/webapp/WEB-INF/spring/security.xml

```
<http auto-config="true" use-expressions="true"
    entry-point-ref="forbiddenAuthEntryPoint">
    ...
</http>
<bean:bean id="forbiddenAuthEntryPoint"
class="org.springframework.security.web.authentication.Http403ForbiddenEntryPoint"/>
```

Now, if a user tries to access a protected resource and is unable to provide a valid certificate, they will be presented with the following page:

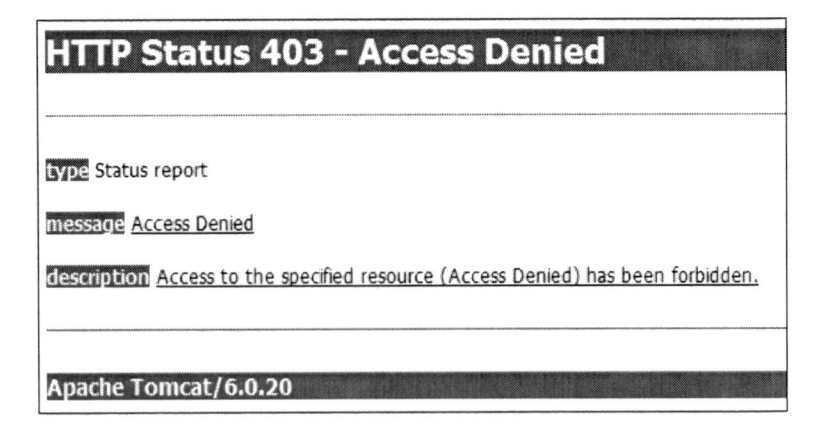

**HTTP Status 403 - Access Denied**

**type** Status report

**message** Access Denied

**description** Access to the specified resource (Access Denied) has been forbidden.

Apache Tomcat/6.0.20

> Your code should now look like `chapter07.02-calendar`.

Other configuration or application flow adjustments that are commonly performed with client certificate authentication are as follows:

- Removal of the form-based login page altogether
- Removal of the **Log Out** link (as there's no reason to log out because the browser will always present the user's certificate)
- Removal of the functionality to rename the user account and change the password
- Removal of the user registration functionality (unless you are able to tie it into the issuance of a new certificate)

## Supporting dual-mode authentication

It is also possible that some environments may support both certificate-based and form-based authentication. If this is the case in your environment, it is also possible (and trivial) to support it with Spring Security 3.1. We can simply leave the default `AuthenticationEntryPoint` interface (redirecting to the form-based login page) intact and allow the user to log in using the standard login form if they do not supply a client certificate.

If you choose to configure your application this way, you'll need to adjust the Tomcat SSL settings (change as appropriate for your application server). Simply change the `clientAuth` directive to `want` instead of `true`:

```
<Connector port="8443" protocol="HTTP/1.1" SSLEnabled="true"
  maxThreads="150" scheme="https" secure="true"
  sslProtocol="TLS"
  keystoreFile="conf/tomcat.keystore"
  keystorePass="password"
  truststoreFile="conf/tomcat.truststore"
  truststorePass="password"
  clientAuth="want"
/>
```

We'll also need to remove the `entry-point-ref` attribute that we configured in the previous exercise, so that the standard form-based authentication workflow takes over if the user isn't able to supply a valid certificate upon the browser first being queried.

Although this is convenient, there are a few things to keep in mind about dual-mode (form- and certificate-based) authentication.

Most browsers will not re-prompt the user for a certificate if they have failed certificate authentication once, so make sure that your users are aware that they may need to re-enter the browser to present their certificate again.

Recall that a password is not required to authenticate users with certificates; however, if you are still using `UserDetailsService` to support your form-based authenticated users, this may be the same `UserDetailsService` that you are also using to give the `PreAuthenticatedAuthenticationProvider` information about your users. This presents a potential security risk, as users who you intend to sign in only with certificates could potentially authenticate using form login credentials. There are several ways to solve this problem, and they are described in the following list:

- Ensure that the users authenticating with certificates have an appropriately strong password in your user store.
- Consider customizing your user store to clearly identify users who are enabled for form-based login. This can be tracked with an additional field in the table holding user account information and minor adjustments to the SQL queries used by the `JdbcDaoImpl` object.
- Configure a separate user details store altogether for users who are logging in as certificate-authenticated users, to completely segregate them from users that are allowed to use form-based login.

Dual-mode authentication can be a powerful addition to your site and can be deployed effectively and securely, provided that you keep in mind the situations under which users will be granted access to it.

# Configuring client certificate authentication using Spring Beans

Earlier in this chapter, we reviewed the flow of the classes involved in client certificate authentication. As such, it should be straightforward for us to configure JBCP Calendar using explicit beans. By using the explicit configuration, we will have additional configuration options at our disposal. Let's take a look and see how to use explicit configuration. We have already created a file named `security-x509-explicitly.xml`. You can view the contents of the file in the following code snippet:

src/main/webapp/WEB-INF/spring/security-x509-explicitly.xml

```xml
<bean id="x509Filter"
  class="org.springframework.security.web.authentication
  .preauth.x509.X509AuthenticationFilter">
  <property name="authenticationManager"
    ref="authenticationManager" />
</bean>
<bean id="preauthAuthenticationProvider"
  class="org.springframework.security.web.authentication
  .preauth.PreAuthenticatedAuthenticationProvider">
  <property name="preAuthenticatedUserDetailsService"
    ref="authenticationUserDetailsService" />
</bean>
<bean id="authenticationUserDetailsService"
  class="org.springframework.security.core.userdetails
  .UserDetailsByNameServiceWrapper">
  <property name="userDetailsService" ref="userDetailsService" />
</bean>
```

We'll also need to remove the `<x509>` element, add `x509Filter` to our filter chain, and add our `AuthenticationProvider` implementation to `AuthenticationManger`.

```xml
<http auto-config="true" use-expressions="true">
   ...
   <x509 user-server-ref="userDetailsService"/>
   <custom-filter ref="x509Filter" position="X509_FILTER"/>
```

```xml
    </http>

    <authentication-manager alias="authenticationManager">
      <authentication-provider ref="preauthAuthenticationProvider"/>
      <authentication-provider>
        <user-service id="userDetailsService">
        <user name="user1@example.com"
          password="user1"
          authorities="ROLE_USER"/>
        <user name="admin1@example.com"
          password="admin1"
          authorities="ROLE_USER,ROLE_ADMIN"/>
        </user-service>
      </authentication-provider>
    </authentication-manager>
```

Lastly, we need to instruct Spring to use our explicit configuration. Open up web.xml, and add our explicit configuration, as follows:

src/main/webapp/WEB-INF/web.xml

```xml
    <param-value>
       ...
       /WEB-INF/spring/security.xml
       /WEB-INF/spring/security-x509-explicitly.xml
    </param-value>
```

Now give the application a try. Nothing much has changed from a user's perspective, but as developers, we have opened the door to a number of additional configuration options.

> Your code should now look like chapter07.03-calendar.

# Additional capabilities of bean-based configuration

The use of Spring bean-based configuration provides us with additional capabilities through the exposure of bean properties that aren't exposed through the security namespace style of configuration.

*Client Certificate Authentication*

Additional properties available on `X509AuthenticationFilter` are as follows:

| Property | Description | Default |
|---|---|---|
| `continueFilterChainOnUnsuccessfulAuthentication` | If `false`, a failed authentication will throw an exception rather than allow the request to continue. This would typically be set in cases where a valid certificate is expected, and required, to access the secured site. If `true`, the filter chain will proceed, even if there is a failed authentication. | `true` |
| `checkForPrincipalChanges` | If `true`, the filter will check to see if the currently authenticated username differs from the username presented in the client certificate. If so, authentication against the new certificate will be performed and the HTTP session will be invalidated (optionally, see the next attribute). If `false`, once the user is authenticated, they will remain authenticated even if they present different credentials. | `false` |
| `invalidateSessionOnPrincipalChange` | If `true`, and the principal in the request changes, the user's HTTP session will be invalidated prior to being reauthenticated. If `false`, the session will remain—note that this may introduce security risks. | `true` |

`PreAuthenticatedAuthenticationProvider` has a couple of interesting properties available to us, which are listed in the following table:

| Property | Description | Default |
|---|---|---|
| `preAuthenticatedUserDetailsService` | Used to build a full `UserDetails` object from the username extracted from the certificate. | None |
| `throwExceptionWhenTokenRejected` | If `true`, a `BadCredentialsException` exception will be thrown when the token is not constructed properly (does not contain a username or certificate). It is typically set to `true` in environments where certificates are used exclusively. | None |

In addition to these properties, there are a number of other opportunities for implementing interfaces or extending classes involved in certificate authentication to further customize your implementation.

# Considerations when implementing Client Certificate authentication

Client certificate authentication, while highly secure, isn't for everyone and isn't appropriate for every situation.

The pros of client certificate authentication are listed as follows:

- Certificates establish a framework of mutual trust and verifiability that both parties (client and server) are who they say they are.
- Certificate-based authentication, if implemented properly, is much more difficult to spoof or tamper with than other forms of authentication.
- If a well-supported browser is used and configured correctly, client certificate authentication can effectively act as a single sign-on solution, enabling transparent login to all certificate-secured applications.

The cons of client certificate authentication are listed as follows:

- Use of certificates typically requires the entire user population to have them. This can lead to both a user training burden and an administrative burden. Most organizations deploying certificate-based authentication on a large scale must have sufficient self-service and helpdesk support for certificate maintenance, expiration tracking, and user assistance.
- Use of certificates is generally an all-or-none affair, meaning that mixed-mode authentication, offering support for non-certificate users, is not provided due to the complexity of web server configuration or poor application support.
- Use of certificates may not be well supported by all users in your user population, including the ones who use mobile devices.
- Correct configuration of the infrastructure required to support certificate-based authentication may require advanced IT knowledge.

As we can see, there are both benefits and drawbacks to client certificate authentication. When implemented correctly, it can be a very convenient mode of access for your users and has extremely attractive security and non-repudiation properties. You will need to determine for your particular situation whether or not this type of authentication is appropriate.

## Summary

In this chapter, we examined the architecture, flow, and Spring Security support for client certificate-based authentication. We have:

- Reviewed the concepts and overall flow of client certificate (mutual) authentication
- Learned the important steps required to configure Apache Tomcat for a self-signed SSL and client certificate scenario
- Configured Spring Security to understand certificate-based credentials presented by clients
- Understood the architecture of Spring Security classes related to certificate authentication
- Discovered how to configure a Spring bean-style client certificate environment
- Weighed the pros and cons of this type of authentication

It's quite common for developers unfamiliar with client certificates to be confused by many of the complexities of this type of environment. We hope that this chapter has made this complicated subject a bit easier to understand and implement! In the next chapter, we will discuss how you can accomplish Single Sign On with OpenID.

# Opening up to OpenID

OpenID is a very popular form of trusted identity management that allows users to manage their identity through a single trusted provider. This convenient feature provides users with the security of storing their password and personal information with the trusted OpenID provider, optionally disclosing this personal information upon request. Additionally, the OpenID-enabled website can have confidence that the users providing OpenID credentials are who they say they are.

In this chapter, you will:

- Learn to set up your own OpenID in less than five minutes
- Configure the JBCP Calendar application with a very rapid implementation of OpenID
- Learn the conceptual architecture of OpenID and how it provides your site with a trustworthy user access
- Implement OpenID-based user registration
- Experiment with OpenID attribute exchange for user profile functionality
- Demonstrate how we can trigger automatic authentication to the previous OpenID Provider
- Examine the security offered by the OpenID-based login

## The promising world of OpenID

The promise of OpenID as a technology is to allow users on the Web to centralize their personal data and information with a trusted provider, and then use the trusted provider as a delegate to establish trustworthiness with the other sites with whom the user wants to interact.

*Opening up to OpenID*

In concept, this type of login through a trusted third party has been in existence for a long time, in many different forms (For example, Microsoft Passport became one of the more notable central login services on the Web for some time). OpenID's distinct advantage is that the OpenID Provider needs to implement only the public OpenID protocol to be compatible with any site seeking to integrate login with OpenID.

Since OpenID is an open specification, there is currently a diverse population of public providers utilizing it. This is an excellent recipe for healthy competition and it is good for consumer choice.

The following diagram illustrates the high-level relationship between a site integrating OpenID during the login process and OpenID providers.

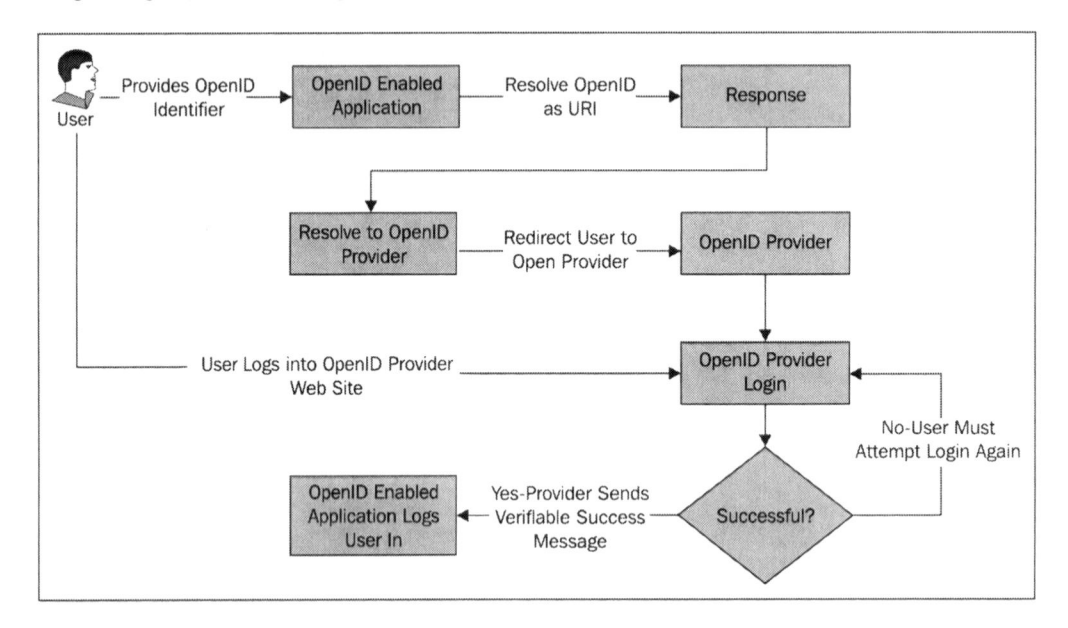

We can see that the user presents his credentials in the form of a unique named identifier, typically a **Uniform Resource Identifier** (**URI**), which is assigned to the user by their OpenID provider, and is used to uniquely identify both the user and the OpenID provider. This is commonly done by either prepending a subdomain to the URI of the OpenID Provider (for example, `https://jamesgosling.myopenid.com/`), or appending a unique identifier to the URI of the OpenID provider URI (for example, `https://me.yahoo.com/springsecurity31`). We can visually see from the presented URI that both methods clearly identify both the OpenID provider (via domain name) and the unique user identifier.

> **Don't trust OpenID unequivocally!**
> Here you can see a fundamental assumption that can fool users of the system. It is possible for us to sign up for an OpenID, which would make it appear as though we were James Gosling, even though we obviously are not. Do not make the false assumption that just because a user has a convincing-sounding OpenID (or OpenID delegate provider) he/she is the authentic person, without requiring additional forms of identification. Thinking about it another way, if someone came to your door just claiming he was James Gosling, would you let him in without verifying his ID?

The OpenID-enabled application then redirects the user to the OpenID provider, at which the user presents his credentials to the provider, which is then responsible for making an access decision. Once the access decision has been made by the provider, the provider redirects the user to the originating site, which is now assured of the user's authenticity.

OpenID is much easier to understand once you have tried it. Let's add OpenID to the JBCP Calendar login screen now!

# Signing up for an OpenID

In order to get the full value of the exercises in this section (and to be able to test login), you'll need your own OpenID from one of the many available providers, of which a partial listing is available at http://openid.net/get-an-openid/. Common OpenID providers with which you probably already have an account are Google, Yahoo!, AOL, Flickr, or MySpace. To get full value out of the exercises in this chapter, we recommend you have accounts with at least:

- myOpenID
- Google

# Enabling OpenID authentication with Spring Security

We'll see a common theme with the external authentication providers examined over the next several chapters. Spring Security provides convenient wrappers around the provider integrations that are actually developed outside the Spring ecosystem.

In this vein, the openid4java project (http://code.google.com/p/openid4java/) provides the underlying OpenID provider discovery and request/response negotiation for the Spring Security OpenID functionality.

# Additional required dependencies

In order to utilize OpenID, we will need to include spring-security-openid and its transitive dependencies. This can be done in Maven by updating the `pom.xml` as shown next.

pom.xml

```xml
<dependency>
    <groupId>org.springframework.security</groupId>
    <artifactId>spring-security-openid</artifactId>
    <version>3.1.0.RELEASE</version>
</dependency>
```

> You should start with the source in `chapter08.00-calendar`.

Writing an OpenID login form, we will need to replace the username and password fields with an OpenID field. Go ahead and make the following updates to your `login.jsp` file.

src/main/webapp/WEB-INF/views/login.jsp

```jsp
<c:url value="/login" var="loginUrl"/>
<form action="${loginUrl}" method="post">
    ...
    <c:if test="${param.logout != null}">
        <div class="alert alert-success">
            You have been logged out.
        </div>
    </c:if>
    <label for="openid_identifer">OpenID</label>
    <input id="openid_identifier" name="openid_identifier"
      type="text" />
    <div class="form-actions">
        <input class="btn" name="submit" type="submit" value="Login"/>
    </div>
</form>
```

You will notice that we have exchanged the `username` and `password` field for an `openid_identifier` field. The name of the form field, `openid_identifier`, is not a coincidence. The OpenID specification recommends that implementing websites use this name for their OpenID login field, so that the user agents (browsers) have the semantic knowledge of the function of this field. There are even browser plugins such as Verisign's OpenID SeatBelt (https://pip.verisignlabs.com/seatbelt.do), which take advantage of this knowledge to pre-populate your OpenID credentials into any recognizable OpenID field on a page.

You'll note that we don't offer the **remember me** option with OpenID login. This is due to the fact that the redirection to and from the vendor causes the **remember me** checkbox value to be lost, such that when the user's successfully authenticated, they no longer have the **remember me** option indicated. This is unfortunate, but ultimately increases the security of OpenID as a login mechanism for our site, as OpenID forces the user to establish a trust relationship through the provider with each and every login.

# Configuring OpenID support in Spring Security

Turning on the basic OpenID support, via the inclusion of a servlet filter in our `FilterChainProxy` and authentication provider, is as simple as removing the `<form-login>` element and adding a directive to our `<http>` configuration element in `security.xml` as follows:

src/main/webapp/WEB-INF/spring/security.xml

```
<http auto-config="true"...>
    ...
    <form-login login-page="/login/form"
            login-processing-url="/login"
            username-parameter="username"
            password-parameter="password"
            authentication-failure-url="/login/form?error"
            default-target-url="/default"/>
    <openid-login login-page="/login/form"
            login-processing-url="/login"
            authentication-failure-url="/login/form?error"
            default-target-url="/default"/>
    <logout logout-url="/logout"
            logout-success-url="/login/form?logout"/>
</http>
```

Keeping all but the username and password attributes of our `<login-form>` element, we have exchanged `<login-form>` for the `<openid-login>` element. Since we use `auto-config="true"`, if we had not chosen to override these defaults, we would only have needed to specify `<openid-login/>` with no additional attributes. You can find a summary of the attributes and their default values in the following table:

| Attribute | Default Value |
| --- | --- |
| `login-page` | `/spring_security_login` |
| `login-processing-url` | `/j_spring_openid_security_check` |
| `authentication-failure-url` | `/spring_security_login?login_error` |
| `default-target-url` | `/` |

After adding this configuration element and restarting the application, you will be able to use the OpenID login form to present an OpenID and navigate through the OpenID authentication process.

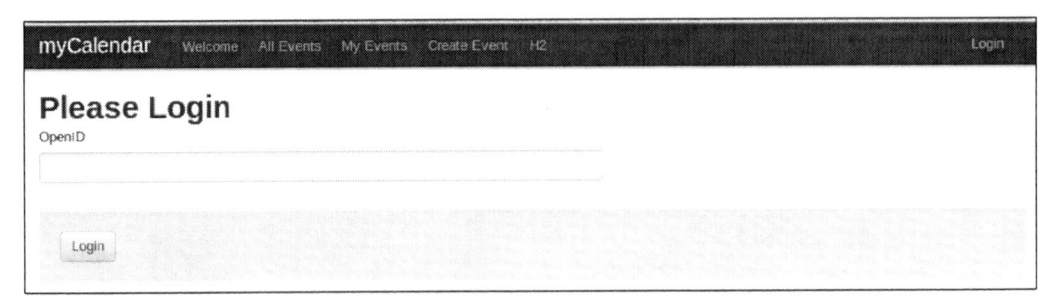

When you are returned to JBCP Calendar, however, you will be denied access. This is because your credentials won't have any roles assigned to them. This is a good example of the difference between authentication and authorization. We were able to successfully authenticate the user, but the user is not authorized to do anything yet. We'll adjust our configuration to grant the use access to the application next.

# Adding OpenID users

As we do not yet have OpenID-enabled new user registration, we'll need to preemptively add the user account to our existing users. To do this you will need to update the `calendar-data.sql` file to include your OpenID. For example, if your OpenID is http://springsecurity31.myopenid.com/, then you will want to update one of the insert statements to use your OpenID as shown next:

src/main/resources/database/h2/calendar-data.sql

```sql
insert into calendar_users(
    id,openid,
    email,password,first_name,last_name)
values (
    0,'http://springsecurity31.myopenid.com/',
    'user1@example.com','user1','User','1'
);
```

You'll note that this is similar to our traditional username and password-based admin account, with the exception that we have added an additional column for the OpenID to act as another alias for the user.

# CalendarUserDetailsService lookup by OpenID

We have included code from the custom authentication we did in *Chapter 3, Custom Authentication*. Previously, we linked Spring Security's `UserDetails` to our `CalendarUser` using its e-mail property. However, the username will now be an OpenID rather than an e-mail, so we need to update our `CalendarUserDetailsService` to lookup the `CalendarUser` user by OpenID. Go ahead and make the following changes:

src/main/java/com/packtpub/springsecurity/core/userdetails/
CalendarUserDetailsService.java

```java
public UserDetails loadUserByUsername(String username) {
    CalendarUser user = calendarUserDao.findUserByOpenid(username);
    ...
}
```

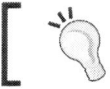

> Your code should look like `chapter08.01-calendar`.

*Opening up to OpenID*

At this point, you should be able to complete a full log in using OpenID. The redirects that occur are as follows:

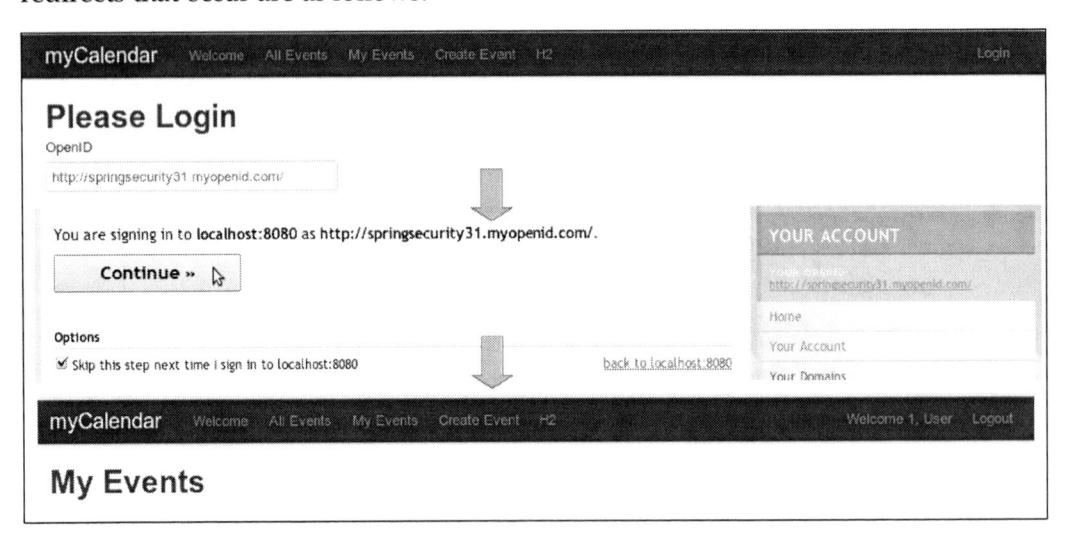

We've now OpenID-enabled JBCP Calendar login! Feel free to test using several OpenID providers. You'll notice that, although the overall functionality is the same, the experience that the provider offers when reviewing and accepting the OpenID request differs greatly from provider to provider.

# The OpenID user registration problem

Try using the same technique that we worked through previously with a Yahoo! OpenID – for example, `https://me.yahoo.com/springsecurity31`. You will find that it doesn't work, as it did with the other OpenID providers. This illustrates a key problem with the structure of OpenID, and highlights the importance of OpenID-enabled user registration.

# How are OpenID identifiers resolved

The actual OpenID that Yahoo! returns will be included in the error message on the login page and will be similar to the following: https://me.yahoo.com/a/MMifyI8ZntF5DvkzM29BhUGVeNr0kEi4Nw--#5a086. In OpenID terminology, the identifier that the user enters in the login box is known as the user-supplied identifier. This identifier may not actually correspond to the identifier that uniquely identifies the user (the user's claimed identifier), but as part of the verification of ownership, the OpenID Provider will take care of translating the user input to the identifier that the provider can actually prove that the user owns.

> The OpenID discovery protocol and the OpenID Provider itself actually have to be smart about figuring out what the user meant, based on what they supply upon OpenID authentication. For example, try entering the name of an OpenID provider (for example, www.yahoo.com) in the OpenID login box—you'll get a slightly different interface that allows you to pick your OpenID, as you didn't supply a unique OpenID in the login box. Pretty clever! For details on this and other aspects of the OpenID specifications, check out the specifications page (on the developers page) of the OpenID Foundation website at http://openid.net/developers/.

Once the user is able to provide proof of ownership of their claimed identifier, the OpenID provider will return a normalized version of the claimed identifier, known as the OpenID Provider Local Identifier (or OP-Local Identifier), to the requesting application. This is the final, unique identifier that the OpenID provider indicates that the user owns, and the one which will always be returned from authentication requests to the provider. Hence, this is the identifier that the JBCP Calendar should be storing for user identification.

*Opening up to OpenID*

The flow of an OpenID login request handled by Spring Security proceeds as follows:

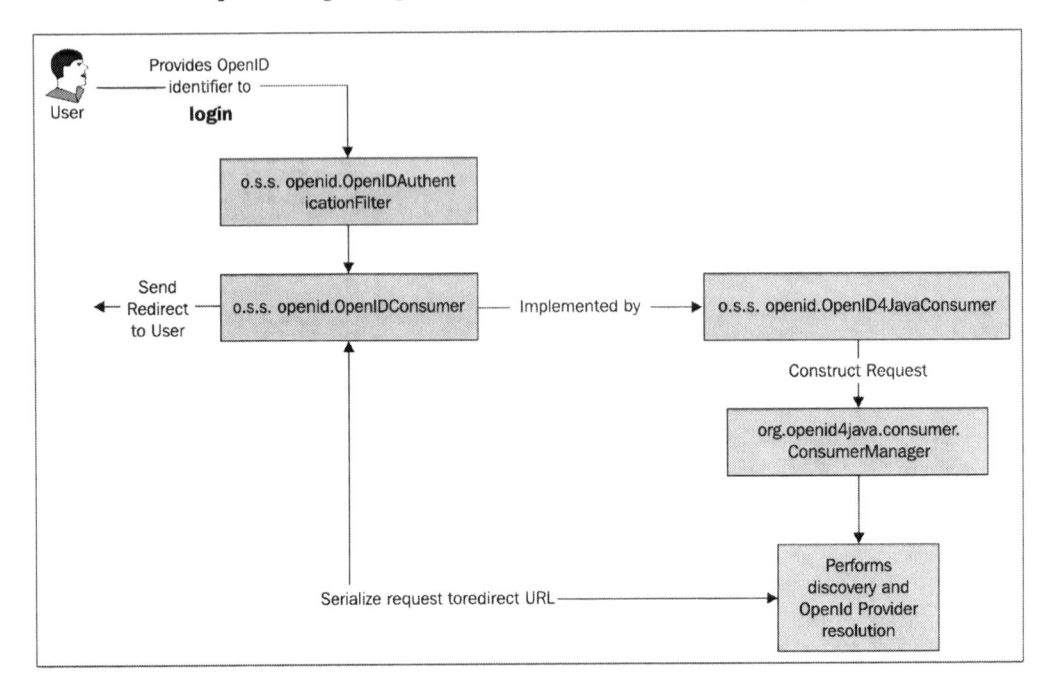

The `o.s.s.openid.OpenIDAuthenticationFilter` is responsible for responding to requests to log in and responding to the user's login request, much as the `UsernamePasswordAuthenticationFilter` did for username password-based authentication. We can see from the diagram that the `o.s.s.openid.OpenID4JavaConsumer` delegates to the `openid4java` library to construct the URL, which ultimately redirects the user to the OpenID Provider. The `openid4java` library (via the `org.openid4java.consumer.ConsumerManager`) is also responsible for the provider discovery process described earlier.

This filter is actually used in both phases of OpenID authentication—both in formulating the redirect to the OpenID Provider, and the handling of the authentication response from the provider. The response from the OpenID Provider is a simple GET request, with a series of well-defined fields, which are consumed and verified by the `openid4java` library. While you won't be dealing with these fields directly, some of the important ones are as follows:

| Field Name | Description |
| --- | --- |
| `openid.op_endpoint` | The OpenID Provider's endpoint URL used for verification. |
| `openid.claimed_id` | The OpenID claimed identifier provided by the user. |

## Chapter 8

| Field Name | Description |
|---|---|
| `openid.response_nonce` | The nonce calculated by the provider, which is a unique value that is used to help prevent replay attacks. |
| `openid.sig` | The OpenID response signature. |
| `openid.association` | The one-time use association generated by the requestor and used to calculate the signature, and determine the validity of the response. |
| `openid.identifier` | The OP-Local Identifier. |

We'll examine how some of these fields are used in verifying the validity of a response. Let's look at the actors involved in processing the vendor's OpenID response:

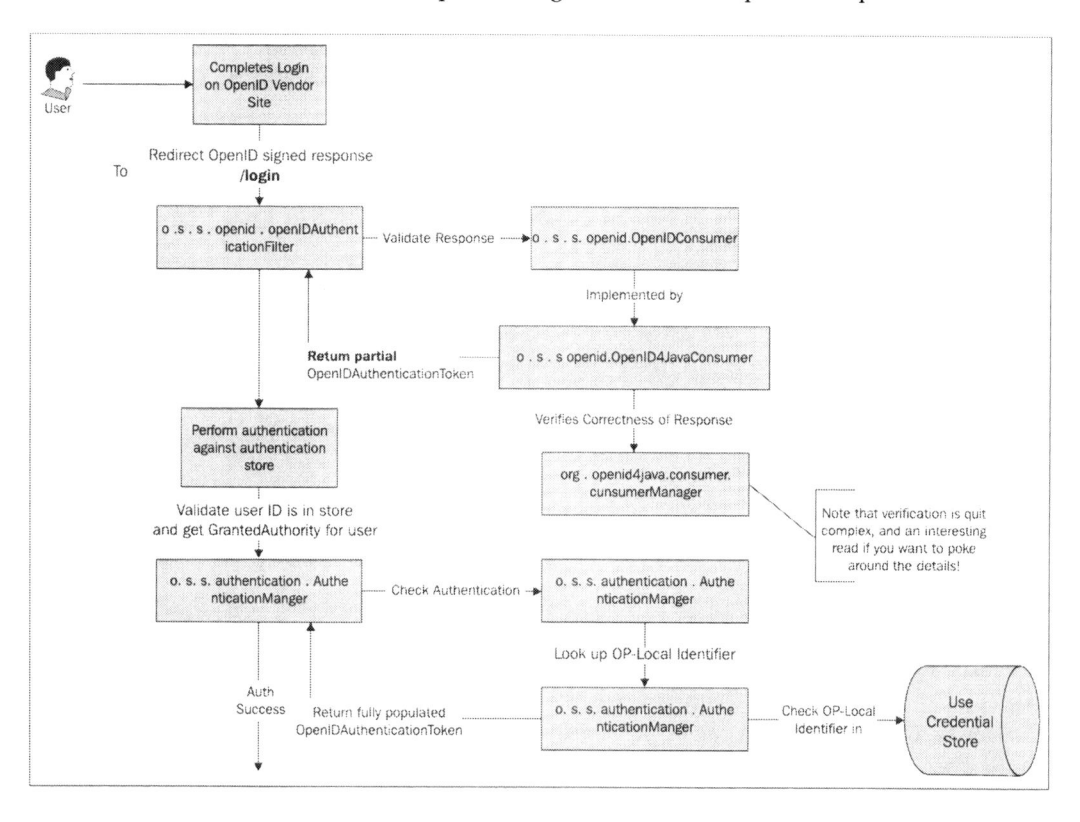

We see that the user is redirected to log in after he/she submits his/her credentials to the OpenID provider's site. The `OpenIDAuthenticationFilter` performs some rather basic checks to see if the invoking request is an OpenID request (from the JBCP Calendar login form), or a possibly valid OpenID response from a provider.

[ 199 ]

Once the request is determined to be an OpenID response, a complex series of validations ensure to validate the correctness and authenticity of the response (refer to the *Is OpenID secure?* section later in this chapter for more details on this). The `OpenID4JavaConsumer` eventually returns a sparsely populated `o.s.s.openid.OpenIDAuthenticationToken`, which is used by the filter to determine whether the initial validation of the response was successful. The token is then passed along to the `AuthenticationManager`, which treats it like any other `Authentication` object.

The `o.s.s.openid.OpenIDAuthenticationProvider` ends up being responsible for performing final verification against the local authentication store (for example, `InMemoryUserDetailsManager`). It's important to remember that what is expected in the authentication store is a username containing the OP-Local Identifier, which may not necessarily match the identifier initially supplied by the user—this is the crux of the OpenID registration problem. The flow from this point onward is very similar to traditional username/password authentication, most notably in the retrieval of appropriate group and role assignments from the `UserDetailsService`.

# Implementing user registration with OpenID

For a user to be able to create an account on the JBCP Calendar application, which will be OpenID enabled, they'll need to first prove that they own the identifier. Thus, we'll integrate the registration with the login process. If desired, you could extend this example to have an explicit registration form that may even have additional parameters.

## Registering OpenIDAuthenticationUserDetailsService

We have already seen the power of Spring Security's `UserDetailsService`, which allows developers to customize the lookup of `UserDetails` by a username. However, there is another more powerful interface that we can leverage to create our users from the OpenID response if the user does not already exist. Let's have a look at the code that is required to do this.

src/main/java/com/packtpub/springsecurity/openid/core/userdetails/
RegisteringOpenIDAuthenticationUserDetailsService.java

```
public UserDetails loadUserDetails(OpenIDAuthenticationToken token)   {
    String openid = token.getIdentityUrl();
    try {
        return userDetailsService.loadUserByUsername(openid);
```

```
        } catch (UsernameNotFoundException e) {
        }

        // user does not exist, so create a new one
        CalendarUser newUser = new CalendarUser();
        newUser.setOpenid(openid);
        newUser.setEmail("mock@example.com");
        newUser.setFirstName("Dynamic");
        newUser.setLastName("Provision");
        newUser.setPassword("notused");
        calendarService.createUser(newUser);

        // now the user exists, try looking them up again
        return userDetailsService.loadUserByUsername(openid);
}
```

The first step is to attempt to lookup the user by the OpenID. You will notice that we are calling the same `CalendarUserDetailsService` that we just updated to lookup our `CalendarUser` by its OpenID. If the user is not found, then we create a new one with mostly mock data and then return the newly created user. Later we will use the `OpenIDAuthenticationToken` to populate the entire `CalendarUser`.

> We could avoid the second lookup by using the `CalendarUserDetails` object we specified in our `CalendarUserDetailsService`. However, we choose to leave the conversion as an implementation detail and perform the lookup again.

Since the `RegisteringOpenIDAuthenticationUserDetailsService` was included with this chapter and it is configured using classpath scanning (as we saw in *Chapter 3, Custom Authentication*), all we need to do is instruct Spring Security to use it. Go ahead and make the following updates to your `security.xml`:

src/main/webapp/WEB-INF/spring/security.xml

```
    <openid-login login-page="/login/form"
        login-processing-url="/login"
        authentication-failure-url="/login/form?error"
        default-target-url="/default"
        user-service-ref=
    "registeringOpenIDAuthenticationUserDetailsService"/>
```

*Opening up to OpenID*

> Keep in mind that OP-Local Identifiers can potentially be quite long—in fact, the OpenID 2.0 specification does not supply a maximum length for an OP-Local Identifier. The default Spring Security JDBC schema provides a relatively small username column (which you may recall that we already extended from the default to 100 characters). Depending on your needs, you may wish to extend the username column further to accommodate long identifiers.
>
> Remember that authentication isn't an issue at this point, merely being able to correctly identify the user in the database, based on their OpenID. Some OpenID-enabled sites go one step further than this, and allow a level of indirection between the OpenID identifier and the username used for authentication (for example, allowing multiple OpenIDs to be associated with the same user account). The abstraction of the OpenID from the user's account name can be helpful for those users who have multiple OpenIDs from different providers that they may wish to use on your site. Although this is somewhat contrary to the goals of OpenID, it does happen, and you need to keep it in mind when designing an OpenID-enabled site.

In order for us to utilize dynamic provisioning, we must have a user that does not exist in the database yet. Go ahead and make changes to the database script so that your OpenID is no longer referenced.

src/main/resources/database/h2/calendar-data.sql

```
insert into calendar_users(
    id,openid,
    email,password,first_name,last_name)
values (
    0,null,
    'user1@example.com','user1','User','1'
);
```

Start up the application and log in with a user that does not yet exist to see that your user is dynamically provisioned. While it is good to no longer have to pre-populate users in the database, using mock data for the e-mail and name leaves a lot to be desired. Fortunately, we can leverage OpenID attribute exchange to obtain this information too.

> Your code should look like chapter08.02-calendar.

[ 202 ]

# Attribute Exchange

One other interesting feature of OpenID is the ability for the OpenID Provider to supply (upon the user's consent) typical user registration data such as name, e-mail, and date of birth, if the OpenID-enabled website requests it. This functionality is called **Attribute Exchange** (**AX**). The following diagram illustrates how a request for attribute exchange makes it into the OpenID request:

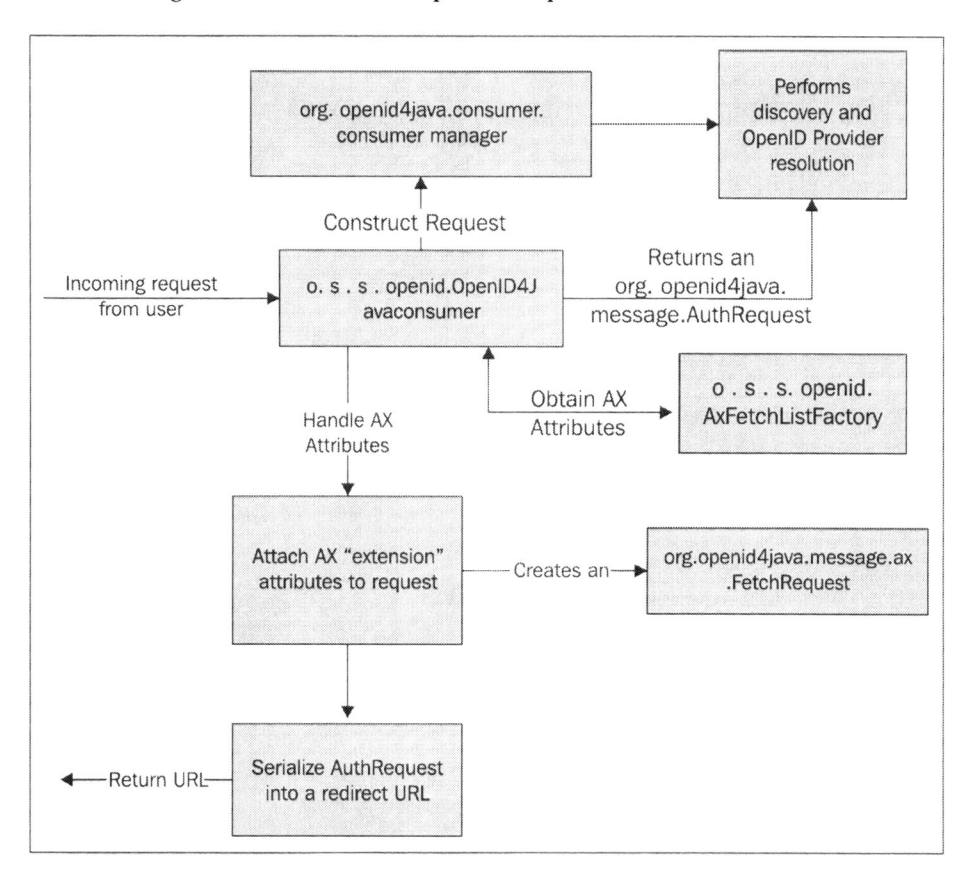

The AX attribute values (if supplied by the provider) are returned along with the rest of the OpenID response, and inserted into the `OpenIDAuthenticationToken` as a list of `o.s.s.openid.OpenIDAttribute`.

AX attributes can be arbitrarily defined by OpenID Providers, but are always uniquely defined by a URI. There has been an effort to standardize the available and common attributes into a schema of sorts. Attributes such as the following are:

| Attribute name | Description |
| --- | --- |
| `http://axschema.org/contact/email` | User's e-mail address |
| `http://axschema.org/namePerson` | User's full name |

The `axschema.org` site used to list over 30 different attributes, with unique URIs and descriptions. While the site is no longer in existence, many OpenID Providers still use the axschema.org definitions. Other OpenID Providers reference `schema.openid.net` instead of `axschema.org`. For additional information, refer to the OpenID Provider's documentation.

Let's see how to configure attribute exchange with Spring Security.

## Enabling AX in Spring Security OpenID

Enabling AX support in Spring Security OpenID is actually quite trivial, once you know the appropriate attributes to request. We can configure AX support so that the user's e-mail address and name is requested as follows:

```
<openid-login ...>
    <attribute-exchange>
        <openid-attribute name="email"
                type="http://schema.openid.net/contact/email"
                required="true"/>
        <openid-attribute name="fullname"
                type="http://schema.openid.net/namePerson"
                required="true" />
    </attribute-exchange>
</openid-login>
```

We can then extract these attributes from the `OpenIDAuthenticationToken` in our `RegisteringOpenIDAuthenticationUserDetailsService`. You will notice that we have provided some helper methods that extract the correct `OpenIDAttribute` for you.

src/main/java/com/packtpub/springsecurity/openid/core/userdetails/
RegisteringOpenIDAuthenticationUserDetailsService.java

```
    private String getAttr(String attrName, List<OpenIDAttribute> attrs) {
        List<String> attrValues = getAttrs(attrName, attrs);
        if (attrValues.isEmpty()) {
```

```
            return null;
    }
    return attrValues.iterator().next();
}

private List<String> getAttrs(String attrName, List<OpenIDAttribute>
attrs) {
    for (OpenIDAttribute attr : attrs) {
        if (attrName.equals(attr.getName())) {
            return new ArrayList<String>(attr.getValues());
        }
    }
    return Collections.emptyList();
}

private String getFirstName(List<OpenIDAttribute> attrs) {
    String firstName = getAttr("firstname", attrs);
    if(firstName != null) {
        return firstName;
    }
    return parseFullName(attrs, true);
}

private String getLastName(List<OpenIDAttribute> attrs) {
    String lastName = getAttr("lastname", attrs);
    if(lastName != null) {
        return lastName;
    }
    return parseFullName(attrs, false);
}
```

The method `getAttrs` will iterate over each `OpenIDAttribute` to find all the values for a particular attribute name. Our `getAttr` method uses the `getAttrs` method to extract the first value. We have also defined a few helper methods to get the first and last name for the current user. If we do not find the first or last name as its own attribute, we extract the appropriate value from an attribute that contains the full name. Update the `loadUserDetails` method to extract out the attributes using the provided utility methods as shown next:

src/main/java/com/packtpub/springsecurity/openid/core/userdetails/
RegisteringOpenIDAuthenticationUserDetailsService.java

```
public UserDetails loadUserDetails(OpenIDAuthenticationToken token) {
    ...
    List<OpenIDAttribute> attrs = token.getAttributes();
```

# Opening up to OpenID

```
        CalendarUser newUser = new CalendarUser();
        newUser.setOpenid(openid);
        newUser.setEmail(getAttr("email", attrs));
        newUser.setFirstName(getFirstName(attrs));
        newUser.setLastName(getLastName(attrs));
        ...
        return userDetailsService.loadUserByUsername(openid);
    }
```

> Your code should look like `chapter08.03-calendar`.

For simplicity, the existing code will return existing users as is without updating the user with the attributes. This means that in order for us to utilize the attribute exchange, we must again use a user that does not exist in the database yet.

For this example, we'd suggest that you log in with your myOpenID identity. You'll see that this time, when you are redirected to the provider, the provider informs you that additional information is being requested by the JBCP Calendar site.

> If you do not see the attributes being shared, you will want to check to ensure that you have entered a full name with at least one space and e-mail in **Your Account | Registration Personas** on the myOpenID site.

You should see something similar to the following screenshot:

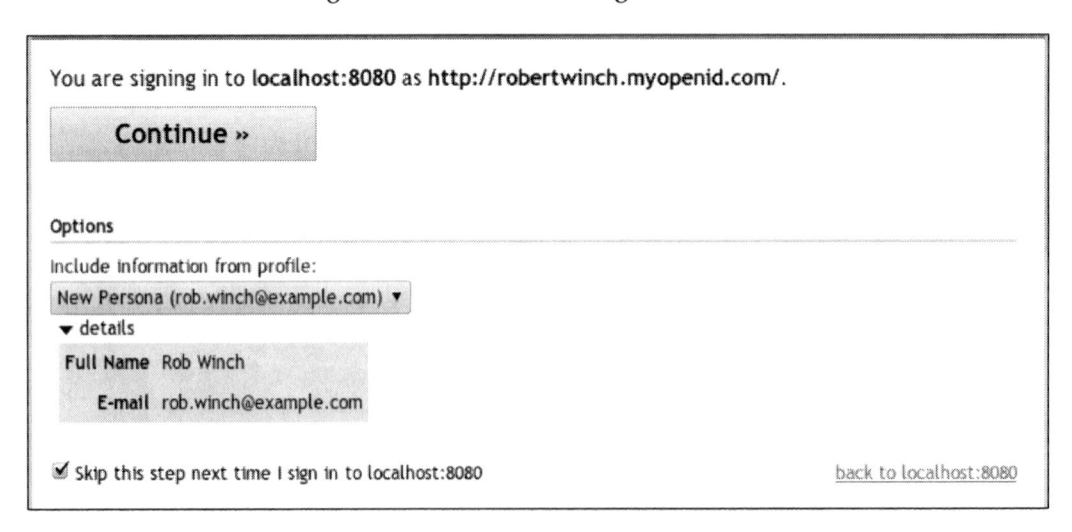

```
You are signing in to localhost:8080 as http://robertwinch.myopenid.com/.

        [ Continue » ]

Options
Include information from profile:
  [ New Persona (rob.winch@example.com) ▼ ]
  ▼ details
    Full Name  Rob Winch
       E-mail  rob.winch@example.com

☑ Skip this step next time I sign in to localhost:8080         back to localhost:8080
```

Afterwards, you will be logged in with the e-mail address you entered and your first and last name. You may notice that our example demonstrates an e-mail coming from example.com, which should not be possible. This is one of the common misconceptions about attribute exchange. In fact, there is no requirement that OpenID Providers verify the e-mail address they return.

Furthermore, realize that anyone (even a malicious user) can create an OpenID Provider. While an OpenID from another provider cannot be impersonated, a malicious OpenID Provider can return arbitrary attributes. This means that using attributes, like e-mail, as a means for access control should be avoided.

# Configuring different attributes for each OpenID Provider

Unfortunately, the promise of AX falls far short in reality. AX is very poorly supported by the available OpenID Providers in the market, with only a handful of providers offering support (myOpenID and Google being the most prominent). Additionally, there is a lot of confusion, even among providers that do support the standard, of what attributes correspond to the data that they are willing to send. For example, to query for a user's e-mail address, the attribute name to request differs even between the two major providers who support AX!

| Provider | AX attribute supported |
| --- | --- |
| myOpenID | http://schema.openid.net/contact/email |
| Google | http://axschema.org/contact/email |

Fortunately, Spring Security makes it easy to request different attributes depending on which OpenID Provider is being used. Let's update our security.xml to take advantage of OpenID Provider's specific attribute exchange.

src/main/webapp/WEB-INF/spring/security.xml

```
<openid-login ...>
    <attribute-exchange identifier-match=".*myopenid.com.*">
        <openid-attribute name="email"
                type="http://schema.openid.net/contact/email"
                required="true"/>
        <openid-attribute name="fullname"
                type="http://schema.openid.net/namePerson"
                required="true"/>
    </attribute-exchange>
    <attribute-exchange identifier-match="https://www.google.com/.*">
        <openid-attribute name="email"
```

```
                type="http://axschema.org/contact/email"
                required="true" count="1"/>
        <openid-attribute name="firstname"
                type="http://axschema.org/namePerson/first"
                required="true" />
        <openid-attribute name="lastname"
                type="http://axschema.org/namePerson/last"
                required="true" />
    </attribute-exchange>
    <attribute-exchange identifier-match=".*yahoo.com.*">
        <openid-attribute name="email"
                type="http://axschema.org/contact/email"
                required="true"/>
        <openid-attribute name="fullname"
                type="http://axschema.org/namePerson"
                required="true" />
    </attribute-exchange>
</openid-login>
```

You will notice that each `<attribute-exchange>` element contains an `identifier-match` attribute, which is a regular expression that is used to compare against the OpenID Provider. If the pattern matches the user provided OpenID, the attributes will be sent to the OpenID Provider. Go ahead and start the application and try logging in with your Google account. We can now authenticate with a Google account just as easily as we did with our myOpenID account.

> Your code should look like `chapter08.04-calendar`.

## Usability enhancements

A number of usability studies have been done on OpenID that have demonstrated it is not as user-friendly as one might want. It is difficult for users to remember their OpenID and even if they remember it, it can be cumbersome to type. One way of dealing with this is by allowing users to select which OpenID Provider they would like to use with a UI.

We have already included the necessary images, css, and JavaScript to use OpenID Selector http://code.google.com/p/openid-selector/ in our sample application at src/main/webapp/resources. Our header.jsp file has already included the JQuery library and the OpenID Selector library in the <head> of our page. To use it we will need to make a few updates to our login.jsp page.

src/main/webapp/WEB-INF/views/login.jsp

```
<form action="${loginUrl}" method="post" id="openid_form">
    ...
    <div id="openid_choice">
        <p>Please click your account provider:</p>
        <div id="openid_btns"></div>
    </div>
    <div id="openid_input_area">
        <input id="openid_identifier"
                name="openid_identifier" type="text" value="http://"
        />
        <input id="openid_submit" type="submit" value="Sign-In"/>
    </div>
</form>
<script type="text/javascript">
    $(document).ready(function() {
        openid.init('openid_identifier');
    });
</script>
```

Observe that we add some additional markup to our OpenID login form. If you have not seen it before, the $(document).ready is utilizing JQuery to initialize our OpenID Selector library after the document is ready. To learn more about JQuery visit their site at http://jquery.com.

Now when you are presented with the login page you will see a listing of various OpenID Providers that can easily be selected.

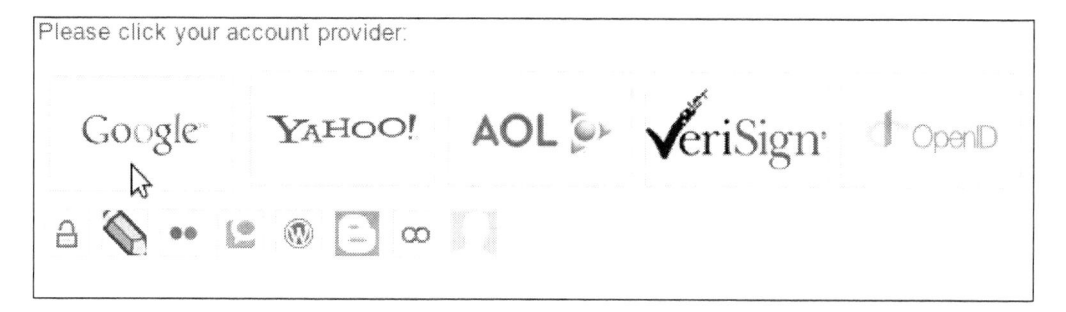

Go ahead and try to use Google to log in. Wasn't this a lot easier? If you are looking for more information on OpenID studies, a good place to start is the article *Thoughts on combining Google & Yahoo UX research* at `https://sites.google.com/site/oauthgoog/UXFedLogin/CombineGoogYahoo`.

> Your code should look like `chapter08.05-calendar`.

# Automatic redirection to the OpenID Provider

At times it may be nice to automatically redirect to a specific OpenID Provider. For example, perhaps we always wanted to use Google for authentication. To do this we only need to make a single configuration update. Update our login page in the `security.xml` as shown next:

src/main/webapp/WEB-INF/spring/security.xml

```
<openid-login ...
    login-page=
        "/login?openid_identifier=https://www.google.com/accounts/o8/id">
    ...
</openid-login>
```

> Your code should look like `chapter08.06-calendar`.

Start up the application and navigate to the **My Events** page. You will find that you are automatically redirected to the Google OpenID Provider. If you are already logged into Google, you will automatically be logged into our Calendar application too.

> Keep in mind that this setup does not prevent a user from using another OpenID Provider. To do this we would need to explicitly check the OpenID Provider's URL before allowing the application to indicate the user is authenticated.

# Conditional automatic redirection

More realistically, we might want to remember if the user last went to the Google OpenID Provider and if so, automatically authenticate with Google. The question now becomes, how do we determine when we should request the login page or automatically redirect the user to Google?

The JavaScript we integrated into our project for enhancing the user experience sets a cookie by the name of `openid_provider` to Google if it was the last OpenID Provider used. We have included a controller that will request automatic log in from Google if the cookie is present and contains the value of Google. Otherwise, the original login page is displayed. As you can see next the implementation is rather trivial:

src/main/java/com/packtpub/springsecurity/web/controllers/ConditionalLoginPageController.java

```
    @Controller
    public class ConditionalLoginPageController {
        @RequestMapping("/login/check")
        public String check( @CookieValue(required = false) String openid_provider) {
            if ("google".equals(openid_provider)) {
                return "redirect:/login?openid_identifier=https://www.google.com/accounts/o8/id";
            }
            return "redirect:/login/form";
        }
    }
```

> This solution should feel very similar to how we set up custom home pages using the `DefaultController` in *Chapter 2, Getting Started with Spring Security*. When possible, creating a controller should be preferred to writing a custom `AuthenticationEntryPoint` since it is not coupled to Spring Security. It should also be noted that while we use Spring MVC, the controller could be implemented using other technologies (such as Struts, a standard Servlet, and so on).

Since we have already included the controller in this chapter, all we need to do now is to update our `security.xml` to send the user to the controller.

src/main/webapp/WEB-INF/spring/security.xml

```
    <openid-login ...
            login-page="/login/check">
        ...
    </openid-login>
```

Go ahead and start the application up and give it a try. Try requesting the **My Events** page and you will find that if you last used Google to log in, you will automatically be redirected to Google. If you are already logged in to Google, you will transparently be logged in to the JBCP Calendar application.

> Your code should look like chapter08.07-calendar.

# Is OpenID Secure

As support for OpenID relies on the trustworthiness of the OpenID Provider and the verifiability of the provider's response, security, and authenticity are critical in order for the application to have confidence in the user's OpenID-based login.

Fortunately, the designers of the OpenID specification were very aware of this concern, and implemented a series of verification steps to prevent response forgery, replay attacks, and other types of tampering, which are explained as follows:

- **Response forgery** is prevented due to the combination of a shared secret key (created by the OpenID-enabled site prior to the initial request), and a one-way hashed message signature on the response itself. A malicious user tampering with the data in any of the response fields without having access to the shared secret key and signature algorithm would generate an invalid response.
- **Replay attacks** are prevented due to the inclusion of a nonce, or a one-time use, random key, that should be recorded by the OpenID-enabled site so that it cannot ever be reused. In this way, even a user attempting to re-issue the response URL would be foiled because the receiving site would determine that the nonce had been previously used and would invalidate the request.

The most likely form of attack that could result in a compromised user interaction would be a man-in-the-middle attack, where a malicious user could intercept the user's interaction between their computer and the OpenID Provider. A hypothetical attacker in this situation could be in a position to record the conversation between the user's browser and the OpenID Provider, and record the secret key used when the request was initiated. The attacker in this case would need a very high level of sophistication and a reasonably complete implementation of the OpenID signature specification—in short, this is not likely to occur with any regularity.

Do note that although the `openid4java` library does support the use of persistent nonce tracking using JDBC, Spring Security OpenID does not currently expose this as a configuration parameter on the namespace configuration—thus nonces are tracked only in memory. This means that a replay attack could occur after a server restart, or in a clustered environment, where the in-memory store would not be replicated between JVMs on different servers.

## Summary

In this chapter, we reviewed OpenID, a relatively recent technology for user authentication and credentials management. OpenID has a very wide reach on the Web, and has made great strides in usability and acceptance within the past year or two. Most public-facing sites on the modern web should plan on some form of OpenID support, and JBCP Calendar application is no exception!

In this chapter we:

- Learned about the OpenID authentication mechanism, and explored its high-level architecture and key terminology
- Implemented OpenID login and automatic user registration with the JBCP Calendar application
- Explored the future of OpenID profile management through the use of **Attribute Exchange (AX)**
- Demonstrated automatic login with OpenID
- Examined the security of OpenID login responses

We covered one of the simplest single sign on mechanisms to implement with Spring Security. One of the downsides is that it does not support a standard mechanism for single logout. In the next chapter, we will explore CAS, another standard single sign on protocol that also supports single logout.

# 9
# Single Sign-on with Central Authentication Service

In this chapter, we'll examine the use of **Central Authentication Service (CAS)** as a single sign-on portal for Spring Security-based applications.

During the course of this chapter, we'll:

- Learn about CAS, its architecture, and how it benefits system administrators and organizations of any size
- Understand how Spring Security can be reconfigured to handle the interception of authentication requests and redirect it to CAS
- Configure the JBCP Calendar application to utilize CAS single sign-on
- Gain an understanding of how a single logout can be performed and configure our application to support it
- Discuss how to use CAS proxy ticket authentication for services, and configure our application to utilize proxy ticket authentication
- Discuss how to customize the out of the box JA-SIG CAS Server using the recommended war overlay approach
- Integrate the CAS Server with LDAP, and pass data from LDAP to Spring Security via CAS

# Introducing Central Authentication Service

CAS is an open source, single sign-on server, providing centralized access control and authentication to web-based resources within an organization. The benefits of CAS are numerous to administrators supporting many applications and diverse user communities, which are as follows:

- Individual or group access to resources (applications) can be configured in one location
- Broad support for a wide variety of authentication stores (to centralize user management) provides a single point of authentication and control to a widespread, cross-machine environment
- Wide authentication support is provided for web-based and non web-based Java applications through CAS client libraries
- A single point of reference for user credentials (via CAS) is provided, so that CAS client applications are not required to have any knowledge of the user's credentials or knowledge of how to verify them

In this chapter, we'll not focus much on the management of CAS but on authentication, and how CAS can act as an authentication point for the users of our site. Although CAS is commonly seen in intranet environments for enterprises or educational institutions, it can also be found in use at high-profile locations such as Sony Online Entertainment's public-facing site.

## High-level CAS authentication flow

At a high level, CAS is composed of a **CAS Server**, which is the central web application for determining authentication and one or more **CAS Services**, which are distinct web applications that use the CAS Server to get authenticated. The basic authentication flow of CAS proceeds via the following actions:

1. The user attempts to access a protected resource on the website.
2. The user is redirected through the browser from the CAS Service to the CAS server to request a login.
3. The CAS server is responsible for user authentication. If the user is not already authenticated to the CAS server, it requests credentials from the user. In the next diagram, the user is presented with a login page.

4. The user submits the credentials (i.e. the username and password).
5. If the user's credentials are valid, the CAS Server responds with a redirect through the browser with a Service Ticket. A **Service Ticket** is a one time use token used to identify a user.
6. The CAS Service calls the CAS Server back to verify that the ticket is valid, has not expired, and so on. Note that this step does not occur through the browser.
7. The CAS Server responds with an assertion indicating that trust has been established. If the ticket is acceptable, trust has been established and the user may proceed via normal authorization checking.

Visually, this behaves as is illustrated in the following diagram:

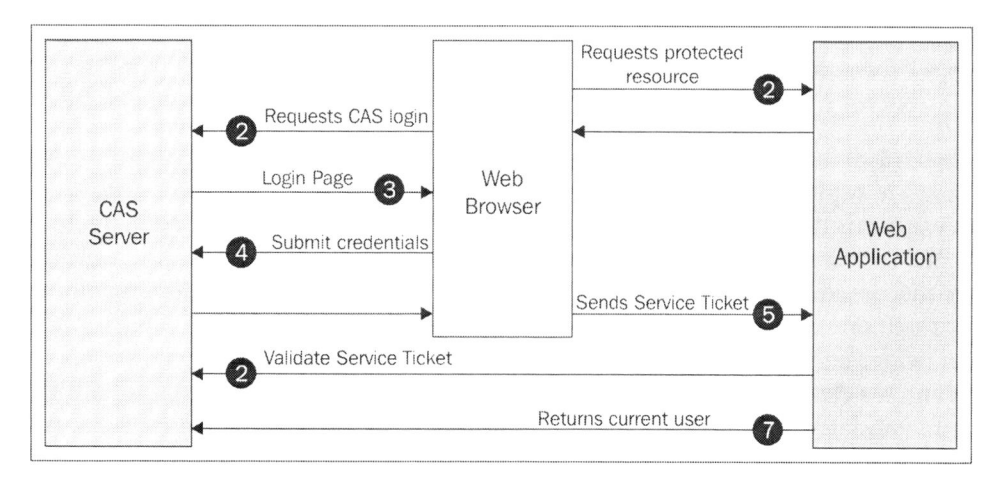

We can see that there is a high level of interaction between the CAS Server and the secured application, with several data exchange handshakes required before trust of the user can be established. The result of this complexity is a single sign-on protocol that is quite hard to spoof through common techniques (assuming other network security precautions, such as the use of SSL and network monitoring are in place).

Now that we understand how CAS authentication works in general, let's see how it applies to Spring Security.

# Spring Security and CAS

Spring Security has a strong integration capability with CAS, although not as tightly integrated into the security namespace style of configuration as the OpenID and LDAP integrations that we've explored thus far in the latter part of this book. Instead, much of the configuration relies on bean wiring and configuration by reference from the security namespace elements to bean declarations.

The two basic pieces of CAS authentication when using Spring Security involve the following:

- Replacement of the standard `AuthenticationEntryPoint` implementation—which typically handles redirection of unauthenticated users to the login page—with an implementation that redirects the user to the CAS Server instead
- Processing the Service Ticket when the user is redirected back from the CAS Server to the protected resource, through the use of a custom servlet filter

An important thing to understand about CAS is that in typical deployments, CAS is intended to replace all the alternative login mechanisms of your application. As such, once we configure CAS for Spring Security, our users must use CAS exclusively as an authentication mechanism to our application. In most cases, this is not a problem; as we discussed in the previous section, CAS is designed to proxy authentication requests to one or more authentication stores (similar to what Spring Security does when delegating to a database or LDAP for authentication). From our previous diagram, we can see that our application is no longer checking its own authentication store to validate users. Instead, it determines the user through the use of the Service Ticket. However, as we will discuss later, initially Spring Security still needs a data store to determine the user's authorization. We will discuss how to remove this restriction later on in the chapter.

After completing the basic CAS integration with Spring Security, we can remove the **Login** link from the home page, and enjoy automatic redirection to CAS's login screen where we attempt to access a protected resource. Of course, depending on the application, it can also be beneficial to still allow the user to explicitly log in (so that they can see customized content, and so on).

# Required dependencies

Before we get too far, we should ensure that our dependencies are updated. A list of the dependencies that we have added with comments about when they are needed can be seen as follows:

pom.xml

```xml
  <!-- needed for any CAS integration
  <dependency>
    <groupId>org.springframework.security</groupId>
    <artifactId>spring-security-cas</artifactId>
    <version>3.1.0.RELEASE</version>
  </dependency>
  <!-- both needed for Single Logout -->
  <dependency>
    <groupId>org.opensaml</groupId>
    <artifactId>opensaml</artifactId>
    <version>1.1</version>
    <scope>runtime</scope>
  </dependency>
  <dependency>
    <groupId>xml-security</groupId>
    <artifactId>xmlsec</artifactId>
    <version>1.3.0</version>
    <scope>runtime</scope>
  </dependency>
  <!-- needed for caching of proxy tickets -->
  <dependency>
    <groupId>net.sf.ehcache</groupId>
    <artifactId>ehcache</artifactId>
    <version>1.6.2</version>
    <scope>runtime</scope>
  </dependency>
```

# CAS installation and configuration

CAS has the benefit of having an extremely dedicated team behind it that has done an excellent job of developing both quality software and accurate, straightforward documentation of how to use it. Should you choose to follow along with the examples in this chapter, you are encouraged to read the appropriate *Getting Started* manual for your CAS platform. You can find this manual at https://wiki.jasig.org/display/CASUM/Demo.

In order to make integration as simple as possible, we have included a cas-server application for this chapter, which can be deployed in Spring Tool Suite along with the Calendar application. For the examples in this chapter, we will assume that CAS is deployed at https://localhost:8443/cas/ and the Calendar application is deployed at https://localhost:8443/calendar/. In order to work, CAS requires the use of HTTPS. For detailed instructions on setting up HTTPS, refer to *Appendix, Additional Reference Material*.

> The examples in this chapter were written using the most recent available version of CAS Server, 3.4.11, at the time of this writing. Be aware that some significant changes to some of the backend classes were made to CAS in the 3.x time frame. So if you are on an earlier version of the server, these instructions may be slightly or significantly different for your environment.

Let's go ahead and configure the components required for CAS authentication.

> You should start the chapter off with the source from chapter09.00-calendar and chapter09.00-cas-server.

# Configuring basic CAS integration

Since the Spring Security namespace does not support CAS configuration, there are quite a few more steps that we need to implement in order to get a basic setup working. In order to get a high-level understanding of what is happening, you can refer to the following diagram. Don't worry about understanding the entire diagram right now, as we will break it into small chunks in order to make it easy to digest.

*Chapter 9*

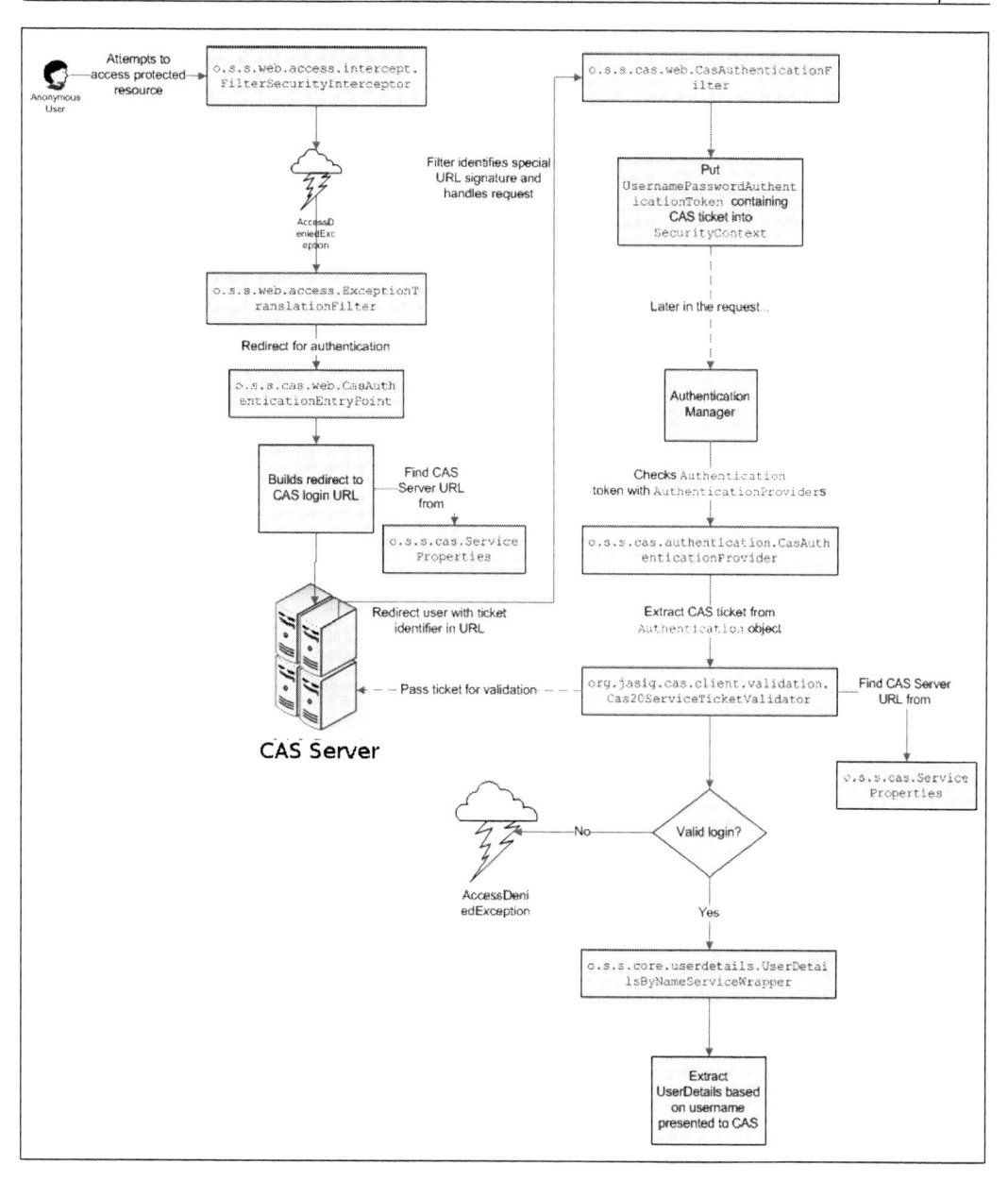

# Creating the CAS ServiceProperties object

The Spring Security setup relies on a o.s.s.cas.ServiceProperties bean in order to store common information about the CAS Service. The ServiceProperties object plays a role in coordinating data exchange between the various CAS components—it is used as a data object to store CAS configuration settings that are shared (and are expected to match) by the varying participants in the Spring CAS stack. You can view the configuration included in the following code snippet:

src/main/webapp/WEB-INF/spring/security-cas.xml

```
<bean id="serviceProperties"
      class="org.springframework.security.cas.ServiceProperties">
  <property name="service"
            value="https://${cas.service.host}/calendar/login"/>
</bean>
<context:property-placeholder
      system-properties-mode="OVERRIDE" properties-ref="environment"/>
<util:properties id="environment">
    <prop key="cas.service.host">localhost:8443</prop>
    <prop key="cas.server.host">localhost:8443</prop>
</util:properties>
```

You probably will have noticed that we leveraged `<context:property-placeholder />` to use variables named `${cas.service.host}` and `${cas.server.host}`. Both of these values can be included in your application, and Spring will automatically replace them with the values provided in `<context:property-placeholder/>`. This is a common strategy when deploying a CAS Service, since the CAS Server will likely change as we progress from development to production. In this instance, we default to using `localhost:8443` for both the CAS Server and the Calendar application. This configuration can be overridden using a system argument when the application is taken to production. Alternatively, the configuration could be externalized into a Java property's files. Either mechanism allows us to externalize our configuration properly.

# Adding the CasAuthenticationEntryPoint

As we briefly mentioned earlier in this chapter, Spring Security uses a `o.s.s.web.AuthenticationEntryPoint` interface to request credentials from the user. Typically, this involves redirecting the user to the login page. With CAS, we will need to redirect the CAS Server to request a login. When we redirect to the CAS Server, Spring Security must include a `service` parameter that indicates where the CAS server should send the Service Ticket. Fortunately, Spring Security provides the `o.s.s.cas.web.CasAuthenticationEntryPoint`, which is specifically designed for this purpose. The configuration that is included in the sample application is as follows:

src/main/webapp/WEB-INF/spring/security-cas.xml

```xml
<bean id="casEntryPoint"
  class="org.springframework.security.cas.web
  .CasAuthenticationEntryPoint">
  <property name="serviceProperties" ref="serviceProperties"/>
  <property name="loginUrl" value=
    "https://${cas.server.host}/cas/login" />
</bean>
```

The `CasAuthenticationEntryPoint` object uses the `ServiceProperties` class to specify where to send the Service Ticket once the user is authenticated. CAS allows for the selective granting of access per user, per application, based on configuration. We'll examine the particulars of this URL in a moment, when we configure the servlet filter that is expected to process it.

Next, we will then need to update Spring Security to utilize the bean with the ID `casEntryPoint`. You will notice that the `autoconfig="true"` attribute is no longer necessary since we are explicitly configuring the `AuthenticationEntryPoint`. Make the following update to our `security.xml` file:

src/main/webapp/WEB-INF/spring/security.xml

```xml
<http use-expressions="true"
      entry-point-ref="casEntryPoint">
    ...
</http>
```

Lastly, we need to ensure that the `security-cas.xml` file is loaded by Spring. Update the `web.xml` file as follows:

src/main/webapp/WEB-INF/web.xml

```xml
<context-param>
  <param-name>contextConfigLocation</param-name>
  <param-value>
    /WEB-INF/spring/services.xml
    /WEB-INF/spring/i18n.xml
    /WEB-INF/spring/security.xml
    /WEB-INF/spring/security-cas.xml
  </param-value>
</context-param>
```

If you start the application at this point and attempt to access the **My Events** page, you will immediately be redirected to the CAS Server for authentication. The default configuration of CAS allows authentication for any user whose username is equal to the password. So, you should be able to log in with a username as `admin1@example.com` and a password as `admin1@example.com` (or `user1@example.com`/`user1@example.com`).

You'll notice, however, that even after the login, you will immediately be redirected back to the CAS Server. This is because although the destination application was able to receive the ticket, it wasn't able to be validated, and as such the `AccessDeniedException` object is handled by CAS as a rejection of the ticket.

## Enabling CAS ticket verification

Referring to the diagram that we saw earlier in the *Configuring Basic CAS Authentication* section, we can see that Spring Security is responsible for identifying an unauthenticated request and redirecting the user to CAS via the `FilterSecurityInterceptor` class. Adding the `CasAuthenticationEntryPoint` object has overridden the standard redirect to the login page functionality and provided the expected redirection from the application to the CAS Server. Now we need to configure things so that, once authenticated to CAS, the user is properly authenticated to the application.

We remember from Chapter 8, Opening up to OpenID, that OpenID uses a similar redirection approach, by redirecting unauthenticated users to the OpenID Provider for authentication and then back to the application with verifiable credentials. CAS differs from OpenID. In the CAS protocol, upon the user's return to the application, the application is expected to call back the CAS server to explicitly validate that the credentials provided are valid and accurate. Contrast this with OpenID that uses the presence of a date-based nonce and key-based signature so that the credentials passed by the OpenID Provider can be independently verified.

The benefit of the CAS approach is that the information passed on from the CAS Server to authenticate the user is much simpler—only a single URL parameter is returned to the application by the CAS server. Additionally, the application itself need not track the active or valid tickets, and instead can wholly rely on CAS to verify this information. Much as we saw with OpenID, a servlet filter is responsible for recognizing a redirect from CAS and processing it as an authentication request. We can see how this is configured in our `security-cas.xml` file, as follows:

src/main/webapp/WEB-INF/spring/security-cas.xml

```xml
<bean id="casFilter"
  class="org.springframework.security.cas.web
  .CasAuthenticationFilter">
  <property name="authenticationManager"
    ref="authenticationManager"/>
  <property name="filterProcessesUrl" value="/login"/>
</bean>
```

We'll then replace the `<form-login>` element with the custom servlet filter declaration in our `security.xml` file:

src/main/webapp/WEB-INF/spring/security.xml

```xml
<http use-expressions="true"
    entry-point-ref="casEntryPoint">
  ...
  <custom-filter ref="casFilter" position="CAS_FILTER"/>
    <logout logout-url="/logout"
        logout-success-url="/login/form?logout"/>
</http>
```

Finally, we noted that a reference to the `AuthenticationManager` was required by the `CasAuthenticationFilter` object—this is added (if not already present) with the `alias` attribute of the `<authentication-manager>` declaration in `security.xml`:

src/main/webapp/WEB-INF/spring/security.xml

```
<authentication-manager
   alias="authenticationManager">
```

> You may have noticed that the CAS service name from the `ServiceProperties` configuration evaluates to `https://localhost:8443/calendar/login`. As we've seen with other authentication filters, it is best to override the default URL `/j_spring_cas_security_check`, to ensure that we do not unnecessarily disclose to malicious users that we are using Spring Security.

The `CasAuthenticationFilter` object populates an `Authentication` implementation (a `UsernamePasswordAuthenticationToken` object) with special credentials that are recognizable by the next and final elements of a minimal CAS configuration.

# Proving authenticity with the CasAuthenticationProvider

If you have been following the logical flow of Spring Security through the rest of this book, hopefully you already know what comes next—the `Authentication` token must be inspected by an appropriate `AuthenticationProvider`. CAS is no different, and as such, the final piece of the puzzle is the configuration of an `o.s.s.cas.authentication.CasAuthenticationProvider` object within the `AuthenticationManager`.

First, we'll declare the Spring Bean in `security-cas.xml`, as follows:

src/main/webapp/WEB-INF/spring/security-cas.xml

```xml
    <bean id="casAuthProvider"
      class="org.springframework.security.cas.authentication
      .CasAuthenticationProvider">
      <property name="ticketValidator" ref="ticketValidator"/>
      <property name="serviceProperties" ref="serviceProperties"/>
      <property name="key" value="casJbcpCalendar"/>
      <property name="authenticationUserDetailsService"
        ref="authenticationUserDetailsService"/>
    </bean>
```

Next, we'll configure a reference to this new `AuthenticationProvider` in `security.xml`, where our `<authentication-manager>` declaration resides:

src/main/webapp/WEB-INF/spring/security.xml

```xml
    </http>
    <authentication-manager alias="authenticationManager">
        <authentication-provider ref="casAuthProvider"/>
    </authentication-manager>
    <user-service id="userDetailsService">
        <user name="user1@example.com"
              password="user1"
              authorities="ROLE_USER"/>
        <user name="admin1@example.com"
              password="admin1"
              authorities="ROLE_USER,ROLE_ADMIN"/>
    </user-service>
</bean:beans>
```

If you have any other `AuthenticationProvider` references remaining from prior exercises, please remember to remove them for our work with CAS. While removing the remaining `<authentication-provider>` references, ensure to move the `<user-service>` tag outside the `<authentication-manager>` tag. It is also important to update the `<user-service>` tag to have an ID that is set to `userDetailsService`. All of these changes are illustrated in the preceding code. Now, we'll need to take care of the other attributes and bean references within the `CasAuthenticationProvider` class.

*Single Sign-on with Central Authentication Service*

The `ticketValidator` attribute refers to an implementation of the `org.jasig.cas.client.validation.TicketValidator` interface; as we are using CAS 2.0 authentication, we'll declare an `org.jasig.cas.client.validation.Cas20ServiceTicketValidator` instance, as follows:

src/main/webapp/WEB-INF/spring/security-cas.xml

```
<bean id="ticketValidator"
  class="org.jasig.cas.client.validation
  .Cas20ServiceTicketValidator">
  <constructor-arg value="https://${cas.server.host}/cas/"/>
</bean>
```

> Astute readers may be confused as to why we are configuring our CAS 3.x Server to use CAS 2.0. The version in the CAS 3.x Server refers to the version of the CAS Server implementation of the protocol; this is distinct from the version in CAS 2.0, which is the version of the CAS protocol being used.

The constructor argument supplied to this class should refer (once again) to the URL used to access the CAS Server. You'll note that at this point, we have moved out of the `org.springframework.security` package into `org.jasig`, which is part of the CAS client JAR files. Later in this chapter, we'll see that the `TicketValidator` interface also has implementations (still within the CAS client JAR files) that support other methods of authentication with CAS, such as the Proxy Ticket and SAML authentication.

Next, we see the `key` attribute; this is simply used to validate the integrity of `UsernamePasswordAuthenticationToken` and can be arbitrarily defined.

Just as we saw in *Chapter 8, Opening up to OpenID* the `authenticationUserDetailsService` attribute refers to an `o.s.s.core.userdetails.AuthenticationUserDetailsService` object that is used to translate the username information from the `Authentication` token to a fully-populated `UserDetails` object. The current implementation does this translation by looking up the username returned by the CAS Server and looking up `UserDetails` using the `UserDetailsService`. Obviously, this technique would only ever be used when we have confirmed that the integrity of the `Authentication` token has not been compromised. We configure this object with a reference to our `InMemoryUserDetailsManager` implementation of the `UserDetailsService` interface.

src/main/webapp/WEB-INF/spring/security-cas.xml

```
<bean id="authenticationUserDetailsService" class="org.springframework.security.core.userdetails.UserDetailsByNameServiceWrapper">
    <property name="userDetailsService" ref="userDetailsService"/>
</bean>
```

We may wonder why a `UserDetailsService` interface isn't directly referenced; it's because, just as we did with OpenID, there will be additional "advanced configuration options" later, which will allow details from the CAS Server to be used, to populate the `UserDetails` object.

> Your code should look like `chapter09.01-calendar` and `chapter09.01-cas-server`.

At this point, we should be able to start both the CAS Server and JBCP Calendar application. You can then visit `https://localhost:8443/calendar/` and select **All Events**, which will redirect you to the CAS Server. You can then log in using the username `admin1@example.com` and the password `admin1@example.com`. Upon successful authentication, you will be redirected back to the JBCP Calendar application. Excellent job!

> If you are experiencing issues, it is most likely due to an improper SSL configuration. Ensure that you have set up the trust store file as `tomcat.keystore`, as described in the *Appendix*.

# Single logout

You may notice that if you log out of the application, you get the logout confirmation page. However, if you click on a protected page, such as the **My Events** page, you are still authenticated. The problem is that the logout is only occurring locally. So when you request for another protected resource in the JBCP Calendar application, a login is requested from the CAS Server. Since the user is still logged in to the CAS Server, it immediately returns a Service Ticket and logs the user back into the JBCP Calendar application.

This also means that if the user had signed in to other applications using the CAS Server, they would still be authenticated to those applications, since our `Calendar` application does not know anything about the other applications. Fortunately, CAS and Spring Security offer a solution to this problem. Just as we can request a login from the CAS Server, we can also request a logout. You can see a high-level diagram of how a logout works within CAS, as follows.

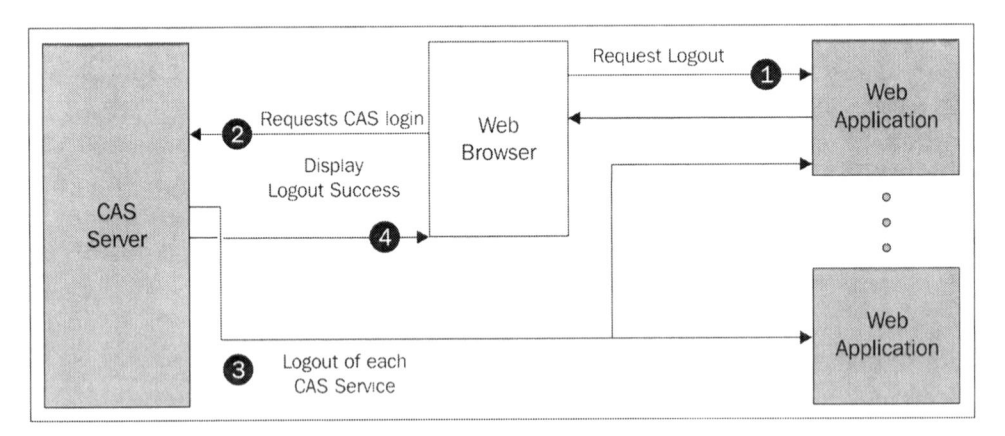

The following steps explain how a single logout takes place:

1. The user requests to log out of the web application.
2. The web application then requests to logout of CAS by sending a redirect through the browser to the CAS server.
3. The CAS Server recognizes the user and then sends a logout request to each CAS Service that was authenticated. Note that these logout requests do not occur through the browser. The CAS Server indicates which user should log out by providing the original Service Ticket that was used to log the user in. The application is then responsible for ensuring that the user is logged out.
4. The CAS Server displays the logout success page to the user.

# Configuring single logout

The configuration for a single logout is relatively simple. The first step is to specify a `logout-success-url` attribute to be the logout URL of the CAS Server in our `security.xml` file. This means that after we log out locally, we will automatically redirect the user to the CAS Server's logout page.

src/main/webapp/WEB-INF/spring/security.xml

```
<http ...>
    ...
    <logout logout-url="/logout"
        logout-success-url="https://${cas.server.host}/cas/logout"/>
</http>
```

Since we only have one application, this is all we need to make it appear as though a single logout is occurring. This is because we log out of our `Calendar` application before redirecting to the CAS Server logout page. This means that by the time the CAS Server sends the logout request to the `Calendar` application, the user has already been logged out.

If there were multiple applications and the user logged out of another application, the CAS Server would send a logout request to our `Calendar` application and not process the logout event. This is because our application is not listening for these log out events. The solution is simple; we must create the `SingleSignoutFilter` object, as follows:

src/main/webapp/WEB-INF/spring/security-cas.xml

```
    <bean id="singleLogoutFilter"
        class="org.jasig.cas.client.session.SingleSignOutFilter"/>
</beans>
```

Next, we need to make Spring Security aware of the `singleLogoutFilter` object in our `security.xml` file by including it as a `<custom-filter>` element. Place the single logout filter before our regular logout to ensure that it receives the logout events, as follows:

src/main/webapp/WEB-INF/spring/security.xml

```
<http ...>
    ...
  <custom-filter ref="casAuthenticationFilter"
    position="CAS_FILTER"/>
  <custom-filter ref="singleLogoutFilter"
    before="LOGOUT_FILTER"/>
  <logout logout-url="/logout"
    logout-success-url="https://${cas.server.host}/cas/logout"/>
</http>
```

Under normal circumstances, we would need to make a few updates to the web.xml file. However, for our Calendar application, we have already made the updates to our web.xml file, as follows:

src/main/webapp/WEB-INF/web.xml

```xml
<listener>
    <listener-class>
        org.jasig.cas.client.session.SingleSignOutHttpSessionListener
    </listener-class>
</listener>
<filter>
    <filter-name>characterEncodingFilter</filter-name>
    <filter-class>
        org.springframework.web.filter.CharacterEncodingFilter
    </filter-class>
    <init-param>
        <param-name>encoding</param-name>
        <param-value>UTF-8</param-value>
    </init-param>
</filter>
<filter-mapping>
    <filter-name>characterEncodingFilter</filter-name>
    <url-pattern>/*</url-pattern>
</filter-mapping>
```

First, we added the SingleSignoutHttpSessionListener object to ensure that the mapping of the Service Ticket to the HttpSession has been removed. We have also added the CharacterEncodingFilter, as recommended by the JA-SIG documentation, to ensure that character encoding is correct when using SingleSignOutFilter.

Go ahead and start up the application, and try logging out now. You will observe that you are actually logged out. Now, try logging back in and visiting the CAS Server's logout URL directly. For our setup, the URL is https://localhost:8443/cas/logout. Now try to visit the JBCP Calendar application. You will observe that you are unable to access the application without authenticating again. This demonstrates that a single logout works.

> Your code should look like chapter09.02-calendar and chapter09.02-cas-server.

# Clustered environments

One of the things that we failed to mention in our initial diagram of a single logout is how the logout is performed. Unfortunately, it is implemented by storing a mapping of the Service Ticket to the `HttpSession` in an in-memory map. This means that a single logout will not work properly within a clustered environment.

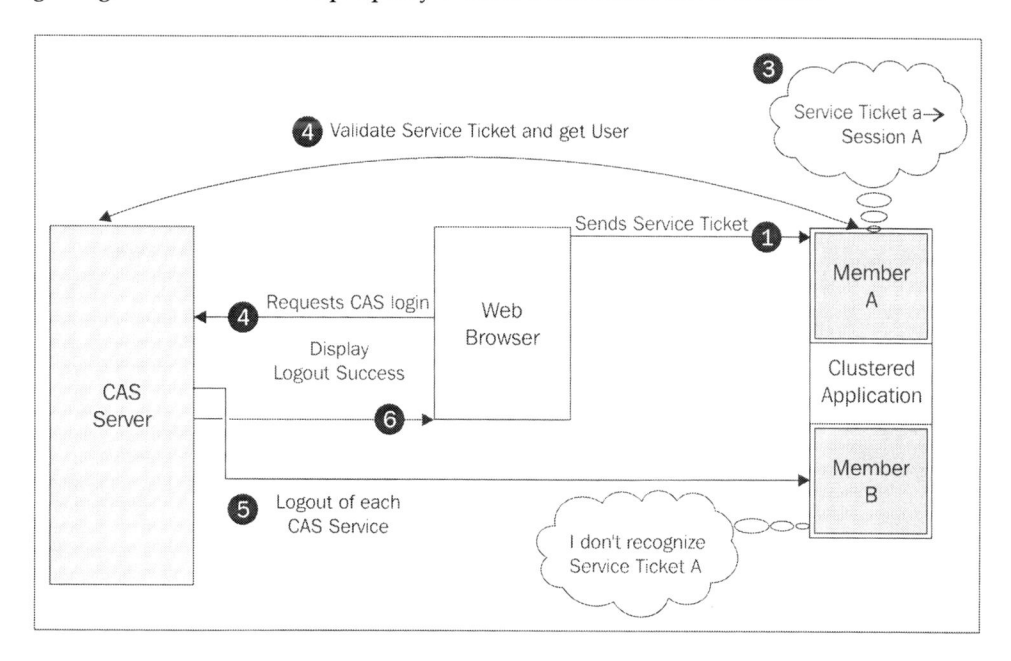

Consider the following situation:

1. The user logs into Cluster **Member A**.
2. Cluster **Member A** validates the Service Ticket.
3. It then remembers, in memory, the mapping of the Service Ticket to the user's session.
4. The user requests to log out from the CAS Server.
5. The CAS Server sends a logout request to the CAS Service, but the Cluster **Member B** receives the logout request. It looks in its memory, but does not find a session for **Service Ticket A**, because it only exists in Cluster **Member A**. This means the user has not been logged out successfully.

Users looking for this functionality might consider looking in the JA-SIG JIRA queue and forums for solutions to this problem. In fact, a working patch has been submitted on `https://issues.jasig.org/browse/CASC-114`. Keep in mind that there are a number of ongoing discussions and proposals on the forums and in the JA-SIG JIRA queue, so you may want to look around before deciding which solution to use. For more information about clustering with CAS, refer to JA-SIG's clustering documentation at `https://wiki.jasig.org/display/CASUM/Clustering+CAS`.

## Proxy ticket authentication for stateless services

Centralizing our authentication using CAS seems to work rather well for web applications, but what if we want to call a web service using CAS? In order to support this, CAS has a notion of **Proxy Tickets (PT)**. Following is a diagram of how it works:

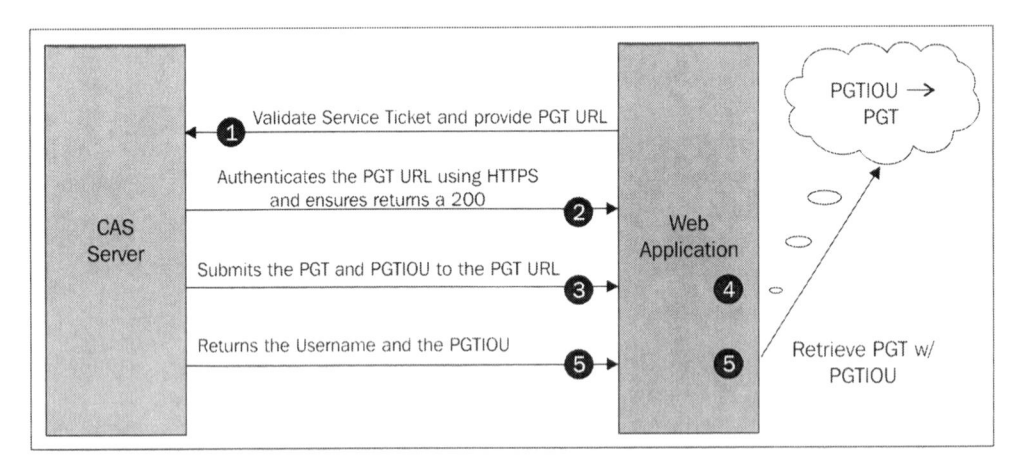

The flow is the same as standard CAS authentication, until the Service Ticket is validated when an additional parameter is included called the **Proxy Ticket callback URL (PGT URL)**.

1. The CAS Server calls the the PGT URL over HTTPS to validate that the PGT URL is what it claims to be. Like most of CAS, this is done by performing an SSL handshake to the appropriate URL.

2. The CAS Server submits the **Proxy Granting Ticket (PGT)** and the **Proxy Granting Ticket I Owe You (PGTIOU)** to the PGT URL over HTTPS to ensure that the tickets are submitted to the source they claim to be.

3. The PGT URL receives the two tickets and must store an association of the PGTIOU to the PGT.

[ 234 ]

4. The CAS Server finally returns a response to the request in step 1 that includes the username and the PGTIOU.
5. The CAS Service can look up the PGT using the PGTIOU.

## Configuring proxy ticket authentication

Now that we know how Proxy Ticket authentication works, we will make updates to our current configuration to obtain a Proxy Granting Ticket.

The first step is to add a reference to a `ProxyGrantingTicketStorage` implementation. Go ahead and add the following code to our `security-cas.xml` file.

src/main/webapp/WEB-INF/spring/security-cas.xml

```
<bean id="pgtStorage"
      class="org.jasig.cas.client.proxy.
ProxyGrantingTicketStorageImpl"/>
<task:scheduled-tasks>
    <task:scheduled ref="pgtStorage"
         method="cleanUp"
         fixed-delay="300000"/>
</task:scheduled-tasks>
</beans>
```

`ProxyGrantingTicketStorageImpl` is an in-memory mapping of the PGTIOU to a PGT. Just as with logging out, this means we would have problems in a clustered environment using this implementation. Refer to the JA-SIG documentation to determine how to set this up in a clustered environment:

https://wiki.jasig.org/display/CASUM/Clustering+CAS

We also need to periodically clean `ProxyGrantingTicketStorage` by invoking its `cleanUp()` method. As you can see, Spring's task abstraction makes this very simple. You may consider tweaking the configuration to clear a schedule, and with a thread pool that makes sense for your environment. For more information, refer to the *Task Execution and Scheduling* section of the Spring Framework reference documentation at http://static.springsource.org/spring/docs/3.1.x/spring-framework-reference/html/scheduling.html.

Now we need to use `ProxyGrantingTicketStorage` that we just created. We just need to update `ticketValidator` to refer to our storage and to know the PGT URL. Make the following updates to `security-cas.xml`:

src/main/webapp/WEB-INF/spring/security-cas.xml

```xml
<bean id="ticketValidator"
  class="org.jasig.cas.client.validation
  .Cas20ServiceTicketValidator">
  <constructor-arg value="https://${cas.server.host}/cas" />

  <property name="proxyCallbackUrl"
    value="https://${cas.service.host}/calendar/pgtUrl"/>
  <property name="proxyGrantingTicketStorage" ref="pgtStorage"/>
</bean>
```

The last update we need to make is to our `CasAuthenticationFilter` object to store the PGTIOU to the PGT mapping in our `ProxyGrantingTicketStorage` implementation when the PGT URL is called. It is critical to ensure that the `proxyReceptorUrl` attribute matches `proxyCallbackUrl` of the `Cas20ProxyTicketValidator` object, to ensure that the CAS Server sends the ticket to the URL that our application is listing to. Make the following changes to `security-cas.xml`:

src/main/webapp/WEB-INF/spring/security-cas.xml

```xml
<bean id="casFilter"
  class="org.springframework.security.cas.web
  .CasAuthenticationFilter">
  ...
  <property name="proxyGrantingTicketStorage" ref="pgtStorage"/>
  <property name="proxyReceptorUrl" value="/pgtUrl"/>
</bean>
```

> You will observe that the `proxyCallBackUrl` attribute matches the absolute path of our context-relative `proxyReceptorUrl` attribute path. Since we are deploying our base application to `https://${cas.serverice.host}/calendar`, the full path of our proxyReceptor URL will be `https://${cas.serverice.host}/calendar/pgtUrl`.

Now that we have a PGT, what do we do with it? A Service Ticket is a one-time use token. However, a PGT can be used to produce **Proxy Tickets (PT)**. Let's see how we can create a PT using a PGT.

## Using proxy tickets

We can now use our PGT to create a PT to authenticate it to a service. The code to do this is quite trivially demonstrated in the `EchoController` class that we included with this chapter. You can see the relevant portions of it in the following code snippet. For additional details, refer to the sample's source code.

src/main/java/com/packtpub/springsecurity/web/controllers/EchoController.java

```java
@ResponseBody
@RequestMapping("/echo")
public String echo() throws UnsupportedEncodingException {
   final CasAuthenticationToken token = (CasAuthenticationToken)
     SecurityContextHolder.getContext().getAuthentication();
   final String proxyTicket =
     token.getAssertion().getPrincipal()
     .getProxyTicketFor(targetUrl);
   return restClient.getForObject(targetUrl+"?ticket={pt}",
     String.class, proxyTicket);
}
```

This controller is a contrived example that will obtain a PT that will be used to authenticate a RESTful call to obtain all the events for the currently logged-in user. It then writes the JSON response to the page. The thing that may confuse some users is that the `EchoController` object is actually making a RESTful call to the `MessagesController` object that is in the same application. This means that the `Calendar` application makes a RESTful call to itself.

Go ahead and visit `https://localhost:8443/calendar/echo` to see it in action. The page looks a lot like the CAS login page (minus the `css`). This is because the controller attempts to echo our **My Events** page, and our application does not yet know how to authenticate a proxy ticket. This means it is redirected to the CAS login page. Let's see how we can authenticate proxy tickets.

> Your code should look like `chapter09.03-calendar` and `chapter09.03-cas-server`.

## Authenticating proxy tickets

We first need to instruct the `ServiceProperties` object that we want to authenticate all the tickets and not just those submitted to the `filterProcessesUrl` attribute. Make the following updates to `security-cas.xml`:

src/main/webapp/WEB-INF/spring/security-cas.xml

```xml
<bean id="serviceProperties"
      class="org.springframework.security.cas.ServiceProperties">
    ...
    <property name="authenticateAllArtifacts" value="true"/>
</bean>
```

We then need to update our `CasAuthenticationFilter` object for it to know that we want to authenticate all artifacts (that is, tickets) instead of only listening to a specific URL. We also need to use an `AuthenticationDetailsSource` that can dynamically provide the CAS Service URL when validating proxy tickets on arbitrary URLs. This is important because when a CAS Service asks whether a ticket is valid or not, it must also provide the CAS Service URL that was used to create the ticket. Since Proxy Tickets can occur on any URL, we must be able to dynamically discover this URL. This is done by leveraging the `ServiceAuthenticationDetailsSource` object, which will provide the current URL from the HTTP request.

src/main/webapp/WEB-INF/spring/security-cas.xml

```xml
<bean id="casFilter"
  class="org.springframework.security.cas.web
  .CasAuthenticationFilter">
  ...
  <property name="serviceProperties" ref="serviceProperties"/>
  <property name="authenticationDetailsSource">
    <bean class="org.springframework.security.cas
      .web.authentication.ServiceAuthenticationDetailsSource"/>
  </property>
</bean>
```

We will also need to ensure that we are using the `Cas20ProxyTicketValidator` object and not the `Cas20ServiceTicketValidator`, and indicate which proxy tickets we will want to accept. We will configure ours to accept a proxy ticket from any CAS Service. In a production environment, you will want to consider restricting yourself to only those CAS Services that are trusted.

src/main/webapp/WEB-INF/spring/security-cas.xml

```xml
<bean id="ticketValidator" class="org.jasig.cas.client
  .validation.Cas20ProxyTicketValidator">
  ...
  <property name="acceptAnyProxy" value="true"/>
</bean>
```

Lastly, we will want to provide a cache for our `CasAuthenticationProvider` object so that we do not need to hit the CAS Service for every call to our service.

src/main/webapp/WEB-INF/spring/security-cas.xml

```xml
<bean id="casAuthProvider" class="org.springframework.security.
  cas.authentication.CasAuthenticationProvider">
  ...
  <property name="statelessTicketCache"
    ref="statelessTicketCache"/>
</bean>
<bean id="statelessTicketCache" class="org.springframework
  .security.cas.authentication.EhCacheBasedTicketCache">
  <property name="cache">
    <bean class="net.sf.ehcache.Cache"
      init-method="initialise" destroy-method="dispose">
      <constructor-arg value="casTickets"/>
      <constructor-arg value="50"/>
      <constructor-arg value="true"/>
      <constructor-arg value="false"/>
      <constructor-arg value="3600"/>
      <constructor-arg value="900"/>
    </bean>
  </property>
</bean>
```

As you might have suspected, the cache requires the `ehcache` dependency that we mentioned at the beginning of the chapter. Go ahead and start the application back up and visit `https://localhost:8443/calendar/echo` again. This time you should see a JSON response of calling our **My Events** page.

> Your code should look like `chapter09.04-calendar` and `chapter09.04-cas-server`.

# Customizing the CAS Server

All of the changes in this section will be to the CAS Server and NOT the `Calendar` application. This section is only meant to be an introduction to configuring the CAS Server, as a detailed setup is certainly beyond the scope of this book. Just as with the changes for the `Calendar` application, we encourage you to follow along with the changes in this chapter. For more information, you can refer to the JA-SIG CAS wiki at `https://wiki.jasig.org/display/CAS/Home`.

## CAS Maven WAR Overlay

The preferred way to customize CAS is to use a Maven War Overlay. With this mechanism, you can change everything from the UI to the method in which you authenticate to the CAS Server. The concept of a WAR overlay is simple. You add a WAR overlay, `cas-server-webapp`, as a Maven dependency, and then provide additional files that will be merged with the existing WAR overlay. For more information about the CAS Maven WAR Overlay, refer to the JA-SIG documentation at `https://wiki.jasig.org/display/CASUM/Best+Practice+-+Setting+Up+CAS+Locally+using+the+Maven2+WAR+Overlay+Method`.

# How CAS internal authentication works

Before we jump into CAS configuration, we'll briefly illustrate the standard behavior of the CAS authentication processing. The following diagram should help you follow the configuration steps required to allow CAS to talk to our embedded LDAP server:

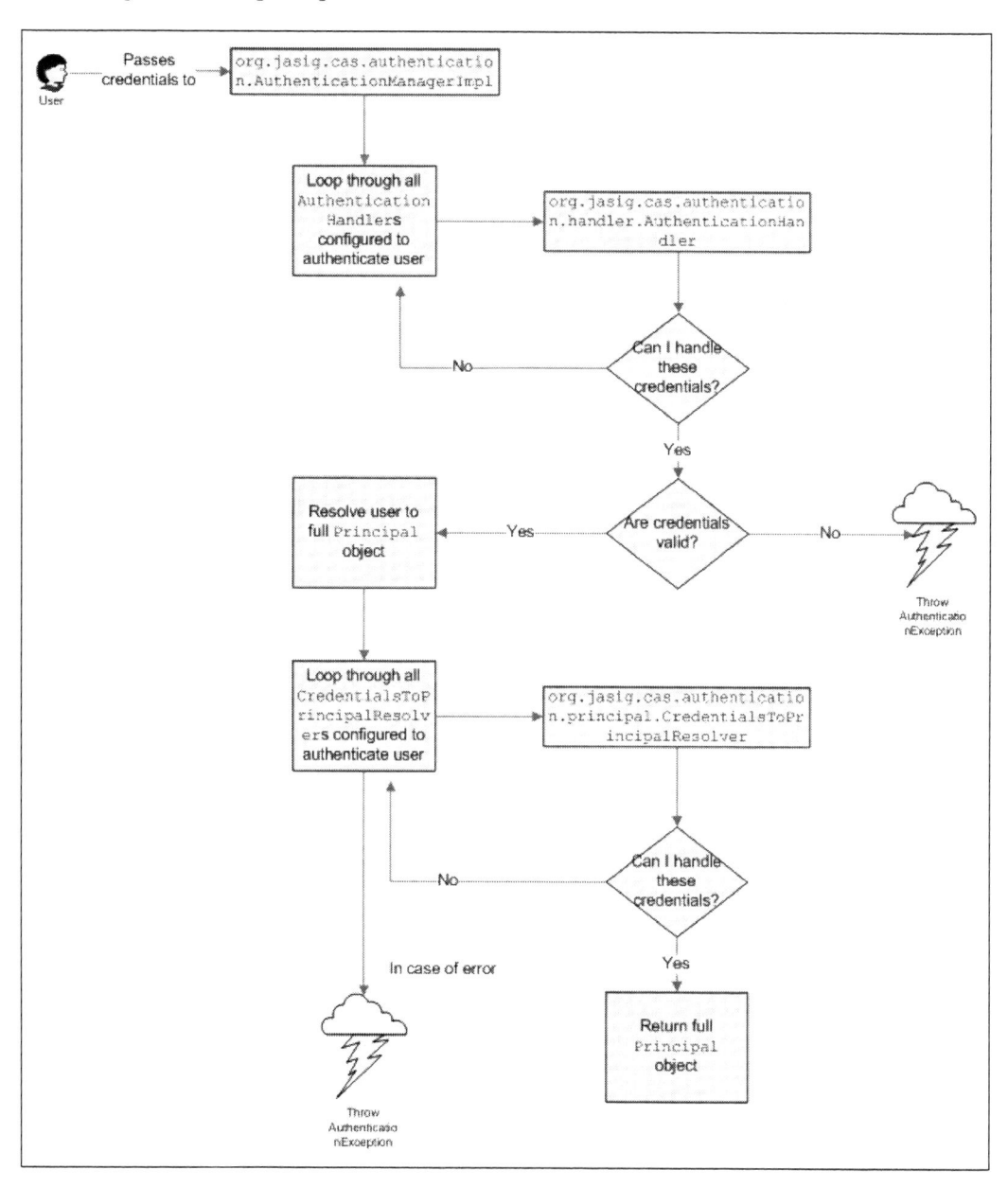

While the previous diagram describes the internal flow of authentication within the CAS server itself, it is likely that if you are implementing integration between Spring Security and CAS, you will need to adjust the configuration of the CAS server as well. It's important, therefore, that you understand how CAS authentication works at a high level.

The CAS server's `org.jasig.cas.authentication.AuthenticationManager` interface (not to be confused with the Spring Security interface of the same name) is responsible for authenticating the user based on the provided credentials. Much as with Spring Security, the actual processing of the credentials is delegated to one (or more) processing class implementing the `org.jasig.cas.authentication.handler.AuthenticationHandler` interface (we recognize that the analogous interface in Spring Security would be `AuthenticationProvider`).

Finally, a `org.jasig.cas.authentication.principal.CredentialsToPrincipalResolver` interface is used to translate the credentials passed into a full `org.jasig.cas.authentication.principal.Principal` object (similar behavior in Spring Security occurs during the implementation of `UserDetailsService`).

While not a full review of the behind-the-scenes functionality of the CAS server, this should help you understand the configuration steps in the next several exercises. We encourage you to read the source code for CAS and consult the web-based documentation available at the JA-SIG CAS wiki, at http://www.ja-sig.org/wiki/display/CAS.

## Configuring CAS to connect to our embedded LDAP server

The `org.jasig.cas.authentication.principal.UsernamePasswordCredentialsToPrincipalResolver` object that comes configured, by default, with CAS doesn't allow us to pass back attribute information and demonstrate this feature of Spring Security CAS integration, so we'd suggest using an implementation that does allow this.

An easy authentication handler to configure and use (especially if you have gone through the previous chapter's LDAP exercises) is `org.jasig.cas.adaptors.ldap.BindLdapAuthenticationHandler`, which communicates with the embedded LDAP server that we used in the previous chapter. We'll lead you through the configuration of CAS that returns user LDAP attributes in the following guide.

All of the CAS configuration will take place in the `WEB-INF/deployerConfigContext.xml` file of the CAS installation, and will typically involve inserting class declarations into configuration file segments that already exist. We have already extracted the default `WEB-INF/deployerConfigContext.xml` file from `cas-server-webapp` and placed it in `cas-server/src/main/webapp/WEB-INF`.

If the contents of this file look familiar to you, it's because CAS uses the Spring Framework for its configuration just like JBCP Calendar! We'd recommend using a good IDE with a handy reference to the CAS source code if you want to dig into what these configuration settings do. Remember that in this section, and all sections where we refer to `WEB-INF/deployerConfigContext.xml`, we are referring to the CAS installation and not JBCP Calendar.

First, we'll add a new `BindLdapAuthenticationHandler` object in place of the `SimpleTestUsernamePasswordAuthenticationHandler` object, which will attempt to bind the user to LDAP (just as we did in *Chapter 5, LDAP Directory Services*).

The `AuthenticationHandler` interface will be placed in the `authenticationHandlers` property of the `authenticationManager` bean:

`cas-server/src/main/webapp/WEB-INF/deployerConfigContext.xml`

```xml
<property name="authenticationHandlers">
  <list>
    ... remove ONLY
      SimpleTestUsernamePasswordAuthenticationHandler ...
    <bean class="org.jasig.cas.adaptors
      .ldap.BindLdapAuthenticationHandler">
      <property name="filter" value="uid=%u"/>
      <property name="searchBase" value="ou=Users"/>
      <property name="contextSource" ref="contextSource"/>
    </bean>
  </list>
</property>
```

> Don't forget to remove the reference to the `SimpleTestUsernamePasswordAuthenticationHandler` object, or at least move its definition to after that of the `BindLdapAuthenticationHandler` object, otherwise your CAS authentication will not use LDAP and use the stub handler instead!

*Single Sign-on with Central Authentication Service*

You'll note the bean reference to a `contextSource` bean; this defines the `org.springframework.ldap.core.ContextSource` implementation, which CAS will use to interact with LDAP (yes, CAS uses Spring LDAP as well). We'll define this at the end of the file, using the Spring Security namespace to simplify its definition:

cas-server/src/main/webapp/WEB-INF/deployerConfigContext.xml

```xml
    <sec:ldap-server id="contextSource"
            ldif="classpath:ldif/calendar.ldif"
            root="dc=jbcpcalendar,dc=com" />
</beans>
```

This creates an embedded LDAP instance that uses the `calendar.ldif` file included with this chapter. Of course in a production environment, you would want to point to a real LDAP server.

Finally, we'll need to configure a new `org.jasig.cas.authentication.principal.CredentialsToPrincipalResolver`, that is responsible for translating the credentials that the user has provided (that CAS has already authenticated using the `BindLdapAuthenticationHandler` object) to a full `org.jasig.cas.authentication.principal.Principal` authenticated principal. You'll notice many configuration options in this class, which we'll skim over, that you are welcome to dive into as you explore CAS further.

Remove `UsernamePasswordCredentialsToPrincipalResolver` and add the following bean definition inline to the `credentialsToPrincipalResolvers` property of the CAS `authenticationManager` bean:

cas-server/src/main/webapp/WEB-INF/deployerConfigContext.xml

```xml
    <property name="credentialsToPrincipalResolvers">
      <list>
      <!-- REMOVE UsernamePasswordCredentialsToPrincipalResolver -->
        <bean class="org.jasig.cas.authentication.principal
          .HttpBasedServiceCredentialsToPrincipalResolver" />
        <bean class="org.jasig.cas.authentication.principal
          .CredentialsToLDAPAttributePrincipalResolver">
          <property name="credentialsToPrincipalResolver">
            <bean class="org.jasig.cas.authentication.principal
              .UsernamePasswordCredentialsToPrincipalResolver"/>
          </property>
          <property name="filter" value="(uid=%u)"/>
          <property name="principalAttributeName" value="uid"/>
          <property name="searchBase" value="ou=Users"/>
          <property name="contextSource" ref="contextSource"/>
          <property name="attributeRepository"
```

```
            ref="attributeRepository"/>
        </bean>
    </list>
</property>
```

You'll notice that as with Spring Security LDAP configuration, much of the same behavior exists in CAS with principals being searched on property matches below a subtree of the directory, based on a DN.

Note that we haven't yet configured the bean with the ID attributeRepository ourselves, which should refer to an implementation of org.jasig.services.persondir.IPersonAttributeDao. CAS ships with a default configuration that includes a simple implementation of this interface, org.jasig.services.persondir.support.StubPersonAttributeDao, which will be sufficient until we configure LDAP-based attributes in a later exercise.

> Your code should look like chapter09.05-calendar and chapter09.05-cas-server.

So now we've configured basic LDAP authentication in CAS. At this point, you should be able to restart CAS, start JBCP Calendar (if it's not already running), and authenticate it using admin1@example.com/admin or user1@example.com/user1. Go ahead and try it to see that it works. If it does not work, try checking the logs and comparing your configuration with the sample configuration.

> Just as discussed in *Chapter 5, LDAP Directory Services* you may encounter issues with starting the application whether the temporary directory named apacheds-spring-security still exists. If the application appears to not exist, check the logs and see if the apacheds-spring-security directory needs to be removed.

# Getting UserDetails from a CAS assertion

Up until this point we have been authenticating with CAS, but by obtaining the roles from our InMemoryUserDetailsManager object. However, we can create the UserDetails from the CAS assertion just as we did with OpenID. The first step is to configure the CAS Server to return the additional attributes.

# Returning LDAP attributes in the CAS Response

We know that CAS can return the username in the CAS Response, but it it can also return arbitrary attributes in the CAS Response. Let's see how we can update the CAS Server to return additional attributes. Again, all the changes in this section are in the CAS Server and NOT in the `Calendar` application.

## Mapping LDAP attributes to CAS attributes

The first step requires us to map LDAP attributes to attributes in the CAS assertion (including the `role` attribute in which we're expecting to contain the user's `GrantedAuthority`).

We'll add another bit of configuration to the `CAS deployerConfigContext.xml` file. This new bit of configuration is required to instruct CAS on how to map attributes from the CAS `Principal` object to the CAS `IPersonAttributes` object, which will ultimately be serialized as a part of ticket validation. This bean configuration should replace the bean of the same name, which is `attributeRepository`.

cas-server/src/main/webapp/WEB-INF/deployerConfigContext.xml

```xml
<bean id="attributeRepository" class="org.jasig.services.persondir
  .support.ldap.LdapPersonAttributeDao">
  <property name="contextSource" ref="contextSource"/>
  <property name="requireAllQueryAttributes" value="true"/>
  <property name="baseDN" value="ou=Users"/>
  <property name="queryAttributeMapping">
    <map>
      <entry key="username" value="uid"/>
    </map>
  </property>
  <property name="resultAttributeMapping">
    <map>
      <entry key="cn" value="FullName"/>
      <entry key="sn" value="LastName"/>
      <entry key="description" value="role"/>
    </map>
  </property>
</bean>
```

The functionality behind the scenes here is definitely confusing—essentially, the purpose of this class is to map `Principal` back to the LDAP directory. (This is the `queryAttributeMapping` property mapping the `username` field of `Principal` to the `uid` attribute in the LDAP query.) The provided `baseDN` Java Bean property is searched using the LDAP query (`uid=user1@example.com`), and attributes are read from the matching entry. The attributes are mapped back to `Principal` using the key/value pairs in the `resultAttributeMapping` property—we recognize that LDAP's `cn` and `sn` attributes are being mapped to meaningful names, and the `description` attribute is being mapped to the role that will be used for determining the authorization of our user.

Part of the complexity comes from the fact that a portion of this functionality is wrapped up in a separate project called **Person Directory** (http://www.ja-sig.org/wiki/display/PD/Home), which is intended to aggregate multiple sources of information about a person into a single view. The design of Person Directory is such that it is not directly tied to the CAS Server and can be re-used as part of other applications. The downside of this design choice is that it makes some aspects of CAS configuration more complex than it initially seems should be required.

> **Troubleshooting LDAP attribute mapping in CAS**
>
> We would love to set up the same type of query in LDAP as we used with Spring Security LDAP in *Chapter 5, LDAP Directory Services* to be able to map `Principal` to a full LDAP-distinguished name, and then to use that DN to look up group membership by matching on the basis of the `uniqueMember` attribute of a `groupOfUniqueNames` entry. Unfortunately, the CAS LDAP code doesn't have this flexibility yet, leading to the conclusion that more advanced LDAP mapping will require extensions to base classes in CAS.

## Authorizing CAS Services to access custom attributes

Next, we will need to authorize any CAS Service over HTTPS to access these attributes. To do this, we can update `RegisteredServiceImpl` that has the description "Only Allows HTTPS URLs" in `InMemoryServiceRegistryDaoImpl`, as follows:

```
cas-server/src/main/webapp/WEB-INF/deployerConfigContext.xml

    <bean class="org.jasig.cas.services.RegisteredServiceImpl">

        <property name="id" value="1" />
        <property name="name" value="HTTPS" />
        <property name="description" value="Only Allows HTTPS Urls" />
        <property name="serviceId" value="https://**" />
```

```xml
        <property name="evaluationOrder" value="10000002" />
        <property name="allowedAttributes">
            <list>
                <value>FullName</value>
                <value>LastName</value>
                <value>role</value>
            </list>
        </property>
    </bean>
```

## Getting UserDetails from a CAS assertion

When we first set up CAS integration with Spring Security, we configured a `UserDetailsByNameServiceWrapper` that simply translated the username presented to CAS into a `UserDetails` object from `UserDetailsService` that we had referenced (in our case, it was `InMemoryUserDetailsManager`). Now that CAS is referencing the LDAP server, we could set up `LdapUserDetailsService` as we discussed at the tail end of *Chapter 5, LDAP Directory Services* and things would work just fine. Note that we have switched back to modifying the `Calendar` application and NOT the CAS Server.

## GrantedAuthorityFromAssertionAttributesUser Details Service

Now that we have modified the CAS server to return custom attributes, we'll experiment with another capability of the Spring Security CAS integration, the ability to populate a `UserDetails` from the CAS assertion itself! This is actually as simple as switching the `AuthenticationUserDetailsService` implementation to the `o.s.s.cas.userdetails.GrantedAuthorityFromAssertionAttributesUserDetailsService` object, whose job it is to read the CAS assertion, look for a certain attribute, and map the value of that attribute directly to `GrantedAuthority` for the user. Let's assume that there is an attribute entitled `role` that will be returned with the assertion. We'll simply configure a new `authenticationUserDetailsService` bean (ensure to replace the previously defined `authenticationUserDetailsService` bean) in `security-cas.xml`:

src/main/webapp/WEB-INF/spring/security-cas.xml

```xml
    <bean id="authenticationUserDetailsService" class=
      "org.springframework.security.cas.userdetails
      .GrantedAuthorityFromAssertionAttributesUserDetailsService">
        <constructor-arg>
            <array>
                <value>role</value>
            </array>
        </constructor-arg>
    </bean>
```

You will also want to remove the `userDetailsService` bean from our `security.xml` file since it is no longer needed.

## Alternative ticket authentication using SAML 1.1

**Security Assertion Markup Language** (**SAML**) is a standard, cross-platform protocol for identity verification through structured XML assertions. SAML is supported by a wide variety of products, including CAS. (In fact, we will look at support for SAML within Spring Security itself in a later chapter.)

While the standard CAS protocol can be extended to return attributes, the SAML security assertion XML dialect solves some of the issues with attribute passing, using the CAS response protocol that we previously described. Happily, switching between CAS ticket validation and SAML ticket validation is as simple as changing the `TicketValidator` implementation configured in `security-cas.xml`. Modify `ticketValidator` as follows:

src/main/webapp/WEB-INF/spring/security-cas.xml

```
<bean id="ticketValidator" class="org.jasig.cas.client.validation
  .Saml11TicketValidator">
  <constructor-arg value="https://${cas.server.host}/cas" />
</bean>
```

You will notice that there is no longer a reference to the PGT URL. This is because the `Saml11TicketValidator` object does not support PGT. While both could exist, we opt to remove any references to the Proxy Ticket authentication since we will no longer be using Proxy Ticket authentication. If you do not want to remove it for this exercise, don't worry; it won't prevent our application from running so long as your `ticketValidator` bean ID looks similar to the previous code snippet.

In general, it's recommended that SAML ticket validation be used over CAS 2.0 ticket validation, as it adds more non-repudiation features, including timestamp validation, and solves the attribute problem in a standard way.

Restart the CAS Server and JBCP Calendar application. You can then visit `https://localhost:8443/calendar/` and see that our calendar application can obtain the `UserDetails` from the CAS response.

> Your code should now look like `chapter09.06-calendar` and `chapter09.06-cas-server`.

# How is attribute retrieval useful

Remember that CAS provides a layer of abstraction for our application, removing the ability for our application to directly access the user repository, and instead forcing all such access to be performed through CAS as a proxy.

This is extremely powerful! It means that our application no longer cares what kind of repository the users are stored in, nor does it have to worry about the details of how to access them—this simply confirms that authentication with CAS is sufficient to prove that a user should be able to access our application. For system administrators, this means that should an LDAP server be renamed, moved, or otherwise adjusted, they only need to reconfigure it in a single location—CAS. Centralizing access through CAS allows for a high level of flexibility and adaptability in the overall security architecture of the organization.

Extend this story to the usefulness of attribute retrieval from CAS; now all applications authenticated through CAS have the same view of a user and can consistently display information across any CAS-enabled environment.

Be aware that, once authenticated, Spring Security CAS does not requery the CAS server unless the user is required to reauthenticate. This means that attributes and other user information stored locally in the application in the user's `Authentication` object may become stale over time and possibly out of sync with the source CAS server. Take care to set session timeouts appropriately to avoid this potential issue!

# Additional CAS capabilities

CAS offers additional advanced configuration capabilities outside of those that are exposed through the Spring Security CAS wrappers. Some of these include the following:

- Providing transparent single sign-on for users who are accessing multiple CAS-secured applications within a configurable (on the CAS server) time window. Applications can force users to authenticate to CAS by setting the `renew` property to `true` on the `TicketValidator`; you may want to conditionally set this property in custom code in the event where the user is attempting to access a highly secured area of the application.
- RESTful API for obtaining Service Tickets.
- JA-SIG's CAS Server can also act as an OpenID server. If you think about it, this makes sense since CAS is very similar to OpenID.
- Provide OAuth support for the CAS server, so that it can obtain access tokens to a delegate OAuth provider (that is, Google) or so that the CAS Server can be the OAuth server itself.

We'd encourage you to explore the full capabilities of the CAS client and server as well as ask questions to the helpful folks in the JA-SIG community forums!

## Summary

In this chapter, we learned about the **Central Authentication System** (**CAS**) single sign-on portal and how it can be integrated with Spring Security, and we also covered the following:

- The CAS architecture and communication paths between actors in a CAS-enabled environment
- The benefits of CAS-enabled applications for application developers and system administrators
- Configuring JBCP Calendar to interact with a basic CAS installation
- How to use CAS's Single Logout support
- How proxy ticket authentication works and how to leverage it to authenticate to stateless services
- Updating CAS to interact with LDAP, and sharing LDAP data with our CAS-enabled application
- Implementing attribute exchange with the industry standard SAML protocol

We hope this chapter was an interesting introduction to the world of single sign-on. There are many other single sign-on systems in the marketplace, mostly commercial, but CAS is definitely one of the leaders of the open source SSO world and an excellent platform to build out SSO capability in any organization.

In the next chapter, we'll learn more about Spring Security authorization.

# 10
# Fine-grained Access Control

Up to this point, we've explored different ways of authenticating users to the JBCP Calendar site. Now that we know who the user is, we are going to use that information to determine if the user is allowed (authorized), to access resources at a more granular level.

In this chapter, we will first examine two ways to implement **fine-grained authorization**—authorization that may affect portions of a page of the application. Next, we will look at Spring Security's approach for securing the business tier through method annotation and the use of interface-based proxies to accomplish aspect-oriented programming. Then, we will review an interesting capability of annotation-based security that allows for role-based filtering on collections of data. Last, we will look at how class-based proxies differ from interface-based proxies.

During the course of this chapter, we'll learn the following:

- Configuring and experimenting with different methods of performing in-page authorization checks on content, given the security context of a user request
- Performing configuration and code annotation to make caller preauthorization a key part of our application's business-tier security
- Several alternative approaches to implement method-level security, and review the pros and cons of each type
- Implementing data-based filters on collections and arrays using method-level annotations
- Implementing method-level security on our Spring MVC controllers to avoid configuring `<intercept-url>` elements

## Maven dependencies

There are a number of optional dependencies that may be required depending on what features you decide to use. You will find that our pom.xml file already includes all of the following dependencies:

pom.xml

```xml
<!-- Required for class based proxy support -->
<dependency>
    <groupId>cglib</groupId>
    <artifactId>cglib-nodep</artifactId>
    <version>2.2.2</version>
    <scope>runtime</scope>
</dependency>
<!-- Required for JSR-250 based security -->
<dependency>
    <groupId>javax.annotation</groupId>
    <artifactId>jsr250-api</artifactId>
    <version>1.0</version>
</dependency>
<!-- Required for protect-pointcut -->
<dependency>
    <groupId>org.aspectj</groupId>
    <artifactId>aspectjweaver</artifactId>
    <version>1.6.12</version>
    <scope>runtime</scope>
</dependency>
```

## Spring Expression Language (SpEL) integration

Spring Security leverages the **Spring Expression Language (SpEL)** in order to easily articulate various authorization requirements. If you recall, we have already seen the use of SpEL in *Chapter 2, Getting Started with Spring Security*, when we defined our <intercept-url> elements.

```xml
<intercept-url pattern="/events/"
    access="hasRole('ROLE_ADMIN')"/>
```

Spring Security provides a `o.s.s.access.expression.SecurityExpressionRoot` object that provides the methods and objects available for use, in order to make an access control decision. For example, one of the methods available for use is `hasRole`, which accepts a string. This corresponds to the value of the `access` attribute (in the preceding code snippet). In fact, there are a number of other expressions available, as shown in the following table:

| Expression | Description |
| --- | --- |
| `hasRole(String role)` `hasAuthority(String role)` | Returns `true` if the current user has the specified authority. |
| `hasAnyRole(String... role)` `hasAnyAuthority(String... authority)` | Returns `true` if the current user has any of the specified authorities. |
| `principal` | Allows access to the current `Authentication` object's `principal` attribute. As discussed in *Chapter 3, Custom Authentication*, this will often be an instance of `UserDetails`. |
| `authentication` | Obtains the current `Authentication` object from the `SecurityContext` interface returned by the `getContext()` method of the `SecurityContextHolder` class. |
| `permitAll` | Always returns `true`. |
| `denyAll` | Always returns `false`. |
| `isAnonymous()` | Returns `true` if the current principal is anonymous (is not authenticated). |
| `isRememberMe()` | Returns `true` if the current principal was authenticated using the remember me feature. |
| `isAuthenticated()` | Returns `true` if the user is not an anonymous user (that is, they are authenticated). |
| `isFullyAuthenticated()` | Returns `true` if the user is authenticated through a means other than remember me. |
| `hasPermission(`<br>`    Object target,`<br>`    Object permission)` | Returns `true` if the user has permission to access the specified object for the given permission. |
| `hasPermission(`<br>`    String targetId,`<br>`    String targetType,`<br>`    Object permission)` | Returns `true` if the user has permission to access the specified identifier for a given type and permission. |

# Fine-grained Access Control

We have provided some examples of using these SpEL expressions in the following code snippet. Keep in mind that we will go into more detail throughout this and the next chapter.

```
// allow users with ROLE_ADMIN
hasRole('ROLE_ADMIN')

// allow users that do not have the ROLE_ADMIN
!hasRole('ROLE_ADMIN')

// allow users that have ROLE_ADMIN or ROLE_ROOT and
// did not use the remember me feature to login
fullyAuthenticated and hasAnyRole('ROLE_ADMIN','ROLE_ROOT')

// allow if Authentication.getName() equals admin
authentication.name == 'admin'
```

## WebSecurityExpressionRoot

The `o.s.s.web.access.expression.WebSecurityExpressionRoot` class makes a few additional properties available to us. These properties, along with the standard properties already mentioned, are made available in the `access` attribute of the `<intercept-url>` tag and in the JSP `access` attribute of the `<sec:authorize>` tag, as we will discuss shortly.

| Expression | Description |
| --- | --- |
| request | The current `HttpServletRequest`. |
| hasIpAddress(String... ipAddress) | Returns `true` if the current IP address matches the `ipAddress` value. This can be an exact IP Address or the IP address/network mask. |

## Using the request attribute

The `request` attribute is fairly self-explanatory, but we have provided a few examples in the following section. Remember, any of these examples could be placed in the `<intercept-url>` element's `access` attribute or the `<sec:authorize>` element's `access` attribute.

```
// allows only HTTP GET
request.method == 'GET'

// allow anyone to perform a GET, but
// other methods require ROLE_ADMIN
request.method == 'GET' ? permitAll : hasRole('ROLE_ADMIN')
```

## Using hasIpAddress

The `hasIpAddress` method is not quite as clear cut as the `request` attribute. The most obvious support is an exact match; for example, the following code would allow access if the current user's IP address was `192.168.1.93`.

```
hasIpAddress('192.168.1.93')
```

However, this is not all that useful. Instead, we can define the following code, which would also match our IP address and any other IP address in our subnet.

```
hasIpAddress('192.168.1.0/24')
```

The question is, how is this calculated? The key is to understand how to calculate the network address and its mask. To learn how to do this, we can take a look at a concrete example. We launch `ifconfig` from our Linux terminal to view our network information (Windows users can use enter `ipconfig /ALL` into the command prompt).

```
$ ifconfig
wlan0     Link encap:Ethernet   HWaddr a0:88:b4:8b:26:64
          inet addr:192.168.1.93  Bcast:192.168.1.255  Mask:255.255.255.0
```

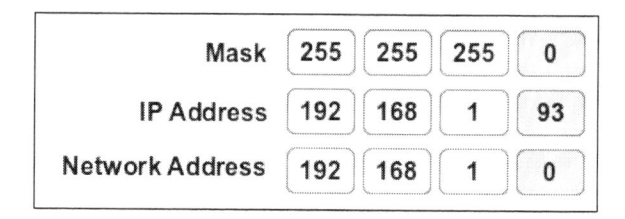

| | | | | |
|---|---|---|---|---|
| Mask | 255 | 255 | 255 | 0 |
| IP Address | 192 | 168 | 1 | 93 |
| Network Address | 192 | 168 | 1 | 0 |

We see that the first three octets of our mask are `255`. This means that the first three octets of our IP address belong to the network address. In our calculation, this means the remaining octets are `0`.

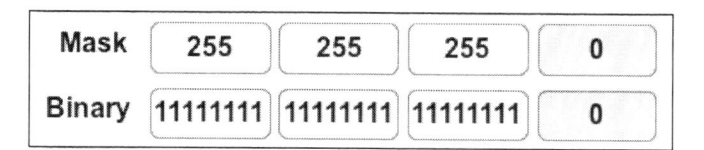

| | | | | |
|---|---|---|---|---|
| Mask | 255 | 255 | 255 | 0 |
| Binary | 11111111 | 11111111 | 11111111 | 0 |

We can then calculate the mask by first transforming each octet into a binary number, and then count how many ones there are. In our instance, we get `24`.

This means our IP address will match `192.168.1.0/24`. A good site for additional information on netmasks is Cisco's documentation, available at http://www.cisco.com/en/US/tech/tk365/technologies_tech_note09186a00800a67f5.shtml.

## MethodSecurityExpressionRoot

Method SpEL expressions also provide a few additional properties that can be used through the `o.s.s.access.expression.method.MethodSecurityExpressionRoot` class.

| Expression | Description |
| --- | --- |
| `target` | Refers to "this" or the current object being secured. |
| `returnObject` | Refers to the object returned by the annotated method. |
| `filterObject` | Can be used on a collection or array in conjunction with `@PreFilter` or `@PostFilter`, to only include the elements that match the expression. `filterObject` represents the loop variable of the collection or array. |
| `#<methodArg>` | Any argument to a method can be referenced by prefixing the argument name with `#`. For example, a method argument named `id` can be referred to using `#id`. |

If the description of these expressions appears a bit brief, don't worry; we'll work through a number of examples later in this chapter.

We hope that you have a decent grasp of the power of Spring Security's SpEL support. To learn more about SpEL, refer to the Spring reference documentation at `http://static.springsource.org/spring/docs/3.1.x/spring-framework-reference/html/`.

## Page-level authorization

**Page-level authorization** refers to the availability of application features based on the context of a particular user's request. Unlike coarse-grained authorization that we explored in *Chapter 2, Getting Started with Spring Security*, fine-grained authorization typically refers to the selective availability of the portions of a page, rather than restricting access to a page entirely. Most real-world applications will spend a considerable amount of time with the details of fine-grained authorization planning.

Spring Security provides us with two methods of selective display of functionality:

- Spring Security JSP Tag Libraries allow conditional access declarations to be placed within a page declaration itself, using the standard JSP tag library syntax.
- Checking user authorization in an MVC application's controller layer allows the controller to make an access decision and bind the results of the decision to the model data provided to the view. This approach relies on standard JSTL conditional page rendering and data binding, and is slightly more complicated than Spring Security tag libraries; however, it is more in line with the standard web application MVC logical design.

Any of these approaches is perfectly valid when developing fine-grained authorization models for a web application. Let's explore how each approach is implemented through a JBCP Calendar use case.

# Conditional rendering with Spring Security tag library

The most common functionality used in the Spring Security tag library is to conditionally render portions of the page based on authorization rules. This is done with the `<authorize>` tag that functions similarly to the `<if>` tag in the core JSTL library, in that the tag's body will render depending on the conditions provided in the tag attributes. We have already seen a very brief demonstration of how the Spring Security tag library can be used to restrict the viewing of content if the user is not logged in.

## Conditional rendering based on URL access rules

The Spring Security tag library provides functionality to render content based on the existing URL authorization rules that are already defined in the security configuration file. This is done by the use of the `<authorize>` tag with the `url` attribute.

> If there are multiple `<http>` elements, the `<authorize>` tag uses the currently matched `<http>` element's rules.

For example, we could ensure that the **All Events** link is displayed only when appropriate, that is, for users who are administrators—recall that the access rules we've previously defined are as follows:

```
<intercept-url pattern="/events/"
    access="hasRole('ROLE_ADMIN')"/>
```

# Fine-grained Access Control

Update our `header.jsp` file to utilize this information to conditionally render the link to the **All Events** page:

> You should start with the code from `chapter10.00-calendar`.

src/main/webapp/WEB-INF/views/includes/header.jsp

```
<%@ taglib prefix="sec" uri="http://www.springframework.org/security/
tags" %>
...
<c:url var="eventsUrl" value="/events/" />
<sec:authorize url="${eventsUrl}">
    <li><a id="navEventsLink" href="${eventsUrl}">All Events</a></li>
</sec:authorize>
```

This will ensure that the content of the tag is not displayed unless the user has sufficient privileges to access the stated URL. It is possible to further qualify the authorization check by the HTTP method, by including the `method` attribute:

```
<c:url var="eventsUrl" value="/events/" />
<sec:authorize url="${eventsUrl}"
        method="GET">
    <li><a id="navEventsLink" href="${eventsUrl}">All Events</a></li>
</sec:authorize>
```

Using the `url` attribute to define authorization checks on blocks of code is convenient, because it abstracts knowledge of the actual authorization checks from your JSPs and keeps them in your security configuration file.

Be aware that the HTTP method should match the case specified in your security `<intercept-url>` declarations, otherwise they may not match as you expect. Also, note that the URL should always be relative to the web application context root (as your URL access rules are).

For many purposes, the use of the `<authorize>` tag's `url` attribute will suffice to correctly display link- or action-related content only when the user is allowed to see it. Remember that the tag need not only surround a link, but it could even surround a whole form if the user doesn't have permission to submit it.

# Conditional rendering using SpEL

An additional, more flexible method of controlling the display of JSP content is available when the `<authorize>` tag is used in conjunction with a SpEL expression. Let's review what we learned in *Chapter 2, Getting Started with Spring Security*. We could hide the **My Events** link from any unauthenticated users by changing our `header.jsp` file as follows:

src/main/webapp/WEB-INF/views/includes/header.jsp

```
<sec:authorize access="authenticated">
    <c:url var="myEventsUrl" value="/events/my" />
    <li><a id="navMyEventsLink" href="${myEventsUrl}">My Events</a></li>
</sec:authorize>
```

The SpEL evaluation is performed by the same code behind the scenes as the expressions utilized in the `<intercept-url>` access declaration rules (assuming the expressions have been configured). Hence, the same set of built-in functions and properties are accessible from the expressions built using the `<authorize>` tag.

Both these methods of utilizing the `<authorize>` tag provide powerful, fine-grained control over the display of page contents based on security authorization rules.

Go ahead and start up the JBCP Calendar application, visit `http://localhost:8080/calendar/`, and log in with the user `user1@example.com` and the password `user1`. You will observe that the **My Events** link is displayed, but the **All Events** link is hidden. Log out and log in as the user `admin1@example.com` and the password `admin1`. Now both links are visible.

# Using controller logic to conditionally render content

In this section, we will demonstrate how we can use Java-based code to determine if we should render some content. We choose to only show the **Create Event** link on the **Welcome** page to users who have a username that contains `user`. This will hide the **Create Event** link on the **Welcome** page from users who are not logged in as administrators.

*Fine-grained Access Control*

The welcome controller from the sample code for this chapter has been updated to populate the model with an attribute named `showCreateLink`, derived from the method name.

src/main/java/com/packtpub/springsecurity/web/controllers/WelcomeController.java

```
@ModelAttribute
public boolean showCreateLink(Authentication authentication) {
    return authentication != null && authentication.getName().
contains("user");
}
```

You may notice that Spring MVC can automatically obtain the `Authentication` object for us. This is because Spring Security maps our current `Authentication` object to the `HttpServletRequest.getPrincipal()` method for us. Since Spring MVC will automatically resolve any object of the type `java.security.Principal` to the value of `HttpServletRequest.getPrincipal()`, specifying `Authentication` as an argument to our controller is an easy way to access the current `Authentication` object. We could also decouple the code from Spring Security by specifying an argument of the type `Principal` instead. However, we choose `Authentication` in this scenario to help demonstrate how everything connects together.

If we were working in another framework that did not know how to do this, we could obtain the `Authentication` object using the `SecurityContextHolder` class, as we did in *Chapter 3, Custom Authentication*. Also note that if we were not using Spring MVC, we could just set the `HttpServletRequest` attribute directly rather than populating it on the model. The attribute that we populated on the request would then be available to our JSP just as it is when using a `ModelAndView` object with Spring MVC.

Next, we will need to use this `HttpServletRequest` attribute in our `index.jsp` file to determine if we should display the **Create Event** link. Update `index.jsp` as follows:

src/main/webapp/WEB-INF/views/index.jsp

```
<c:if test="${showCreateLink}">
    <li><a id="createEventLink" ... </li>
</c:if>
```

Now start the application, log in using admin1@example.com as the username and admin1 as the password, and visit the **All Events** page. You should no longer see the **Create Events** link within the page (although it will still be present in the main navigation).

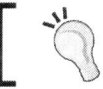

> Your code should look like chapter10.02-calendar.

## WebInvocationPrivilegeEvaluator

There may be times when an application will not be written using JSPs and will need to be able to determine access based upon a URL, as we did with `<sec:authorize url="${eventsUrl}">`. This can be done by using the `o.s.s.web.access.WebInvocationPrivilegeEvaluator` interface, which is the same interface that backs the JSP tag library. In the following code snippet, we demonstrate its use by populating our model with an attribute named `showAdminLink`. We are able to obtain `WebInvocationPrivilegeEvaluator` using the `@Autowired` annotation.

src/main/java/com/packtpub/springsecurity/web/controllers/WelcomeController.java

```
@ModelAttribute
public boolean showAdminLink(Authentication authentication) {
    return webInvocationPrivilegeEvaluator.
        isAllowed("/admin/", authentication);
}
```

If the framework you are using is not being managed by Spring, `@Autowire` will not be able to provide you with `WebInvocationPrivilegeEvaluator`. Instead, you can use Spring's `org.springframework.web.context.WebApplicationContextUtils` interface to obtain an instance of `WebInvocationPrivilegeEvaluator`, as follows:

```
ApplicationContext context = WebApplicationContextUtils
    .getRequiredWebApplicationContext(servletContext);
WebInvocationPrivilegeEvaluator privEvaluator =
    context.getBean(WebInvocationPrivilegeEvaluator.class)
```

To try it out; go ahead and update `index.jsp` to use the `showAdminLink` request attribute, as follows:

src/main/webapp/WEB-INF/views/index.jsp

```
<c:if test="${showAdminLink}">
    <li>
        <a id="h2Link" href="admin/h2/">
            H2 Database Console
        </a>
        ...
    </li>
</c:if>
```

Restart the application and view the welcome page before you have logged in. The **H2** link should not be visible. Log in as `admin1@example.com`/`admin1`, and you should see it.

> Your code should look like `chapter10.03-calendar`.

# What is the best way to configure in-page authorization

The major advances in the Spring Security `<authorize>` tag in Spring Security 3 removed many of the concerns about the use of this tag in prior versions of the library. In many cases, the use of the `url` attribute of the tag can appropriately isolate the JSP code from changes in authorization rules. You should use the `url` attribute of the tag in the following scenarios:

- The tag is preventing display of functionality that can be clearly identified by a single URL
- The contents of the tag can be unambiguously isolated to a single URL

Unfortunately, in a typical application, the likelihood that you will be able to use the `url` attribute of the tag frequently is somewhat low. The reality is that applications are usually much more complex than this, and require more involved logic when deciding to render portions of a page.

It's tempting to use the Spring Security tag library to declare bits of rendered pages off-limits based on security criteria in the other ways. However, there are a number of reasons why (in many cases) this isn't a great idea:

- Complex conditions beyond role membership are not supported by the tag library. For example, if our application incorporated customized attributes on the `UserDetails` implementation, IP filters, geo-location, and so on—none of these would be supported using the standard `<authorize>` tag.

    These could, however, conceivably be supported by a custom JSP tag or using SpEL expressions. Even in this case, the JSP is more likely to be directly tied to business logic rather than what is typically encouraged.

- The `<authorize>` tag must be referenced on every page that it's used in. This leads to potential inconsistencies between the rulesets that are intended to be common, but may be spread across different physical pages. A good object-oriented system design would suggest that conditional rule evaluations be located in only one place and logically referred to from where they should be applied.

  It is possible (and we illustrate this using our common header JSP include) to encapsulate and reuse portions of JSP pages to reduce the occurrence of this type of problem, but it is virtually impossible to eliminate in a complex application.

- There is no way to validate the correctness of rules stated at compile time. Whereas compile-time constants can be used in typical Java-based, object-oriented systems, the JSP tag library requires (in typical use) hardcoded role names where a simple typo might go undetected for some time.

  To be fair, such typos could be caught easily by comprehensive functional tests of the running application, but they are far easier to test using a standard Java component unit testing techniques.

We can see that although the JSP-based approach for conditional content rendering is convenient, there are some significant downsides.

All of these issues can be solved through the use of code in controllers that can be used to push data into the application view model. Additionally, performing advanced authorization determinations in code allows the benefits of re-use, compile-time checks, and proper logical separation of the model, view, and controller.

# Method-level security

Our primary focus up to this point in the book has been on securing the web-facing portion of the JBCP Calendar application; however, in the real-world planning of secured systems, equal attention should be paid to securing the service methods that allow users access to the most critical part of any system—its data.

## Why we secure in layers

Let's take a minute to see why it is important to secure our methods even though we have already secured our URLs. Start the JBCP Calendar application up. Log in using `user1@example.com` as the username and `user1` as the password, and visit the **All Events** page. You will see our custom **Access Denied** page. Now add `.json` to the end of the URL in the browser so that the URL is now `http://localhost:8080/calendar/events/.json`. You will now see a JSON response with the same data as the HTML **All Events** page. This data should only be visible to an administrator, but we have bypassed it by finding a URL that was not configured properly.

We can also view the details of an event that we do not own and are not invited to. Change `.json` to be `102` so that the URL is now `http://localhost:8080/calendar/events/102`. You will now see a **Lunch** event that is not listed in your **My Events** page. This should not be visible to us because we are not an administrator and this is not our event.

As you can see, our URL rules are note quite strong enough to entirely secure our application. These exploits do not even need to take advantage of more complex problems, such as differences in how containers handle URL normalization. In short, there are often ways to bypass URL-based security. Let's see how adding a security layer to our business tier can help with our new security vulnerability.

## Securing the business tier

Spring Security has the ability to add a layer of authorization (or authorization-based data pruning) to the invocation of any Spring-managed bean in your application. While many developers focus on web-tier security, business-tier security is arguably just as important, as a malicious user may be able to penetrate the security of your web tier or access services exposed through a non-UI frontend, such as a web service.

Let's examine the following logical diagram to see where we're interested in applying a secondary layer of security:

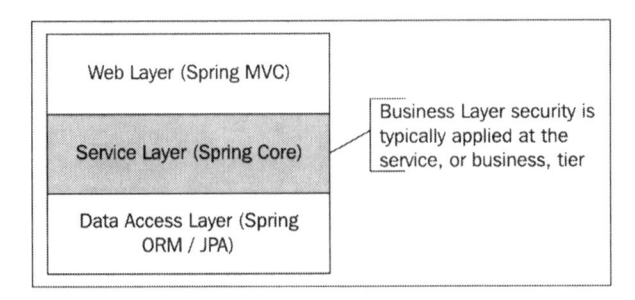

Spring Security has two main techniques for securing methods:

- Preauthorization ensures that certain constraints are satisfied prior to the execution of a method that is being allowed—for example, if a user has a particular `GrantedAuthority`, such as `ROLE_ADMIN`. Failure to satisfy the declared constraints means that the method call will fail.
- Postauthorization ensures that the calling principal still satisfies declared constraints after the method returns. This is used rarely, but can provide an extra layer of security around some complex, interconnected business tier methods.

Pre and postauthorization provide formalized support for what are generally termed **preconditions** and **postconditions** in a classic, object-oriented design. Preconditions and postconditions allow a developer to declare through runtime checks that certain constraints around a method's execution must always hold true. In the case of security pre and postauthorization, the business tier developer makes a conscious decision about the security profile of particular methods by encoding expected runtime conditions as part of an interface or class API declaration. As you may imagine, this can require a great deal of forethought to avoid unintended consequences!

## Adding @PreAuthorize method annotation

Our first design decision will be to augment method security at the business tier by ensuring that a user must be logged in as a user with `ROLE_ADMIN` before he/she is allowed to access the `getEvents()` method. This is done with a simple annotation added to the method in the service interface definition, as follows:

```
import org.springframework.security.access.prepost.PreAuthorize;
...
public interface CalendarService {
    ...
    @PreAuthorize("hasRole('ROLE_ADMIN')")
    List<Event> getEvents();
}
```

This is all that is required to ensure that anyone invoking our `getEvents()` method is an administrator. Spring Security will use a runtime **Aspect Oriented Programming** (**AOP**) pointcut to execute before an advice on the method, and throw `o.s.s.access.AccessDeniedException` if the security constraints aren't met.

## Instructing Spring Security to use method annotations

We'll also need to make a one-time change to `security.xml`, where we've got the rest of our Spring Security configuration. Simply add the following element right before the `<http>` declaration:

src/main/webapp/WEB-INF/spring/security.xml

```
<global-method-security
        pre-post-annotations="enabled"/>
<http ...>
```

## Validating method security

Don't believe it was that easy? Log in with `user1@example.com` as the username and `user1` as the password, and try accessing `http://localhost:8080/calendar/events/.json`. You should see the **Access Denied** page now.

> Your code should look like `chapter10.04-calendar`.

If you look at the Tomcat console, you'll see a very long stack trace, starting with the following output:

```
DEBUG ExceptionTranslationFilter - Access is denied (user is not
anonymous); delegating to AccessDeniedHandler
org.s.s.access.AccessDeniedException: Access is denied
   at org.s.s.access.vote.AffirmativeBased.decide
   at org.s.s.access.intercept.AbstractSecurityInterceptor.
beforeInvocation
   at org.s.s.access.intercept.aopalliance.MethodSecurityInterceptor.
invoke
   ...
   at $Proxy16.getEvents
   at com.packtpub.springsecurity.web.controllers.EventsController.
events
```

Based on the access denied page, and the stack trace clearly pointing to the `getEvents` method invocation, we can see that the user was appropriately denied access to the `business` method because it lacked `GrantedAuthority` of `ROLE_ADMIN`. If you run the same with the username `admin1@example.com` and the password `admin1`, you will discover that access will be granted.

Isn't it amazing that with a simple declaration in our interface, we're able to ensure that the method in question has been secured? How does AOP work?

## Interface-based proxies

In the preceding example, Spring Security uses an interface-based proxy to secure our `getEvents` method. Let's take a look at simplified pseudo code of what is happening to understand how this works.

```
DefaultCalendarService originalService = context.getBean(CalendarService.class)
CalendarService secureService = new CalendarService() {
    … other methods just delegate to originalService …
    public List<Event> getEvents() {
        if(!permitted(originalService.getEvents)) {
            throw AccessDeniedException()
        }
        return originalCalendarService.getEvents()
    }
};
```

You can see that Spring creates the original `CalendarService` just as it normally does. However, it instructs our code to use another implementation of the `CalendarService` that performs a security check before returning the result of the original method. The secure implementation can be created with no prior knowledge of our interface because Spring uses Java's `java.lang.reflect.Proxy` APIs to dynamically create new implementations of the interface. Note that the object returned is no longer an instance of `DefaultCalendarService` since it is a new implementation of `CalendarService` (that is, it is an anonymous implementation of `CalendarService`). This means that we must program against an interface in order to use the secure implementation, otherwise a `ClassCastException` would occur. To learn more about Spring AOP, refer to the Spring reference documentation at http://static.springsource.org/spring/docs/current/spring-framework-reference/html/aop.html#aop-introduction-proxies.

In addition to the `@PreAuthorize` annotation, there are several other ways of declaring security preauthorization requirements on methods. We can examine these different ways of securing methods and then evaluate their pros and cons in different circumstances.

## JSR-250 compliant standardized rules

JSR-250, Common Annotations for the Java Platform, defines a series of annotations, some that are security-related, which are intended to be portable across JSR-250 compliant runtime environments. The Spring Framework became compliant with JSR-250 as part of the Spring 2.x release, including the Spring Security framework.

While the JSR-250 annotations are not as expressive as the Spring native annotations, they have the benefit that the declarations they provide are compatible across implementing Java EE application servers such as Glassfish or service-oriented runtime frameworks such as Apache Tuscany. Depending on your application's needs and requirements for portability, you may decide that the trade-off of reduced specificity is worth the portability of the code.

To implement the rule we specified in the first example, we would make a few changes. First, we need to update our `security.xml` file to use the JSR-250 annotations.

src/main/webapp/WEB-INF/spring/security.xml

```
<global-method-security
    jsr250-annotations="enabled"/>
```

Lastly, the `@PreAuthorize` annotation needs to change to the `@RolesAllowed` annotation. As we might anticipate, the `@RolesAllowed` annotation does not support SpEL expressions, so we edit `CalendarService` as follows:

```
@RolesAllowed("ROLE_ADMIN")
List<Event> getEvents();
```

Restart the application, log in as `user1@example.com/user1`, and try to access `http://localhost:8080/calendar/events/.json`. You should see the **Access Denied** page again.

> Your code should look like `chapter10.05-calendar`.

Note that it's also possible to provide a list of allowed `GrantedAuthority` names using the standard Java 5 String array annotation syntax:

```
@RolesAllowed({"ROLE_USER","ROLE_ADMIN"})
List<Event> getEvents();
```

There are also two additional annotations specified by JSR-250, namely `@PermitAll` and `@DenyAll`, which function as you might expect, permitting and denying all requests to the method in question.

> **Annotations at the class level**
>
> Be aware that the method-level security annotations can be applied at the class level as well! Method-level annotations, if supplied, will always override annotations specified at the class level. This can be helpful if your business needs to dictate specification of security policies for an entire class at a time. Take care to use this functionality in conjunction with good comments and coding standards so that developers are very clear about the security characteristics of a class and its methods.

# Method security using Spring's @Secured annotation

Spring itself provides a simpler annotation style that is similar to the JSR-250 `@RolesAllowed` annotation. The `@Secured` annotation is functionally and syntactically the same as `@RolesAllowed`. The only notable differences are that it does not require the external dependency, cannot be processed by other frameworks, and the processing of these annotations must be explicitly enabled with another attribute on the `<global-method-security>` element:

src/main/webapp/WEB-INF/spring/security.xml

```
<global-method-security
    secured-annotations="enabled"/>
```

As `@Secured` functions in the same way as the JSR standard `@RolesAllowed` annotation does, there's no real compelling reason to use it in new code, but you may run across it in older Spring code.

# Method security rules using aspect-oriented programming

The final technique for securing methods has the benefit that it doesn't require code modification at all. Instead, it uses aspect-oriented programming to declare a pointcut at a method or set of methods, with an advice that performs checks for role membership when the pointcut matches. The AOP declarations are only present in the Spring Security XML configuration file and do not involve any annotations.

# Fine-grained Access Control

Following is an example of a declaration protecting all the `CalendarService` interface methods with administrative rights:

```
<global-method-security>
    <protect-pointcut access="ROLE_ADMIN" expression=
            "execution(* com.packtpub.springsecurity.service.
CalendarService.*(..))"/>
</global-method-security>
```

The pointcut expressions are supported under the hood with Spring AOP support via AspectJ. Unfortunately, Spring AspectJ AOP only supports a very small subset of the AspectJ pointcut expression language—refer to the Spring AOP documentation for more details on supported expressions and other important elements of programming with Spring AOP.

That said, be aware that it's possible to specify a series of pointcut declarations that target different roles and pointcut targets. Update your configuration to add a pointcut to target a method in your DAO:

src/main/webapp/WEB-INF/spring/security.xml

```
<global-method-security>
    <protect-pointcut access="ROLE_ADMIN" expression="execution(* com.
packtpub.springsecurity.dataaccess.EventDao.getEvents(..)) &amp;&amp;
args()"/>
</global-method-security>
```

Note that the new pointcut we added uses some more advanced AspectJ syntax, illustrating Boolean logic and the other supported pointcuts, `args`, that can be used to specify the type declaration of arguments.

> Your code should look like `chapter10.06-calendar`.

Start up the application and try accessing the **All Events** page with the user `user1@example.com` and password `user1`. You should get the **Access Denied** page.

Much as with other areas of Spring Security that allow a series of security declarations, AOP-style method security is processed from top to bottom, so it's a good idea to write the pointcuts in a most-specific to least-specific order.

Programming using AOP can be confusing for even seasoned developers. If you intend to use AOP heavily for security declarations, it is highly suggested that you review the Spring AOP reference documentation.

## Method security rules using bean decorators

An alternative form for declaring method security rules involves the use of declarative XML, which can be included within a Spring Bean definition. Although easier to read, this form of method security is far less expressive than pointcuts and far less comprehensive than the annotation-based approaches that we've reviewed so far. Nonetheless, for certain types of projects, using an XML declarative approach may be sufficient for your needs.

We can experiment by replacing the rules we declared in the prior examples with XML-based declarations to secure the `getEvents` method. As we have used bean auto-wiring upto this point, which is unfortunately not compatible with XML method decorators, we'll need to explicitly declare the service layer beans in order to demonstrate this technique.

The security decorators are part of the security XML namespace. When including Spring Security configuration, it is important to specify the security namespace. We have already updated our `services.xml` file to have the Security namespace defined, as follows:

src/main/webapp/WEB-INF/spring/services.xml

```
<?xml version="1.0" encoding="UTF-8"?>
<beans xmlns="http://www.springframework.org/schema/beans"
    xmlns:xsi="http://www.w3.org/2001/XMLSchema-instance"
    ...
    xmlns:security="http://www.springframework.org/schema/security"
    xsi:schemaLocation="...
        http://www.springframework.org/schema/security http://www.springframework.org/schema/security/spring-security-3.1.xsd">
```

Next (for the purposes of this exercise), remove any security annotations that you may have on the `DefaultCalendarService.getEvents` method. Also, remove any `<pointcut-protect>` elements from your `security.xml` file.

*Fine-grained Access Control*

Finally, declare the bean in Spring XML syntax with the following additional decorator that will declare that anyone wishing to invoke the `getEvents` method must be of the type ROLE_ADMIN:

src/main/webapp/WEB-INF/spring/services.xml

```xml
<bean id="calendarService"
      class="com.packtpub.springsecurity.service.DefaultCalendarService"
      autowire="constructor">
   <security:intercept-methods>
      <security:protect access="ROLE_ADMIN" method="getEvents"/>
   </security:intercept-methods>
</bean>
```

As with the earlier examples in this chapter, this protection can be easily verified by changing ROLE_USER to ROLE_ADMIN and attempting to view the **All Events** page with user1@example.com as the username and user1 as the password.

> Your code should look like chapter10.07-calendar now.

Behind the scenes, the functionality of this type of method access protection uses a `MethodSecurityInterceptor` object wired to `MapBasedMethodSecurityMetadataSource`, which the interceptor uses, to determine appropriate access. Unlike the more expressive SpEL-aware `@PreAuthorize` annotation, the `<protect>` declaration takes only a comma-separated list of roles in the `access` attribute (similar to the JSR-250 `@RolesAllowed` annotation).

It is also possible to use a simple wildcard match as part of the stated method name, for example, we might protect all getters of a given bean as follows:

```xml
<security:intercept-methods>
  <security:protect access="ROLE_ADMIN" method="get*"/>
</security:intercept-methods>
```

Method name matching can be performed by including a leading or trailing regular expression wildcard indicator (*). The presence of such an indicator will perform a wildcard search on the method name, adding the interceptor to any method matching the regular expression. Please note that other common regular expression operators (such as ? or []) are not supported. Please consult the relevant Java documentation for assistance on formulating and understanding basic regular expressions.

It is not common to see this type of security declaration in new code, as more expressive options exist, but it is good to be aware of this type of security decoration so that you can recognize it as an option in your method security tool belt. This type of method security declaration can be especially useful in cases where adding annotations to relevant interfaces or classes is not an option, such as when you are dealing with securing components in third-party libraries.

## Method security rules incorporating method parameters

Logically, writing rules that refer to method parameters in their constraints seems sensible for certain types of operations. For example, it might make sense for us to restrict the `findForUser(int userId)` method to meet the following constraints:

- The `userId` argument must be equal to the the current user's ID
- The user must be an administrator (in this case, it is valid for the user to see any event)

While it's easy to see how we could alter the rule to restrict the method invocation only to administrators, it's not clear how we would determine if the user is attempting to change their own password.

Fortunately, the SpEL binding used by the Spring Security method annotations supports more sophisticated expressions, including expressions that incorporate method parameters.

Remove the `<security:intercept-methods>` element from `services.xml` so that our bean with the ID `calendarService` is as follows:

src/main/webapp/WEB-INF/spring/services.xml

```
<bean id="calendarService"
      class="com.packtpub.springsecurity.service.DefaultCalendarService"
      autowire="constructor">
<!-- this should be empty -->
</bean>
```

You will also want to ensure that you have enabled `pre-post-annotations` in the `security.xml` file, as follows:

src/main/webapp/WEB-INF/spring/security.xml

```
<global-method-security
       pre-post-annotations="enabled"/>
```

*Fine-grained Access Control*

Lastly, we can update our `CalendarService` interface as follows:

```
@PreAuthorize("hasRole('ROLE_ADMIN') or principal.id == #userId")
List<Event> findForUser(int userId);
```

You can see here that we've augmented the SpEL directive we used in the first exercise with a check against the ID of the principal against the `userId` method parameter (`#userId`—the method parameter name is prefixed with a # symbol). The fact that this powerful feature of method parameter binding is available should get your creative juices flowing and allow you to secure method invocations with a very precise set of logical rules.

> Our `principal` is currently an instance of `CalendarUser` due to the custom authentication setup from *Chapter 3, Custom Authentication*. This means that `principal` has all the properties that our `CalendarUser` has on it. If we had not done this customization, only the properties on the `UserDetails` would be available.

SpEL variables are referenced with the hash (#) prefix. One important note is that in order for method argument names to be available at runtime, debugging symbol table information must be retained after compilation. Common methods of enabling this are listed as follows:

- If you are using the `javac` compiler, you will need to include the `-g` flag when building your classes
- When using the `<javac>` task in `ant`, add the attribute `debug="true"`
- In Maven, ensure the property `maven.compiler.debug=true` (the default is `true`)

Consult your compiler, build tool, or IDE documentation for assistance on configuring this same setting in your environment.

Start up your application and try logging in with `user1@example.com` as the username and `user1` as the password. On the **Welcome** page, request the **My Events (userId=0)** link to see an **Access denied** page. Try again with the **My Events (userId=1)** to see it work. Note that the displayed user on the **My Events** page matches the currently logged-in user. Now try the same steps and log in as `admin1@example.com` / `admin1`. We will be able to see both pages since we are logged in as a user with `ROLE_ADMIN`.

> Your code should look like `chapter10.08-calendar`.

# Method security rules incorporating returned values

Just as we were able to leverage the parameters to the method, we can also leverage the returned value of the method call. Let's update the getEvent method to meet the following constraints on the returned value:

- The attendee's ID must be the current user's ID or
- The owner's ID must be the current user's ID or
- The user must be an administrator (in this case, it is valid for the user to see any event)

Add the following code to our CalendarService interface:

```
@PostAuthorize("hasRole('ROLE_ADMIN') or " +
        "principal.id == returnObject.owner.id or " +
        "principal.id == returnObject.attendee.id")
Event getEvent(int eventId);
```

Now try logging in with the username user1@example.com and the password user1. Next, try accessing the **Lunch** event using the link on the **Welcome** page. You should now see the **Access Denied** page. If you log in using the username user2@example.com and the password user2, the event will display as expected since user2@example.com is the attendee on the **Lunch** event.

> Your code should look like chapter10.09-calendar.

# Securing method data through role-based filtering

Two, final, Spring Security-dependent annotations are @PreFilter and @PostFilter, which are used to apply security-based filtering rules to collections or arrays (with @PostFilter only). This type of functionality is referred to as **security trimming** or **security pruning**, and involves using the security credentials of principal at runtime, to selectively remove members from a set of objects. As you might expect, this filtering is performed using the SpEL expression notation within the annotation declaration.

We'll work through an example with JBCP Calendar, where we want to filter the getEvents method to only return the events that this user is allowed to see. In order to do this, we remove any existing security annotations and add the @PostFilter annotation to our CalendarService interface, as follows:

```
@PostFilter("principal.id == filterObject.owner.id or " +
        "principal.id == filterObject.attendee.id")
List<Event> getEvents();
```

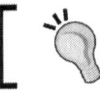

> Your code should look like chapter10.10-calendar.

Remove the `<intercept-url>` element restricting access to `/events/` URL so that we can test our annotation. Start up the application and view the **All Events** page when logged in with user1@example.com and password user1. You will observe that only the events that are associated to our user are displayed.

With `filterObject` acting as the loop variable that refers to the current event, Spring Security will iterate over the `List<Event>` returned by our service and modify it to only contain the `Event` objects that match our SpEL expression.

In general, the `@PostFilter` method behaves in the following way. For brevity, we refer to collection as the method return value, but be aware that `@PostFilter` works with either collection or array method return types.

- `filterObject` is rebound to the SpEL context for each element in the collection. This means that if your method is returning a collection with 100 elements, the SpEL expression will be evaluated for each.
- The SpEL expression must return a Boolean value. If the expression evaluates to `true`, the object will remain in the collection, while if the expression evaluates to `false`, the object will be removed.

In most cases, you'll find that collection post filtering saves you from the complexity of writing boilerplate code that you would likely be writing anyway.

Take care that you understand how `@PostFilter` works conceptually; unlike `@PreAuthorize`, `@PostFilter` specifies method behavior and not a precondition. Some object-oriented purists may argue that `@PostFilter` isn't appropriate for inclusion as a method annotation, and such filtering should instead be handled through code in a method implementation.

> **Safety of collection filtering**
>
> Be aware that the actual collection returned from your method will be modified! In some cases, this isn't desirable behavior, so you should ensure that your method returns a collection that can be safely modified. This is especially important if the returned collection is an ORM-bound one, as postfilter modifications could inadvertently be persisted to the ORM data store!

Spring Security also offers functionality to prefilter method parameters that are collections; let's try implementing it now.

## Pre-filtering collections with @PreFilter

The `@PreFilter` annotation can be applied to a method to filter collection elements that are passed into a method based on the current security context. Functionally once it has a reference to a collection, this annotation behaves exactly the same as the `@PostFilter` annotation, with a couple of exceptions:

- `@PreFilter` supports only collection arguments and does not support array arguments
- `@PreFilter` takes an additional, optional attribute `filterTarget` that is used to specifically identify the method parameter to filter it when the annotated method has more than one argument

As with `@PostFilter`, keep in mind that the original collection passed to the method is permanently modified. This may not be desirable behavior, so ensure that callers know that the collection's security may be trimmed after the method is invoked!

Imagine if we had a `save` method that accepted a collection of event objects, and we wanted to only allow the saving of events that are owned by the currently logged-in user. We could do this as follows:

```
@PreFilter("principal.id == filterObject.owner.id")
void save(Set<Event> events);
```

Much like our `@PostFilter` method, this annotation causes Spring Security to iterate over each event with the loop variable `filterObject`. It then compares the current user's ID against the event owner's ID. If they match, the event is retained. If they do not match, the result is discarded.

## Comparing method authorization types

The following quick reference chart may assist you in selecting a type of method authorization checking to use:

| Method authorization type | Specified as | JSR standard | Allows SpEL expressions |
|---|---|---|---|
| `@PreAuthorize` `@PostAuthorize` | Annotation | No | Yes |
| `@RolesAllowed` `@PermitAll` `@DenyAll` | Annotation | Yes | No |
| `@Secure` | Annotation | No | No |
| `protect-pointcut` | XML | No | No |

[ 279 ]

*Fine-grained Access Control*

Most Java 5 consumers of Spring Security will probably opt to use the JSR-250 annotations for maximum compatibility and re-use of their business classes (and relevant constraints) across the IT organization. Where needed, these basic declarations can be replaced with the annotations that tie the code to the Spring Security implementation itself.

If you are using Spring Security in an environment that doesn't support annotations (Java 1.4 or previous), unfortunately your choices are somewhat limited with method security enforcement. Even in this situation, the use of AOP provides a reasonably rich environment in which we can develop basic security declarations.

# Practical considerations for annotation-based security

One thing to consider is that when returning a collection in real-world applications, there is likely to be some sort of paging. This means that our `@PreFilter` and `@PostFilter` annotations cannot be used as the sole means of selecting which objects to return. Instead, we need to ensure that our queries only select the data that the user is allowed to access. This means that the security annotations become redundant checks. However, it is important to remember our lesson at the beginning of this chapter; we want to secure in layers in the event that one layer is able to be bypassed.

# Method security on Spring MVC controllers

Rather than typing the URL configuration in our Spring Security configuration, we may want to add `@PreAuthorize` annotations to our MVC controllers. We already have our `global-method-security` setup, so the setup seems like it is straightforward. Let's demonstrate this functionality with the `/events/` URL. First, we will demonstrate that we are securing our controller. Start by ensuring the following code has been removed from our `security.xml` file:

src/main/webapp/WEB-INF/spring/security.xml

```
<intercept-url pattern="/events/"
    access="hasRole('ROLE_ADMIN')"/>
```

We will also want to ensure that we remove any annotations from the `getEvents()` method of `CalendarService`.

src/main/java/com/packtpub/springsecurity/service/CalendarService.java

```
// ensure no annotations on this method
List<Event> getEvents();
```

Next, we will add the `@PreAuthorize` tag to our `EventsController` as follows:

```
@PreAuthorize("hasRole('ROLE_ADMIN')")
@RequestMapping("/")
public ModelAndView events() {
    return new ModelAndView("events/list", "events", calendarService.getEvents());
}
```

Now start up the application and visit the **All Events** page, ensuring to log in with the username `user1@example.com` and the password `user1` to see that the method is not secured. How can this be done? We have just encountered one of the most common problems when trying to secure a Spring MVC controller. Remember in *Chapter 2, Getting Started with Spring Security* we briefly discussed that the `ContextLoaderListener` typically loads the Spring Security configuration and the `DispatcherServlet` loads our Spring MVC configuration? The problem is that our `<global-method-security>` is loaded by our `ContextLoaderListener`, which has no visibility to our MVC configuration (that is, our `EventsController`) and so does not secure it. Add the following code to `mvc-config.xml`.

src/main/webapp/WEB-INF/mvc-config.xml

```
<sec:global-method-security
    pre-post-annotations="enabled"/>
```

Try starting the application, ensuring to log in with the username `user1@example.com` and the password `user1`, and visiting the **All Events** page. We now see a `404` error rather than our **Access Denied** page. Now what is wrong?

The problem this time is that Spring's AOP support has created an interface-based proxy of the `Serializable` interface that is on our `EventsController`. The result is an object that looks similar to the following code snippet:

```
Serializable secureController = new Serializable() {
    private CalendarController insecureController;
}
```

Since there are no methods on the `Serializable` interface, no methods have been exposed to process our **All Events** page. To get around this, we can modify our `mvc-config.xml` file as follows:

src/main/webapp/WEB-INF/mvc-config.xml

```
<sec:global-method-security
    proxy-target-class="true"
    pre-post-annotations="enabled"/>
```

*Fine-grained Access Control*

This will instruct Spring to create a class-based proxy using `cglib` instead of using an interface-based proxy.

## Class-based proxies

A class-based proxy looks much like our interface-based proxy except that instead of an anonymous implementation of an interface, it creates an anonymous implementation of the class. This means the object still has all the same methods on it and so there are methods to process the requests unlike our interface-based proxy. A simplified pseudo code would look similar to the following code snippet:

```
EventsController secureController = new EventsController() {
    ... other methods just delegate to originalService ...
    public ModelAndView events() {
        if(!permitted(insecureController.events)) {
            throw AccessDeniedException()
        }
        return insecureController.events();
    }
};
```

## Class-based proxy limitations

Start up the application again and you will get an error stating `Cannot subclass final class class ...EventsController`. If you look at our example, you can see that in order to secure our `EventsController`, Spring must create an anonymous inner class (which is trying to extend a final class). This is not possible since final classes cannot be extended. Remove the final declaration from our `EventsController`.

src/main/java/com/packtpub/springsecurity/web/controllers/EventsController.java

```
public class EventsController implements Serializable {
```

## Chapter 10

When we try to start our application this time, we get another exception stating `Superclass has no null constructors but no arguments were given`. The problem is that Spring will not create a proxy of an object that does not have a default constructor. This is a safety precaution to ensure that the arguments are not processed twice (that is, once for the secure proxy and once for the actual implementation) in the event that the constructor modifies the state. For example, consider if the argument was a `DataSource` and the constructor tried to create the schema. Passing it in twice would cause the schema to be created twice, resulting in an error. Add a default constructor to the `EventsController` to resolve this error. Note that the constructor can be in the default scope rather than in public.

src/main/java/com/packtpub/springsecurity/web/controllers/EventsController.java

```
EventsController() {
    calendarService = null;
    userContext = null;
}
```

> Your code should now look like chapter10.11-calendar.

We are finally able to start the application; log in with the username user1@example.com and password user1, visit the **All Events** page, and see the expected **Access Denied** page.

> It should be noted that switching to using annotations means that our `<sec:authorize>` JSP tag will no longer work since it uses the information in our `<intercept-url>` elements. This makes sense since Spring Security is unaware of our Spring MVC mappings.

# Summary

In this chapter, we have covered most of the remaining areas in standard Spring Security implementations that deal with authorization. We've learned enough to take a thorough pass through the JBCP Calendar application and verify that proper authorization checks are in place at all tiers of the application, to ensure that malicious users cannot manipulate or access data to which they do not have access.

Specifically, we:

- Developed two techniques for micro-authorization, namely filtering out in-page content based on authorization or other security criteria using the Spring Security JSP tag library and Spring MVC controller data binding
- Explored several methods of securing business functions and data in the business tier of our application and supporting a rich, declarative security model that is tightly integrated with the code
- Learned how to secure our Spring MVC controllers and the differences between interface and class proxy objects

At this point, we've wrapped up coverage of much of the important Spring Security functionality that you're likely to encounter in most standard, secure web application development scenarios.

In the next chapter, we will discuss the access control list (domain object model) module of Spring Security. This will allow us to explicitly declare authorization rather than relying on existing data.

# 11
# Access Control Lists

In this chapter, we will address the complex topic of **Access Control Lists** (ACL), which can provide a rich model of the domain object instance-level authorization. Spring Security ships with a robust, but complicated, access control list module that can serve the needs of small to medium-sized implementations reasonably well.

During the course of this chapter we'll:

- Understand the conceptual model of access control lists
- Review the terminology and application of access control list concepts in the Spring Security ACL module
- Build and review the database schema required to support Spring ACL
- Configure JBCP Calendar to use ACL secured business methods via annotations and Spring Beans
- Perform advanced configuration, including customized ACL permissions, ACL-enabled JSP tag checks and method security, mutable ACLs, and smart caching
- Examine architectural considerations and plan scenarios for ACL deployment

# Using access control lists for business object security

The final piece of the non web tier security puzzle is security at the business object level, applied at or below the business tier. Security at this level is implemented using a technique known as access control lists, or ACLs. Summing up the objective of ACLs in a single sentence — ACLs allow specification of a set of group permissions based on the unique combination of a group, business object, and logical operation.

For example, an ACL declaration for JBCP Calendar might declare that a given user has write access to his or her own event. This might be shown as follows:

| Username | Group | Object | Permissions |
|---|---|---|---|
| rob |  | event_01 | read, write |
|  | ROLE_USER | event_123 | read |
|  | ANONYMOUS | Any Event | none |

You can see that this ACL is eminently readable by a human—rob has read and write access to his own event (event_01); other registered users can read the events of rob, but anonymous users cannot. This type of rule matrix is, in a nutshell, what ACL attempts to synthesize about a secured system and its business data into a combination of code, access checking, and metadata. Most true ACL-enabled systems have extremely complex ACL lists, and may conceivably have millions of entries across the entire system. Although this sounds frighteningly complex, proper up-front reasoning and implementation with a capable security library can make ACL management quite feasible.

If you use a Microsoft Windows or Unix/Linux-based computer, you experience the magic of ACLs every single day. Most modern computer operating systems use ACL directives as part of their file storage systems, allowing permission granting based on a combination of a user or group, file or directory, and permission. In Microsoft Windows, you can view some of the ACL capabilities of a file by right-clicking on a file and examining its security properties (**Properties | Security**):

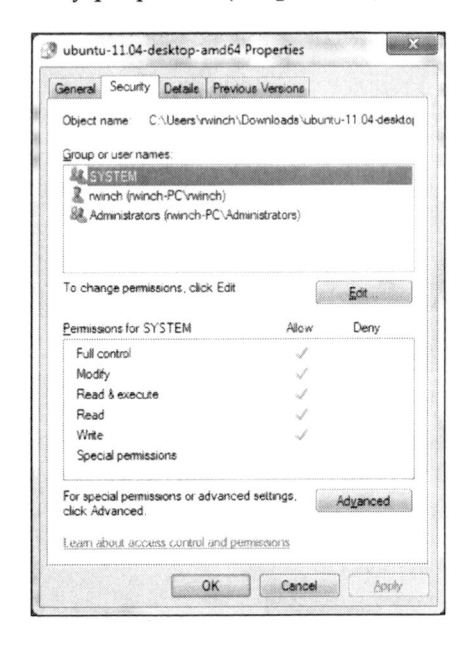

You will be able to see that the combinations of inputs to the ACL are visible and intuitive as you navigate through the various groups or users and permissions.

# Access control lists in Spring Security

Spring Security supports ACL-driven authorization checks against access to individual domain objects by individual users of the secured system. Much as in the OS filesystem example, it is possible to use the Spring Security ACL components to build logical tree structures of both business objects and groups or principals. The intersection of permissions (inherited or explicit) on both the **requestor** and the **requestee** is used to determine allowed access.

It's quite common for users approaching the ACL capability of Spring Security to be overwhelmed by its complexity, combined with a relative dearth of documentation and examples. This is compounded by the fact that setting up the ACL infrastructure can be quite complicated, with many interdependencies and a reliance on bean-based configuration mechanisms, which are quite unlike much of the rest of Spring Security (as you'll see in a moment when we set up the initial configuration).

The Spring Security ACL module was written to be a reasonable baseline, but users intending to build extensively on the functionality will likely run into a series of frustrating limitations and design choices, which have gone (for the most part) uncorrected as they were first introduced in the early days of Spring Security. Don't let these limitations discourage you! The ACL module is a powerful way to embed rich access controls in your application, and further scrutinize and secure user actions and data.

Before we dig into configuring Spring Security ACL support, we need to review some key terminology and concepts.

The main unit of secured actor identity in the Spring ACL system is the **Security Identity** (**SID**). The SID is a logical construct that can be used to abstract the identity of either an individual principal or a group (`GrantedAuthority`). The SIDs defined by the ACL data model you construct are used as the basis for explicit and derived access control rules, when determining the allowed level of access for a particular principal.

If SIDs are used to define actors in the ACL system, the opposite half of the security equation is the definition of the secured objects themselves. The identification of individual secured objects is called (unsurprisingly) an **object identity**. The default Spring ACL implementation of an object identity requires ACL rules to be defined at the individual object instance level, which means, if desired, every object in the system can have an individual access rule.

Individual access rules are known as **Access Control Entries (ACEs)**. An ACE is the combination of the following factors:

- The SID for the actor to which the rule applies
- The object identity to which the rule applies
- The permission that should be applied to the given SID and the stated object identity
- Whether or not the stated permission should be allowed or denied for the given SID and object identity

The purpose of the Spring ACL system as a whole is to evaluate each secured method invocation and determine whether the object or objects being acted on in the method should be allowed as per the applicable ACEs. Applicable ACEs are evaluated at runtime, based on the caller and the objects in play.

Spring Security ACL is flexible in its implementation. Although the majority of this chapter details the out-of-the-box functionality of the Spring Security ACL module, keep in mind, however, that many of the rules indicated represent default implementations, which in many cases can be overridden based on more complex requirements.

Spring Security uses helpful value objects to represent the data associated with each of these conceptual entities. These are listed in the following table:

| ACL conceptual object | Java object |
| --- | --- |
| SID | o.s.s.acls.model.Sid |
| Object identity | o.s.s.acls.model.ObjectIdentity |
| ACL | o.s.s.acls.model.Acl |
| ACE | o.s.s.acls.model.AccessControlEntry |

Let's work through the process of enabling Spring Security ACL components for a simple demonstration in the JBCP Calendar application.

# Basic configuration of Spring Security ACL support

Although we hinted previously that configuring ACL support in Spring Security requires bean-based configuration (which it does), you can use ACL support while retaining the simpler security XML namespace configuration if you choose.

## Maven dependencies

As with most of the chapters, we will need to add some dependencies in order to use the functionality in this chapter. A list of the dependencies we have added with comments about when they are needed can be seen as follows:

pom.xml

```
    <!-- needed for any ACL integration --->
    <dependency>
      <groupId>org.springframework.security</groupId>
      <artifactId>spring-security-acl</artifactId>
      <version>3.1.0.RELEASE</version>
    </dependency>
    <!-- needed for caching of ACLs -->
    <dependency>
      <groupId>net.sf.ehcache</groupId>
      <artifactId>ehcache</artifactId>
      <version>1.6.2</version>
      <scope>runtime</scope>
    </dependency>
```

## Defining a simple target scenario

Our simple target scenario is to grant `user2@example.com` read access to only the **Birthday Party** event. All other users will not have any access to any events. You will observe that this differs from our other examples since `user2@example.com` is not otherwise associated with the Birthday Party event.

Although there are several ways to set up ACL checking, our preference is to follow the annotation-based approach that we used in this chapter's method-level annotations. This nicely abstracts the use of ACLs away from the actual interface declarations, and allows for replacement (if you want) of the role declarations with something other than ACLs at a later date (should you so choose).

## Access Control Lists

We'll add an annotation to the `CalendarService.getEvents` method, which filters each event based upon the current user's permission to the event:

src/main/java/com/packtpub/springsecurity/service/CalendarService.java

```
@PostFilter("hasPermission(filterObject, 'read')")
List<Event> getEvents();
```

> You should start with the code from `chapter11.00-calendar`.

When we are done, the events listed on the **All Events** page will be filtered based upon the configured permissions. Let's get started with our configuration changes!

## Adding ACL tables to the H2 database

The first thing we'll need to do is add the required tables and data to support persistent ACL entries in our in-memory H2 database. To do this, we'll add a new SQL DDL file and the corresponding data to our embedded-database declaration in `services.xml`. We will break down each of these files later in the chapter.

src/main/webapp/WEB-INF/spring/services.xml

```
<jdbc:embedded-database id="dataSource" type="H2">
  <jdbc:script location="classpath:/database/h2/calendar-
    schema.sql"/>
  <jdbc:script location="classpath:/database/h2/calendar-
    data.sql"/>
  <jdbc:script
    location="classpath:/database/h2/security-acl-schema.sql"/>
  <jdbc:script location="classpath:/database/h2/security-acl-
    data.sql"/>
</jdbc:embedded-database>
```

We have included the following `security-acl-schema.sql` file with this chapter's source code, which is based upon the schema files included in the Spring Security reference's *Appendix, Additional Reference Material*.

src/main/resources/database/h2/security-acl-schema.sql

```
create table acl_sid (
  id bigint generated by default as identity(start with 100) not
    null primary key,
  principal boolean not null,
```

```
    sid varchar_ignorecase(100) not null,
    constraint uk_acl_sid unique(sid,principal) );

create table acl_class (
    id bigint generated by default as identity(start with 100) not
      null primary key,
    class varchar_ignorecase(500) not null,
    constraint uk_acl_class unique(class) );

create table acl_object_identity (
    id bigint generated by default as identity(start with 100) not
      null primary key,
    object_id_class bigint not null,
    object_id_identity bigint not null,
    parent_object bigint,
    owner_sid bigint not null,
    entries_inheriting boolean not null,
    constraint uk_acl_objid
      unique(object_id_class,object_id_identity),
    constraint fk_acl_obj_parent foreign
      key(parent_object)references acl_object_identity(id),
    constraint fk_acl_obj_class foreign
      key(object_id_class)references acl_class(id),
    constraint fk_acl_obj_owner foreign key(owner_sid)references
      acl_sid(id) );

create table acl_entry (
    id bigint generated by default as identity(start with 100) not
      null primary key,
    acl_object_identity bigint not null,
    ace_order int not null,
    sid bigint not null,
    mask integer not null,
    granting boolean not null,
    audit_success boolean not null,
    audit_failure boolean not null,
    constraint uk_acl_entry unique(acl_object_identity,ace_order),
    constraint fk_acl_entry_obj_id foreign key(acl_object_identity)
      references acl_object_identity(id),
    constraint fk_acl_entry_sid foreign key(sid) references

      acl_sid(id) );
```

The preceding code will result in the following database schema:

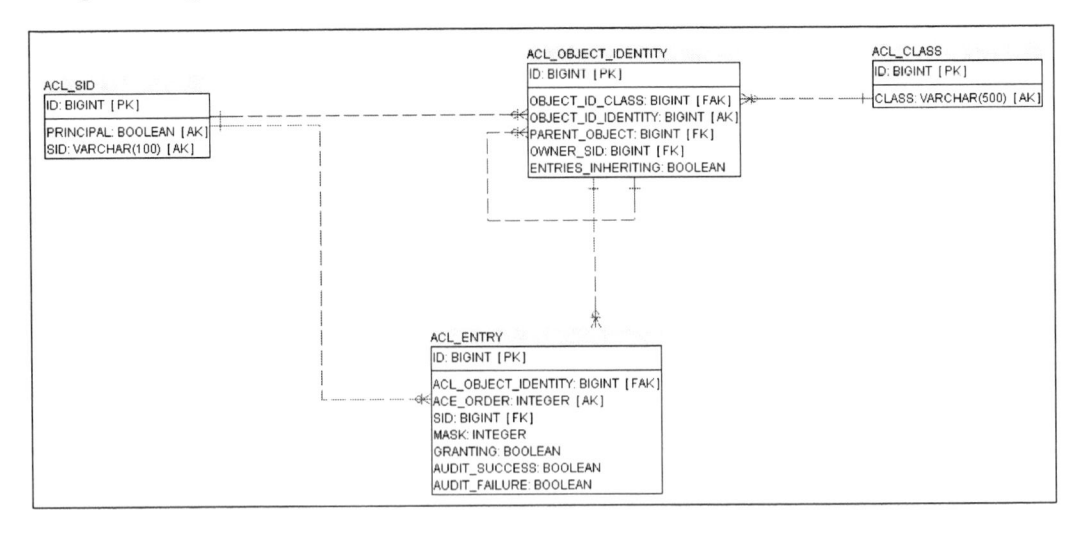

```
ACL_SID                              ACL_OBJECT_IDENTITY                    ACL_CLASS
ID: BIGINT [PK]                      ID: BIGINT [PK]                        ID: BIGINT [PK]
PRINCIPAL: BOOLEAN [AK]              OBJECT_ID_CLASS: BIGINT [FAK]          CLASS: VARCHAR(500) [AK]
SID: VARCHAR(100) [AK]               OBJECT_ID_IDENTITY: BIGINT [AK]
                                     PARENT_OBJECT: BIGINT [FK]
                                     OWNER_SID: BIGINT [FK]
                                     ENTRIES_INHERITING: BOOLEAN

                                     ACL_ENTRY
                                     ID: BIGINT [PK]
                                     ACL_OBJECT_IDENTITY: BIGINT [FAK]
                                     ACE_ORDER: INTEGER [AK]
                                     SID: BIGINT [FK]
                                     MASK: INTEGER
                                     GRANTING: BOOLEAN
                                     AUDIT_SUCCESS: BOOLEAN
                                     AUDIT_FAILURE: BOOLEAN
```

You can see how the concepts of SIDs, object identity, and ACEs map directly to the database schema. Conceptually, this is convenient, as we can map our mental model of the ACL system and how it is enforced directly to the database.

If you've cross referenced this with the H2 database schema supplied with the Spring Security documentation, you'll note that we've made a few tweaks that commonly bite users. These are as follows:

- Change the `ACL_CLASS.CLASS` column to `500` characters, from the default value of `100`. Some long, fully-qualified class names don't fit in 100 characters.
- Name the foreign keys with something meaningful so that failures are more easily diagnosed.

> If you are using another database, such as Oracle, you'll have to translate the DDL into DDL and data types specific to your database.

Once we configure the remainder of the ACL system, we'll return to the database to set up some basic ACEs to prove the ACL functionality in its most primitive form.

# Configuring SecurityExpressionHandler

We'll need to configure `<global-method-security>` to enable annotations (where we'll annotate based on the expected ACL privilege), and reference a custom access decision manager.

We will also need to provide a `o.s.s.access.expression.SecurityExpressionHandler` implementation that is aware of how to evaluate permissions. Update your `security.xml` configuration as follows:

src/main/webapp/WEB-INF/spring/security.xml

```xml
<global-method-security
        pre-post-annotations="enabled">
    <expression-handler ref="expressionHandler"/>
</global-method-security>
<http pattern="/resources/**" security="none"/>
```

This is a bean reference to the `DefaultMethodSecurityExpressionHandler` object that we have defined in `security-acl.xml` for you:

src/main/webapp/WEB-INF/spring/security-acl.xml

```xml
<bean id="expressionHandler"
    class="org.springframework.security.access.expression
    .method.DefaultMethodSecurityExpressionHandler">
    <property name="permissionEvaluator" ref="permissionEvaluator"/>
    <property name="permissionCacheOptimizer"
        ref="permissionCacheOptimizer"/>
</bean>
```

With even a relatively straightforward ACL configuration, as we have in our scenario, there are a number of required dependencies to set up. As we mentioned previously, the Spring Security ACL module comes out of the box with a number of components that you can assemble to provide a decent set of ACL capabilities. Take note that all of the components that we'll reference in the following diagram are part of the framework:

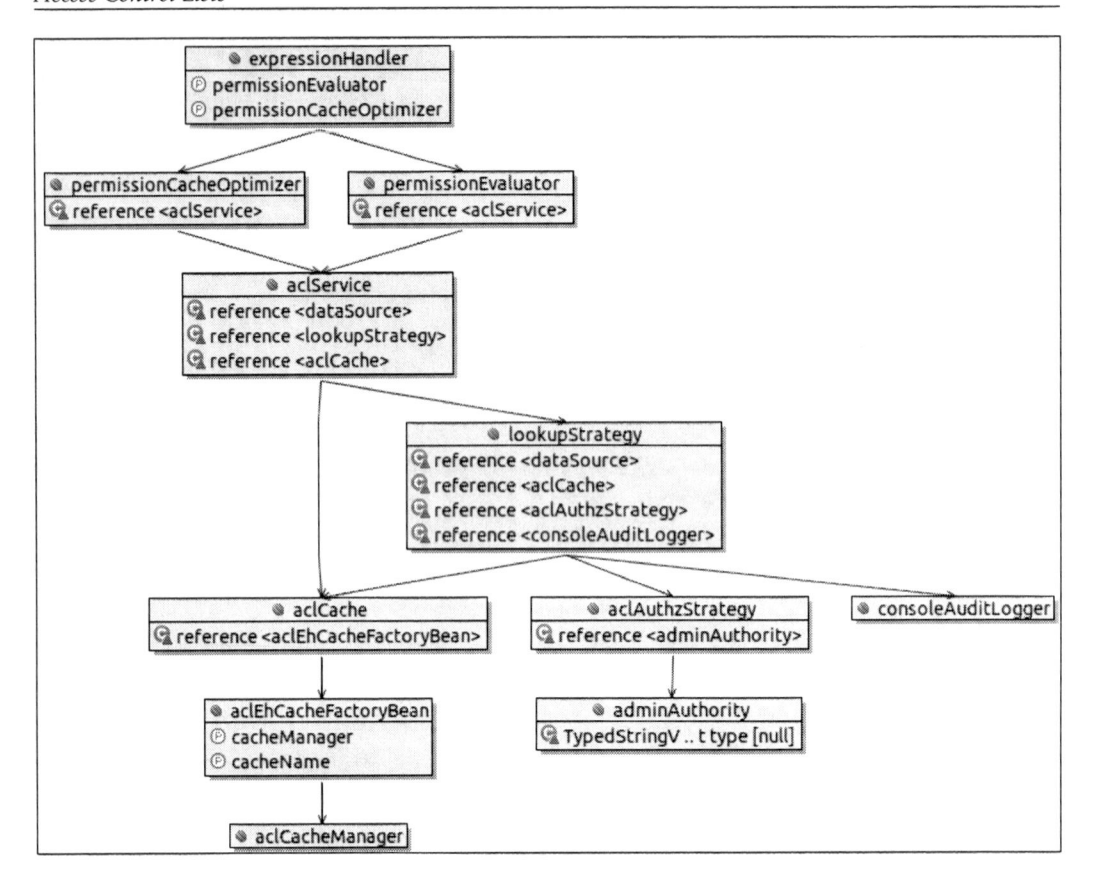

## AclPermissionCacheOptimizer

The `DefaultMethodSecurityExpressionHandler` object has two dependencies. The `AclPermissionCacheOptimizer` object is used to prime the cache with all the ACLs for a collection of objects in a single JDBC `select` statement. The relatively simple configuration included with this chapter can be seen as follows:

src/main/webapp/WEB-INF/spring/security-acl.xml

```
<bean id="permissionCacheOptimizer"
  class="org.springframework.security.acls
  .AclPermissionCacheOptimizer">
  <constructor-arg ref="aclService"/>
</bean>
```

# PermissionEvaluator

`DefaultMethodSecurityExpressionHandler` then delegates to a `PermissionEvalulator` instance. For the purposes of this chapter, we are using ACLs so that the bean we will use `AclPermissionEvaluator`, which will read the ACLs that we define in our database. You can view the provided configuration for `permissionEvaluator` as follows:

src/main/webapp/WEB-INF/spring/security-acl.xml

```
<bean id="permissionEvaluator"
  class="org.springframework.security.acls
  .AclPermissionEvaluator">
  <constructor-arg ref="aclService"/>
</bean>
```

# JdbcMutableAclService

At this point, we have seen a reference to the bean with ID as `aclService` twice. `aclService` resolves to an implementation of `o.s.s.acls.model.AclService` that is responsible (through delegation) for translating information about the object being secured by ACLs into expected ACEs.

src/main/webapp/WEB-INF/spring/security-acl.xml

```
<bean id="aclService" class="org.springframework.security.acls
  .jdbc.JdbcMutableAclService">
  <constructor-arg ref="dataSource"/>
  <constructor-arg ref="lookupStrategy"/>
  <constructor-arg ref="aclCache"/>
</bean>
```

We'll use `o.s.s.acls.jdbc.JdbcMutableAclService`, which is the default implementation of `o.s.s.acls.model.AclService`. This implementation comes out of the box, and is ready to use the schema that we defined earlier in the chapter. `JdbcMutableAclService` will additionally use recursive SQL and post-processing to understand object and SID hierarchies, and ensure representations of these hierarchies are passed back to `AclPermissionEvaluator`.

*Access Control Lists*

## BasicLookupStrategy

The `JdbcMutableAclService` class uses the same JDBC `dataSource` instance that we've defined with the embedded-database declaration, and also delegates to an implementation of `o.s.s.acls.jdbc.LookupStrategy`, which is solely responsible for actually making database queries and resolving requests for ACLs. The only `LookupStrategy` implementation supplied with Spring Security is `o.s.s.acls.jdbc.BasicLookupStrategy`, and is defined as follows:

src/main/webapp/WEB-INF/spring/security-acl.xml

```
<bean id="lookupStrategy"
  class="org.springframework.security.acls
  .jdbc.BasicLookupStrategy">
  <constructor-arg ref="dataSource" />
  <constructor-arg ref="aclCache" />
  <constructor-arg ref="aclAuthzStrategy"/>
  <constructor-arg ref="consoleAuditLogger"/>
</bean>
```

Now, `BasicLookupStrategy` is a relatively complex beast. Remember that its purpose is to translate a list of `ObjectIdentity` declarations to be protected into the actual, applicable ACE list from the database. As `ObjectIdentity` declarations can be recursive, this proves to be quite a challenging problem, and a system which is likely to experience heavy use should consider the SQL that's generated for performance impact on the database.

> **Querying with the lowest common denominator**
>
> Be aware that `BasicLookupStrategy` is intended to be compatible with all databases by strictly sticking with standard ANSI SQL syntax, notably `left [outer]` joins. Some older databases (notably, Oracle 8*i*) did not support this join syntax, so be sure to verify that the syntax and structure of SQL is compatible with your particular database!
>
> There are also most certainly more efficient database-dependent methods of performing hierarchical queries using non-standard SQL, for example, Oracle's `CONNECT BY` statement and the **Common Table Expression** (**CTE**) capability of many other databases, including PostgreSQL and Microsoft SQL Server.
>
> Much as we learned in the example in *Chapter 4, JDBC-based Authentication*, using a custom schema for the `JdbcDaoImpl` implementation of the `UserDetailsService` properties are exposed to allow for configuration of the SQL utilized by `BasicLookupStrategy`. Please consult the Javadoc and the source code itself to see how they are used, so that they can be correctly applied to your custom schema.

We can see that `LookupStrategy` requires a reference to the same JDBC `dataSource` instance that `AclService` utilizes. The other three references bring us almost to the end of the dependency chain.

## EhCacheBasedAclCache

`o.s.s.acls.model.AclCache` declares an interface for a caching `ObjectIdentity` to ACL mappings, to prevent redundant (and expensive) database lookups. Spring Security ships with only one implementation of **AclCache**, using the third-party library **Ehcache**.

Ehcache is an open-source, memory and disk-based caching library that is widely used in many open-source and commercial Java products. As mentioned earlier in the chapter, Spring Security ships with a default implementation of ACL caching, which relies on the availability of a configured Ehcache instance, which it uses to store ACL information in preference to reading ACLs from the database.

While deep configuration of Ehcache is not something we want to cover in this section, we'll cover how Spring ACL uses the cache, and walk you through a basic, default configuration.

Setting up Ehcache is trivial—we'll simply declare `o.s.s.acls.domain.EhCacheBasedAclCache` along with its two dependent beans from Spring Core that manage Ehcache instantiation and expose several helpful configuration properties. Like our other beans, we have already provided the following configuration in `security-acl.xml`.

src/main/webapp/WEB-INF/spring/security-acl.xml

```
<bean id="aclCache"
  class="org.springframework.security.acls
  .domain.EhCacheBasedAclCache">
  <constructor-arg ref="aclEhCacheFactoryBean"/>
</bean>
<bean id="aclEhCacheFactoryBean"
  class="org.springframework.cache.ehcache.EhCacheFactoryBean">
  <property name="cacheManager" ref="aclCacheManager"/>
  <property name="cacheName" value="aclCache" />
</bean>
<bean id="aclCacheManager"
  class="org.springframework.cache.ehcache
  .EhCacheManagerFactoryBean"/>
```

## ConsoleAuditLogger

The next simple dependency hanging off of `o.s.s.acls.jdbc.BasicLookupStrategy` is an implementation of the `o.s.s.acls.domain.AuditLogger` interface, which is used by the `BasicLookupStrategy` class to audit ACL and ACE lookups. Similar to the `AclCache` interface, only one implementation is supplied with Spring Security that simply logs to the console. We'll configure it with another one-line bean declaration:

src/main/webapp/WEB-INF/spring/security-acl.xml

```
    <bean id="consoleAuditLogger"
      class="org.springframework.security.acls.domain
      .ConsoleAuditLogger" />
```

## AclAuthorizationStrategyImpl

The final dependency to resolve is to an implementation of the `o.s.s.acls.domain.AclAuthorizationStrategy` interface, which actually has no immediate responsibility at all during the load of the ACL from the database. Instead, the implementation of this interface is responsible for determining whether a runtime change to an ACL or ACE is allowed, based on the type of change. We'll explain more on this later when we cover mutable ACLs, as the logical flow is both somewhat complicated and not pertinent to getting our initial configuration complete. The final configuration requirements are as follows:

src/main/webapp/WEB-INF/spring/security-acl.xml

```
    <bean id="aclAuthzStrategy"
      class="org.springframework.security.acls
      .domain.AclAuthorizationStrategyImpl">
      <constructor-arg ref="adminAuthority"/>
    </bean>
    <bean id="adminAuthority"
      class="org.springframework.security.core
      .authority.SimpleGrantedAuthority">
      <constructor-arg value="ROLE_ADMINISTRATOR" />
    </bean>
```

You might wonder what the reference to the bean with ID as `adminAuthority` is for—`AclAuthorizationStrategyImpl` provides the ability to specify `GrantedAuthority` that is required to allow specific operations at runtime on mutable ACLs. We'll cover these later in the chapter.

Last we need to update our `web.xml` file to load our `security-acl.xml` file as follows:

src/main/webapp/WEB-INF/web.xml

```
<param-value>
    ...
    /WEB-INF/spring/security-acl.xml
</param-value>
```

We're finally done with basic configuration of an out-of-the-box Spring Security ACL implementation. The next and final step requires that we insert a simple ACL and ACE into the H2 database, and test it out!

# Creating a simple ACL entry

Recall that our very simple scenario is to only allow user2@example.com access to the Birthday Party event and ensure that no other events are accessible. You may find it helpful to refer back several pages to the database schema diagram to follow which data we are inserting and why.

We have already included a file named `security-acl-data.sql` in the sample application. All the SQL explained in this section will be from the file — you may feel free to experiment and add more test cases based on the sample SQL we've provided — in fact, we'd encourage that you experiment with sample data!

First, we'll need to populate the ACL_CLASS table with any or all of the domain object classes, which may have ACL rules — in the case of our example, this is simply our Event class:

src/main/resources/database/h2/security-acl-data.sql

```
insert into acl_class (id, class)
values (10, 'com.packtpub.springsecurity.domain.Event');
```

> We chose to use primary keys that are between 10 to 19 for the ACL_CLASS table, 20 to 29 for the ACL_SID table, and so on. This will help to make it easier to understand which data associates to which table. Note that our EVENTS table starts with a primary key of 100. These conveniences are done for example purposes and are not suggested for production purposes.

Next, the ACL_SID table is seeded with SIDs that will be associated to the ACEs. Remember that SIDs can either be roles or users — we'll populate the roles and user2@example.com here.

## Access Control Lists

While the SID for roles is straightforward, the SID for a user is not quite as clear cut. For our purposes, the username is used for the SID. To learn more about how the SIDs are resolved for roles and users, refer to `o.s.s.acls.domain. SidRetrievalStrategyImpl`. If the defaults do not meet your needs, a custom `o.s.s.acls.model.SidRetrievalStrategy` default can be injected into `AclPermissionCacheOptimizer` and `AclPermissionEvaluator`. We will not need this sort of customization for our example, but it is good to know that it is available if necessary.

src/main/resources/database/h2/security-acl-data.sql

```
insert into acl_sid (id, principal, sid) values (20, true, 'user2@example.com');
insert into acl_sid (id, principal, sid) values (21, false, 'ROLE_USER');
insert into acl_sid (id, principal, sid) values (22, false, 'ROLE_ADMIN');
```

The table where things start getting complicated is the `ACL_OBJECT_IDENTITY` table that is used to declare individual domain object instances, their parent (if any), and owning SID. For example, this table represents the `Event` objects that we are securing. We'll insert a row with the following properties:

- Domain Object of type `Event` that is a foreign key, `10`, to our `ACL_CLASS` via the `OBJECT_ID_CLASS` column.
- Domain Object primary key of `100` (the `OBJECT_ID_IDENTITY` column). This is a foreign key (although not enforced with a database constraint) to our `Event` object.
- Owner SID of `user2@example.com`, which is a foreign key, `20`, to `ACL_SID` via the `OWNER_SID` column.

The SQL to represent our events with IDs of `100` (Birthday Event), `101`, and `102` is:

src/main/resources/database/h2/security-acl-data.sql

```
insert into acl_object_identity
    (id,object_id_identity,object_id_class,parent_object,owner_sid,entries_inheriting)
    values (30, 100, 10, null, 20, false);
insert into acl_object_identity
    (id,object_id_identity,object_id_class,parent_object,owner_sid,entries_inheriting)
    values (31, 101, 10, null, 21, false);
insert into acl_object_identity
    (id,object_id_identity,object_id_class,parent_object,owner_sid,entries_inheriting)
    values (32, 102, 10, null, 21, false);
```

Keep in mind that the owning SID could also represent a role—both types of rules function equally well as far as the ACL system is concerned.

Finally, we'll add an ACE related to this object instance, which declares that `user2@example.com` is allowed read access to the the Birthday event.

src/main/resources/database/h2/security-acl-data.sql

```
insert into acl_entry
    (acl_object_identity, ace_order, sid, mask, granting, audit_success, audit_failure)
    values(30, 1, 20, 1, true, true, true);
```

The `MASK` column here represents a bitmask, which is used to grant permission assigned to the stated SID on the object in question. We'll explain the details of this later in this chapter—unfortunately, it doesn't tend to be as useful as it may sound.

Now, we can start the application and run through our sample scenario. Try logging in with `user1@example.com` / `user1` and accessing the **All Events** page. You will see that only the Birthday event is listed. When logged in with `admin1@example.com` / `admin1` and viewing the **All Events** page, no events will be displayed. However, if we navigated directly to an event, it would not be protected. Can you figure out how to secure direct access to an event based upon what we learned in this chapter?

If you have not figured it out yet, you can secure direct access to an event by making the following update to `CalendarService`:

src/main/java/com/packtpub/springsecurity/service/CalendarService.java

```
@PostAuthorize("hasPermission(filterObject, 'read') " +
        "or hasPermission(filterObject, 'admin_read')")
Event getEvent(int eventId);
```

We now have a basic working setup of ACL-based security (albeit, a very simple scenario). Let's move on to some more explanation about concepts we saw during this walkthrough, and then review a couple of considerations in a typical Spring ACL implementation that you should consider before using it.

```
@PostAuthorize("hasPermission(returnObject, 'read')")
```

> Your code should look like `calendar11.01-calendar`.

# Advanced ACL topics

Some high-level topics that we skimmed over during the configuration of our ACL environment had to do with ACE permissions, and the use of GrantedAuthority indicators to assist the ACL environment in determining whether certain types of runtime changes to ACLs were allowed. Now that we have a working environment, we'll review these more advanced topics.

## How permissions work

Permissions are no more than single logical identifiers represented by bits in an integer. An access control entry grants permissions to SIDs based on the bitmask, which comprises the logical ANDing of all permissions applicable to that access control entry.

The default permission implementation, o.s.s.acls.domain.BasePermission, defines a series of integer values representing common ACL authorization verbs. These integer values correspond to single bits set in an integer, so a value of BasePermission, WRITE, with integer value 1 has a bitwise value of $2^1$ or 2.

These are illustrated in the following diagram:

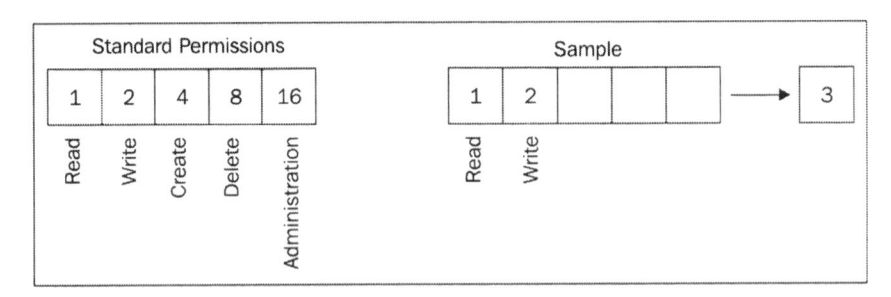

| Standard Permissions | | | | | | Sample | | | | | |
|---|---|---|---|---|---|---|---|---|---|---|---|
| 1 | 2 | 4 | 8 | 16 | | 1 | 2 | | | → | 3 |
| Read | Write | Create | Delete | Administration | | Read | Write | | | | |

We can see that the sample permission bitmask would have an integer value of 3, due to the application of both the **Read** and **Write** permissions to the permission value. All of the standard integer single permission values shown in the diagram are defined in the BasePermission object as static constants.

The logical constants that are included in BasePermission are just a sensible baseline of commonly used permissions in access-control entries, and have no semantic meaning within the Spring Security framework. It's quite common for very complex ACL implementations to invent their own custom permissions, augmenting best practice examples with domain- or business-dependent ones.

One issue that often confuses users is how the bitmasks are used in practice, given that many databases either do not support bitwise logic, or do not support it in a scalable way. Spring ACL intends to solve this problem by putting more of the load of calculating appropriate permissions vis-à-vis bitmasks on the application, rather than on the database.

It's important to review the resolution process, where we see how `AclPermissionEvaluator` resolves permissions declared on the method itself (in our example, with the `@PostFilter` annotation) to real ACL permissions. The following diagram illustrates the process that Spring ACL performs to evaluate the declared permission against the relevant ACEs for the requesting principal:

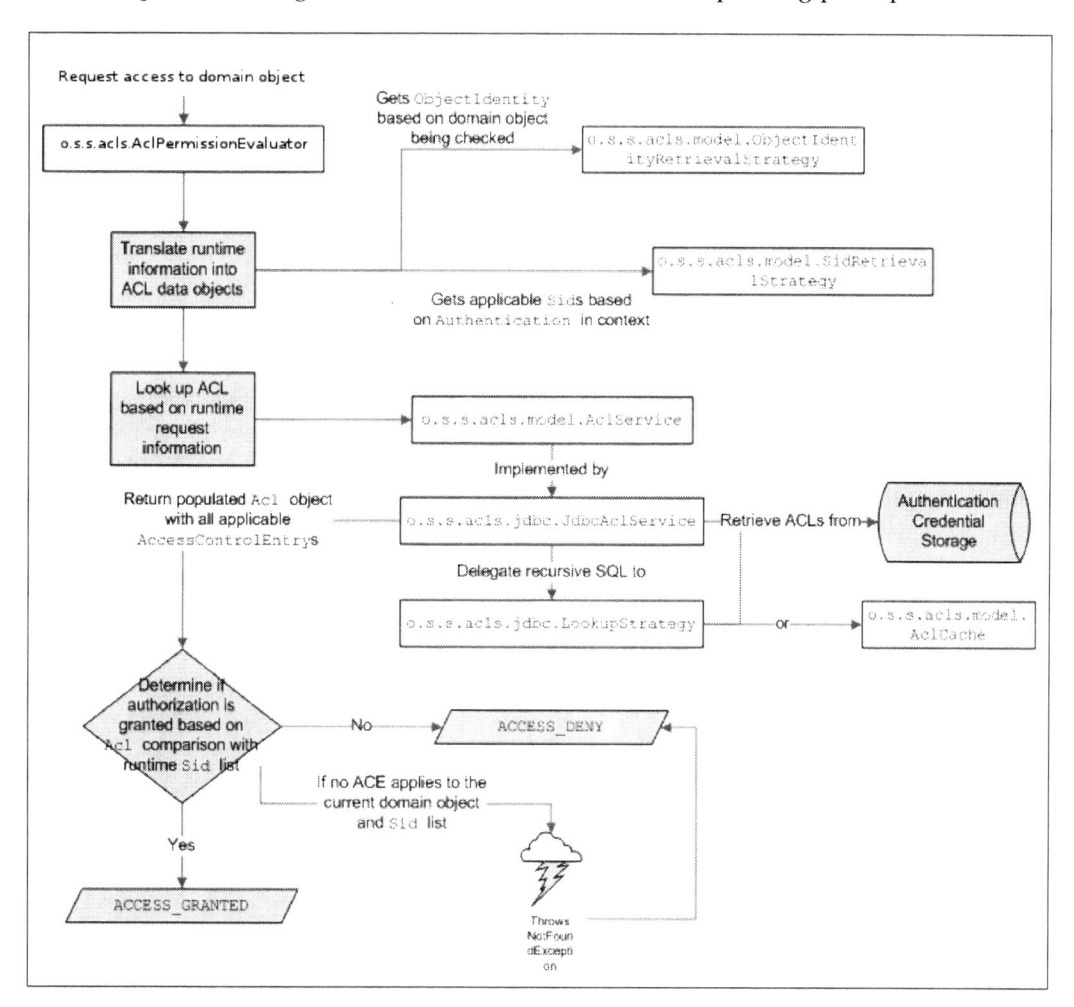

We see that `AclPermissionEvaluator` relies on classes implementing two interfaces, `o.s.s.acls.model.ObjectIdentityRetrievalStrategy` and `o.s.s.acls.model.SidRetrievalStrategy`, to retrieve `ObjectIdentity` and SIDs appropriate for the authorization check. The important thing to note about these strategies is how the default implementation classes actually determine `ObjectIdentity` and SIDs to return, based on the context of the authorization check.

`ObjectIdentity` has two properties, `type` and `identifier`, that are derived from the object being checked at runtime, and used to declare ACE entries. The default `ObjectIdentityRetrievalStrategy` uses the fully-qualified class name to populate the `type` property. The `identifier` property is populated with the result of a method with the signature `Serializable getId()`, invoked on the actual object instance.

As your object isn't required to implement an interface to be compatible with ACL checks, the requirement to implement a method with a specific signature can be surprising for developers implementing Spring Security ACL. Plan ahead and ensure that your domain objects contain this method! You may also implement your own `ObjectIdentityRetrievalStrategy` (or subclass the out-of-the-box implementation) to call a method of your choice. The name and type signature of the method is, unfortunately, not configurable.

Unfortunately, the actual implementation of `AclImpl` directly compares the permission specified in our SpEL expression in our `@PostFilter` annotation, and the permission stored on the ACE in the database, without using bitwise logic. The Spring Security community is in debate about whether this is unintentional or working as intended, but regardless, you will need to take care when declaring a user with a combination of permissions; as either `AclEntryVoter` must be configured with all combinations of permission, or the ACEs need to ignore the fact that the permission field is intended to store multiple values, and instead store a single permission per ACE.

If you want to verify this with our simple scenario, change the **Read** permission we granted to the `user2@example.com` SID to the bitmask combination of **Read** and **Write**, which translates to a value of 3. This would be changed in `security-acl-data.sql`:

src/main/resources/database/h2/security-acl-data.sql

```
    insert into acl_entry
        (acl_object_identity, ace_order, sid, mask, granting, audit_success, audit_failure)
        values(30, 1, 20, 3, true, true, true);
```

You can see that if you now try to view the **All Events** page with `user2@example.com` / `user2`, you will not be able to view the Birthday event, even though we've declared that you have both **Read** and **Write** access in a single ACE.

> Your code should look like `chapter11.02-calendar`.

# Custom ACL permission declaration

As stated in the earlier discussion on permission declarations, permissions are nothing but logical names for integer bit values. As such, it's possible to extend the `o.s.s.acls.domain.BasePermission` class and declare your own permissions. We'll cover a very straightforward scenario here, where we create a new ACL permission called `ADMIN_READ`. This is a permission that will be granted only to administrative users, and will be assigned to protect resources that only administrators could read. Although a contrived example for the JBCP Calendar application, this type of use of custom permissions occurs quite often in situations dealing with personally identifiable information (for example, social security number, and so on—recall that we covered PII in *Chapter 1, Anatomy of an Unsafe Application*).

Let's get started making the changes required to support this. The first step is to extend `BasePermission` with our own `com.packtpub.springsecurity.acls.domain.CustomPermission` class:

```
package com.packtpub.springsecurity.acls.domain;

public class CustomPermission extends BasePermission {
    public static final Permission ADMIN_READ = new CustomPermission(1 << 5, 'M'); // 32

    public CustomPermission(int mask, char code) {
        super(mask, code);
    }
}
```

Next, we will need to configure the `o.s.s.acls.domain.PermissionFactory` default implementation, `o.s.s.acls.domain.DefaultPermissionFactory`, to register our custom permission logical value. The role of the `PermissionFactory` is to resolve permission bitmasks into logical permission values (which can be referenced by constant value, or by name, such as `ADMIN_READ`, in other areas of the application). The `PermissionFactory` requires that any custom permissions be registered with it for proper lookup. We have included the following configuration that registers our `CustomPermission` as follows:

src/main/webapp/WEB-INF/spring/security-acl.xml

```
    <bean id="permissionFactory"
      class="org.springframework.security.acls
      .domain.DefaultPermissionFactory">
      <constructor-arg value="com.packtpub.springsecurity.acls
        .domain.CustomPermission"/>
    </bean>
```

Next, we will need to override the default `PermissionFactory` instance for our `BasicLookupStrategy` and our `AclPermissionEvaluator` with the customized `DefaultPermissionFactory`. Make the following updates to your `security-acl.xml` file:

src/main/webapp/WEB-INF/spring/security-acl.xml

```
    <bean id="permissionEvaluator" ...>
        ...
        <property name="permissionFactory" ref="permissionFactory"/>
    </bean>
    ...
    <bean id="lookupStrategy" ...>
        ...
        <property name="permissionFactory" ref="permissionFactory"/>
    </bean>
```

We also need to add the SQL query to utilize the new permission to grant access to the Conference Call (`acl_object_identity` ID of 31) event to admin1@example.com the following lines into `security-acl.xml`:

src/main/resources/database/h2/security-acl-data.sql

```
    insert into acl_sid (id, principal, sid) values (23, true, 'admin1@example.com');
    insert into acl_entry
        (acl_object_identity, ace_order, sid, mask, granting, audit_success, audit_failure)
        values(31, 1, 23, 32, true, true, true);
```

We can see that the new integer bitmask value of 32 has been referenced in the ACE data. This intentionally corresponds to our new `ADMIN_READ` ACL permission, as defined in Java code. The Conference Call event is referenced by its primary key (stored in the `object_id_identity` column) value of 31, in the `ACL_OBJECT_IDENTITY` table.

The last step is to update our `CalendarService`'s `getEvents()` method, to utilize our new permission.

```
@PostFilter("hasPermission(filterObject, 'read') " +
     "or hasPermission(filterObject, 'admin_read')")
List<Event> getEvents();
```

With all these configurations in place, we can start up the site again and test out the custom ACL permission. Based on the sample data we have configured, here is what should happen when the various available users click on categories:

| Username/password | Birthday Party event | Conference Call event | Other events |
|---|---|---|---|
| user2@example.com/ user2 | Allowed via READ | Denied | Denied |
| admin1@example.com/ admin1 | Denied | Allowed via ADMIN_READ | Denied |
| user1@example.com/ user1 | Denied | Denied | Denied |

We can see that even with the use of our simple cases, we've now been able to extend the Spring ACL functionality in a very limited way to illustrate the power of this fine-grained access control system.

> Your code should look like `chapter11.03-calendar`.

# Enabling your JSPs with the Spring Security JSP tag library through ACL

We saw in *Chapter 2*, *Getting Started with Spring Security*, that the Spring Security JSP tag library offers functionality to expose authentication-related data to the user, and to restrict what the user can see based on a variety of rules.

The very same tag library can also interact with an ACL-enabled system right out of the box! From our simple experiments, we have configured a simple ACL authorization scenario around the first two categories in the list on the home page.

First, we will need to remove our `@PostFilter` annotation from the `getEvents()` method in our `CalendarService` interface in order to give our JSP tag library a chance to filter out the events that are not allowed for display. Go ahead and remove `@PostFilter` now:

src/main/java/com/packtpub/springsecurity/service/CalendarService.java

```
    List<Event> getEvents();
```

Now that we have removed `@PostFilter`, we can utilize the `<sec:accesscontrollist>` tag to hide the events that the user doesn't actually have access to. Please refer to the table in the previous section as a refresher of the access rules we've configured up to this point!

We'll wrap the display of each event with the `<sec:accesscontrollist>` tag, declaring the list of permissions to check on the object to be displayed:

src/main/webapp/WEB-INF/views/events/list.jsp

```
    <c:forEach items="${events}" var="event">
      <sec:authorize access="hasPermission(#event,'read') or
        hasPermission(#event,'admin_read')">
        <tr>
          <fmt:formatDate value="${event.when.time}" type="both"
            pattern="yyyy-MM-dd HH:mm" var="when"/>
          <td><c:out value="${when}"/></td>
          <td><c:out value="${event.owner.name}" /></td>
          <td><c:out value="${event.attendee.name}" /></td>
          <c:url var="eventUrl" value="${event.id}"/>
          <td><a href="${eventUrl}">
            <c:out value="${event.summary}" />
          </a></td>
        </tr>
      </sec:authorize>
    </c:forEach>
```

Think for a moment about what we want to occur here—we want the user to see only the items to which they actually have the READ or ADMIN_READ (our custom permission) access.

Behind the scenes, the tag implementation utilizes the same `SidRetrievalStrategy` and `ObjectIdentityRetrievalStrategy` discussed earlier in this chapter. So, the computation of access checking follows the same workflow as it does with ACL-enabled voting on method security. As we will see in a moment, the tag implementation will also use the same `PermissionEvaluator`.

We have already configured our `<global-method-security>` element with an `<expression-handler>` element that references a `DefaultMethodSecurityExpressionHandler`. `DefaultMethodSecurityExpressionHandler` is aware of our `AclPermissionEvaluator`, but we must also make Spring Security's web tier aware of `AclPermissionEvalulator`. If you think about it, this symmetry makes sense, since securing methods and an HTTP request are protecting two very different resources. Fortunately, Spring Security's abstractions make this rather simple. Add `DefaultWebSecurityExpressionHandler` that references the bean with ID as `permissionEvaluator` that we have already defined.

src/main/webapp/WEB-INF/spring/security-acl.xml

```xml
<bean id="webExpressionHandler"
        class="org.springframework.security.web.access.expression.DefaultWebSecurityExpressionHandler">
    <property name="permissionEvaluator" ref="permissionEvaluator"/>
</bean>
```

Now update `security.xml` to refer to our `webExpressionHandler` as follows:

src/main/webapp/WEB-INF/spring/security.xml

```xml
<http auto-config="true" use-expressions="true">
    ...
    <expression-handler ref="webExpressionHandler"/>
</http>
```

You can see how these steps are very similar to how we added support for permission handling to our method security. This time it was a bit simpler, since we were able to reuse the same bean with ID as `PermissionEvaluator` that we already configured.

Start up our application and try accessing the **All Events** page as different users. You will find that the events that are not allowed for a user are now hidden using our tag library instead of the `@PostFilter` annotation. We are still aware that accessing an event directly would allow a user to see it. However, this could easily be added by combining what we learned in this chapter with what we learned about the `@PostAuthorize` annotation in this chapter.

> Your code should look like `chapter11.04-calendar`.

# Mutable ACLs and authorization

Although the JBCP Calendar application doesn't implement full user administration functionality, it's likely that your application will have common features, such as new user registration and administrative user maintenance. To this point, lack of these features—which we have worked around using SQL inserts at application startup—hasn't stopped us from demonstrating many of the features of Spring Security and Spring ACL.

However, the proper handling of runtime changes to declared ACLs, or the addition or removal of users in the system, is critical to maintaining the consistency and security of the ACL-based authorization environment. Spring ACL solves this issue through the concept of the mutable ACL (o.s.s.acls.model.MutableAcl).

Extending the standard ACL interface, the MutableAcl interface, allows for runtime manipulation of ACL fields in order to change the in-memory representation of a particular ACL. This additional functionality includes the ability to create, update, or delete ACEs, change ACL ownership, and other useful functions.

We might expect, then, that the Spring ACL module would come out of the box with a way to persist runtime ACL changes to the JDBC data store, and indeed it does. The o.s.s.acls.jdbc.JdbcMutableAclService class may be used to create, update, and delete MutableAcl instances in the database, as well as to do general maintenance on the other supporting tables for ACLs (handling SIDs, ObjectIdentity, and domain object class names).

Recall from earlier in the chapter that the AclAuthorizationStrategyImpl class allows us to specify the administrative role for actions on mutable ACLs. These are supplied to the constructor as part of the bean configuration. The constructor arguments and their meanings are as follows:

| Arg # | What it does |
| --- | --- |
| 1 | Indicates the authority that a principal is required to have in order to take ownership of an ACL-protected object at runtime |
| 2 | Indicates the authority that a principal is required to have in order to change the auditing of an ACL-protected object at runtime |
| 3 | Indicates the authority that a principal is required to have in order to make any other kind of change (create, update, and delete) to an ACL-protected object at runtime. |

> It may be confusing that we only specified a single constructor argument when there are three arguments listed. `AclAuthorizationStrategyImpl` can also accept a single `GrantedAuthority`, which will then be used for all three arguments. This is convenient if we want the same `GrantedAuthority` to be used for all of the operations.

`JdbcMutableAclService` contains a number of methods used to manipulate ACL and ACE data at runtime. While the methods themselves are fairly understandable (`createAcl`, `updateAcl`, `deleteAcl`), the correct way to configure and use `JdbcMutableAclService` is often difficult for even advanced Spring Security users.

Let's modify `CalendarService` to create a new ACL for newly-created events.

## Adding ACLs to newly created Events

Currently, if a user creates a new event, it will not be visible to the user in the **All Events** view since we are using the `<sec:authorize>` JSP tag to only display `Event` objects that the user has access to. Let's update our `DefaultCalendarService`, so that when a user creates a new event, they are granted read access to that event and it will be displayed for them on the **All Events** page. The first step is to update our constructor to accept `MutableAclService` and `UserContext`:

src/main/java/com/packtpub/springsecurity/service/DefaultCalendarService.java

```
public class DefaultCalendarService implements CalendarService {
    ...
    private final MutableAclService aclService;
    private final UserContext userContext;

    @Autowired
    public DefaultCalendarService(EventDao eventDao,
            CalendarUserDao userDao,
            MutableAclService aclService,
            UserContext userContext) {
        ...
        this.aclService = aclService;
        this.userContext = userContext;
    }
```

# Access Control Lists

Then we need to update our `createEvent` method to also create an ACL for the current user. Make the following changes:

src/main/java/com/packtpub/springsecurity/service/DefaultCalendarService.java

```
    @Transactional
    public int createEvent(Event event) {
        int result = eventDao.createEvent(event);
        event.setId(result);

        MutableAcl acl = aclService.createAcl(new
ObjectIdentityImpl(event));
        PrincipalSid sid =
                new PrincipalSid(userContext.getCurrentUser().getEmail());
        acl.setOwner(sid);
        acl.insertAce(0, BasePermission.READ, sid, true);
        aclService.updateAcl(acl);

        return result;
    }
```

`JdbcMutableAclService` uses the current user as the default owner for the created `MutableAcl`. We chose to explicitly set the owner again to demonstrate how this can be overridden. We then add a new ACE and save our ACL. That's all there is to it.

Start the application and log in as user1@example.com/user1. Visit the **All Events** page and see that there are no events currently listed. Then, create a new event and it will be displayed the next time you visit the **All Events** page. If you log in as any other user, the event will not be visible on the **All Events** page. However, it will potentially be visible to the user since we have not applied security to other pages. Again, we encourage you to attempt to secure these pages on your own.

> Your code should look like `chapter11.05-calendar`.

# Considerations for a typical ACL deployment

Actually deploying Spring ACL in a true business application tends to be quite involved. We wrap up coverage of Spring ACL with some considerations that arise in most Spring ACL implementation scenarios.

# About ACL scalability and performance modelling

For small and medium-sized applications, the addition of ACLs is quite manageable, and while it adds overhead to database storage and runtime performance, the impact is not likely to be significant. However, depending on the granularity with which ACLs and ACEs are modeled, the numbers of database rows in a medium- to large-sized application can be truly staggering, and can task even the most seasoned database administrator.

Let's assume we were to extend ACLs to cover an extended version of the JBCP Calendar application. Let's assume that users can manage accounts, post pictures to events, and administer (add/remove users) from an event. We'll model the data as follows:

- All users have accounts.
- 10 percent of users are able to administer an event. The average number of events that a user can administer will be two.
- Events will be secured (read-only) per customer, but also need to be accessible (read/write) by administrators.
- 10 percent of all customers will be allowed to post pictures. The average number of posts per user will be 20.
- Posted pictures will be secured (read-write) per user, as well as administrators. Posted pictures will be read-only for all other users.

Given what we know about the ACL system, we know that the database tables have the following scalability attributes:

| Table | Scales with data | Scalability notes |
| --- | --- | --- |
| ACL_CLASS | No | One row is required per domain class. |
| ACL_SID | Yes (users) | One row is required per role (GrantedAuthority). One row is required for each user account (if individual domain objects are secured per user). |
| ACL_OBJECT_IDENTITY | Yes (domain class * instances per class) | One row is required per instance of secured domain object. |
| ACL_ENTRY | Yes (domain object instances * individual ACE entries) | One row is required per ACE; may require multiple rows for a single domain object. |

Access Control Lists

We can see that ACL_CLASS doesn't really have scalability concerns (most systems will have fewer than 1000 domain classes). ACL_SID will scale linearly based on the number of users in the system. This is probably not a matter of concern because other user-related tables will scale in this fashion as well (user account, and so on).

The two tables of concern are ACL_OBJECT_IDENTITY and ACL_ENTRY. If we model the estimated rows required to model an order for an individual customer, we come up with the following estimates:

| Table | ACL data per event | ACL data per picture post |
| --- | --- | --- |
| ACL_OBJECT_IDENTITY | One row is required for a single event. | One row required for a single post. |
| ACL_ENTRY | Three Rows—one row is required for read access by the owner (the user SID), two rows are required (one for read access, one for write access) for the administrative group SID. | Four rows—one row is required for read access by the user group SID, one row is required for write access by the owner, two rows are required for the administrative group SID (as with events) |

We can then take the usage assumptions from the previous page and calculate the following ACL scalability matrix:

| Table/Object | Scale factor | Estimates (Low) | Estimates (High) |
| --- | --- | --- | --- |
| Users | | 10,000 | 1,000,000 |
| Events | # Users * 0.1 * 2 | 2,000 | 200,000 |
| Picture Posts | # Users * 0.1 * 20 | 20,000 | 2,000,000 |
| ACL_SID | # Users | 10,000 | 1,000,000 |
| ACL_OBJECT_IDENTITY | # Events + # Picture Posts | 22,0000 | 2,200,000 |
| ACL_ENTRY | (# Events * 3) + (# Picture Posts * 4) | 86,000 | 8,600,000 |

From these projections based on only a subset of the business objects likely to be involved and secured in a typical ACL implementation, you can see that the number of database rows devoted to storing ACL information is likely to grow linearly (or faster) in relation to your actual business data. Especially in large system planning, forecasting the amount of ACL data that you are likely to use is extremely important. It is not uncommon for very complex systems to have hundreds of millions of rows related to ACL storage.

# Do not discount custom development costs

Utilizing a Spring ACL-secured environment often requires significant development work above and beyond the configuration steps we've described to this point. Our sample configuration scenario has the following limitations:

- No facility is provided for responding to the manipulation modification of events or modification of permissions
- Not all of the application is using permissions. For example, the **My Events** page and directly navigating to an event are both not secured

The application does not effectively use ACL hierarchies. These limitations would significantly impact the functionality where we were to roll out ACL security to the whole site. This is why it is critical that when planning Spring ACL rollout across an application, you must carefully review all places where the domain data is manipulated and ensure that these locations correctly update ACL and ACE rules, and invalidate caches. Typically, the securing of methods and data takes place at the service or business application layer, and the hooks required to maintain ACLs and ACEs occur at the data access layer:

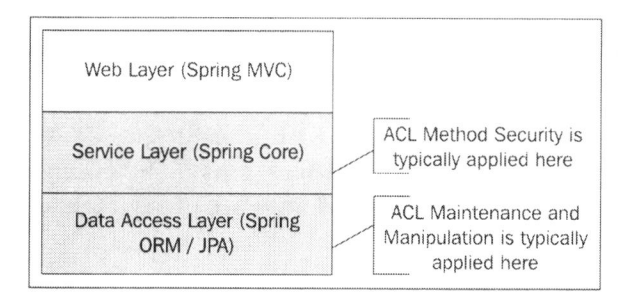

```
Web Layer (Spring MVC)

Service Layer (Spring Core)      ACL Method Security is
                                 typically applied here

Data Access Layer (Spring        ACL Maintenance and
ORM / JPA)                       Manipulation is typically
                                 applied here
```

If you are dealing with a reasonably standard application architecture, with proper isolation and encapsulation of functionality, it's likely that there's an easily identified central location for these changes. On the other hand, if you're dealing with an architecture that has devolved (or was never designed well in the first place), then adding ACL functionality and supporting hooks in data manipulation code can prove to be very difficult.

As previously hinted, it's important to keep in mind that the Spring ACL architecture hasn't changed significantly since the days of Acegi 1.x. During that time, many users have attempted to implement it, and have logged and documented several important restrictions, many of which are captured in the Spring Security JIRA repository (http://jira.springframework.org/). Issue SEC-479 functions as a useful entry point for some of the key limitations, many of which remain unaddressed with Spring Security 3, and (if they are applicable to your situation) can require significant custom coding to work around.

The following are some of the most important and commonly encountered, issues:

- The ACL infrastructure requires a numeric primary key. For applications that use a GUID or UUID primary key (which occurs more frequently due to more efficient support in modern databases), this can be a significant limitation.
- As of this writing, the JIRA issue, SEC-1140, documents the issue that the default ACL implementation does not correctly compare permission bitmasks using bitwise operators. We covered this earlier in the section on permissions.
- Several inconsistencies exist between the method of configuring Spring ACL and the rest of Spring Security. In general, it is likely that you will run into areas where class delegates or properties are not exposed through DI, necessitating an override and rewrite strategy that can be time-consuming and expensive to maintain.
- The permission bitmask is implemented as an integer, and thus has 32 possible bits. It's somewhat common to expand the default bit assignments to indicate permissions on individual object properties (for example, assigning a bit to read the social security number of an employee). Complex deployments may have well over 32 properties per domain object, in which case the only alternative would be to remodel your domain objects around this limitation.

Depending on your specific application's requirements, it is likely that you will encounter additional issues, especially with regards to the number of classes requiring change when implementing certain types of customizations.

## Should I use Spring Security ACL

Just as the details of applying Spring Security as a whole tend to be highly business dependent, so too is the application of Spring ACL support—in fact, this tends to be even more true of ACL support due to its tight coupling to business methods and domain objects. We hope that this guide to Spring ACL explained the important high- and low-level configurations and concepts required to analyze Spring ACL for use in your application, and can assist you in determining and matching its capabilities to real-world use.

# Summary

In this chapter, we focused on security based on access control list and the specific details of how this type of security is implemented by the Spring ACL module.

We did the following:

- Reviewed the basic concept of access control lists, and the many reasons why they can be very effective solutions to authorization.
- Learned the key concepts related to the Spring ACL implementation, including access control entries, SIDs, and object identity.
- Examined the database schema and logical design required to support a hierarchical ACL system.
- Configured all the required Spring Beans to enable the Spring ACL module, and enhanced one of the service interfaces to use annotated method authorization. We then tied the existing users in our database, and business objects used by the site itself, into a sample set of ACE declarations and supporting data.
- Reviewed the concepts around Spring ACL Permission handling.
- Expanded our knowledge of the Spring Security JSP tag library and SpEL expression language (for method security) to utilize ACL checks.
- Discussed the mutable ACL concept, and reviewed the basic configuration and custom coding required in a mutable ACL environment.
- Developed a custom ACL permission, and configured the application to demonstrate its effectiveness.
- Configured and analyzed the use of the Ehcache cache manager to reduce the database impact of Spring ACL.
- Analyzed the impact and design considerations of using the Spring ACL system in a complex business application.

This wraps up our discussion about Spring Security ACLs. In the next chapter, we'll dig a bit further into how Spring Security works.

# 12
# Custom Authorization

In this chapter, we will write custom implementations of Spring Security's key authorization APIs. Once we have done this, we will use the understanding of the custom implementations to understand how Spring Security's authorization architecture works.

Throughout this chapter, we'll:

- Gain an understanding of how authorization works
- Write a custom `SecurityMetaDataSource` backed by a database instead of `<intercept-url>` elements.
- Create a custom SpEL expression
- Implement a custom `PermissionEvaluator` that allows our permissions to be encapsulated

## How requests are authorized

Similar to authentication, Spring Security provides a servlet filter, `o.s.s.web.access.intercept.FilterSecurityInterceptor`, which is responsible for coming up with a decision on whether or not a particular request will be accepted or denied. At the point the filter is invoked, the principal has already been authenticated, so the system knows that a valid user has logged in; remember that we implemented a method (`List<GrantedAuthority> getAuthorities()`), which returns a list of authorities for the principal in *Chapter 3, Custom Authentication*. In general, the authorization process will use the information from this method (defined by the `Authentication` interface) to determine, for a particular request, whether or not the request should be allowed.

Remember that authorization is a binary decision—a user either has access to a secured resource or he does not. There is no ambiguity when it comes to authorization.

Smart object-oriented design is pervasive within the Spring Security framework, and authorization decision management is no exception.

In Spring Security, the `o.s.s.access.AccessDecisionManager` interface specifies two simple and logical methods that fit sensibly into the processing decision flow of requests:

- `supports`: This logical operation actually comprises two methods that allow the `AccessDecisionManager` implementation to report whether or not it supports the current request.
- `decide`: This allows the `AccessDecisionManager` implementation to verify, based on the request context and security configuration, whether or not access should be allowed and the request be accepted. `decide` actually has no return value, and instead reports the denial of a request by throwing an exception to indicate rejection.

Specific types of exceptions can further dictate the action to be taken by the application to resolve authorization decisions. `o.s.s.access.AccessDeniedException` is the most common exception thrown in the area of authorization and merits special handling by the filter chain.

The implementation of `AccessDecisionManager` is completely configurable using standard Spring Bean binding and references. The default `AccessDecisionManager` implementation provides an access granting mechanism based on `AccessDecisionVoter` and vote aggregation.

A voter is an actor in the authorization sequence whose job is to evaluate any or all of the following:

- The context of the request for a secured resource (such as a URL requesting an IP address)
- The credentials (if any) presented by the user
- The secured resource being accessed
- The configuration parameters of the system, and the resource itself

The `AccessDecisionManager` implementation is also responsible for passing the access declaration (referred to in the code as implementations of the `o.s.s.access.ConfigAttribute` interface) of the resource being requested to the voter. In the case of web URLs, the voter will have information about the access declaration of the resource. If we look at our very basic configuration file's URL intercept declaration, we'll see `ROLE_USER` being declared as the access configuration for the resource the user is trying to access:

```
<intercept-url pattern="/**" access="ROLE_USER"/>
```

Based on the voter's knowledge, it will decide whether the user should have access to the resource or not. Spring Security allows the voter to make one of three decisions, whose logical definition is mapped to constants in the interface:

| Decision type | Description |
| --- | --- |
| `Grant (ACCESS_GRANTED)` | The voter recommends giving access to the resource. |
| `Deny (ACCESS_DENIED)` | The voter recommends denying access to the resource. |
| `Abstain (ACCESS_ABSTAIN)` | The voter abstains (does not make a decision) on access to the resource. This may happen for a number of reasons, such as:<br>• The voter doesn't have conclusive information<br>• The voter can't decide on a request of this type |

As you may have guessed from the design of access decision-related objects and interfaces, this portion of Spring Security has been designed so that it can be applicable to authentication and access control scenarios that aren't exclusively in the web domain. We'll encounter voters and access decision managers when we look at method-level security later in this chapter.

# Custom Authorization

When we put this all together, the overall flow of the "default authorization check for web requests" is similar to the following diagram:

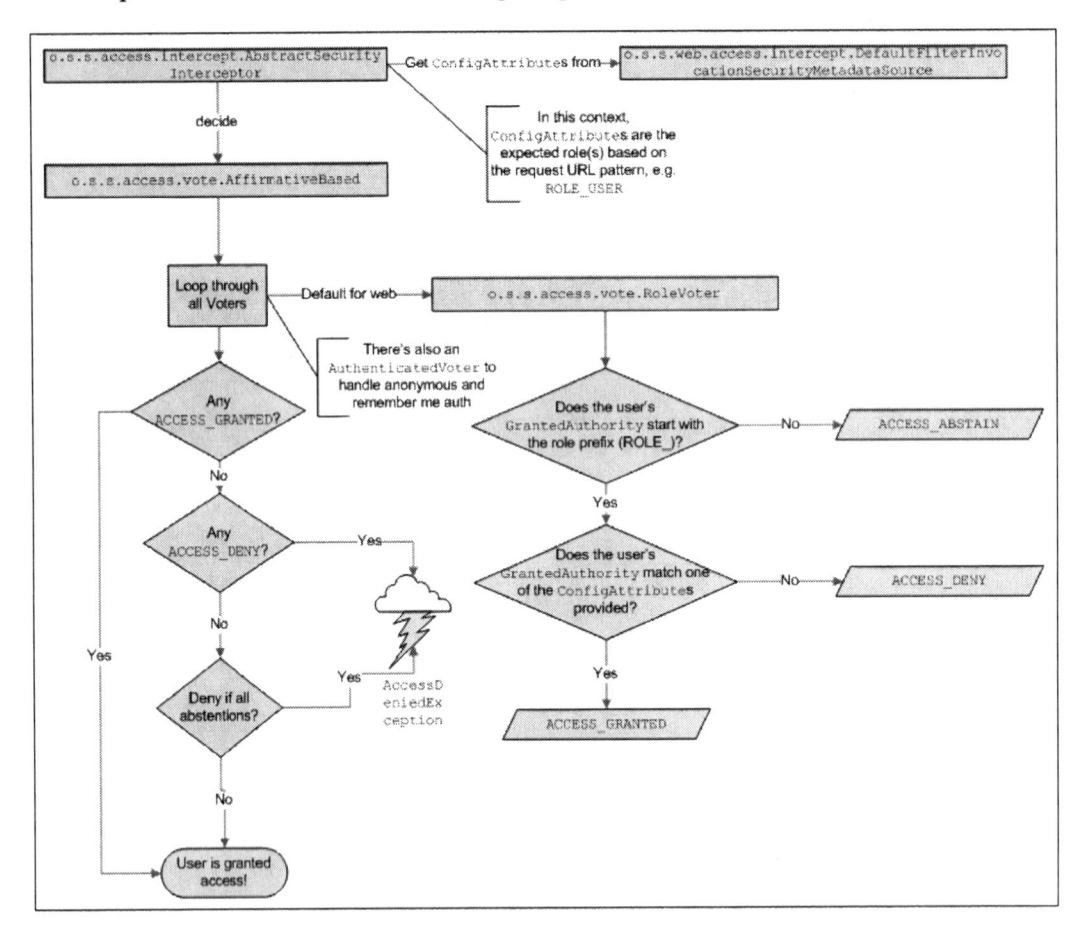

We can see that the abstraction of `ConfigAttribute` allows for data to be passed from the configuration declarations (retained in the `o.s.s.web.access.intercept.DefaultFilterinvocationSecurityMetadataSource`) to the voter responsible for acting on `ConfigAttribute` without any intervening classes needing to understand the contents of `ConfigAttribute`. This separation of concerns provides a solid foundation for building new types of security declarations (such as the declarations we will see with method security) while utilizing the same access decision pattern.

# Configuration of access decision aggregation

Spring Security does actually allow configuration of `AccessDecisionManager` in the security namespace. The `access-decision-manager-ref` attribute on the `<http>` element allows you to specify a Spring Bean reference to an implementation of `AccessDecisionManager`. Spring Security ships with three implementations of this interface, all in the `o.s.s.access.vote` package. They are as follows:

| Class name | Description |
| --- | --- |
| `AffirmativeBased` | If any voter grants access, access is immediately granted, regardless of previous denials. |
| `ConsensusBased` | The majority vote (grant or deny) governs the decision of the `AccessDecisionManager`. Tie-breaking and handling of empty votes (containing only abstentions) is configurable. |
| `UnanimousBased` | All voters must grant access, otherwise access is denied. |

# Configuring to use a UnanimousBased access decision manager

If we want to modify our application to use the access decision manager, we'd require two modifications. In order to do this, we would add the `access-decision-manager-ref` attribute to the `<http>` element in our `security.xml` file as follows:

src/main/webapp/WEB-INF/spring/security.xml

```
<http auto-config="true"
      access-decision-manager-ref="unanimousBased">
```

This is a standard Spring Bean reference, so this should correspond to the `id` attribute of a bean. We could then define the `UnanimousBased` bean, as shown in the following code snippet. Note that we will not actually utilize this configuration in our exercises.

src/main/webapp/WEB-INF/spring/security-accessdecisionmanager.xml

```
<bean id="unanimousBased"
      class="org.springframework.security.access.vote.
UnanimousBased">
    <constructor-arg>
        <list>
            <ref bean="roleVoter" />
            <ref bean="authenticatedVoter" />
        </list>
```

# Custom Authorization

```
        </constructor-arg>
    </bean>
    <bean id="roleVoter"
            class="org.springframework.security.access.vote.RoleVoter"/>
    <bean id="authenticatedVoter"
            class="org.springframework.security.access.vote.
AuthenticatedVoter"/>
```

You may be wondering what the `decisionVoters` property is about. This property is auto-configured until we declare our own `AccessDecisionManager`. The default `AccessDecisionManager` requires us to declare the list of voters who are consulted to arrive at the authentication decisions. The two voters listed here are the defaults supplied by the security namespace configuration.

Spring Security doesn't come supplied with a wide variety of voters, but it would be trivial to implement a new one. As we will see later in the chapter, in most situations, creating a custom voter is not necessary, since it can typically be implemented using custom expressions or even a custom `o.s.s.access.PermissionEvaluator`.

The two voter implementations that we reference here do the following:

| Class name | Description | Example |
| --- | --- | --- |
| `o.s.s.access.vote.RoleVoter` | Checks that the user has the matching the declared role. Expects the attribute to define a comma-delimited list of names. The prefix is expected, but optionally configurable. | `access="ROLE_USER,ROLE_ADMIN"` |
| `o.s.s.access.vote.AuthenticatedVoter` | Supports special declarations allowing wildcard matches: `IS_AUTHENTICATED_FULLY` allows access if a fresh username and password are supplied. `IS_AUTHENTICATED_REMEMBERED` allows access if the user has authenticated with the **remember me** functionality. `IS_AUTHENTICATED_ANONYMOUSLY` allows access if the user is anonymous | `access="IS_AUTHENTICATED_ANONYMOUSLY"` |

# Expression-based request authorization

As you might expect, the SpEL handling is supplied by a different `Voter` implementation, `o.s.s.web.access.expression.WebExpressionVoter`, which understands how to evaluate the SpEL expressions. The `WebExpressionVoter` class relies on an implementation of the `SecurityExpressionHandler` interface for this purpose. The `SecurityExpressionHandler` is responsible both for evaluating the expressions, as well as for supplying the security-specific methods that are referenced in the expressions. The default implementation of this interface exposes methods defined in the `o.s.s.web.access.expression.WebSecurityExpressionRoot` class.

The flow and relationship between these classes is shown in the following diagram:

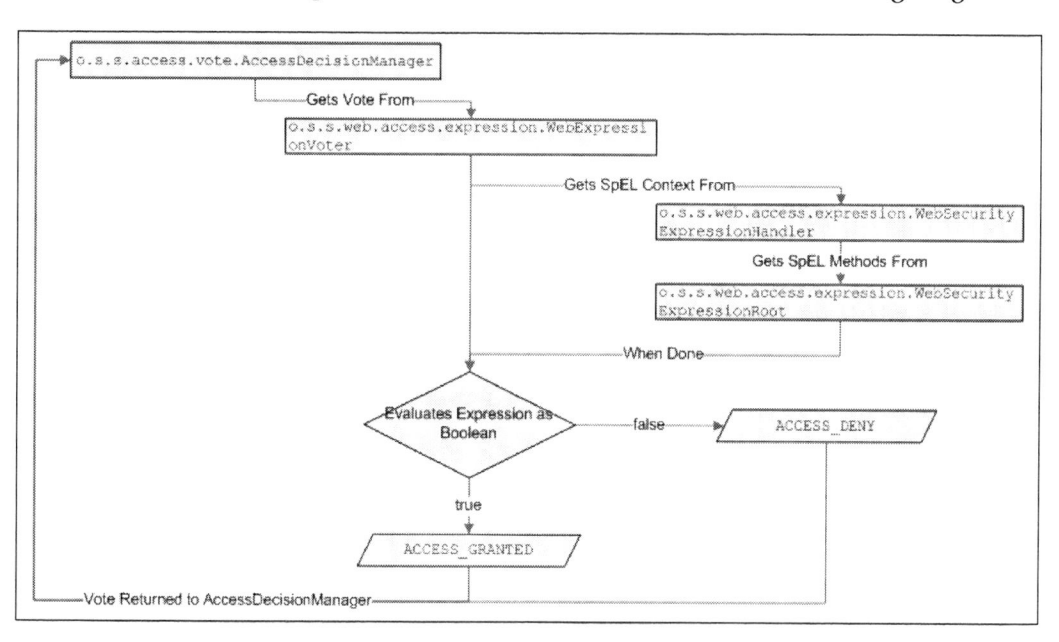

Now that we know how request authorization works, let's solidify our understanding by making a few custom implementations of key interfaces.

# Customizing request authorization

The real power of Spring Security's authorization is demonstrated by how adaptable it is to custom requirements. Let's explore a few scenarios that will help reinforce our understanding of the overall architecture.

# Dynamically defining access control to URLs

Spring Security provides several methods for mapping `ConfigAttribute` objects to a resource. For example, the `<intercept-url>` element to ensure it is simple for developers to restrict access to specific HTTP requests in their web application. Under the covers, an implementation of `o.s.s.acess.SecurityMetadataSource` is populated with these mappings and queried to determine what is required in order to be authorized to make any given HTTP request.

While the `<intercept-url>` method is very simple, there may be times that it would be desirable to provide a custom mechanism for determining the URL mappings. An example of this might be if an application needs to be able to dynamically provide the access control rules. Let's demonstrate what it would take to move our URL authorization configuration into a database.

## JdbcRequestConfigMappingService

The first step is to be able to obtain the necessary information from the database. This will replace the logic that reads in the `<intercept-url>` elements from our security bean configuration. In order to do this, the chapter's sample code contains `JdbcRequestConfigMappingService`, which will obtain a mapping of an **ant pattern** and an expression from the database represented as a `RequestConfigMapping`. The rather simple implementation is as follows:

src/main/java/com/packtpub/springsecurity/web/access/intercept/
JdbcRequestConfigMappingService.java

```
@Repository("requestConfigMappingService")
public class JdbcRequestConfigMappingService implements
RequestConfigMappingService {
    private static final String SELECT_SQL = "select ant_pattern,
expression from security_filtermetadata order by sort_order";
    private final JdbcOperations jdbcOperations;

    public JdbcRequestConfigMappingService(JdbcOperations
jdbcOperations) {
        this.jdbcOperations = jdbcOperations;
```

```
        }

    public List<RequestConfigMapping> getRequestConfigMappings() {
        return jdbcOperations.query(SELECT_SQL,
                new RequestConfigMappingMapper());
    }

    private static final class RequestConfigMappingMapper implements
RowMapper<RequestConfigMapping> {
        public RequestConfigMapping mapRow(ResultSet rs, int rowNum)
throws SQLException {
            String pattern = rs.getString("ant_pattern");
            String expressionString = rs.getString("expression");
            AntPathRequestMatcher matcher = new AntPathRequestMatcher
(pattern);
            return new RequestConfigMapping(matcher,
                    new SecurityConfig(expressionString));
        }
    }
}
```

It is important to notice that, just as with the `<intercept-url>` element, order matters. Therefore, we ensure the results are sorted by the column named, `sort_order`. The service creates an `AntRequestMatcher` and associates it to `SecurityConfig`, an instance of `ConfigAttribute`. This will provide a mapping of HTTP request to `ConfigAttribute` objects that can be used by Spring Security to secure our URLs.

In order for the new service to work, we will need to initialize our database with the schema and the access control mappings. Just as with the service implementation, our schema is rather straightforward.

src/main/resources/database/h2/security-metadata-schema.sql

```
create table security_filtermetadata (
    id bigint identity,
    ant_pattern varchar(1024) not null unique,
    expression varchar(1024) not null,
    sort_order bigint not null
);
```

# Custom Authorization

We can then use the same `<intercept-url>` mappings from our `security.xml` file to produce the `security-metadata-data.sql` file.

src/main/resources/database/h2/security-metadata-data.sql

```sql
insert into security_filtermetadata(ant_pattern,expression,sort_order)
    values ('/','permitAll',10);
...
insert into security_filtermetadata(ant_pattern,expression,sort_order)
    values ('/admin/**','hasRole("ROLE_ADMIN")',60);
...
```

We can then instruct Spring to load our newly defined SQL scripts at startup time, in order to properly initialize our database. Make the following updates to `services.xml`:

> You should be starting with `chapter12.00-calendar`.

src/main/webapp/WEB-INF/spring/services.xml

```xml
<jdbc:embedded-database id="dataSource" type="H2">
    ...
    <jdbc:script location="classpath:/database/h2/security-metadata-schema.sql"/>
    <jdbc:script location="classpath:/database/h2/security-metadata-data.sql"/>
</jdbc:embedded-database>
```

## FilterInvocationServiceSecurityMetadataSource

In order for Spring Security to be aware of our URL mappings, we need to provide a custom `FilterInvocationSecurityMetadataSource` implementation. `FilterInvocationSecurityMetadataSource` extends the `SecurityMetadataSource` interface which given a particular HTTP request is what provides Spring Security the information necessary for determining if access should be granted. Let's take a look at how we can utilize our `RequestConfigMappingService` to implement a `SecurityMetadataSource` interface.

src/main/java/com/packtpub/springsecurity/web/access/intercept/FilterInvocationServiceSecurityMetadataSource.java

```java
@Component("filterInvocationServiceSecurityMetadataSource")
public class FilterInvocationServiceSecurityMetadataSource implements
        FilterInvocationSecurityMetadataSource, InitializingBean{
```

```
        ... constructor  and member variables omitted ...

    public Collection<ConfigAttribute> getAllConfigAttributes() {
        return this.delegate.getAllConfigAttributes();
    }

    public Collection<ConfigAttribute> getAttributes(Object object) {
        return this.delegate.getAttributes(object);
    }

    public boolean supports(Class<?> clazz) {
        return this.delegate.supports(clazz);
    }

    public void afterPropertiesSet() throws Exception {
        List<RequestConfigMapping> requestConfigMappings =
                requestConfigMappingService.getRequestConfigMappings();
        LinkedHashMap requestMap =
                new LinkedHashMap(requestConfigMappings.size());
        for(RequestConfigMapping requestConfigMapping : requestConfigMappings) {
            RequestMatcher matcher = requestConfigMapping.getMatcher();
            Collection<ConfigAttribute> attributes =
                    requestConfigMapping.getAttributes();
            requestMap.put(matcher,attributes);
        }
        this.delegate =
            new ExpressionBasedFilterInvocationSecurityMetadataSource(requestMap,
                expressionHandler);
    }
}
```

We are able to use our `RequestConfigMappingService` to create a map of `RequestMatcher` to the `ConfigAttribute` objects. We then delegate to an instance of `ExpressionBasedFilterInvocationSecurityMetadataSource` to do all the work. For simplicity, the current implementation would require restarting the application to pick up changes. However, with a few minor changes, we could avoid this inconvenience.

# BeanPostProcessor to extend namespace configuration

Now, all that is left is for us to configure `FilterInvocationServiceSecurityMetadataSource`. The only problem is that the Spring Security namespace does not support configuring a custom `FilterInvocationServiceSecurityMetadataSource`. If we abandon the namespace configuration, the amount of work to configure Spring Security quickly gets out of control. Instead, we will use `o.s.beans.factory.config.BeanPostProcessor` to customize our configuration.

`BeanPostProcessor` is a standard Spring interface that allows any object configured through Spring to be manipulated before the application starts up. We will use a custom `BeanPostProcessor` to replace the standard `FilterInvocationServiceSecurityMetadataSource` with our custom implementation. Make sure to uncomment the `@Component` annotation.

src/main/java/com/packtpub/springsecurity/config/FilterInvocationServiceSecurityMetadataSourceBeanPostProcessor.java

```
@Component
public class FilterInvocationServiceSecurityMetadataSourceBeanPostProcessor implements BeanPostProcessor {
    @Autowired
    private FilterInvocationServiceSecurityMetadataSource metadataSource;

    public Object postProcessBeforeInitialization(Object bean, String beanName) {
        if(bean instanceof FilterInvocationSecurityMetadataSource) {
            return metadataSource;
        }
        return bean;
    }

    public Object postProcessAfterInitialization(Object bean, String beanName) {
        return bean;
    }
}
```

To customize our configuration if the passed in bean is an instance of `FilterInvocationSecurityMetadataSource`, we will return our `FilterInvocationServiceSecurityMetadataSource` instead of the default implementation. Otherwise we simply return the original bean.

## Removing our <intercept-url> elements

Now that the database is being used to map our security configuration, we can remove the `<intercept-url>` elements from our `security.xml` file. Go ahead and remove them, so that the configuration looks similar to the following code snippet:

src/main/webapp/WEB-INF/spring/security.xml

```xml
<http auto-config="true" use-expressions="true">
    <!-- no intercept-url elements -->
    <access-denied-handler .../>
    <form-login .../>
    <logout .../>
</http>
```

You should now be able to start the application and test to ensure that our URLs are secured as they have been. Our users will not notice a difference, but we know that our URL mappings are persisted in a database now.

> Your code should look like `chapter12.01-calendar`.

## Creating a custom expression

The `o.s.s.access.expression.SecurityExpresssionHandler` interface is how Spring Security abstracts how the Spring Expressions are created and initialized. Just as with the `SecurityMetadataSource` interface, there is an implementation for creating expressions for web requests and creating expressions for securing methods. In this section, we will explore how we can easily add new expressions.

### CustomWebSecurityExpressionRoot

Let's assume that we want to support a custom web expression named `isLocal` that will return `true` if the host is `localhost` and `false` otherwise. This new method could be used to provide additional security for our SQL console by ensuring that it is only accessed from the same machine that the web application is deployed from.

# Custom Authorization

> This is an artificial example that does not add any security benefit since the host comes from the headers of the HTTP request. This means a malicious user could inject a header stating the host is localhost even if they are requesting to an external domain.

All the expressions that we have seen are available because the SecurityExpressionHandler makes them available via an instance of o.s.s.access.expression.SecurityExpressionRoot. If you open this object, you will find the methods and properties we use in our Spring Expressions (that is, hasRole, hasPermission, and so on) that are common to both web and method security. A subclass provides the methods that are specific to web and method expressions. For example, o.s.s.web.access.expression.WebSecurityExpressionRoot provides the hasIpAddress method for web requests.

To create a custom web SecurityExpressionhandler, we will first need to create a subclass of WebSecurityExpressionRoot that defines our isLocal method.

src/main/java/com/packtpub/springsecurity/web/access/expression/CustomWebSecurityExpressionRoot.java

```java
public class CustomWebSecurityExpressionRoot extends
        WebSecurityExpressionRoot {

    public CustomWebSecurityExpressionRoot(Authentication a,
FilterInvocation fi) {
        super(a, fi);
    }

    public boolean isLocal() {
        return "localhost".equals(request.getServerName());
    }
}
```

> It is important to note that getServerName() returns the value that is provided in the Host header value. This means a malicious user can inject a different value in the header to bypass constraints. However, most application servers and proxies can enforce the value of the Host header. Please read the appropriate documentation before leveraging such an approach to ensure that malicious users do not inject a Host header value to bypass such a constraint.

## CustomWebSecurityExpressionHandler

In order for our new method to become available, we need to create a custom `SecurityExpressionHandler` interface that utilizes our new `root` object. This is as simple as extending `WebSecurityExpressionHandler` as follows:

src/main/java/com/packtpub/springsecurity/web/access/expression/CustomWebSecurityExpressionHandler.java

```java
@Component
public class CustomWebSecurityExpressionHandler extends
        DefaultWebSecurityExpressionHandler {
    private final AuthenticationTrustResolver trustResolver =
            new AuthenticationTrustResolverImpl();

    protected SecurityExpressionOperations
            createSecurityExpressionRoot(Authentication authentication,
    FilterInvocation fi) {
        WebSecurityExpressionRoot root =
                new CustomWebSecurityExpressionRoot(authentication, fi);
        root.setPermissionEvaluator(getPermissionEvaluator());
        root.setTrustResolver(trustResolver);
        root.setRoleHierarchy(getRoleHierarchy());
        return root;
    }
}
```

We perform the same steps that the `super` class does except that we use our `CustomWebSecurityExpressionRoot`, which contains the new method. `CustomWebSecurityExpressionRoot` becomes the root of our **Spring Expression Language (SpEL)** expression. For further details, refer to the SpEL documentation within the Spring Reference at http://static.springsource.org/spring/docs/current/spring-framework-reference/html/expressions.html.

## Configuring and using CustomWebSecurityExpressionHandler

We now need to configure `CustomWebSecurityExpressionHandler`. Fortunately, this can be done easily using the Spring Security namespace configuration support. Add the following configuration to `security.xml`:

src/main/webapp/WEB-INF/spring/security.xml

```
<http ...>
    ...
    <expression-handler ref="customWebSecurityExpressionHandler"/>
</http>
```

Now, let's update our initialization SQL query to use the new expression. Update our `security-metadata-data.sql` file, so that it requires the user to be ROLE_ADMIN and requested from the local machine. You will notice that we are able to write `local` instead of `isLocal`, since SpEL supports Java Bean conventions.

src/main/resources/database/h2/security-metadata-data.sql

```
insert into security_filtermetadata(ant_pattern,expression,sort_order)
    values ('/admin/**','local and hasRole("ROLE_ADMIN")',60);
```

Restart the application and access the H2 console using http://localhost:8080/calendar/admin/h2 and admin1@example.com/admin1 to see the admin console. If the H2 console is accessed using http://127.0.0.1:8080/calendar/admin/h2 and admin1@example.com admin1, the access denied page will be displayed.

> Your code should look like chapter12.03-calendar.

## How does method security work

The access decision mechanism for method security—whether or not a given request is allowed—is conceptually the same as the access decision logic for web request access. `AccessDecisionManager` polls a set of `AccessDecisionVoters`, each of which can provide a decision to grant or deny access, or abstain from voting. The specific implementation of `AccessDecisionManager` aggregates the voter decisions and arrives at an overall decision to allow the method invocation.

Web request access decision making is less complicated, due to the fact that the availability of servlet filters makes interception (and summary rejection) of securable requests relatively straightforward. As method invocation can happen from anywhere, including areas of code that are not directly configured by Spring Security, Spring Security designers chose to use a Spring-managed AOP approach to recognize, evaluate, and secure method invocations.

The following high-level flow illustrates the main players involved in authorization decisions for method invocation:

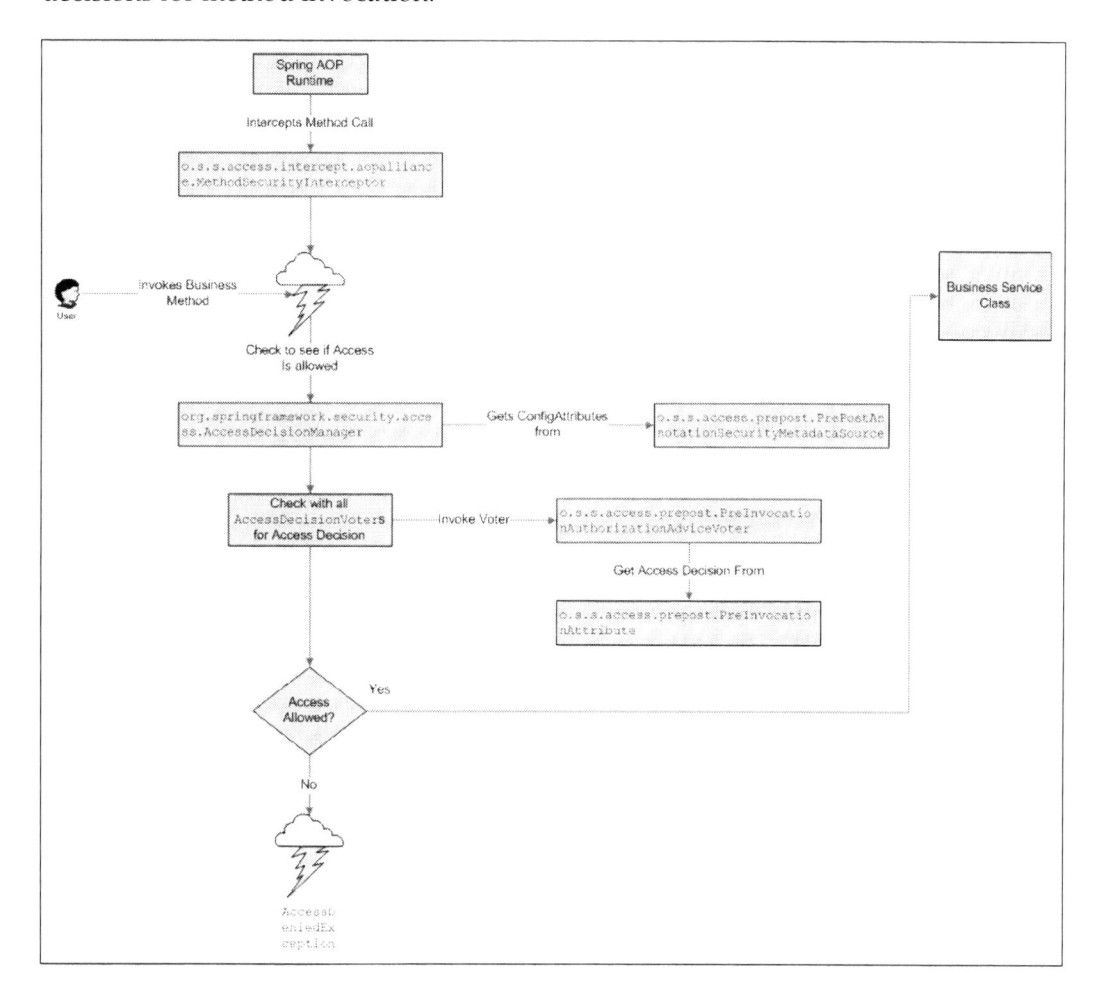

We can see that Spring Security's `o.s.s.access.intercept.aopalliance.MethodSecurityInterceptor` is invoked by the standard Spring AOP runtime to intercept method calls of interest. From here, the logic of whether or not to allow a method call is relatively straightforward, as per the previous flow diagram.

# Custom Authorization

At this point, we might wonder about the performance of the method security feature. Obviously, MethodSecurityInterceptor couldn't be invoked for every method call in the application—so how do annotations on methods or classes result in AOP interception?

First of all, AOP proxying isn't invoked for all Spring-managed beans by default. Instead, if <global-method-security> is defined in the Spring Security configuration, a standard Spring AOP o.s.beans.factory.config.BeanPostProcessor will be registered that will introspect the AOP configuration to see if any AOP advisors indicate that proxying (and interception) is required. This workflow is a standard Spring AOP handling (known as **AOP auto-proxying**), and doesn't inherently have any functionality specific to Spring Security. All registered BeanPostProcessor run at initialization of the spring ApplicationContext, after all Spring Bean configurations have occurred.

The AOP auto-proxy functionality queries all registered PointcutAdvisor to see if there are AOP pointcuts that resolve to method invocations that should have AOP advice applied. Spring Security implements the o.s.s.access.intercept.aopalliance.MethodSecurityMetadataSourceAdvisor class, which examines any and all configured method security and sets up appropriate AOP interception. Take note that only interfaces or classes with declared method security rules will be proxied for AOP!

> Be aware that it is strongly encouraged to declare AOP rules (and other security annotations) on interfaces, and not on implementation classes. The use of classes, while available using CGLIB proxying with Spring, may unexpectedly change certain behavior of your application, and is generally less semantically correct than security declarations (through AOP) on interfaces. MethodSecurityMetadataSourceAdvisor delegates the decision to affect methods with AOP advice to an o.s.s.access.method.MethodSecurityMetadataSource instance. The different forms of method security annotation each have their own MethodSecurityMetadataSource implementation, which is used to introspect each method and class in turn and add AOP advice to be executed at runtime.

The following diagram illustrates how this process occurs:

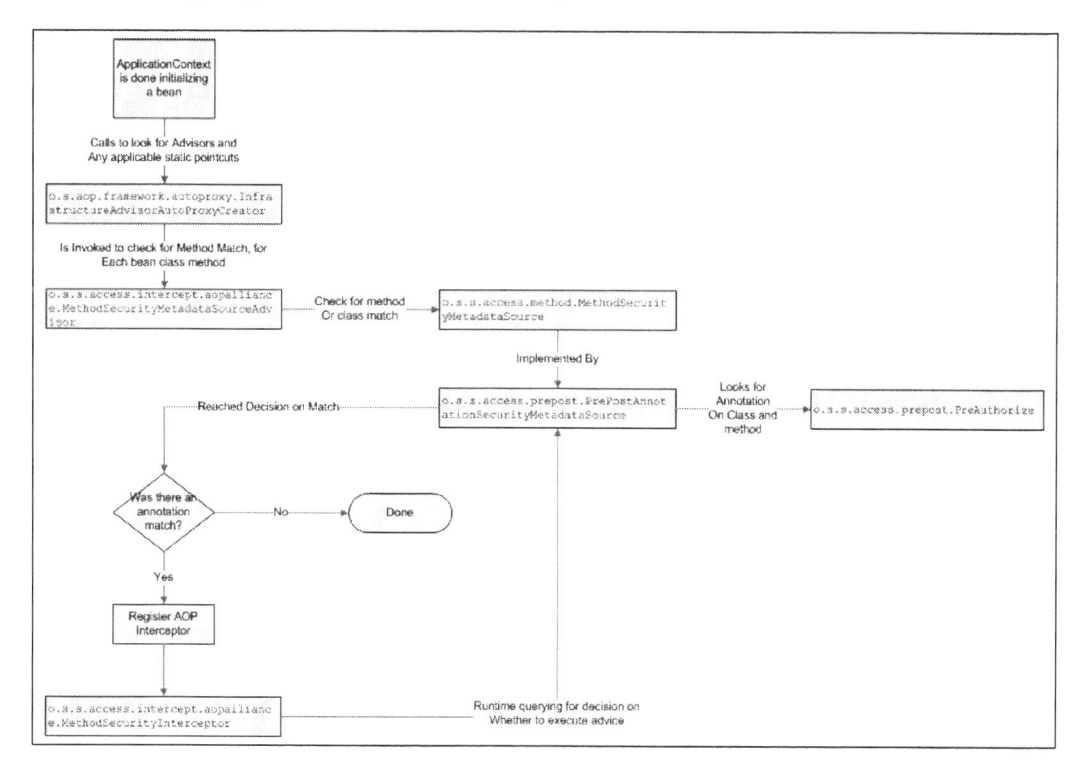

Depending on the number of Spring Beans configured in your application, and the number of secured method annotations you have, adding method security proxying may increase the time required to initialize your `ApplicationContext`. Once your Spring context is initialized, however, there is a negligible performance impact on individual proxied beans.

Now that we have an understanding of how we use AOP to apply Spring Security, let's strengthen our grasp of Spring Security authorization by creating a custom `PermissionEvaluator`.

# Creating a custom PermissionEvaluator

In the previous chapter, we demonstrated that we could use Spring Security's built-in `PermissionEvaluator` implementation, `AclPermissionEvaluator`, to restrict access to our application. While powerful, this can often at times be more complicated than necessary. We have also discovered how Spring's Expression language can formulate complex expressions that are able to secure our application. While simple, one of the downsides of using complex expressions is that the logic is not centralized. Fortunately, we can easily create a custom `PermissionEvaluator` that is able to centralize our authorization logic and still avoid the complexity of using ACLs.

## CalendarPermissionEvaluator

A simplified version of our custom `PermissionEvaluator` that does not contain any validation can be seen as follows:

src/main/java/com/packtpub/springsecurity/access/CalendarPermissionEvaluator.java

```
public final class CalendarPermissionEvaluator implements
PermissionEvaluator {
    private final EventDao eventDao;

    public CalendarPermissionEvaluator(EventDao eventDao) {
        this.eventDao = eventDao;
    }

    public boolean hasPermission(Authentication authentication, Object
targetDomainObject, Object permission) {
        // should do instanceof check since could be any domain object
        return hasPermission(authentication, (Event)
targetDomainObject, permission);
    }

    public boolean hasPermission(Authentication authentication,
Serializable targetId, String targetType,
        Object permission) {
        // missing validation and checking of the targetType
        Event event = eventDao.getEvent((Integer)targetId);
```

```java
            return hasPermission(authentication, event, permission);
    }

    private boolean hasPermission(Authentication authentication, Event event, Object permission) {
        if(event == null) {
            return true;
        }
        String currentUserEmail = authentication.getName();
        String ownerEmail = extractEmail(event.getOwner());
        if("write".equals(permission)) {
            return currentUserEmail.equals(ownerEmail);
        } else if("read".equals(permission)) {
            String attendeeEmail = extractEmail(event.getAttendee());
            return currentUserEmail.equals(attendeeEmail) ||
currentUserEmail.equals(ownerEmail);
        }
        throw new IllegalArgumentException("permission "+permission+" is not supported.");
    }

    private String extractEmail(CalendarUser user) {
        if(user == null) {
            return null;
        }
        return user.getEmail();
    }
}
```

The logic is fairly similar to the Spring Expressions that we have already used except that it differentiates read and write access. If the current user's username matches the owner's e-mail of the `Event` object, then both read and write access are granted. If the current user's e-mail matches the attendee's e-mail, then read access is granted. Otherwise access is denied.

> It should be noted that a single `PermissionEvaluator` is used for every domain object. So, in a real world situation, we must perform `instanceof` checks first. For example, if we were also securing our `CalendarUser` objects, these could be passed into this same instance. For a full example with these minor changes, refer to the sample code included in the text.

## Configuring CalendarPermissionEvaluator

We can then leverage the `security-globalsecurity.xml` configuration that is provided with this chapter to provide `ExpressionHandler` that uses our `CalendarPermissionEvaluator`.

src/main/webapp/WEB-INF/spring/security-globalsecurity.xml

```
<bean id="defaultExpressionHandler" class="org.springframework
  .security.access.expression.method
  .DefaultMethodSecurityExpressionHandler">
  <property name="permissionEvaluator">
    <bean autowire="constructor"
      class="com.packtpub.springsecurity.access
      .CalendarPermissionEvaluator"/>
  </property>
</bean>
```

The configuration should look similar to the configuration from *Chapter 12, Access Control Lists*, except that we now use our `CalendarPermissionEvaluator` instead of the `AclPermissionEvaluator`.

Next, we inform Spring Security to use our customized `ExpressionHandler` by adding the following configuration to `security.xml`.

src/main/webapp/WEB-INF/spring/security.xml

```
<global-method-security pre-post-annotations="enabled">
    <expression-handler ref="defaultExpressionHandler"/>
</global-method-security>
```

In the configuration, we ensure that `pre-post-annotations` is enabled and point the configuration to our `ExpressionHandler` definition. Once again, the configuration should look very similar to our configuration from *Chapter 12, Access Control Lists*.

## Securing our CalendarService

Lastly, we can secure our `CalendarService getEvent(int eventId)` method with a `@PostAuthorize` annotation. You will notice that this step is exactly the same as we did in *Chapter 1, Anatomy of an Unsafe Application* since we have only changed the implementation of `PermissionEvaluator`.

src/main/java/com/packtpub/springsecurity/service/CalendarService.java

```
@PostAuthorize("hasPermission(returnObject,'read')")
Event getEvent(int eventId);
```

If you have not done so already, restart the application, log in as admin1@example.com/admin1, and visit the Conference Call event using the link on the **Welcome** page. The access denied page will be displayed. However, we would like users with ROLE_ADMIN to be able to access all events.

## Benefits of a custom PermissionEvaluator

With only a single method being protected, it would be trivial to update the annotation to check if the user has the role ROLE_ADMIN or has permission. However, if we had protected all of our service methods that use an event, it would become quite cumbersome. Instead, we could just update our CalendarPermissionEvaluator. Make the following changes:

```
private boolean hasPermission(Authentication authentication, Event event, Object permission) {
    if(event == null) {
        return true;
    }
    GrantedAuthority adminRole =
            new SimpleGrantedAuthority("ROLE_ADMIN");
    if(authentication.getAuthorities().contains(adminRole)) {
        return true;
    }
    ...
}
```

Now, restart the application and repeat our previous exercise. This time, the Conference Call event will display successfully. You can see that the ability to encapsulate our authorization logic can be extremely beneficial. However, sometimes it may be useful to extend the expressions themselves.

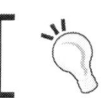

> Your code should look like chapter12.03-calendar.

# Summary

After reading this chapter, you should have a firm understanding of how Spring Security authorization works for HTTP requests and methods. With this knowledge and the provided concrete examples, you should also know how to extend authorization to meet your needs. Specifically in this chapter, we:

- Covered the Spring Security authorization architecture for both HTTP requests and methods
- Demonstrated how to configure secured URLs from a database
- Created a custom `PermissionEvaluator`
- Created a custom Spring Security expression

In the next chapter, we will explore how Spring Security performs session management. We will also gain an understanding of how it can be used to restrict access to our application.

# 13
# Session Management

This chapter discusses Spring Security's session management functionality. It starts off with an example of how Spring Security defends against session fixation. We will then discuss how concurrency control can be leveraged to restrict access to software licensed on a per user basis. We will also see how session management can be leveraged for administrative functions. Last, we will explore how HttpSession is used in Spring Security and how we can control its creation.

The following is a list of topics that will be covered in the chapter:

- Session Management/session fixation
- Concurrency control
- Managing logged in users
- How HttpSession are used in Spring Security and how to control their creation
- How to use the DebugFilter class to discover where HttpSession was created

## Configuring session fixation protection

As we are using the security namespace style of configuration, session fixation protection is already configured on our behalf. If we wanted to explicitly configure it to mirror the default settings, we would do the following: *IN SECURITY.XML*

```
<http auto-config="true" use-expressions="true">
  ...
  <session-management
      session-fixation-protection="migrateSession"/>
</http>
```

*Session Management*

**Session fixation protection** is a feature of the framework that you most likely won't even notice unless you try to act as a malicious user. We'll show you how to simulate a session-stealing attack; but before we do, it's important to understand what session fixation does and the type of attack it prevents.

# Understanding session fixation attacks

**Session fixation** is a type of attack whereby a malicious user attempts to steal the session of an unauthenticated user of your system. This can be done by using a variety of techniques that result in the attacker obtaining the unique session identifier of the user (for example, JSESSIONID). If the attacker creates a cookie or a URL parameter with the user's JSESSIONID identifier in it, they can access the user's session.

Although this is obviously a problem, typically, if a user is unauthenticated, they haven't entered any sensitive information. This becomes a more critical problem if the same session identifier continues to be used after a user has been authenticated. If the same identifier is used after authentication, the attacker may now gain access to the authenticated user's session without ever having to know their username or password!

> At this point, you may scoff in disbelief and think this is extremely unlikely to happen in the real world. In fact, session-stealing attacks happen frequently. We would suggest that you spend some time reading the very informative articles and case studies on the subject, published by the **Open Web Application Security Project (OWASP)** organization (http://www.owasp.org/). Specifically, you will want to read the OWASP Top 10 list. Attackers and malicious users are real, and they can do very real damage to your users, your application, or your company, if you don't understand the techniques that they commonly use and know how to avoid them.

The following diagram illustrates how a session fixation attack works:

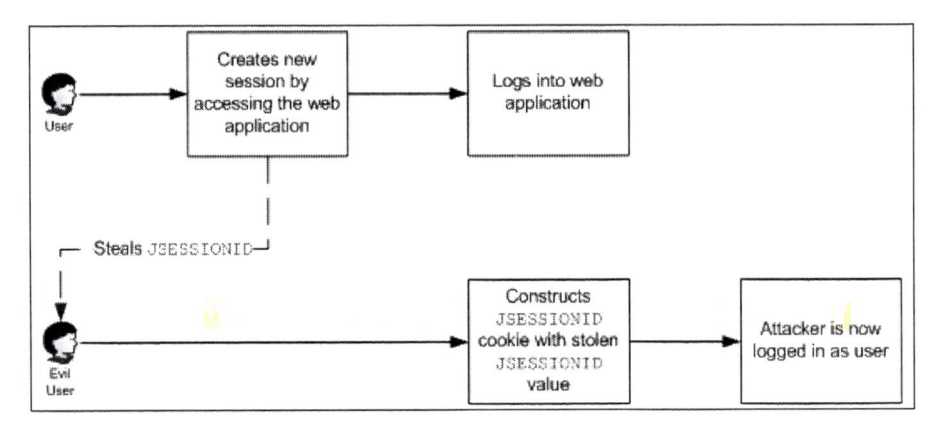

[ 344 ]

Now that we have seen how an attack like this works, we'll see what Spring Security can do to prevent it.

# Preventing session fixation attacks with Spring Security

If we can prevent the same session that the user had prior to authentication from being used after authentication, we can effectively render the attacker's knowledge of the session ID useless. Spring Security session fixation protection solves this problem by explicitly creating a new session when a user is authenticated, and invalidating their old session.

Let's see the following screenshot:

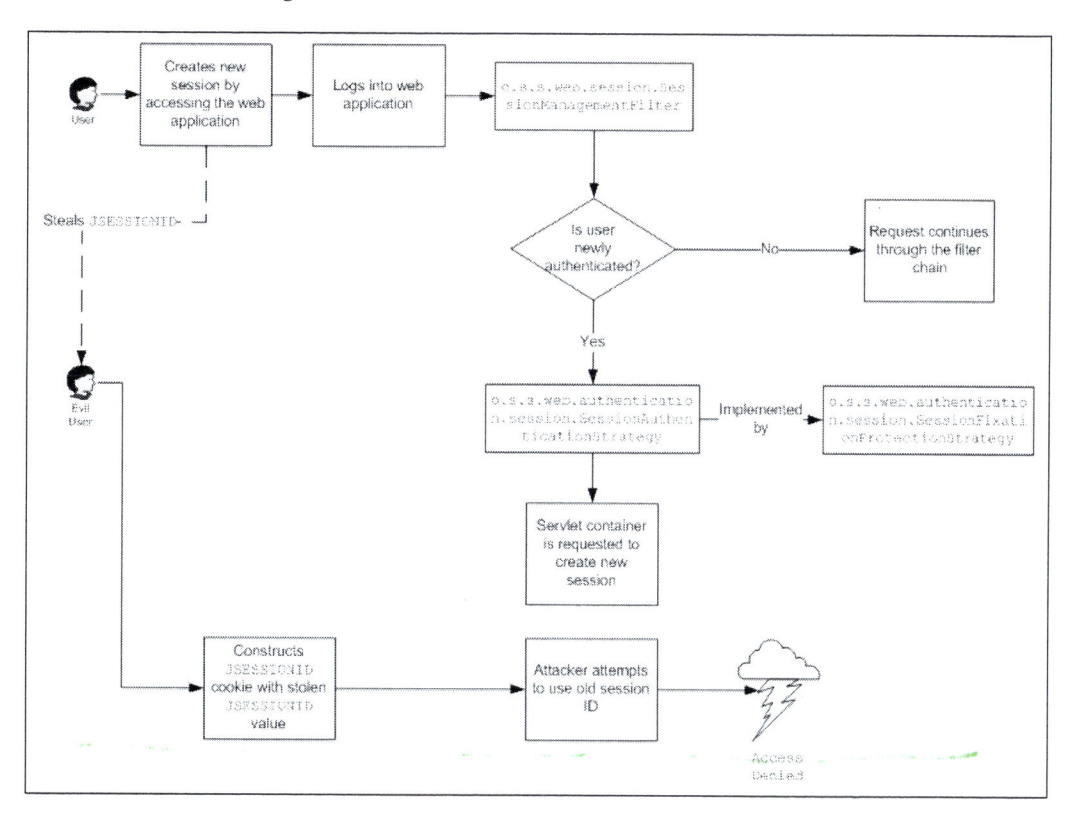

# Session Management

We can see that a new filter, o.s.s.web.session.SessionManagementFilter, is responsible for evaluating if a particular user is newly authenticated. If the user is newly authenticated, a configured o.s.s.web.authentication.session.SessionAuthenticationStrategy determines what to do. o.s.s.web.authentication.session.SessionFixationProtectionStrategy will create a new session (if the user already had one), and copy the contents of the existing session to the new one. That's pretty much it—seems simple; however, as we can see in the diagram, it effectively prevents the evil user from reusing the session ID after the unknowing user is authenticated.

## Simulating a session fixation attack

At this point, you may want to see what's involved in simulating a session-fixation attack. To do this, you'll first need to disable session fixation protection in security.xml by adding the <session-management> element as a child of the <http> element.

> You should start with the code from chapter13.00-calendar.

src/main/webapp/WEB-INF/spring/security.xml

```
<http ...>
    ...
    <session-management
        session-fixation-protection="none"/>
</http>
```

> Your code should now look like chapter13.01-calendar.

Next, you'll need to open two browsers. We'll initiate the session in Google Chrome, steal it from there, and our attacker will log in using the stolen session in Firefox. We will use the Chrome and the Firefox web developer add-on in order to view and manipulate cookies. The Firefox web developer add-on can be downloaded from https://addons.mozilla.org/en-US/firefox/addon/web-developer/. Chrome's web developer tools are built-in.

Open the JBCP Calendar home page in Chrome. Next, from the main menu, navigate to **Edit | Preferences | Under the Hood**. In the **Privacy** category, press **the Content Settings...** button. Next, in **Cookies Settings**, press the **All Cookies and Site Data...** button. Finally, enter `localhost` into the **Search** field.

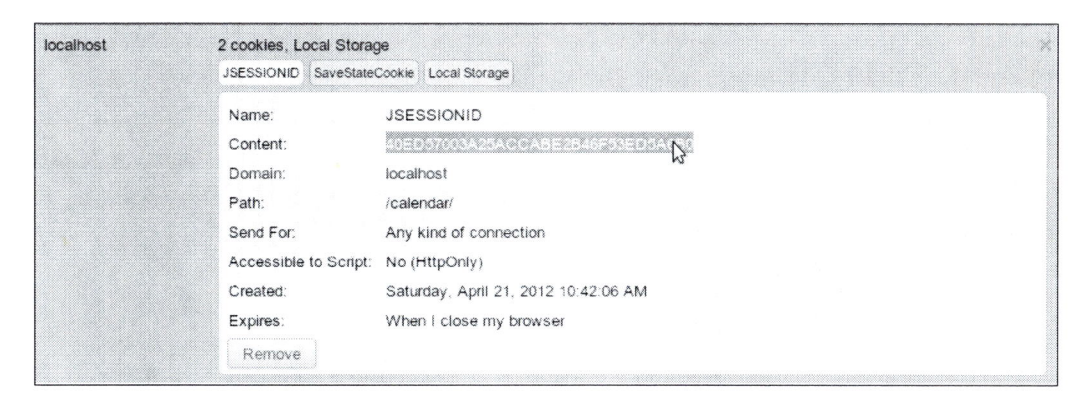

Select the **JSESSIONID** cookie, copy the value of **Content** to the clipboard, and log in to the JBCP Calendar application. If you repeat the **View Cookie Information** command, you'll see that **JSESSIONID** did not change after you logged in, making you vulnerable to a session-fixation attack!

In Firefox, open the JBCP Calendar website. You will have been assigned a session cookie, which we can view by navigating to **Tools | Web Developer | Cookies | View Cookie Information...** from the main menu. Keep in mind that newer versions of Firefox include web developer tools too. However, you will need to ensure that you are using the extension and not the built-in one, as it provides additional capabilities.

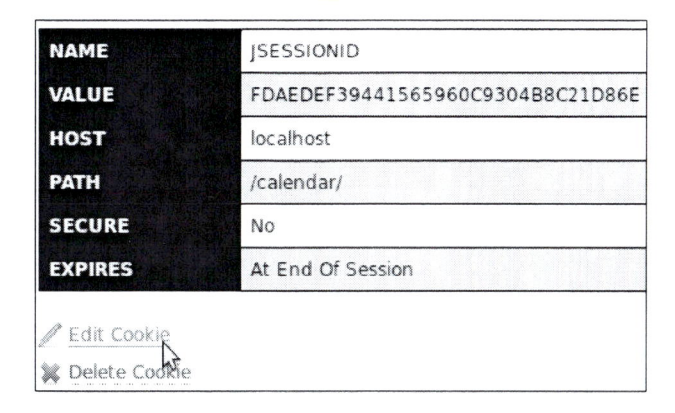

*Session Management*

To complete our hack, we'll click on the **Edit Cookie** option, and paste in the `JSESSIONID` cookie that we copied to the clipboard from Chrome, as shown in the following screenshot:

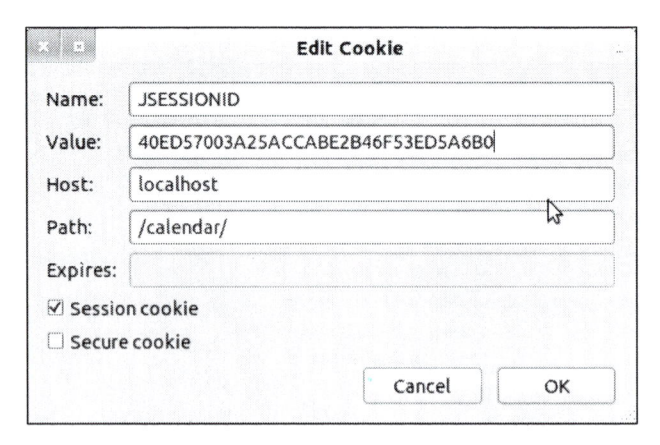

| | |
|---|---|
| Name: | JSESSIONID |
| Value: | 40ED57003A25ACCABE2B46F53ED5A6B0 |
| Host: | localhost |
| Path: | /calendar/ |
| Expires: | |

☑ Session cookie
☐ Secure cookie

Our session fixation hack is complete! If you now reload the page in Firefox, you will see that you are logged in as the same user that was logged in using Chrome, without requiring the knowledge of the username and password. Are you scared of malicious users yet?

Now, re-enable session fixation protection and try this exercise again. You'll see that, in this case, the **JSESSIONID** changes after the user logs in. Based on our understanding of how session-fixation attacks occur, this means that we have reduced the likelihood of an unsuspecting user falling victim to this type of attack. Excellent job!

Cautious developers should take note that there are many methods of stealing session cookies, some of which, such as **Cross-Site Scripting** (**XSS**), may make even session fixation protected sites vulnerable. Please consult the OWASP site for additional resources on preventing these types of attacks.

# Comparing session-fixation-protection options

The `session-fixation-protection` attribute has three options that allow you to alter its behavior:

| Attribute value | Description |
| --- | --- |
| None | This option disables session fixation protection, and (unless other `<session-management>` attributes are non-default) does not configure `SessionManagementFilter`. |
| migrateSession | When the user is authenticated and a new session is allocated, it ensures that all attributes of the old session are moved to the new session. |
| newSession | When the user is authenticated, a new session is created and no attributes from the old (unauthenticated) session will be migrated. |

In most cases, the default behavior of `migrateSession` will be appropriate for sites that wish to retain important attributes of the user's session (such as click interest and shopping carts) after the user has been authenticated.

# Restricting the number of concurrent sessions per user

In the software industry, software is often times sold on a per user basis. This means that, as software developers, we have an interest in ensuring that only a single session per user exists, to combat sharing of accounts. Spring Security's concurrent session control ensures that a single user cannot have more than a fixed number of active sessions simultaneously (typically one). Ensuring that this maximum limit is enforced involves several components working in tandem to accurately track changes in user session activity.

Let's configure the feature, review how it works, and then test it out!

*Session Management*

# Configuring concurrent session control

Now that we have understood the different components involved in concurrent session control, setting it up should make much more sense. To do this, update your `security.xml` file as follows:

src/main/webapp/WEB-INF/spring/security.xml

```xml
<http ...>
    ...
    <session-management>
        <concurrency-control max-sessions="1"/>
    </session-management>
</http>
```

Next, we need to enable `o.s.s.web.session.HttpSessionEventPublisher` in the `web.xml` deployment descriptor, so that the servlet container will notify Spring Security (through `HttpSessionEventPublisher`) of session lifecycle events.

src/main/webapp/WEB-INF/web.xml

```xml
<listener>
    <listener-class>
        org.springframework.web.context.ContextLoaderListener
    </listener-class>
</listener>
<listener>
    <listener-class>
        org.springframework.security.web.session.HttpSessionEventPublisher
    </listener-class>
</listener>
```

With these two configuration bits in place, concurrent session control will now be activated. Let's see what it actually does, and then we'll demonstrate how it can be tested.

# Understanding concurrent session control

Concurrent session control uses `o.s.s.core.session.SessionRegistry` to maintain a list of active HTTP sessions and the authenticated users with which they are associated. As sessions are created and expired, the registry is updated in real-time, based on the session lifecycle events published by `HttpSessionEventPublisher` to track the number of active sessions per authenticated user.

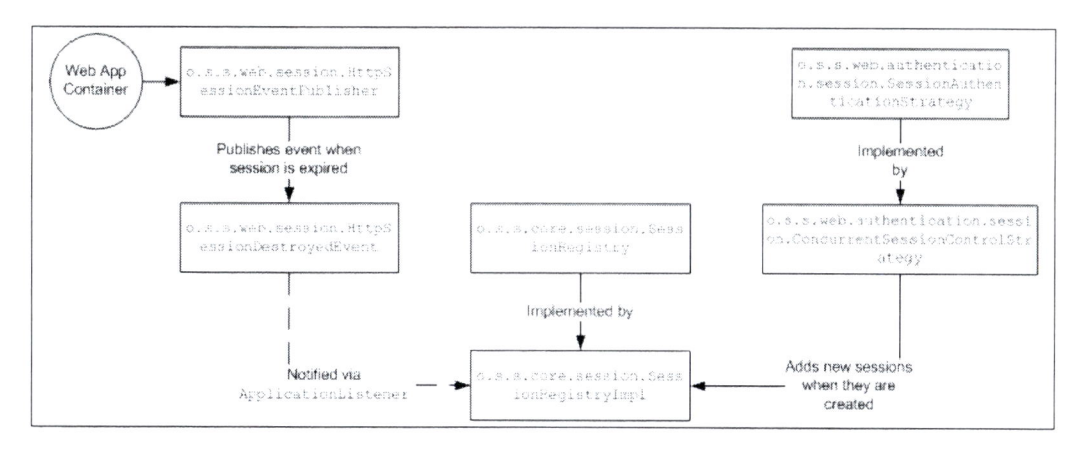

An extension of `SessionAuthenticationStrategy`, `o.s.s.web.authentication.session.ConcurrentSessionControlStrategy` is the method by which new sessions are tracked and the method by which concurrency control is actually enforced. Each time a user accesses the secured site, `SessionManagementFilter` is used to check the active session against `SessionRegistry`. If the user's active session isn't in the list of active sessions tracked in `SessionRegistry`, the least recently used session is immediately expired.

The secondary actor in the modified concurrent session control filter chain is `o.s.s.web.session.ConcurrentSessionFilter`. This filter will recognize expired sessions (typically, sessions that have been expired either by the servlet container or forcibly by the `ConcurrentSessionControlStrategy` interface) and notify the user that their session has expired.

Now that we have understood how concurrent session control works, it should be easy for us to reproduce a scenario in which it is enforced.

> Your code should now look like `chapter13.02-calendar`.

# Testing concurrent session control

As we did with verifying session fixation protection, we will need to access two web browsers. Follow these steps:

1. In Chrome, log in to the site as `user1@example.com/user1`.
2. Now, in Firefox, log in to the site as the same user.
3. Finally, go back to Chrome, and take any action. You will see a message indicating that your session has expired.

The following message will appear:

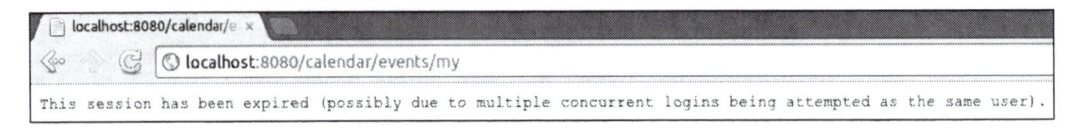

```
This session has been expired (possibly due to multiple concurrent logins being attempted as the same user).
```

If you were using the application, you'd probably be confused. This is because it's obviously not a friendly method of being notified that only a single user can access the application at a time. However, it does illustrate that the session has been forcibly expired by the software.

> Concurrent session control tends to be a very difficult concept for new Spring Security users to grasp. Many users try to implement it without truly understanding how it works, and what the benefits are. If you're trying to enable this powerful feature, and it doesn't seem to be working as you expect, make sure you have everything configured correctly; and then review the theoretical explanations in this section—hopefully they will help you understand what may be wrong!

When this event occurs, we should probably redirect the user to the login page, and provide them a message to indicate what went wrong.

# Configuring expired session redirect

Fortunately, there is a simple method for directing users to a friendly page (typically, the login page) when they are flagged by concurrent session control—simply specify the `expired-url` attribute, and set it to a valid page in your application. Update your `security.xml` file as follows:

src/main/webapp/WEB-INF/spring/security.xml

```
<http ...>
  <session-management>
    <concurrency-control max-sessions="1"
```

```
        expired-url="/login/form?expired"/>
    </session-management>
</http>
```

In the case of our application, this will redirect the user to the standard login form. We will then use the query parameter to display a friendly message indicating that we determined that they had multiple active sessions, and should log in again. Update your `login.jsp` page to use this parameter to display our message.

src/main/webapp/WEB-INF/views/login.jsp

```
...
<c:if test="${param.expired != null}">
    <div class="alert alert-success">
        You have been forcibly logged out due to multiple
        sessions on the same account (only one active
        session per user is allowed).
    </div>
</c:if>
<label for="username">Username</label>
```

Go ahead and give it a try by logging in with `admin1@example.com/admin1` using both Chrome and Firefox. This time, you should see a login page with a custom error message.

> Your code should now look like `chapter13.03-calendar`.

## Common problems with concurrency control

There are a few common reasons that logging in with the same user does not trigger a logout event. The first occurs when using a custom `UserDetails` (as we did in Chapter 3, *Custom Authentication*) while the equals and hashCode methods are not properly implemented. This occurs because the default `SessionRegistry` implementation uses an in-memory map to store `UserDetails`. In order to resolve this, you must ensure that you have properly implemented the `hashCode` and `equals` methods.

# Session Management

The second problem occurs when restarting the application container while the user sessions are persisted to a disk. When the container has started back up, the users who were already logged in with a valid session are logged in. However, the in-memory map of `SessionRegistry` that is used to determine if the user is already logged in, will be empty. This means that Spring Security will report that the user is not logged in even though the user is. To solve this problem, either a custom `SessionRegistry` is required along with disabling session persistence within the container, or implementing a container-specific way to ensure that the persisted sessions get populated into the in-memory map at startup.

Yet another reason is that at the time of this writing, concurrency control was not implemented for the Remember Me feature. If users are authenticated with Remember Me, that concurrency control is not enforced. There is a JIRA to implement this feature, so refer to it for any updates if your application requires both Remember Me and concurrency control, at https://jira.springsource.org/browse/SEC-2028.

The last common reason we will cover is that concurrency control will not work in a clustered environment with the default `SessionRegistry` implementation. As mentioned previously, the default implementation uses an in-memory map. This means that if `user1` logs in to Application Server A, the fact that they are logged in will be associated to that server. Thus, if `user1` then authenticates to Application Server B, the previously associated authentication will be unknown to Application Server B.

## Preventing authentication instead of forcing logout

Spring Security can also prevent a user from being able to log in to the application if the user already has a session. This means that instead of forcing the original user to be logged out, Spring Security will prevent the second user from being able to log in. The configuration changes can be seen as follows:

src/main/webapp/WEB-INF/spring/security.xml

```
<session-management>
    <concurrency-control max-sessions="1"
        expired-url="/login/form?expired"
        error-if-maximum-exceeded="true"/>
</session-management>
```

Make the updates and log in to the `Calendar` application with Chrome. Now, attempt to log in to the `Calendar` application with Firefox using the same user. You should see our custom error message from our `login.jsp` file.

> Your code should now look like `chapter13.04-calendar`.

There is a disadvantage to this approach that may not be apparent without some thought. Try closing Chrome without logging out and then opening it up again. Now, attempt to log in to the application again. You will observe that you are unable to log in. This is because when the browser is closed, the `JSESSIONID` cookie is deleted. However, the application is not aware of this, so the user is still considered to be authenticated. You can think of this as a kind of memory leak, since `HttpSession` still exists but there is no pointer to it (the `JSESSIONID` cookie is gone). It is not until the session times out that our user will be able to authenticate again. Thankfully, once the session times out, our `SessionEventPublisher` will remove the user from our `SessionRegistry`. Our take away is that if a user forgets to log out and closes the browser, they will not be able to log in to the application until the session times out.

> Just as with the *Chapter 6, Remember-me Services*, this experiment may not work if the browser decides to remember a session even after the browser is closed. Typically, this will happen if a plugin or the browser is configured to restore sessions. In this event, you might want to delete the `JSESSIONID` cookie manually to simulate the browser being closed.

## Other benefits of concurrent session control

Another benefit of concurrent session control is that `SessionRegistry` exists to track active (and, optionally, expired) sessions. This means that we can get runtime information about what user activity exists in our system (for authenticated users, at least).

You can even do this if you don't want to enable concurrent session control. Simply set `max-sessions` to `-1`, and session tracking will remain enabled, even though no maximum will be enforced. Unfortunately, the namespace support will not allow us to use a negative number. Instead, we will use the explicit bean configuration provided in the `security-session.xml` file of this chapter.

src/main/webapp/WEB-INF/spring/security-session.xml

```
<bean id="concurrentSessionManager"
        class="org.springframework.security.web.authentication.
session.ConcurrentSessionControlStrategy">
    <constructor-arg ref="sessionRegistry"/>
```

# Session Management

```xml
        <property name="maximumSessions" value="-1"/>
</bean>
<bean id="concurrencyControlFilter"
        class="org.springframework.security.web.session.ConcurrentSessionFilter">
    <constructor-arg ref="sessionRegistry"/>
    <constructor-arg value="/login/form?expired"/>
</bean>
<bean id="sessionRegistry"
        class="org.springframework.security.core.session.SessionRegistryImpl"/>
```

We have already added the import of the `security-session.xml` file to the `web.xml` file. So, all that we need to do is reference the custom configuration in our `security.xml` file. Go ahead and replace our current `<session-management>` and `<concurrency-control>` configurations with the following code:

src/main/webapp/WEB-INF/spring/security.xml

```xml
    <http ...>
    ...
        <custom-filter
            ref="concurrencyControlFilter"
            position="CONCURRENT_SESSION_FILTER"/>
        <session-management
            session-authentication-strategy-ref="concurrentSessionManager"/>
    </http>
```

Now, our application will allow an unlimited number of authentications for the same user. However, we can use `SessionRegistry` to forcibly log out the users. Let's see how we can use this information to enhance the security of our users.

> Your code should now look like chapter13.05-calendar.

# Displaying active sessions for a user

You've probably seen how many websites allow a user to view and forcibly log out sessions for their account. We can easily use this functionality to do the same. We have already provided `UserSessionController` that obtains the active sessions for the currently logged in user. You can see the implementation as follows:

src/main/java/com/packtpub/springsecurity/web/controllers/UserSessionController.java

```java
@Controller
public class UserSessionController {
    private final SessionRegistry sessionRegistry;

    @Autowired
    public UserSessionController(SessionRegistry sessionRegistry) {
        this.sessionRegistry = sessionRegistry;
    }

    @RequestMapping("/user/sessions/")
    public String sessions(Authentication authentication, ModelMap model) {
        List<SessionInformation> sessions =
                sessionRegistry.getAllSessions(authentication.getPrincipal(), false);
        model.put("sessions", sessions);
        return "user/sessions";
    }

    @RequestMapping(value="/user/sessions/{sessionId}",
            method=RequestMethod.DELETE)
    public String removeSession(@PathVariable String sessionId,
            RedirectAttributes redirectAttrs) {
        SessionInformation sessionInformation =
                sessionRegistry.getSessionInformation(sessionId);
        if(sessionInformation != null) {
            sessionInformation.expireNow();
        }
        redirectAttrs.addFlashAttribute("message", "Session was removed");
        return "redirect:/user/sessions/";
    }
}
```

*Session Management*

Our `sessions` method will use Spring MVC to automatically obtain the current Spring Security `Authentication`. If we were not using Spring MVC, we could also get the current `Authentication` from `SecurityContextHolder`, as discussed in *Chapter 3, Custom Authentication*. The principal is then used to obtain all the `SessionInformation` objects for the current user. The information is easily displayed by iterating over the `SessionInformation` objects in our `sessions.jsp` file.

src/main/webapp/WEB-INF/views/user/sessions.jsp

```
...
<c:forEach items="${sessions}" var="session">
    <tr>
        <fmt:formatDate value="${session.lastRequest}" type="both"
pattern="yyyy-MM-dd HH:mm" var="lastUsed"/>
        <td><c:out value="${lastUsed}"/></td>
        <td><c:out value="${session.sessionId}" /></td>
        <c:url var="deleteUrl" value="./${session.sessionId}"/>
        <td>
            <form action="${deleteUrl}" ...>
                ...
            </form>
        </td>
    </tr>
</c:forEach>
...
```

You can now safely start the JBCP Calendar application and log in to it using `user1@example.com`/`user1` in Chrome. Now, log in using Firefox and click on the **user1@example.com** link in the upper-right corner. You will then see both sessions listed in the display:

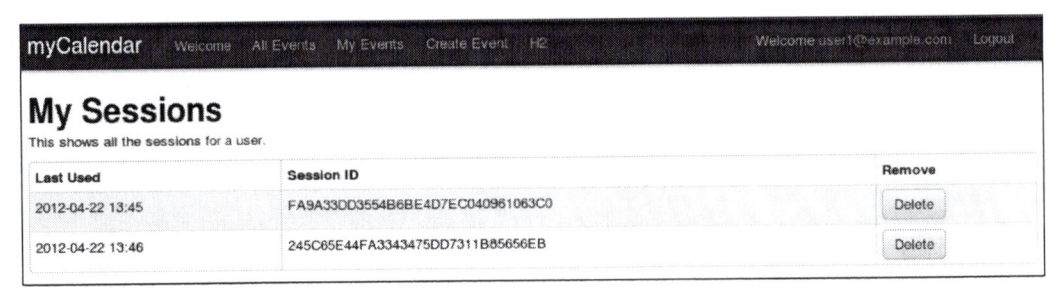

| Last Used | Session ID | Remove |
|---|---|---|
| 2012-04-22 13:45 | FA9A33DD3554B6BE4D7EC040961063C0 | Delete |
| 2012-04-22 13:46 | 245C65E44FA3343475DD7311B85656EB | Delete |

While in Firefox, click on the **Delete** button for the first session. This sends the request to our `deleteSession` method of `UserSessionsController`. This indicates that the session should be terminated. Now, navigate to any page within Chrome. You will see our custom message saying the session has been forcibly terminated. While the message could use updating, we see that this is a nice feature for users to terminate other active sessions.

Other possible uses include allowing an administrator to list and manage all active sessions, displaying the number of active users on the site, or even extending the information to include things like an IP Address or location information.

# How Spring Security uses the HttpSession

We have already discussed how Spring Security uses `SecurityContextHolder` to determine the currently logged in user. However, we have not explained how `SecurityContextHolder` gets automatically populated by Spring Security. The secret to this lies in the `o.s.s.web.context.SecurityContextPersistenceFilter` and o.s.s.web.context.SecurityContextRepository interfaces.

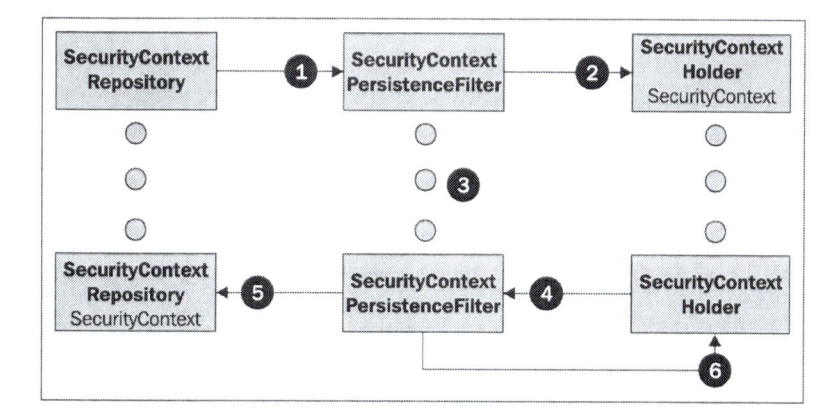

1. At the beginning of each web request, `SecurityContextPersistenceFilter` is responsible for obtaining the current `SecurityContext` using `SecurityContextRepository`.
2. Immediately afterwards, it sets `SecurityContext` on `SecurityContextHolder`.

3. For the remainder of the web request, `SecurityContext` is available via `SecurityContextHolder`. For example, if a Spring MVC controller or `CalendarService` wanted to access `SecurityContext`, it could use `SecurityContextHolder` to access it.

4. Then, at the end of each request, `SecurityContextPersistenceFilter` gets `SecurityContext` from `SecurityContextHolder`.

5. Immediately afterwards, `SecurityContextPersistenceFilter` saves `SecurityContext` in `SecurityContextRepository`. This ensures that if `SecurityContext` is updated at any point during the web requests (that is, when a user creates a new account, as done in *Chapter 3, Custom Authentication*) `SecurityContext` is saved.

6. Last, `SecurityContextPersistenceFilter` clears `SecurityContextHolder`.

The question that comes into place is how is this related to `HttpSession`? This is all tied together by the default `SecurityContextRepository` implementation, which uses `HttpSession`.

# HttpSessionSecurityContextRepository

The default implementation of `SecurityContextRepository`, `o.s.s.web.context.HttpSessionSecurityContextRepository`, uses `HttpSession` to retrieve and store the current `SecurityContext`. There are no other `SecurityContextRepository` implementations provided out of the box. However, since the usage of `HttpSession` is abstracted behind the `SecurityContextRepository` interface, we could easily write our own implementation if we desired.

# Configuring how Spring Security uses HttpSession

Spring Security has the ability to configure when the session is created by Spring Security. This can be done with the `<http>` element's `create-session` attribute. A summary of the options can be seen in the following table:

| Attribute value | Description |
| --- | --- |
| `ifRequired` | Spring Security will create a session only if one is required (default value). |
| `always` | Spring Security will proactively create a session if one does not exist. |

| Attribute value | Description |
|---|---|
| never | Spring Security will never create a session, but will make use of one if the application does. This means if there is `HttpSession`, `SecurityContext` will be persisted or retrieved from it. |
| stateless | Spring Security will not create a session and ignore the session for obtaining a Spring Authentication. In such instances, `NullSecurityContextRepository` is used, which will always state that the current `SecurityContext` is `null`. |

In practice, controlling session creation can be more difficult than it first appears. This is because the attributes only control a subset of Spring Security's usage of `HttpSession`. It does not apply to any other components, such as JSPs, in the application. To help figure out when `HttpSession` was created, we can add Spring Security's `DebugFilter`.

## Debugging with Spring Security's DebugFilter

Update your `security.xml` file to have a session policy of `never`. Also add the `<debug>` element so that we can track when the session is created. The updates can be seen as follows:

src/main/webapp/WEB-INF/spring/security.xml

```
<debug/>
<http auto-config="true"
      use-expressions="true"
      create-session="never">
```

When you start up the application, you should see something similar to the following code written to standard out. If you do not, ensure that you have logging enabled for all levels on the Spring Security Debugger category.

```
********************************************************************
**********          Security debugging is enabled.
*************
**********       This may include sensitive information.
*************
**********          Do not use in a production system!
*************
********************************************************************
```

## Session Management

Now, clear out your cookies (this can be done in Firefox with *Shift + Ctrl + Del*), start up the application, and navigate directly to `http://localhost:8080/calendar/`. When we look at the cookies, as we did earlier in the chapter, we see that `JSESSIONID` is created even though we stated that Spring Security should never create `HttpSession`. Look at the logs again, and you will see a call stack of the code that created `HttpSession`:

```
New HTTP session created: 66E512273121EEECC242EA1D2A334A1C

Call stack:
    at Logger.log(Logger.java:29)
    at DebugRequestWrapper.getSession(DebugFilter.java:90)
    ...
    at JspFactoryImpl.internalGetPageContext(JspFactoryImpl.java:112)
    at JspFactoryImpl.getPageContext(JspFactoryImpl.java:65)
    at WEB_002dINF.views.login_jsp._jspService(login_jsp.java:66)
```

In this instance, our JSP page is responsible for creating the new `HttpSession`. In fact, all JSPs will create a new `HttpSession` by default unless you include the following at the top of each JSP:

```
<%@ page session="false" %>
```

There are a number of other uses for `DebugFilter`, which we encourage you to explore on your own. For example, determining when a request will match a particular URL, which Spring Security Filters are being invoked, and so on.

# Summary

After reading this chapter you should:

- Understand how Spring Security manages sessions and protects against session-fixation attacks
- Know how to use Spring Security's concurrency control to prevent the same user from being authenticated multiple times
- Be able to utilize concurrency control to allow a user to terminate sessions associated with their account
- Know how to configure Spring Security's creation of sessions
- Know how to use Spring Security's `DebugFilter` to troubleshoot issues related to Spring
- Learn about security, including determining when `HttpSession` was created and what caused it to be created

This concludes our discussion about Spring Security's session management. In the next chapter we will discuss specifics about integrating Spring Security with other frameworks.

# 14
# Integrating with Other Frameworks

In this chapter, we explore how to integrate Spring Security with other frameworks. The chapter aims to assist you in setting up a very basic project with Spring Security and the respective framework. It is out of the scope of this chapter to provide details of the frameworks we integrate with, other than how they relate to Spring Security, as entire books have been written on all of these frameworks. In this chapter, we will cover how to integrate Spring Security with a number of frameworks and technologies including the following:

- **Java Server Faces (JSF)** applications
- AJAX-enabled applications
- **Google Web Toolkit (GWT)** applications
- Spring Roo applications   *see p 383, 386...*
- AspectJ

Before you read this chapter, you should already have an understanding of how Spring Security works. This means you should already be able to set up authentication and authorization in a simple web application. If you are unable to do this, you will want to ensure you have read up to *Chapter 3, Custom Authentication*, before proceeding with this chapter. If you keep the basic concepts of Spring Security in mind and you understand the framework you are integrating with, then integrating with other frameworks is fairly straightforward.

As we have already mentioned, we will only provide details about the particular framework we are integrating with, when it pertains to integration with Spring Security. This means that you will need an understanding of the framework you are integrating with, in order to get the most out of this chapter.

# Integrating with Java Server Faces (JSF)

Using Spring Security with JSF is fairly straightforward, but there are a few challenges that can make it a bit difficult. In this section, we will go over the steps that are specific to integrating Spring Security with JSF. Our sample application integrates with the JBoss Richfaces project, but the steps should be similar for other JSF implementations.

> The entire source code for the JSF sample code can be found in chapter14.00-richfaces. When started it can be found at `http://localhost:8080/richfaces/`. You may log into it using the username `admin1@example.com` and the password `admin1`.

## Customizations to support AJAX

The first problem that users will probably encounter when integrating with JSF, or any framework that makes heavy use of **Asynchronous JavaScript and XML (AJAX)** requests, is that when the application times out, a redirect to the login page is sent. This does not work very well when making AJAX requests. The problem is that we want to support requesting that the user logs in for both AJAX requests and standard web requests. The answer involves using `o.s.s.web.authentication.DelegatingAuthenticationEntryPoint`, a custom `o.s.s.web.util.RequestMatcher`, and a custom `o.s.s.web.AuthenticationEntryPoint`.

## DelegatingAuthenticationEntryPoint

`o.s.s.web.authentication.DelegatingAuthenticationEntryPoint` uses a `LinkedHashMap` of the `RequestMatcher` implementations to the `AuthenticationEntryPoint` implementations to determine which `AuthenticationEntryPoint` to use.

> Remember from *Chapter 7, Client Certificate Authentication*, that `AuthenticationEntryPoint` is Spring Security's way of requesting credentials. For example, `LoginUrlAuthenticationEntryPoint` performs a redirect to a page that typically has a form to submit a username and password.

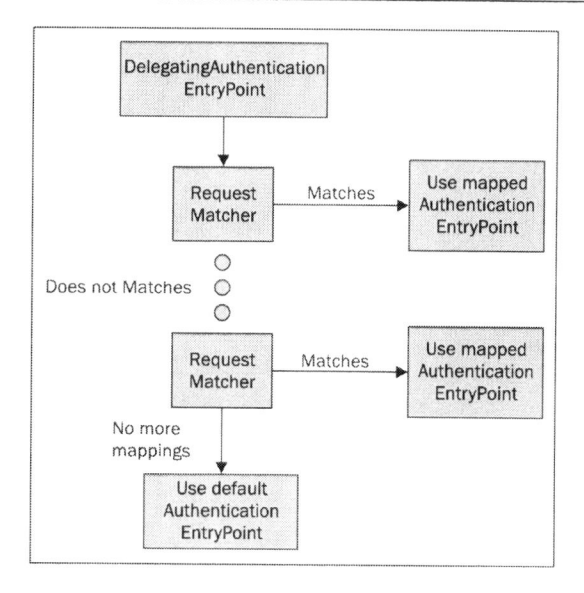

If there are no more mappings, the default `AuthenticationEntryPoint` is used. This means that if we can create `RequestMatcher` that identifies all AJAX requests, we can take a different action when login is required for an AJAX request than when a full page request is made.

## AjaxRequestMatcher

Most AJAX frameworks will have something that uniquely identifies an AJAX request from a standard web request. In the case of **Richfaces**, a header by the name of `faces-request` can be found in AJAX requests. This means that we can create a request matcher as follows:

richfaces/src/main/java/com/packtpub/springsecurity/
RichfacesRequestMatcher.java

```
public class RichfacesRequestMatcher implements RequestMatcher {
    public boolean matches(HttpServletRequest request) {
        return request.getHeader("faces-request") != null;
    }
}
```

*Integrating with Other Frameworks*

While this request matcher works for Richfaces, it will not work for other frameworks making AJAX requests. Inspect the request to figure out what is unique about the AJAX requests. Some options are the `X-Requested-With` header, the content type, and so on.

> You can use Firefox Tamper Data or Chrome Developer Tools to inspect the requests.

## Http401EntryPoint

As we mentioned previously, Spring Security's default behavior when using form-based login is to redirect the user to a page that contains a form to submit their username and password. This will not behave very well with a JavaScript client. Therefore, we now need to provide a mechanism that can indicate to the JavaScript client that it should request the user to log in.

richfaces/src/main/java/com/packtpub/springsecurity/Http401EntryPoint.java

```java
public class Http401EntryPoint implements AuthenticationEntryPoint {
    public void commence(HttpServletRequest request,
            HttpServletResponse response, AuthenticationException authException)
            throws IOException, ServletException {
        response.sendError(401);
    }
}
```

`Http401EntryPoint` indicates that login is required by returning an HTTP status of `401`. This is much easier for a JavaScript client to process. If it sees an error status code of `401`, it can then take appropriate measures to allow the user to log in. We demonstrate how to do this with Richfaces later in this chapter.

## Configuration updates

Now that we have explained all the moving parts, we can discuss the necessary configuration updates. The first set of updates can be found in our `security-ajax.xml` file:

richfaces/src/main/webapp/WEB-INF/spring/security-ajax.xml

```xml
<?xml version="1.0" encoding="UTF-8"?>
<beans xmlns="http://www.springframework.org/schema/beans"
    xmlns:xsi="http://www.w3.org/2001/XMLSchema-instance"
```

```xml
        xsi:schemaLocation="http://www.springframework.org/schema/beans 
http://www.springframework.org/schema/beans/spring-beans.xsd">

        <bean id="entryPoint"      class="org.springframework.security.
web.authentication.DelegatingAuthenticationEntryPoint">
            <constructor-arg>
                <map>
                    <entry>
                        <key>
                            <bean class="com.packtpub.springsecurity.
RichfacesRequestMatcher" />
                        </key>
                        <bean class="com.packtpub.springsecurity.
Http401EntryPoint" />
                    </entry>
                </map>
            </constructor-arg>
            <property name="defaultEntryPoint">
                <bean
                    class="org.springframework.security.web.
authentication.LoginUrlAuthenticationEntryPoint">
                    <property name="loginFormUrl" value="/login" />
                </bean>
            </property>
    </bean>
</beans>
```

This specifies the `DelegatingAuthenticationEntryPoint` class, which will delegate to the appropriate `AuthenticationEntryPoint` depending on whether the request is a Richfaces AJAX request or not.

The next configuration change is to update `security.xml` to instruct Spring Security to utilize the custom `AuthenticationEntryPoint`.

richfaces/src/main/webapp/WEB-INF/spring/security.xml

```xml
<http security="none" pattern="/org.richfaces.resources/**"/>
<http auto-config="true"
      use-expressions="true"
      entry-point-ref="entryPoint">
    <intercept-url pattern="/jsf-login.jsf" access="permitAll"/>
```

Recall that Spring Security will send the browser to the last requested page that requires authentication after the user logs in. It would not work very well if the user had requested a JSON resource using AJAX. A simple method to avoid redirecting to the JSON resources is to always send the user to the `default-target-url` attribute. This can be done with the following changes to the `security.xml` file:

```
<form-login login-page="/login.jsf"
        authentication-failure-url="/login.jsf?error"
        default-target-url="/"
        always-use-default-target="true"/>
```

## JavaScript updates

The last change we need to make is to have the JavaScript framework handle the `401` response sent by Spring Security when a login is required. The method in which this is done will vary depending on the JavaScript framework being used. The following example demonstrates how to add a global handler that redirects the user to the default target URL page if the HTTP response status is a `401` when using JBoss Richfaces:

richfaces/src/main/webapp/templates/template.xhtml

```
<script type="text/javascript">
    jsf.ajax.addOnError(handleError);

    function handleError(data) {
        if(data.responseCode == 401) {
            window.location = "${request.contextPath}"
        }
    }
</script>
```

Assuming the default target URL is protected, redirecting to the default target URL when an AJAX request requires authentication can be used as an alternative to setting `always-use-default-target` to `true`. The advantage to this approach is that Spring Security can still remember non-AJAX requests.

## Proxy-based authorization with JSF

As we discussed in *Chapter 10, Fine-grained Access Control*, Spring must create our objects in order to support proxy-based authorization. This conflicts with the fact that JSF will typically create and inject the managed beans. However, there is a very simple method to allow Spring to create our managed beans. In order for Spring to create our beans, we need to update our `faces-config.xml` file to use `o.s.web.jsf.el.SpringBeanFacesElResolver`. This allows JSF to resolve standard Spring beans, allowing Spring Security to restrict access to secure our service tier using proxy objects just as we did in *Chapter 10, Fine-grained Access Control*. If you are unsure of the steps that are required to set up proxy-based authorization with Spring Security, we invite you to revisit *Chapter 10, Fine-grained Access Control* in order to refresh your memory. You can refer to this chapter's `richfaces` sample project for a working example of proxy-based authorization in JSF. The relevant code is as follows:

richfaces/src/main/webapp/WEB-INF/faces-config.xml

```
<application>
  <el-resolver>
    org.springframework.web.jsf.el.SpringBeanFacesELResolver
  </el-resolver>
</application>
```

## Custom login page in JSF

For developers who are accustomed to using JSF, it can be challenging to create a custom login page for their application when using Spring Security. Typically, the problem is that developers want to use all of the standard JSF tag libraries, but this does not work, since Spring Security provides a hook for authenticating the user in a servlet filter and the standard JSF tags cannot point to a servlet filter. There are a couple of techniques that we can use to more easily create our custom login page in a JSF application.

The first approach to creating a custom login page with JSF is to use a standard HTML form tag rather than the JSF tag. This has the downside of no longer integrating with JSF. However, we are able to reuse Spring Security's servlet filters for processing the username and password. You can find an example of how this works as follows:

richfaces/src/main/webapp/login.xhtml

```
<c:if test="${param.error != null}">
  <div class="alert alert-error">
    Failed to login.
    <c:if test="${SPRING_SECURITY_LAST_EXCEPTION != null}">
```

## Integrating with Other Frameworks

```
      Reason: <h:outputText value="#
        {sessionScope.SPRING_SECURITY_LAST_EXCEPTION.message}"/>
    </c:if>
  </div>
</c:if>
<c:if test="${param.logout != null}">
  <div class="alert alert-success">
    You have been logged out.
  </div>
</c:if>
<form action="${request.contextPath}/j_spring_security_check"
    method="post">
  <label for="username">Username</label>
  <input type="text" id="username" name="j_username"/>
  <label for="password">Password</label>
  <input type="password" id="password" name="j_password"/>
  <div class="form-actions">
    <input id="submit" class="btn" name="submit" type="submit"
      value="Login"/>
  </div>
</form>
```

This should look nearly identical to the login page that we created for a standard JSP page. For a working example, refer to the `richfaces` sample application that is provided with this chapter.

The second approach to creating a custom login page with JSF leverages the fact that any part of our application can authenticate the user. This means that we can use `AuthenticationManager` in a JSF-managed bean to authenticate the user. In order to ensure that `AuthenticationManager` is injected into the managed bean:

1. Add `SpringBeanFacesElResolver` to the `faces-config.xml` file, as discussed previously in this chapter.
2. Create the Spring Security configuration as you would normally.
3. Use Spring to create the managed bean so that the `AuthenticationManager` can be injected into the managed bean.

The relevant portion of the example `LoginBean` provided in the chapter's sample code can be seen in the following code. You will need to ensure to map the navigation rules for `success` and `fail` for this bean to work properly. We have already done so in the sample application.

richfaces/src/main/java/com/packtpub/springsecurity/LoginBean.java

```java
@Component
@Scope("request")
public class LoginBean {
   … members and getter/setters omitted …

   @Autowired
   public LoginBean(AuthenticationManager authenticationManager) {
      this.authenticationManager = authenticationManager;
   }

   public String login() {
      UsernamePasswordAuthenticationToken token =
        new UsernamePasswordAuthenticationToken(username, password);
      try {
         Authentication authentication =
            authenticationManager.authenticate(token);
         SecurityContext sContext =
            SecurityContextHolder.getContext();
         sContext.setAuthentication(authentication);
         return "success";
      } catch (AuthenticationException loginError) {
         FacesContext fContext = FacesContext.getCurrentInstance();
         FacesMessage message =
            new FacesMessage("Invalid username/password. Reason "
            + loginError.getMessage());
         fContext.addMessage(null,  message);
         return "fail";
      }
   }
}
```

*Integrating with Other Frameworks*

Since authentication is performed in the managed bean (rather than Spring Security's servlet filters), we can now use the standard JSF tag libraries for creating our custom login form. You can see the relevant portion of `jsf-login.xhtml` provided within the chapter's sample code, as follows:

richfaces/src/main/webapp/jsf-login.xhtml

```
    <h:message for="login" styleClass="alert alert-error"/>
    <div>
      <h:form id="login" method="post">
        <h:outputLabel for="username" value="Username"/>
        <h:inputText id="username" value="#{loginBean.username}"/>
        <h:outputLabel for="password" value="Username"/>
        <h:inputSecret id="password" value="#{loginBean.password}"/>
        <div class="form-actions">
          <h:commandButton value="Login" class="btn"
            action="#{loginBean.login}" />
        </div>
      </h:form>
    </div>
```

If you would like to give this method of authenticating the user a try, replace any occurrence of `login.jsf` with `jsf-login.jsf` within the `security.xml` and `security-ajax.xml` files of the `richface` example, and try out the application.

## Spring Security Facelets tag library

The `spring-faces` project is a part of Spring Web Flow and provides JSF tag library integration with Spring Security.

The first step to integrating Spring Security and JSF is to add the `spring-faces` dependency, which provides tight integration with Spring and JSF. You can see an example of adding the `spring-faces` dependency as follows:

richfaces/pom.xml

```
    <dependency>
        <groupId>org.springframework.webflow</groupId>
        <artifactId>spring-faces</artifactId>
        <version>2.3.1.RELEASE</version>
    </dependency>
```

The next step is to supply the `taglib` definition based upon the JSF version you are using. The `richfaces` sample project provides the JSF 2 definition that is shown as follows:

src/main/webapp/WEB-INF/springsecurity.taglib.xml

```xml
<?xml version="1.0"?>
<!DOCTYPE facelet-taglib PUBLIC
  "-//Sun Microsystems, Inc.//DTD Facelet Taglib 1.0//EN"
  "http://java.sun.com/dtd/facelet-taglib_1_0.dtd">
<facelet-taglib>
  <namespace>
    http://www.springframework.org/security/tags
  </namespace>
  <tag>
    <tag-name>authorize</tag-name>
    <handler-class>
      org.springframework.faces.security
        .FaceletsAuthorizeTagHandler
    </handler-class>
  </tag>
  <function>
    <function-name>areAllGranted</function-name>
    <function-class>
      org.springframework.faces.security.FaceletsAuthorizeTagUtils
    </function-class>
    <function-signature>
      boolean areAllGranted(java.lang.String)
    </function-signature>
  </function>
  <function>
    <function-name>areAnyGranted</function-name>
    <function-class>
      org.springframework.faces.security.FaceletsAuthorizeTagUtils
    </function-class>
    <function-signature>
      boolean areAnyGranted(java.lang.String)
    </function-signature>
  </function>
  <function>
    <function-name>areNotGranted</function-name>
    <function-class>
      org.springframework.faces.security.FaceletsAuthorizeTagUtils
    </function-class>
    <function-signature>
```

*Integrating with Other Frameworks*

```xml
          boolean areNotGranted(java.lang.String)
        </function-signature>
    </function>
    <function>
      <function-name>isAllowed</function-name>
      <function-class>
         org.springframework.faces.security.FaceletsAuthorizeTagUtils
      </function-class>
      <function-signature>
         boolean isAllowed(java.lang.String, java.lang.String)
      </function-signature>
    </function>
</facelet-taglib>
```

Next, update `web.xml` to inform JSF to use the custom tag library as follows:

richfaces/src/main/webapp/WEB-INF/web.xml

```xml
<context-param>
    <param-name>javax.faces.FACELETS_LIBRARIES</param-name>
    <param-value>/WEB-INF/springsecurity.taglib.xml</param-value>
</context-param>
```

You can then use the authorized tag just as we did in *Chapter 10, Fine-grained Access Control*. As shown in the `taglib` definition file, there are additional methods that are also supported. We have provided a few examples within the `richfaces` application. For example, the `index.xhtml` page demonstrates the use of the `ifAnyGranted` attribute:

```xml
<!DOCTYPE html PUBLIC "-//W3C//DTD XHTML 1.0 Transitional//EN"
  "http://www.w3.org/TR/xhtml1/DTD/xhtml1-transitional.dtd">
<html ...
    xmlns:sec="http://www.springframework.org/security/tags">
...
<sec:authorize ifAnyGranted="ROLE_ADMIN">
    This is an admin
</sec:authorize>
```

The expressions can be used in the rendered attribute of JSF components. For example, we can prevent a link from being rendered, as demonstrated by the `template.xhtml` in the sample application.

richfaces/src/main/webapp/templates/template.xhtml

```
<h:outputLink
  value="${request.contextPath}/j_spring_security_logout"
  rendered="#{sec:isAllowed('/j_spring_security_logout','GET')}">
    <f:verbatim>Logout</f:verbatim>
</h:outputLink>
```

This should provide a fairly good foundation for integrating with a JSF application. For more details about Spring Web Flow including JSF 1.2 taglib definition, consult the spring web flow project documentation at http://www.springsource.org/spring-web-flow.

# Google Web Toolkit (GWT) integration

There are a number of ways to set up a GWT-based application to communicate with the server. This section describes how to use Spring Security when utilizing GWT's `com.google.web.bindery.requestfactory.shared.RequestFactory`. We have chosen to use `RequestFactory`, because it is optimal for larger data-driven applications that are more likely to be found in real-world applications. Another benefit of using `RequestFactory` is that we can utilize the `ServiceLocator` interface to allow Spring to create our objects.

While the initial complexity of setting up `RequestFactory` can be difficult for developers; the long-term benefits of `RequestFactory` are likely to outweigh the initial complexity. For more information about `RequestFactory` and its benefits, refer to the GWT documentation at https://developers.google.com/web-toolkit/.

## Spring Roo and GWT

If you are new to using GWT or just want a rapid way to create GWT applications, Spring Roo provides scaffolding support for GWT and simplifies integrating Spring and GWT. In fact, the sample application that we will be securing was generated using Spring Roo. For additional information, refer to the Spring Roo documentation at http://www.springsource.org/spring-roo.

*Integrating with Other Frameworks*

# Spring Security setup

The first steps are the same as that of any application that you would want to run Spring Security in. If you do not remember the details of these steps, please revisit *Chapter 2, Getting Started with Spring Security*. The following is a high-level checklist of items that are covered in *Chapter 2, Getting Started with Spring Security* that will need to be done:

- Ensure that the necessary dependencies are added. No additional Spring or Spring Security dependencies are required for this sample.
- Update `web.xml` to refer to the necessary Spring configuration, `ContextLoaderListener` and `springSecurityFilterChain`.

# GwtAuthenticationEntryPoint

By now you should be getting rather familiar with Spring Security's `AuthenticationEntryPoint` interface. This is how Spring Security determines what to do when a user is not yet authenticated, but should be. Normally, Spring Security will redirect to a login page to prompt for a username and password. However, just as with JSF, we will need to customize the behavior to allow the GWT JavaScript library to understand that a login is required. You can view `GwtEntryPoint` that we have included with the chapter's sample code.

events/src/main/java/com/packtpub/springsecurity/web/authentication/GwtEntryPoint.java

```
public class GwtEntryPoint implements AuthenticationEntryPoint {
    private final String loginUrl = "/spring_security_login";

    public void commence(HttpServletRequest request,
            HttpServletResponse response,
            AuthenticationException authException)
            throws IOException, ServletException {

        String scheme = request.getScheme();
        String serverName = request.getServerName();
        int serverPort = request.getServerPort();
        String url = request.getContextPath() + loginUrl;

        String login =
                UrlUtils.buildFullRequestUrl(scheme, serverName,
     serverPort, url, null);
        response.setHeader("login", login);     response.
    sendError(HttpServletResponse.SC_UNAUTHORIZED);
    }
}
```

In this example, Spring Security will return an HTTP status of 401 and a custom header with the URL to redirect to in order for the user to log in. Just as with JSF, we do not use a redirect so that the JavaScript can process the response as a request to log in.

# GWT client updates

We now need to instruct GWT to interpret the response from our GwtEntryPoint into an action to send the user to the login page. All the code in this section occurs within the context of the GWT client code and is GWT-specific. You will notice that the code has no dependencies on Spring Security.

## AuthRequestTransport

We now need to instruct GWT to translate the response from our GwtEntryPoint into a notification that authentication is required.

> If you are familiar with the GWT examples, you may have noticed that we are using a similar pattern to integrate Spring Security that is demonstrated by the expenses sample provided with the GWT 2.4 distribution at http://google-web-toolkit.googlecode.com/files/gwt-2.4.0.zip. Studying the expenses sample will demonstrate that integrating with Spring Security is trivial once you understand the framework you are integrating with. Inspection of the expenses sample may also help if you are new to GWT and have trouble implementing some of the topics not covered in this chapter.

You can find the implementation in the following sample code:

events/src/main/java/com/packtpub/springsecurity/events/client/scaffold/request/AuthRequestTransport.java

```
  protected RequestCallback
    createRequestCallback(final TransportReceiver receiver) {
      final RequestCallback superCallback =
        super.createRequestCallback(receiver);
      return new AuthCallbackWrapper(superCallback, receiver);
  }

  private final class AuthCallbackWrapper implements RequestCallback {
    private final RequestCallback delegate;
    private final TransportReceiver receiver;

    public AuthCallbackWrapper(RequestCallback delegate,
      TransportReceiver receiver) {
      this.delegate = delegate;
```

```
    this.receiver = receiver;
  }

  public void onResponseReceived(Request request, Response response) {
    if (Response.SC_UNAUTHORIZED == response.getStatusCode()) {
      String loginUrl = response.getHeader("login");
      if (loginUrl != null) {
        boolean fatal = false;
        ServerFailure failure =
          new ServerFailure("Unauthenticated user", null, null,
            fatal);
        receiver.onTransportFailure(failure);
        eventBus.fireEvent(new AuthRequiredEvent(loginUrl));
        return;
      }
    }
    delegate.onResponseReceived(request, response);
  }

  public void onError(Request request, Throwable exception) {
    delegate.onError(request, exception);
  }
}
```

To translate the response we create a custom `RequestTransport` that wraps the standard `RequestCallback` to determine if a log in is required. If an `HTTP 401` error is found, we use `EventBus` to fire `AuthRequiredEvent` containing the login URL from the response headers. In order to simplify our code, we have extended the `DefaultRequestTransport` class and overridden the `createRequestCallback` method.

## AuthRequiredEvent

`AuthRequiredEvent` is a very simple `GwtEvent` that stores the login URL and provides hooks for listening to events from `EventBus` using `AuthRequiredEvent.Handler` implementation.

events/src/main/java/com/packtpub/springsecurity/events/client/scaffold/request/AuthRequiredEvent.java

```
  public class AuthRequiredEvent extends
    GwtEvent<AuthRequiredEvent.Handler> {
      public interface Handler extends EventHandler {
        void onAuthFailure(AuthRequiredEvent requestEvent);
```

```
        }

        // constructor and getters omitted
        private static final Type<Handler> TYPE = new Type<Handler>();

        private String loginUrl;

        public static HandlerRegistration register(EventBus eventBus,
                AuthRequiredEvent.Handler handler) {
            return eventBus.addHandler(TYPE, handler);
        }

        protected void dispatch(Handler handler) {
            handler.onAuthFailure(this);
        }
    }
```

## LoginOnAuthRequired

We need to listen for and take some sort of action when `AuthRequiredEvent` is fired. To do this, we will create an implementation of the `AuthRequiredEvent.Handler` interface that sets the URL with the login URL from the header when `AuthRequiredEvent` is received.

events/src/main/java/com/packtpub/springsecurity/events/client/scaffold/request/LoginOnAuthRequired.java

```
    public class LoginOnAuthRequired implements AuthRequiredEvent.Handler {

        public HandlerRegistration register(EventBus eventBus) {
            return AuthRequiredEvent.register(eventBus, this);
        }

        public void onAuthFailure(AuthRequiredEvent requestEvent) {
            Location.replace(requestEvent.getLoginUrl());
        }
    }
```

## Configuring GWT

Explaining all the details of how GWT works would be a book all by itself, and thus it is out of the scope of this book. Instead, we will simply go through the specific pieces necessary in order for GWT to use our customizations. If you are unfamiliar with the GWT architecture, we encourage you to review the GWT documentation.

Spring Roo generates a Gin module named ScaffoldModule, which is used for configuring, among other things, RequestFactory that should be used.

> **GWT INjection (GIN)** utilizes a subset of Google Guice to support automatic dependency injection to GWT client-side code. For details about Gin, visit their website at http://code.google.com/p/google-gin/.

We can update RequestFactoryProvider to utilize our custom AuthRequestTransport. The relevant updates are as follows:

events/src/main/java/com/packtpub/springsecurity/events/client/scaffold/ioc/ScaffoldModule.java

```java
public class ScaffoldModule ... {
    ...
    static class RequestFactoryProvider ... {
        ...
        public RequestFactoryProvider(EventBus eventBus) {
            requestFactory = GWT.create(ApplicationRequestFactory.class);
            AuthRequestTransport authReqTransport =
                new AuthRequestTransport(eventBus);
            EventSourceRequestTransport transport =
                new EventSourceRequestTransport(eventBus, authReqTransport);
            requestFactory.initialize(eventBus, transport);
        }
    }
}
```

We also need to instruct our GWT `EntryPoint` to utilize our `LoginOnAuthRequired` handler. In order to do this, we will update the `init` method of `ScaffoldDesktopApp` that invokes our `EntryPoint` named `Scaffold`. The following code provides relevant updates to register our `LoginOnAuthRequired` handler:

events/src/main/java/com/packtpub/springsecurity/events/client/scaffold/ScaffoldDesktopApp.java

```
public class ScaffoldDesktopApp extends ScaffoldApp {

    ...
    private void init() {
        ...
        // Check for Authentication failures or mismatches
        new LoginOnAuthRequired().register(eventBus);
        ...
    }
}
```

## Spring Security configuration

We will also need to ensure to update our Spring Security configuration in order to use our new security extensions.

> Observant readers will notice that our Spring Security configuration is in a different location than we have placed it in the past. We tried to minimize the changes between a standard Spring Roo application, which places the security configuration in the META-INF folder. The location does not matter so long as the configuration is referenced in web.xml.

events/src/main/resources/META-INF/spring/applicationContext-security.xml

```
<http entry-point-ref="entryPoint" ...>
  ...
  <form-login
    default-target-url="/ApplicationScaffold
    .html?gwt.codesvr=127.0.0.1:9997"
    always-use-default-target="true"/>
    <intercept-url pattern="/gwtRequest*/**"
      access="hasRole('ROLE_USER')" />
    <!-- <intercept-url pattern="/**"
      access="hasRole('ROLE_USER')" /> -->
</http>
<beans:bean id="entryPoint"
  class="com.packtpub.springsecurity.web
  .authentication.GwtEntryPoint"/>
```

*Integrating with Other Frameworks*

Our configuration updates `AuthenticationEntryPoint` to use our `GwtEntryPoint` that we created earlier. We ensure that our servlet is protected so that only users can request resources from it.

Start up the application and give the configuration a try. You can refer to the README file in the sample code for special instructions on how to run this application, since it is set up to run in Google App Engine.

> When you request the application, you will notice that the page flickers with the application prior to displaying the login page. This is because we are only protecting the `gwtRequest` URL and not the host page. In practice, we should protect the host page. However, this allows us to easily test scenarios where security integration is different from a standard application. For example, we need to process an AJAX request that requires a login differently from a standard application.

Since we are testing AJAX requests we have set our `default-target-url` attribute, and instructed Spring Security to always use it. Otherwise, when we log in, we would be redirected to a page that would be made with JavaScript. Observant readers have probably already realized that `DelegatingAuthenticationEntryPoint` could be used, as we did in the JSF section, to support a login page from an HTML request and a JSON request. If you are feeling ambitious, go ahead and try to update the application to use this strategy now.

## Method security

Since we utilized Spring Roo to generate this application, there are no special steps required to utilize method-level security. If you are not using Spring Roo in your application, the secret to integrating with GWT is creating a custom `ServiceLocator` that integrates with GWT's `RequestFactory`. A rather straightforward implementation is displayed as follows:

events/src/main/java/com/packtpub/springsecurity/events/server/CustomServiceLayerDecorator.java

```java
public class CustomServiceLayerDecorator extends
  ServiceLayerDecorator {
  public <T extends Locator<?, ?>> T createLocator(Class<T> clazz)
  {
    ApplicationContext context =
      WebApplicationContextUtils.getWebApplicationContext(
        CustomRequestFactoryServlet
        .getThreadLocalServletContext());
    return context.getBean(clazz);
  }
}
```

This is then tied together by our `CustomRequestFactoryServlet`, which extends the standard `RequestFactoryServlet` to inject our `CustomServiceLayerDecorator`.

events/src/main/java/com/packtpub/springsecurity/events/server/CustomRequestFactoryServlet.java

```
public class CustomRequestFactoryServlet extends
  RequestFactoryServlet {
  public CustomRequestFactoryServlet() {
    this(new DefaultExceptionHandler(), new
      CustomServiceLayerDecorator());
  }
  ...
}
```

Our `CustomRequestFactoryServlet` is configured in our `web.xml` file instead of the standard `RequestFactoryServlet`, which ensures that Spring is used to lookup the `Locator` implementations.

The `Locator` implementations object itself can then be annotated just as we did in *Chapter 10, Fine-grained Access Control*. For example, we could update our `EventLocator` to require `ROLE_ADMIN` as follows:

events/src/main/java/com/packtpub/springsecurity/events/server/locator/EventLocator.java

```
@PreAuthorize("hasRole('ROLE_ADMIN')")
public Event find(...) {
```

In fact, we can use all the techniques we used to restrict access to our services, as we did in *Chapter 10, Fine-grained Access Control*, *Chapter 11, Access Control Lists*, and *Chapter 12, Custom Authorization*. For details on how to implement authorization with Spring Security, refer back to the relevant chapters.

Go ahead and try to update the application to require `ROLE_ADMIN` for the `find` method. Then, authenticate with `user1@example.com/user1`. Spring Security will prevent the user from accessing the protected data.

Note that in order to gracefully handle the failure, we would need to customize how GWT handled the failed authorization attempt, similar to what we did for authentication required.

## Method security with Spring Roo

You may notice that there are not many methods on the `EventLocator`. This is because Spring Roo generates a `Event_Roo_Jpa_ActiveRecord` aspect, which adds the data access methods as static methods to the `Event` class itself. We do not want to modify the aspect generated by Roo, since it may get updated if we decide to add more fields. Instead, we can create our own aspect named `EventSecurity` that specifies our security annotations. The result would look similar to the following code snippet:

src/main/java/com/packtpub/springsecurity/events/server/domain/EventSecurity.aj

```
public aspect EventSecurity {
    declare @method: public long Event.countEvents(): @PreAuthorize("hasRole('ROLE_ADMIN')");
}
```

The `countEvents` method was added by the aspects generated by Spring Roo. We create our own aspect to add the `@PreAuthorize` annotation to the method introduced by Spring Roo. This gives us a very nice separation of concerns. Additionally, we can continue to use Spring Roo without accidentally removing our Security annotations.

## Authorization with AspectJ

We will need to make a few other changes in order for this to work. Spring Roo already weaves advice into the `Event` object using AspectJ at compile time. This means that we are not able to weave advice using proxy-based AOP as we did in *Chapter 13, Session Management*. Instead, we will configure Spring Security to use AspectJ compile-time weaving.

> AspectJ is an alternative to using proxy-based AOP as we saw in *Chapter 10, Fine-grained Access Control*. It is important to note that when adding security using AspectJ, we must add the security annotations to implementations and not interfaces. For further details about using AspectJ in your Spring projects, refer to the Spring reference at http://static.springsource.org/spring/docs/3.1.x/spring-framework-reference/html/.

The first step is to update our maven dependencies to include `spring-security-aspects` as follows:

events/pom.xml

```xml
<dependency>
    <groupId>org.springframework.security</groupId>
    <artifactId>spring-security-aspects</artifactId>
    <version>3.1.0.RELEASE</version>
</dependency>
```

The next step is to configure `aspectj-maven-plugin` to compile with the `spring-security-aspects.jar` file.

events/pom.xml

```xml
<plugin>
    <groupId>org.codehaus.mojo</groupId>
    <artifactId>aspectj-maven-plugin</artifactId>
    ...
    <configuration>
        ...
        <aspectLibraries>
            ...
            <aspectLibrary>
                <groupId>org.springframework.security</groupId>
                <artifactId>spring-security-aspects</artifactId>
            </aspectLibrary>
        </aspectLibraries>
    </configuration>
</plugin>
```

This configuration informs AspectJ to compile the additional code instructions that secure any method that has a Spring Security annotation on it. For our sample, this means that our `Events.countEvents()` method is secured.

We will also need to instruct Spring Security to use AspectJ to secure methods annotated with the security annotations. This is a simple change in our security configuration.

events/src/main/resources/META-INF/spring/applicationContext-security.xml

```xml
<global-method-security pre-post-annotations="enabled"
    mode="aspectj" />
```

Start up the application and you will find that now if you log in with `user1@example.com`/`user1`, it will give an error before an event is even added. This is because the `countEvents` method has now been secured. If you log in with `admin1@example.com`/`admin1`, you will be able to access the application without problems.

There are a number of features that still need to be implemented in our GWT. For example, we do not display a username, there is no way to log out, we do not handle access denied errors cleanly, and so on. However, these should be simple so long as you understand the basics of GWT, since they do not involve special knowledge of Spring Security that has not been covered in the book already.

# Summary

We have covered integrating Spring Security in a number of different frameworks and contexts, but there will always be some left uncovered. It is our belief that the concepts learned from this chapter combined with the rest of the book are a solid foundation for integrating with other frameworks. After reading this chapter, you should know how to do the following:

- Integrate Spring Security with Java Server Faces (JSF)
- Use Spring Security in AJAX-enabled web applications
- Secure Google Web Toolkit (GWT) applications using Spring Security
- Leverage Spring Security in a Spring Roo application and integrate Spring Security using AspectJ

In the next chapter, we will discuss how to migrate from Spring Security 2.0 to Spring Security 3.1.

# 15
# Migration to Spring Security 3.1

In this final chapter, we will review information relating to common migration issues when moving from Spring Security 2 to Spring Security 3. We'll spend much more time discussing the differences between Spring Security 2 and Spring Security 3, because this is what most users will struggle with. This is due to the fact that the updates from Spring Security 2 to Spring Security 3 contain a lot of non-passive refactoring.

At the end of the chapter, we will also highlight some of the new features that can be found in Spring Security 3.1. However, we do not explicitly cover changes from Spring Security 2 to Spring Security 3.1. This is because by explaining the differences between Spring Security 2 and Spring Security 3, users should be able to update to Spring Security 3.1 with ease, since the changes to Spring Security 3.1 are passive.

During the course of this chapter we'll:

- Review important enhancements in Spring Security 3
- Understand configuration changes required in your existing Spring
- Review Security 2 applications when moving them to Spring Security 3
- Illustrate the overall movement of important classes and packages in Spring Security 3
- Highlight some of the new features found in Spring Security 3.1

Once you have completed the review of this chapter, you will be in a good position to migrate an existing application from Spring Security 2 to Spring Security 3.

# Migrating from Spring Security 2

You may be planning to migrate an existing application to Spring Security 3.1, or trying to add functionality to a Spring Security 2 application and looking for guidance in the pages of this book. We'll try to address both of your concerns in this chapter.

First, we'll run through the important differences between Spring Security 2 and 3.1—both in terms of features and configuration. Second, we'll provide some guidance in mapping configuration or class name changes. These will better enable you to translate the examples in the book from Spring Security 3.1 back to Spring Security 2 (where applicable).

A very important migration note is that Spring Security 3+ mandates a migration to Spring Framework 3 and Java 5 (1.5) or greater. Be aware that in many cases, migrating these other components may have a greater impact on your application than the upgrade of Spring Security!

# Enhancements in Spring Security 3

Significant enhancements in Spring Security 3 over Spring Security 2 include the following:

- The addition of **Spring Expression Language (SpEL)** support for access declarations, both in URL patterns and method access specifications, which we covered in *Chapter 2, Getting Started with Spring Security* and *Chapter 10, Fine-grained Access Control*.

- Additional fine-grained configuration around authentication and accessing successes and failures.

- Enhanced capabilities of method access declaration, including annotation-based pre- and post-invocation access checks and filtering, as well as highly configurable security namespace XML declarations for custom backing bean behavior. These capabilities are examined in *Chapter 10, Fine-grained Access Control*.

- Fine-grained management of session access and concurrency control using the namespace, covered in *Chapter 13, Session Management*.

- Noteworthy revisions to the ACL module, with the removal of the legacy ACL code in `o.s.s.acl` and some important issues with the ACL framework are addressed. ACL configuration and support is reviewed in *Chapter 11, Access Control Lists*.

- Support for OpenID Attribute Exchange, and other general improvements to the robustness of OpenID, illustrated in *Chapter 8, Opening up to OpenID*.

Other more innocuous changes encompassed a general restructuring and cleaning up of the code base and the configuration of the framework, such that the overall structure and usage makes much more sense. The authors of Spring Security have made efforts to add extensibility where none previously existed, especially in the areas of login and URL redirection.

If you are already working in a Spring Security 2 environment, you may not find compelling reasons to upgrade if you aren't pushing the boundaries of the framework. However, if you have found limitations in the available extension points, code structure, or configurability of Spring Security 2, you'll welcome many of the minor changes that we discuss in detail in the remainder of this chapter.

# Changes to configuration in Spring Security 3

Many of the changes in Spring Security 3 will be visible in the namespace style of configuration. Although this chapter cannot cover all of the minor changes in detail, we'll try to cover those changes that will be most likely to affect you as you move to Spring Security 3.

# Rearranged AuthenticationManager configuration

The most obvious changes in Spring Security 3 deal with the configuration of the `AuthenticationManager` and any related `AuthenticationProvider` elements. In Spring Security 2, the `AuthenticationManager` and `AuthenticationProvider` configuration elements were completely disconnected—declaring an `AuthenticationProvider` didn't require any notion of an `AuthenticationManager` at all.

```
<authentication-provider>
    <jdbc-user-service data-source-ref="dataSource" />
</authentication-provider>
```

In Spring Security 2, it was possible to declare the `<authentication-manager>` element as a sibling of any `AuthenticationProvider`.

```
<authentication-manager alias="authManager"/>
<authentication-provider>
    <jdbc-user-service data-source-ref="dataSource"/>
</authentication-provider>
<ldap-authentication-provider server-ref="ldap://localhost:10389/"/>
```

## Migration to Spring Security 3.1

In Spring Security 3, all `AuthenticationProvider` elements must be the children of the `<authentication-manager>` element, so this would be rewritten as follows:

```
<authentication-manager alias="authManager">
    <authentication-provider>
        <jdbc-user-service data-source-ref="dataSource" />
    </authentication-provider>
    <ldap-authentication-provider server-ref= "ldap://localhost:10389/"/>
</authentication-manager>
```

Of course, this means that the `<authentication-manager>` element is now required in any security namespace configuration.

If you had defined a custom `AuthenticationProvider` in Spring Security 2, you would have decorated it with the `<custom-authentication-provider>` element as part of its bean definition. An example using the `CalendarUserAuthenticationProvider` from *Chapter 3, Custom Authentication*, is shown as follows:

```
<bean id="calendarUserAuthenticationProvider"
class="com.packtpub.springsecurity.authentication.
CalendarUserAuthenticationProvider">
    ...
    <security:custom-authentication-provider/>
</bean>
```

While moving this custom `AuthenticationProvider` to Spring Security 3, we would remove the decorator element and instead configure the `AuthenticationProvider` as we saw in *Chapter 3, Custom Authentication* using the `ref` attribute of the `<authentication-provider>` element as follows:

```
<authentication-manager alias="authenticationManager">
<authentication-provider ref= "calendarUserAuthenticationProvider"/>
</authentication-manager>
```

Of course, the source code of our custom provider would change due to class relocations and renaming in Spring Security 3—look later in the chapter for basic guidelines.

# New configuration syntax for session management options

In addition to continuing support for the session fixation and concurrency control features from prior versions of the framework, Spring Security 3 adds new configuration capabilities for customizing URLs and classes involved in session and concurrency control management, as described in detail in *Chapter 14, Integrating with Other Frameworks*. If your older application was configuring session fixation protection or concurrent session control, the configuration settings have a new home in the `<session-management>` directive of the `<http>` element.

In Spring Security 2, these options would be configured as follows:

```
<http ... session-fixation-protection="none">
    ...
    <concurrent-session-control max-sessions="1"
            exception-if-maximum-exceeded ="true"/>
</http>
```

The analogous configuration in Spring Security 3 removes the `session-fixation-protection` attribute from the `<http>` element, and consolidates as follows:

```
<http ...>
    <session-management session-fixation-protection="none">
        <concurrency-control max-sessions="1"
            error-if-maximum-exceeded ="true" />
    </session-management>
</http>
```

You can see that the new logical organization of these options is much more sensible and leaves room for future expansion.

# Changes to custom filter configuration

Many users of Spring Security 2 have developed custom authentication filters (or other filters to alter the flow of a secured request). As with custom authentication providers, such filters were previously indicated through decoration of a bean with the `<custom-filter>` element. This made it a bit difficult in some cases to tie the configuration of a filter directly to the Spring Security configuration.

*Migration to Spring Security 3.1*

Let's see an example of the configuration for the signed request header filter from *Chapter 6, Remember-me Services*, as applied to a Spring Security 2 environment.

```
<bean id="domainUsernamePasswordAuthenticationFilt
er" class="com.packtpub.springsecurity.web.authentication.
DomainUsernamePasswordAuthenticationFilter">
    ...
    <security:custom-filter
        after="AUTHENTICATION_PROCESSING_FILTER"/>
</bean>
```

Contrast this with the same configuration from Spring Security 3, and you can see that the bean definition and security wiring are done independently. The custom filter is declared within the `<http>` element as follows:

```
<http ...>
    ...
    <custom-filter ref="domainUsernamePasswordAuthenticationFilter"
        position="FORM_LOGIN_FILTER"/>
</http>
```

The bean declaration remains the same as in Spring Security 2, although, as you'd expect, the code for a custom filter is quite different. You can find a sample of a custom filter in *Chapter 3, Custom Authentication*.

Also, the logical filter names for some of the filters have changed in Spring Security 3. We present the list of changes in the following figure and a full table for reference is provided in *Appendix, Additional Reference Material*:

| Spring Security 2 | Spring Security 3 |
| --- | --- |
| SESSION_CONTEXT_INTEGRATION_FILTER | SECURITY_CONTEXT_FILTER |
| CAS_PROCESSING_FILTER | CAS_FILTER |
| AUTHENTICATION_PROCESSING_FILTER | FORM_LOGIN_FILTER |
| OPENID_PROCESSING_FILTER | OPENID_FILTER |
| BASIC_PROCESSING_FILTER | BASIC_AUTH_FILTER |
| NTLM_FILTER | Removed in Spring Security 3 |

You must make these changes in your configuration files in addition to relocating the `<custom-filter>` element.

# Changes to CustomAfterInvocationProvider

One final bean decoration from Spring Security 2 has been replaced by a straight, inline element reference, a `CustomAfterInvocationProvider` declared by the `<custom-after-invocation-provider>` element.

```
<bean id="customAfterInvocationProvider"
      class="com.packtpub.springsecurity.security
.CustomAfterInvocationProvider">
    <security:custom-after-invocation-provider/>
</bean>
```

Similar to what we saw with the other bean decorators from Spring Security 2, in Spring Security 3, this element has been moved within the `<global-method-security>` declaration, with a simple bean reference.

```
<global-method-security ...>
    <after-invocation-provider ref="customAfterInvocationProvider"/>
</global-method-security>
```

# Minor configuration changes

The following points will briefly state the additional changes in configuration attributes between Spring Security 2 and 3:

- While using the `auto-config` attribute in Spring Security 3, remember-me services are no longer configured by default. You will need to explicitly add the `<remember-me>` declaration within your `<http>` element.
- For LDAP configuration, the default value for `group-search-base-attribute` (used in LDAP authorities search) changed in Spring Security 3 from `ou=Groups` to an empty string (the root of the LDAP tree). We used this attribute in *Chapter 5, LDAP Directory Services*.
- The `<filter-invocation-definition-source>` decoration element, used for configuring a filter chain manually, has been renamed in Spring Security 3 to `<filter-security-metadata-source>`.
- The attribute `exception-if-maximum-exceeded`, related to the `<concurrent-session-control>` element, has been moved and renamed in Spring Security 3 to `error-if-maximum-exceeded`, on the new `<concurrency-control>` element.
- While using the in-memory DAO `UserDetailsService`, the `password` attribute is no longer required in Spring Security 3 when declaring users in the configuration file.

The remainder of the changes in the XML configuration dialect for Spring Security 3 represent additions to functionality, and will not cause migration issues for existing applications configured with the security namespace.

# Changes to packages and classes

Although in very straightforward applications of Spring Security 2, the locations of classes in packages may not matter, most applications of Spring Security don't end up being free from some kind of ties with the underlying code. So, we felt it would be helpful to point you in the direction of many of the overall package migrations and class renames that occurred between Spring Security 2 and 3.

Wherever possible, we have tried to map classes as accurately as we could—an overview of the major package moves are provided here, and (should you need it) a more comprehensive list is provided as a download with the source code. The following table indicates the biggest relocations of classes from Spring Security 2 to Spring Security 3—we've truncated the table to include the majority of changes you're likely to see:

| Number of classes | Location in Spring 2 | Location in Spring 3 |
| --- | --- | --- |
| 13 | o.s.s | o.s.s.authentication |
| 13 | o.s.s.acls | o.s.s.acls.model |
| 13 | o.s.s.event.authentication | o.s.s.authentication.event |
| 12 | o.s.s.vote | o.s.s.access.vote |
| 11 | o.s.s.ui.rememberme | o.s.s.authentication.rememberme |
| 10 | o.s.s.providers.jaas | o.s.s.authentication.jaas |
| 10 | o.s.s.securechannel | o.s.s.web.access.channel |
| 10 | o.s.s.userdetails.ldap | o.s.s.ldap.userdetails |
| 9 | o.s.s.providers.encoding | o.s.s.authentication.encoding |
| 8 | o.s.s.config | o.s.s.config.authentication |
| 8 | o.s.s.util | o.s.s.web.util |
| 7 | o.s.s.config | o.s.s.config.http |
| 7 | o.s.s.context | o.s.s.core.context |
| 7 | o.s.s.userdetails | o.s.s.core.userdetails |
| 6 | o.s.s | o.s.s.access |
| 6 | o.s.s.afterinvocation | o.s.s.acls.afterinvocation |

| Number of classes | Location in Spring 2 | Location in Spring 3 |
|---|---|---|
| 6 | o.s.s.event.authorization | o.s.s.access.event |
| 6 | o.s.s.util | o.s.s.web |
| 5 | o.s.s.annotation | o.s.s.access.annotation |
| 5 | o.s.s.authoritymapping | o.s.s.core.authority.mapping |
| 5 | o.s.s.providers | o.s.s.authentication |
| 5 | o.s.s.token | o.s.s.core.token |
| 5 | o.s.s.ui | o.s.s.web.authentication |

If it appears to you that classes have moved substantially, you are correct! Very few classes were untouched in the overall package reorganization as part of Spring Security 3. Hopefully, this overview points you in the right direction for classes that you may be looking for. Again, please consult the downloads for this chapter to review a detailed class-by-class mapping.

The benefit to this reorganization is that the entire framework is now much more modular, and fits into discrete JAR files containing only particular elements of functionality, as indicated in the following table (we used <version> in place of the release number):

| JAR name | Functionality |
|---|---|
| spring-security-acl-<version>.jar | ACL support (see *Chapter 12, Custom Authorization*) |
| spring-security-cas-client-<version>.jar * | CAS support (see *Chapter 9, Single Sign-on with Central Authentication Service*) |
| spring-security-config-<version>.jar | Namespace configuration support |
| spring-security-core-<version>.jar | Core framework and classes |
| spring-security-ldap-<version>.jar | LDAP support (see *Chapter 5, LDAP Directory Services*) |
| spring-security-openid-<version>.jar | OpenID support (see *Chapter 8, Opening Up To OpenID*) |
| spring-security-tablibs-<version>.jar | JSP Tag Library support (see *Chapter 2, Getting Started with Spring Security* and *Chapter 11, Access Control Lists*) |
| spring-security-web-<version>.jar | Web tier support |

> Note that the CAS JAR file was renamed to `spring-security-cas-<version>.jar` in Spring Security 3.1.
>
> This modularization means that, for example, it is possible to deploy Spring Security to a non-web application without any web dependencies (and might even be enough for your needs).

# Updates in Spring Security 3.1

Fortunately, the path from Spring Security 3 to Spring Security 3.1 is a rather passive one. There have been a number of updates that are found in Spring Security 3.1 that we have already gone over, but we will highlight some of the most significant features added in Spring Security 3.1 shown as follows:

- One of the biggest updates is that Spring Security 3.1 was the first release to allow multiple `<http>` elements as discussed in *Chapter 2, Getting Started with Spring Security*. For example, the following code would not be allowed in Spring Security 3:

```
<http security="none" pattern="/resources/**"/>
<http auto-config="true">
  <intercept-url pattern="/**" access="ROLE_USER"/>
</http>
```

- Spring Security 3.1 added support for using CAS to authenticate with RESTful services using proxy tickets as discussed in *Chapter 9, Single Sign-on with Central Authentication Service*.

- Support for stateless authentication as discussed in *Chapter 13, Session Management*.

- A Google App Engine sample application is now included in the sample applications. You can find additional information on the Spring Source blog post that introduces this new sample application at http://blog.springsource.org/2010/08/02/spring-security-in-google-app-engine/.

- Improved Active Directory LDAP support as discussed in *Chapter 5, LDAP Directory Services*.

Unfortunately, we did not have space for discussing Spring Security's JAAS integration. However, there is a JAAS sample application included in the Spring Security samples at http://static.springsource.org/spring-security/site/docs/3.1.x/reference/sample-apps.html. In fact, there is also excellent documentation about the JAAS integration available in the Spring Security reference at http://static.springsource.org/spring-security/site/docs/3.1.x/reference/jaas.html. When looking at the JAAS reference documentation, you will notice that starting with Spring Security 3.1, there is added support for using JAAS login modules using arbitrary JAAS configuration implementations. Spring Security 3.1 also adds the jaas-api-provision attribute to the <http> element that ensures that the JAAS Subject is populated for applications that may also rely on the JAAS Subject.

# Summary

This chapter reviewed the major and minor changes that you will find when upgrading an existing Spring Security 2 project to Spring Security 3. In this chapter we have:

- Reviewed the significant enhancements to the framework that are likely to motivate an upgrade
- Examined upgrade requirements, dependencies, and common types of code and configuration changes that will prevent applications from working post-upgrade
- Investigated (at a high level) the overall code-reorganization changes that the Spring Security authors made as part of codebase restructuring

If this is the first chapter you've read, we hope that you return to the rest of the book, using this chapter as a guide, to allow your upgrade to Spring Security 3 to proceed as smoothly as possible!

# Additional Reference Material

In this appendix, we will cover some reference material that we feel is helpful (and largely undocumented) but too comprehensive to insert into the text of the chapters.

## Getting started with the JBCP Calendar sample code

As we described in *Chapter 1*, *Anatomy of an Unsafe Application*, we have made the assumption that you have installed a **Java Development Kit** (**JDK**). You can download a JDK from Oracle's website, at http://www.oracle.com/technetwork/java/javase/downloads/index.html.

We also assume you have access to **Spring Tool Suite** (**STS**) 3.1.0. You can download STS from http://www.springsource.org/springsource-tool-suite-download. At the time of this writing, if you prefer not to fill out the form, you can accept the terms and select the link to take you to the download page.

> **Downloading the example code**
> You can download the example code files for all Packt books you have purchased from your account at http://www.PacktPub.com. If you purchased this book elsewhere, you can visit http://www.PacktPub.com/support and register to have the files e-mailed directly to you.

# Creating a new workspace

It is best to create a fresh workspace in order to minimize discrepancies with your environment. When you first open STS, it will prompt you for the workspace location. If you were previously using STS, you may need to use **File | Switch Workspace | Other** to create a new workspace. We recommend entering a workspace location that does NOT contain any spaces. For example:

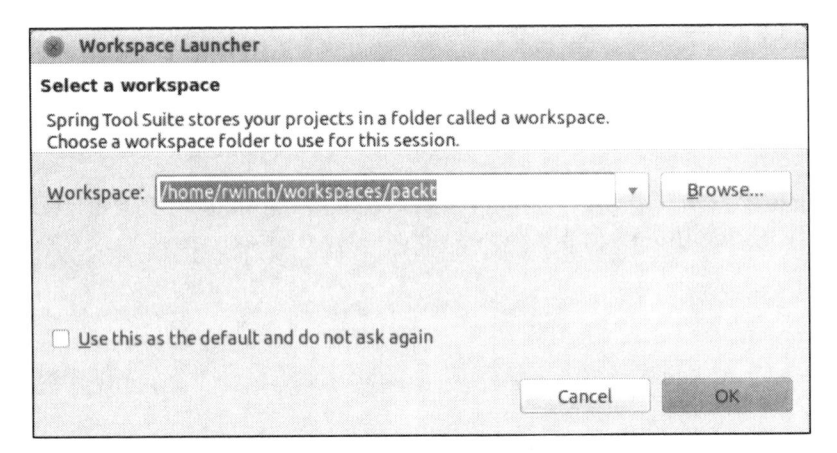

Once you have created a new workspace, you will want to exit the **Welcome** screen by clicking on the close button on the **Welcome** tab.

# Sample code structure

The sample code is structured in a `.zip` file and contains folders of Maven projects named `chapterNN.mm-project`, where `NN` is the chapter number and `mm` is the milestone within that chapter. For simplicity, we recommend that you extract the source to a path that does NOT contain any spaces. Each milestone is a checkpoint within the chapter and allows you to easily compare your code with the book's code. For example, `chapter02.03-calendar` contains milestone number `03` within *Chapter 2, Getting Started with Spring Security*, of the `Calendar` application.

In order to keep each chapter as independent as possible, most chapters in the book are built off of *Chapter 2, Getting Started with Spring Security* or *Chapter 3, Custom Authentication*. This means that, in most cases, you can read through *Chapter 3, Custom Authentication* and then skip around to the other parts of the book. However, this also means that it is important to start each chapter with the chapter's milestone 00 source code rather than continuing to work on the code from the previous chapter. This ensures that your code starts in the same place that the chapter does.

While you can get through the entire book without performing any of the steps, we recommend starting each chapter with milestone 00 and implementing the steps in the book. This will ensure that you get the most out of the book. You can use the milestone versions to copy large portions of code or to compare your code if you run into problems.

# Importing the samples

Starting with our fresh workspace, perform the following steps:

1. Go to **File** | **Import** and select **Existing Maven Projects**.

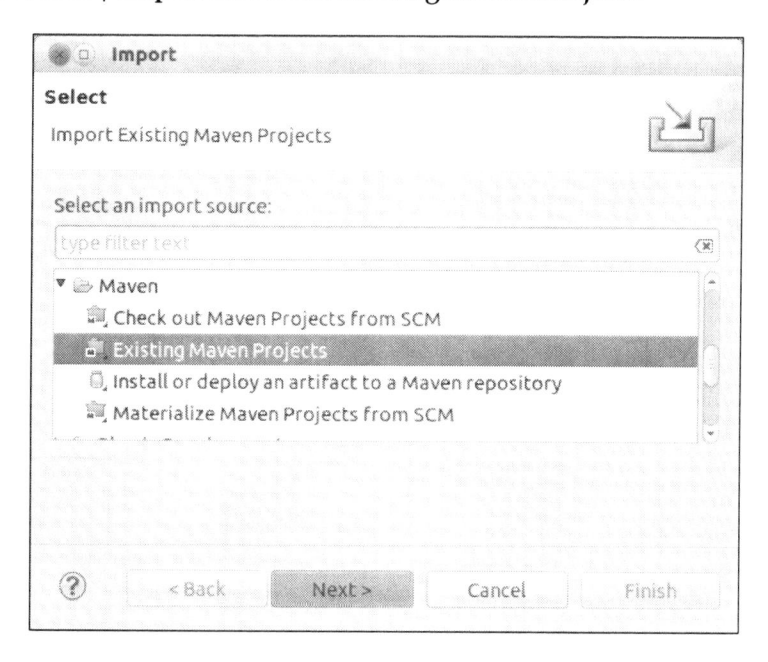

*Additional Reference Material*

2. Click on **Next**.

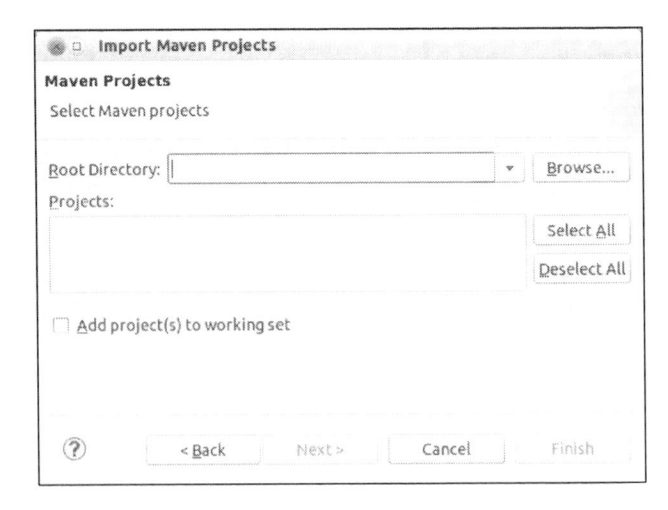

3. Browse to the location you exported the code to, and select the parent folder of the code.

    You will see all of the projects listed. You can select the projects you are interested in, or you can leave all of the projects selected. If you decide to import all of the projects, you can easily focus on the current chapter since the naming conventions will ensure the projects are sorted in the order that they are presented in, in the book.

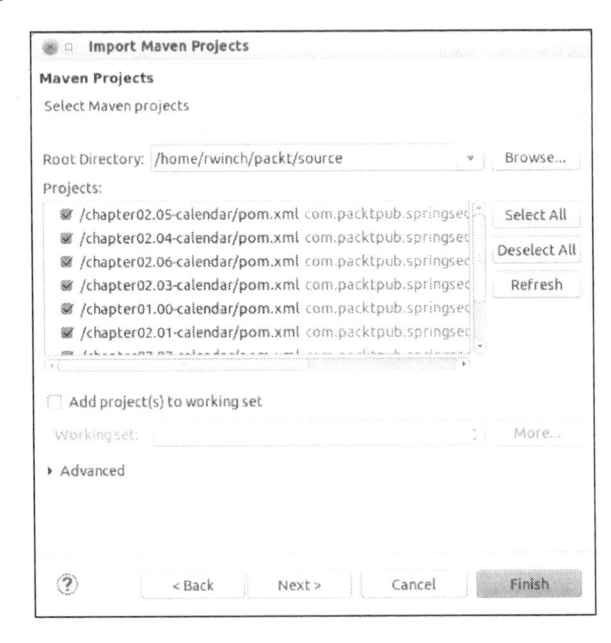

*Appendix*

4. Click on **Finish**. All of the selected projects will be imported. If you have not used Maven frequently, it will take a while to download your dependencies.

> An Internet connection is required to download the dependencies.

Updated instructions for running the projects will be found in the README file. This ensures that, as updates are made to STS, the code can still be built and run with the latest tools.

# Running the samples in Spring Tool Suite

There are a few things that are necessary in order to run the sample applications within Spring Tool Suite. In the following section, we have included instructions to run the samples on Tomcat within STS to get you started fast.

## Creating a Tomcat v7.0 server

In order to run the application, you will first need to configure a **server**. To do so, you will need to download the latest Tomcat 7 Core distribution and extract it onto your local hard drive. You can navigate to the Tomcat 7 Download page at http://tomcat.apache.org/download-70.cgi to download the latest Core distribution.

After you have extracted Tomcat 7 to your local hard drive (or if you have already done this), you will need to perform the following steps within STS:

1. Go to **File | New | Other...**.
2. Enter Server into the filter and select **Server** from the listing of **Wizards**:

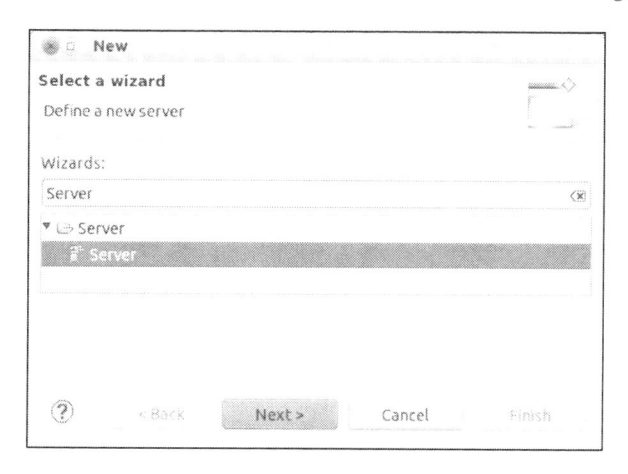

*Additional Reference Material*

3. Click on **Next**.
4. Under **Select the server type:**, enter `Tomcat v7`, and then select **Tomcat v7.0 Server**:

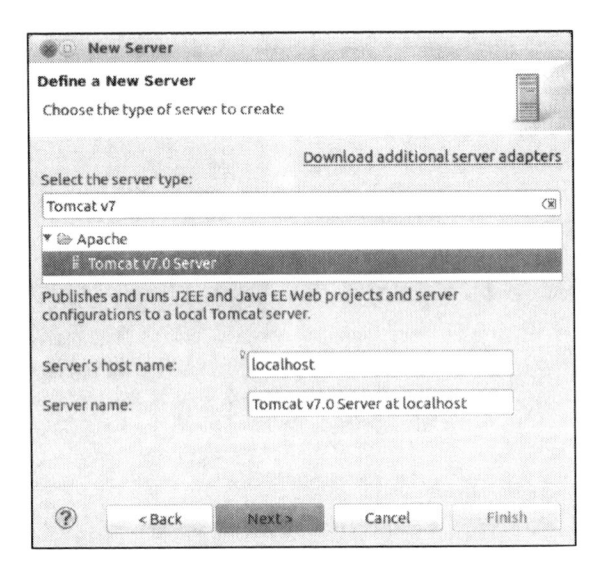

5. Click on **Next**.
6. Click on **Browse...** and navigate to the location you extracted the Tomcat 7 distribution to:

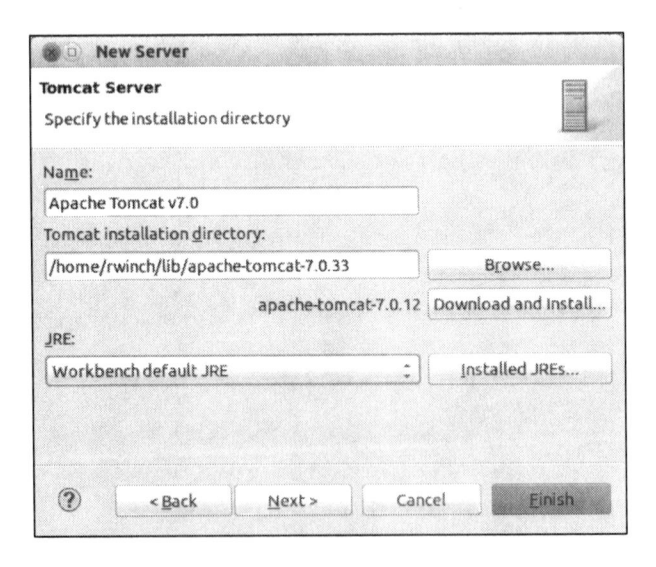

7. Click on **Finish**.

*Appendix*

You should now see the Tomcat v7.0 server at localhost in the **Servers** view. If you cannot find the **Servers** view, you can open it using **Window | Show View | Servers**:

## Starting the samples within Spring Tool Suite

Now that you have created a Tomcat v7.0 server within Spring Tool Suite, you can run the `Calendar` application on it. Use the following steps to run the `Calendar` application on the Tomcat v7.0 server we created in the previous section:

1. Locate the project that you wish to run on the server. For example, if you want to run the unsecured application from *Chapter 1, Anatomy of an Unsafe Application* you can select the `chapter01.00-calendar` project from **Package Explorer** view. If you cannot find the **Package Explorer** view, use **Window | Show View | Package Explorer**:

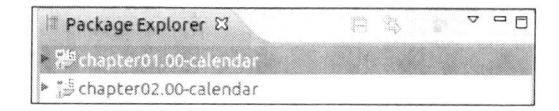

2. Right-click on the project and select **Run As | Run on Server**.
3. Select the server we created previously (**Tomcat v7.0 Server at localhost**):

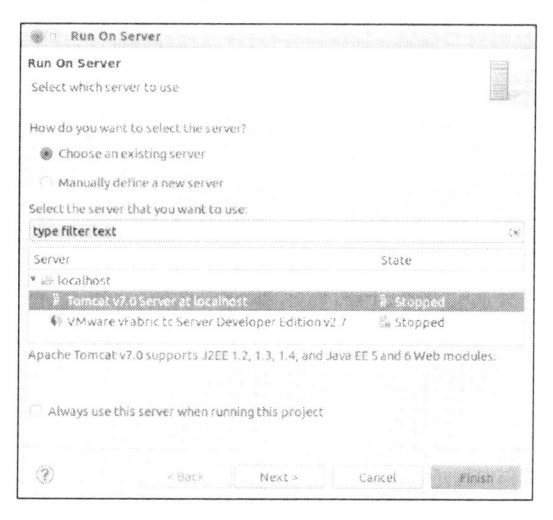

4. Click on **Finish**.

[ 407 ]

*Additional Reference Material*

Tomcat will be started and the application will be opened in STS. You can observe the standard output from Tomcat in the console view. If you have any issues running the application (that is, if you get a **Page Not Found** error), you will want to look in the console for any clues as to why the application did not start properly.

Many developers may want to copy the URL from STS and paste it into an external web browser such as Firefox in order to use browser plugins for development.

## Shutting down the samples within Spring Tool Suite

To shut down the application, you can select the Tomcat server in the **Servers** view and click on the **Stop** button (the red square):

## Removing previous versions of the samples

Since all the `Calendar` projects use the same context root, you must remove any other versions of the `Calendar` application before adding a new version. This can be done by using the following steps:

1. When it is stopped, right-click the server named **Tomcat v7.0 Server at localhost** from within the **Servers** view.
2. Select the **Add and Remove...** menu item:

*Appendix*

3. Click on the **Remove All...** button.
4. Click on **Finish**.

## Using HTTPS within Spring Tool Suite

Some of the chapters' sample code (that is, *Chapter 8, Opening up to OpenID* and *Chapter 9, Single Sign-on with Central Authentication Service*) require the use of HTTPS in order for the sample code to work. You can find the simplified steps for getting these samples working within Spring Tool Suite, as follows:

1. The source code included with the book contains a directory named `etc` that contains a file named `server.xml`. Open the `server.xml` file using your favorite text editor and copy the entire contents of the file to your clipboard.
2. Within the **Package Explorer** view of Spring Tool Suite, navigate to **Servers | Tomcat v7.0 Server at localhost-config**:

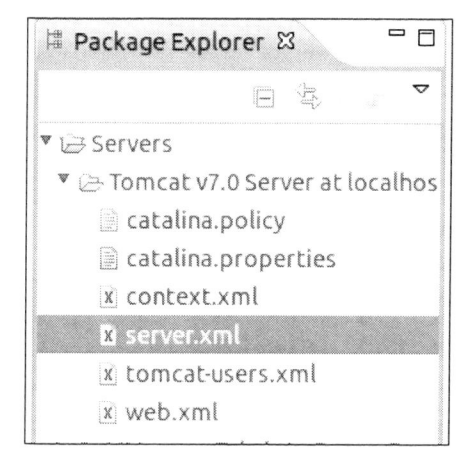

3. Open `server.xml`, select the **Source** tab, and paste the contents of your clipboard. For *Chapter 7, Client Certificate Authentication*, copy the contents of the `server-clientauth.xml` file instead.
4. Copy the path to the folder where you found the `server.xml` file.

[ 409 ]

*Additional Reference Material*

5. Open the `catalina.properties` file found in the same directory, and at the bottom, and add a new property with the name of `keystore.folder` and the value `<server-path>`, where `<server-path>` is the value you copied previously. For example, if `server.xml` from the sample source was found at `/home/rwinch/packt/source/etc/`, a new entry in `catalina.properties` should look similar to the following screenshot:

```
#tomcat.util.buf.StringCache.cacheSize=5000
keystore.folder=/home/rwinch/packt/source/etc/
```

Ensure that the value of `keystore.folder` ends with a / character.

The preceding steps are enough to get the server to run using HTTPS. However, we will need to ensure that when our application makes HTTPS calls to another application, the SSL handshake succeeds. To do this, we need to update the system properties on the JVM, as follows:

1. In the **Servers** view, double-click on the **Tomcat v7.0** server:
2. In the **Overview** tab, locate the **General Information** section and click on **Open launch configuration**:

```
General Information
Specify the host name and other common settings.
Server name:          Tomcat v7.0 Server at localhost
Host name:            localhost
Runtime Environment:  Apache Tomcat v7.0
Configuration path:   /Servers/Tomcat v7.0 Server at localhost-config
Open launch configuration
```

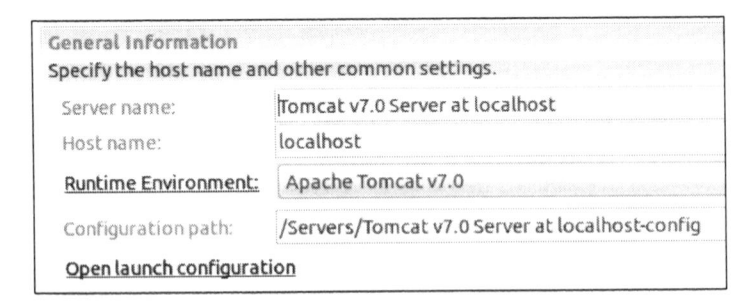

3. In the **Arguments** tab, locate the VM arguments and append the following system arguments to the end. Take care to replace `<server-path>` with the path to the folder the `server.xml` file was in, and ensure that there is a space before each entry, but no other spaces:

    `-Djavax.net.ssl.trustStore=<server-path>/tomcat.keystore`
    `-Djavax.net.ssl.trustStorePassword=changeit`

```
VM arguments:
packt/.metadata/.plugins/org.eclipse.wst.server.core/tmp0/wtpwebapps" -
Djava.endorsed.dirs="/home/rwinch/lib/apache-tomcat-7.0.33/endorsed" -
Djavax.net.ssl.trustStore=/home/rwinch/packt/source/etc/tomcat.keystore
-Djavax.net.ssl.trustStorePassword=changeit
```

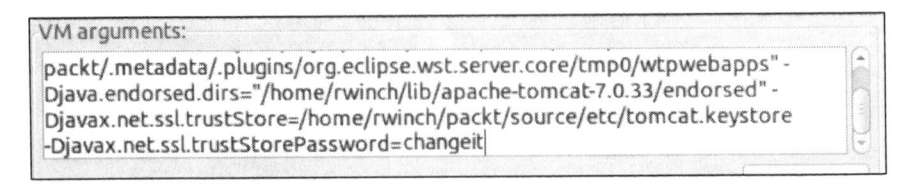

Now, when you run the sample code on the Tomcat Server within Spring Tool Suite, you can connect to `http://localhost:8080/calendar/` or to `https://localhost:8443/calendar/`.

# Default URLs processed by Spring Security

The following URLs are the default URLs (all of which can be customized through configuration) processed by the filters that are looked up in Spring Security's `FilterChainProxy`. Remember that these URLs are relative to your web application's context root.

- `/j_spring_security_check`: It is checked by `UsernamePasswordAuthenticationFilter` for username/password form authentication
- `/j_spring_openid_security_check`: It is checked by `OpenIDAuthenticationFilter` for OpenID returning authentication (from the OpenID provider)
- `/j_spring_cas_security_check`: It is used by CAS authentication upon return from the CAS SSO login
- `/spring_security_login`: It is the URL used by the `DefaultLoginPageGeneratingFilter` when configured to auto-generate a login page
- `/j_spring_security_logout`: It is used by `LogoutFilter` to detect a logout action
- `/saml/SSO`: It is used by the Spring Security SAML SSO extension, `SAMLProcessingFilter`, to process a SAML SSO sign-on request
- `/saml/logout`: It is used by the Spring Security SAML SSO extension, `SAMLLogoutFilter`, to process a SAML SSO sign-out request
- `/j_spring_security_switch_user`: It is used by `SwitchUserFilter` to switch users to another user
- `/j_spring_security_exit_user`: It is used to exit the switch user functionality

# Logical filter names migration reference

As discussed in *Chapter 15, Migration to Spring Security 3*, many of the logical filter names (used in the `<custom-filter>` element) change when we migrate from Spring Security 2 and 3. We present a full table of the changes here, to ease your migration of custom filter configuration from Spring Security 2 to 3:

| Spring Security 2 | Spring Security 3/3.1 |
| --- | --- |
| CHANNEL_FILTER | CHANNEL_FILTER |
| CONCURRENT_SESSION_FILTER | CONCURRENT_SESSION_FILTER |
| SESSION_CONTEXT_INTEGRATION_FILTER | SECURITY_CONTEXT_FILTER |
| LOGOUT_FILTER | LOGOUT_FILTER |
| PRE_AUTH_FILTER | PRE_AUTH_FILTER |
| CAS_PROCESSING_FILTER | CAS_FILTER |
| AUTHENTICATION_PROCESSING_FILTER | FORM_LOGIN_FILTER |
| OPENID_PROCESSING_FILTER | OPENID_FILTER |
| LOGIN_PAGE_FILTER is not present in Spring Security 2 | LOGIN_PAGE_FILTER |
| DIGEST_AUTH_FILTER is not present in Spring Security 2 | DIGEST_AUTH_FILTER |
| BASIC_PROCESSING_FILTER | BASIC_AUTH_FILTER |
| REQUEST_CACHE_FILTER is not present in Spring Security 2 | REQUEST_CACHE_FILTER |
| SERVLET_API_SUPPORT_FILTER | SERVLET_API_SUPPORT_FILTER |
| JAAS_API_SUPPORT_FILTER is not present in Spring Security 2 | JAAS_API_SUPPORT_FILTER (only in Spring Security 3.1) |
| REMEMBER_ME_FILTER | REMEMBER_ME_FILTER |
| ANONYMOUS_FILTER | ANONYMOUS_FILTER |
| SESSION_MANAGEMENT_FILTER is not present in Spring Security 2 | SESSION_MANAGEMENT_FILTER |
| EXCEPTION_TRANSLATION_FILTER | EXCEPTION_TRANSLATION_FILTER |
| NTLM_FILTER | NTLM_FILTER is removed in Spring Security 3 |
| FILTER_SECURITY_INTERCEPTOR | FILTER_SECURITY_INTERCEPTOR |
| SWITCH_USER_FILTER | SWITCH_USER_FILTER |

# HTTPS setup in Tomcat

In this section, we outline how to set up HTTPS in Tomcat to provide **Transport Layer Security** to our application. If you are just trying to run the sample applications, you can refer to documentation in the *Using HTTPS within Spring Tool Suite* section of this appendix.

## Generating a server certificate

If you do not already have a certificate, you must first generate one. If you wish, you can skip this step and use the `tomcat.keystore` file, which contains a certificate that is located in the `etc` directory in the book's sample source. Enter the following at the command prompt:

```
$ keytool -genkey -alias jbcpcalendar -keypass changeit -keyalg RSA \
            -keystore tomcat.keystore


Enter keystore password:
changeit
Re-enter new password:
changeit
What is your first and last name?

   [Unknown]:  localhost

What is the name of your organizational unit?

   [Unknown]:  JBCP Calendar

What is the name of your organization?

   [Unknown]:  JBCP

What is the name of your City or Locality?

   [Unknown]:  Anywhere

What is the name of your State or Province?
```

```
  [Unknown]:  IL
```

What is the two-letter country code for this unit?

```
  [Unknown]:  US


Is CN=localhost, OU=JBCP Calendar, O=JBCP, L=Anywhere, ST=IL, C=US
correct?

  [no]:  yes
```

Most of the values are self-explanatory, but you will want to ensure that the answer to "What is your first and last name?" is the host that you will be accessing your web application from. This is necessary to ensure that the SSL handshake will succeed.

You should now have a file in the current directory named `tomcat.keystore`. You can view its contents using the following command from within the same directory:

```
$ keytool -list -v -keystore tomcat.keystore
 Enter keystore password: changeit


Keystore type: JKS

Keystore provider: SUN




...


Alias name: jbcpcalendar

...
Owner: CN=localhost, OU=JBCP Calendar, O=JBCP, L=Anywhere, ST=IL, C=US


Issuer: CN=localhost, OU=JBCP Calendar, O=JBCP, L=Anywhere, ST=IL, C=US
```

> As you may have guessed, it is insecure to use `changeit` as a password as this is the default password used with many JDK implementations. In a production environment, you should use a secure password rather than something as simple as `changeit`.

For additional information about the keytool, refer to the documentation found on Oracle's website, at `http://docs.oracle.com/javase/6/docs/technotes/tools/solaris/keytool.html`. If you are having issues, you might also find the CAS SSL Troubleshooting and Reference Guide to be helpful (`https://wiki.jasig.org/display/CASUM/SSL+Troubleshooting+and+Reference+Guide`).

# Configuring Tomcat Connector to use SSL

In this section we will discuss how to configure a Tomcat 7 Connector to SSL.

1. Open the `server.xml` file that was included with the download of Tomcat 7. You can find this in the `conf` directory of your Tomcat server's home directory.

2. Find the following entry in your `server.xml` file:

   ```
   <!--
       <Connector port="8443" protocol="HTTP/1.1" SSLEnabled="true"
                  maxThreads="150" scheme="https" secure="true"
                  clientAuth="false" sslProtocol="TLS" />
   ```

3. Uncomment the Connector and modify the value of the `keystoreFile` attribute to be the location of the keystore from the previous section. Also ensure to update the value of the `keystorePass` attribute to be the password used when generating the keystore. An example is shown in the following code snippet, but ensure to update the values of both `keystoreFile` and `keystorePass`:

   ```
   <Connector port="8443" protocol="HTTP/1.1" SSLEnabled="true"
       maxThreads="150" scheme="https" secure="true"
       clientAuth="false" sslProtocol="TLS"
       keystoreFile="/home/rwinch/packt/etc/tomcat.keystore"
       keystorePass="changeit"/>
   ```

You should now be able to start Tomcat and access it at `https://localhost:8443/`. For more information on configuring SSL on Tomcat, refer to the SSL Configuration How-To at `http://tomcat.apache.org/tomcat-7.0-doc/ssl-howto.html`.

# Basic Tomcat SSL termination guide

This section is intended to help set up Tomcat to use SSL when using an SSL termination. The idea is that an external entity, such as a load balancer, is managing the SSL connection instead of Tomcat. This means that the connection from the client (that is, the web browser) to the load balancer is over HTTPS and is secured. The connection from the load balancer to Tomcat is over HTTP and insecure. For this sort of setup to provide any layer of security, the connection from the load balancer to Tomcat should be over a private network.

The problem this setup causes is that Tomcat will now believe that the client is using HTTP and thus redirects will be sent as though there is an HTTP connection. To get around this, you can modify the configuration to instruct Tomcat that it is behind a proxy server.

Starting with our configuration in *Chapter 7, Client Certificate Authentication*, we can add the following code to our connector:

server.xml

```
<Connector
    scheme="https"
    secure="true"
    proxyPort="443"
    proxyHost="example.com"
    port="8443"
    protocol="HTTP/1.1"
    redirectPort="443"
    maxThreads="750"
    connectionTimeout="20000" />
```

> The server.xml file can be found at TOMCAT_HOME/conf/server.xml. If you are interacting with Tomcat using Eclipse or Spring Tool Suite, you will find a project named Servers that contains server.xml. For example, if you are using Tomcat 7, the path in your Eclipse workspace might look similar to /Servers/Tomcat v7.0 Server at localhost-config/server.xml.

Note that there is no reference to a keystore because Tomcat does not manage the SSL connection. This setup will override the `HttpServletRequest` object to believe that the connection is HTTPS so that redirects are performed correctly. However, it will continue to accept HTTP connections. If the client can make an HTTP connection as well, a separate Connector can be created, one that does not include the HTTPS setup. The proxy server can then send requests to the appropriate connector depending on whether the original request was HTTP or HTTPS.

For more information, refer to the *Tomcat Proxy How To* documentation at `http://tomcat.apache.org/tomcat-7.0-doc/proxy-howto.html`. If you are working with a different application, you can refer to their documentation for working with proxy servers.

# Supplimentary materials

This section contains a listing of additional resources to technologies and concepts that are used throughout the book.

- **Java Development Kit Downloads**: `http://www.oracle.com/technetwork/java/javase/downloads/index.html`.
- **MVC Architecture**: `http://en.wikipedia.org/wiki/Model%E2%80%93view%E2%80%93controller`.
- **Spring Security Site**: `http://www.springsource.org/spring-security`. You can find links to the Spring Security Javadoc, Downloads, Source Code, and Reference from this link.
- **Spring Framework**: `http://www.springsource.org/spring-framework`. You can find links to the Spring Framework Javadoc, Downloads, Source Code, and Reference from this link.
- **Maven**: For more information about Maven, visit their site at `http://maven.apache.org/`. For more information about Maven Transitive dependencies, refer to the *Introduction to the Dependency Mechanism* documentation at `http://maven.apache.org/guides/introduction/introduction-to-dependency-mechanism.html#Transitive_Dependencies`.
- **Building with Gradle**: Spring Security builds with Gradle (`http://gradle.org/`) instead of using Maven. You can refer to the samples, for examples of how to build with Gradle at `http://static.springsource.org/spring-security/site/docs/3.1.x/reference/sample-apps.html`.

- **Object Relational Mapping (ORM)**: You can find more general information on Wikipedia at `http://en.wikipedia.org/wiki/Object-relational_mapping`. If you want more hands-on instruction, you may also be interested in the Hibernate (a common Java ORM Framework) documentation at `http://www.hibernate.org/`.

The following are UI technologies:

- **JSP**: You can find more information about JSPs on Oracle's site at `http://docs.oracle.com/javaee/5/tutorial/doc/bnagx.html`.
- **Thymeleaf**: It is a modern, tempting framework that provides an excellent alternative to JSPs. An additional benefit is that it provides support for both Spring and Spring Security out of the box. You can find more information about Thymeleaf at `http://www.thymeleaf.org`.
- **Freemarker**: It is a templating library that provides an alternative to JSPs. You can learn more about Freemarker at `http://freemarker.sourceforge.net`.
- **Velocity**: It is a templating library that provides an alternative to JSPs. You can learn more about Velocity at `http://velocity.apache.org`.

# Index

## Symbols

\<login-form> element 194
\<openid-login> element 194
\<password-encoder> element 100
@PostFilter method 279
@PreAuthorize annotation 270
@PreAuthorize method annotation 267
@PreFilter
  using, for pre-filtering collections 279
\<sec:authentication /> tag 45

## A

access control lists
  about 285
  in Spring Security 287, 288
  using, for business object security 286, 287
Access Control Lists. *See* ACL
AccountController
  configuring, for LdapUserDetailsService usage 130
ACL 285
AclAuthorizationStrategyImpl class 310
AclAuthorizationStrategyImpl
  object 298, 299
AclCache 297
AclPermissionCacheOptimizer
  object 294, 295
Active Directory (AD) 83
ActiveDirectoryLdapAuthentication
  Provider class 141
additional user details
  viewing 125-127
Administrators 83

advanced ACL topics
  about 302
  permissions, working 302-304
advanced LDAP
    configurationUserDetails 120
AffirmativeBased class 323
AJAX 366
AJAX supported customization
  about 366
  AjaxRequestMatcher 367, 368
  DelegatingAuthenticationEntryPoint 366, 367
  Http401EntryPoint 368
  JavaScript updates 370
  updates, configuring 368-370
All Events page 17, 281
alternate password attribute
  using 127, 128
always attribute 360
AOP auto-proxying 336
Apache Directory Studio 111
application technology
  about 11
  audit results, reviewing 12, 13
  sample code, integrating 11
AspectJ 365, 386
Asynchronous JavaScript and XML. *See* AJAX
attribute name, LDAP
  about 106
  c 106
  cn 106
  dc 106
  o 106
  ou 106

uid 107
userPassword 107
**authentication**
  about 14, 15
  credential-based authentication 14
  hardware authentication 14
  two-factor authentication 14
**AuthenticationException exception 66**
**authentication-failure-url attribute 194**
**authentication method**
  AuthenticationProvider 74
  SecurityContextHolder 73
  UserDetailsService 74
**AuthenticationProvider method 74**
**authorization**
  about 16-18
  unauthorized user 18
**auto-config attribute 395**
**AX**
  attributes 204
  enabling, in Spring Security OpenID 207

# B

**Base64-encoded string 146**
**basic CAS integration configuration**
  about 220
  authenticity proving, CasAuthenticationProvider interface used 226-229
  CasAuthenticationEntryPoint interface, adding 223, 224
  CAS ServiceProperties object, creating 222
  CAS ticket verification, enabling 224, 225
**basic configuration, Spring Security ACL support**
  ACL tables, adding to H2 database 290, 292
  Maven dependencies 289
  simple target scenario, defining 289
**BasicLookupStrategy object 296**
**basic password comparison**
  configuring 121
**basic Tomcat SSL termination guide 416, 417**
**bcrypt hashing function 99**
**BeanPostProcessor 330**

**bind authentication**
  versus password comparison 120
**Birthday Party event 289**
**boolean userExists() method 81**
**bootstrap process 92**
**business tier security**
  about 266
  aspect-oriented programming, using 271, 272
  bean decorators, using 273, 274
  interface-based proxies 269
  JSR-250 compliant standardized rules 270, 271
  method authorization types, comparing 279
  method data security, role-based filtering used 277, 278
  method parameters 275, 276
  method security, validating 268, 269
  post authorization 267
  preauthorization 267
  @PreAuthorize method annotation, adding 267
  @PreFilter, using 279
  returned values 277
  Spring Security, instructing 268
  Spring's @Secured annotation, using 271
  techniques 267

# C

**calendar application 8**
**CalendarPermissionEvaluator**
  about 338
  configuring 340
**CalendarService**
  about 50, 51
  securing 340
**CalendarUser 50**
**CAS**
  about 215, 216
  capabilities 250
  configuring 220
  high-level authentication flow 216, 217
  installing 220
  required dependencies 219

Spring Security 218
**CAS assertion**
  attribute retrieval, using 250
  GrantedAuthorityFromAssertion
      AttributesUserDetailsService 248
  ticket authentication, SAML 1.1 used 249
  UserDetails, getting 248
**CAS capabilities 250**
**CAS Maven WAR Overlay 240**
**CAS Server**
  about 240
  CAS Maven WAR Overlay 240
  configuring, to LDAP server 242-245
  internal authentication, working 241, 242
**Central Authentication Service.** *See* **CAS**
**certificate authority (CA) 168**
**certificate key pair, importing**
  Chrome, using 173
  Firefox, using 172
  Internet Explorer, using 173, 174
**certificates 166**
**checkForPrincipalChanges property 186**
**client certificate authentication**
  about 166
  bean-based configuration capabilities,
      adding 185
  configuring, in Spring Security 176
  configuring, security namespace used 177
  configuring, Spring Beans used 184-187
  cons 187
  implementing, considerations 187
  pros 187
  Spring Security certificate authentication
      178
  working 166-168
**client certificate authentication**
    **infrastructure**
  about 168
  certificate key pair, importing 172
  client certificate key pair, creating 169, 170
  public key infrastructure 168, 169
  setting up 168
  testing 174, 175
  Tomcat trust store, configuring 170-172
  troubleshooting 175
**Common Table Expression.** *See* **CTE**

**concurrent session control**
  about 351
  authentication, preventing 354
  benefits 355-359
  common problems 353
  configuring 350
  expired session redirect,
      configuring 352, 353
  per user count, restricting 349
  testing 352
**conditional rendering**
  SpEL, using 261
  Spring Security tag library, using 259
  URL access rules based 259, 260
**configuration changes, Spring Security 3**
  custom filter configuration,
      changes 393, 394
  rearranged AuthenticationManager
      configuration 391, 392
  session management options, configuration
      syntax 393
**connector 171**
**ConsensusBased class 323**
**ConsoleAuditLogger object 298**
**ContextLoaderListener 27**
**continueFilterChainOnUnsuccessful**
    **Authentication property 186**
**controller logic**
  used, for content rendering 262
  WebInvocationPrivilegeEvaluator 263
**cookie 144**
**countEvents method 386**
**createRequestCallback method 380**
**credential-based authentication 14**
**Cross-Site Scripting.** *See* **XSS**
**cryptographic hash algorithms 147**
**CTE 296**
**custom ACL permission**
  declaring 305-307
  JSPs, enabling with Spring Security JSP tag
      307-309
**CustomAfterInvocationProvider changes**
  about 395
  minor changes 395
**custom AuthenticationProvider object**
  authentication, parameters used 66

CalendarUserAuthenticationProvider 64, 65
CalendarUserAuthenticationProvider, configuring 66
configuration, updating 70-73
creating 63
domain, adding to page 68
DomainUsernamePasswordAuthenticationFilter 69, 70
DomainUsernamePasswordAuthenticationToken 67
updating 68
**custom expression, creating**
CustomWebSecurityExpressionHandler 333
CustomWebSecurityExpressionHandler, using 334
CustomWebSecurityExpressionRoot 331, 332
method security, working 334-337
**custom PermissionEvaluator**
benefits 341
CalendarPermissionEvaluator 338, 339
CalendarPermissionEvaluator, configuring 340
CalendarService, securing 340
creating 338
custom PermissionEvaluator, benefits 341
**custom schema support**
about 86
CalendarUser authority SQL 88
custom authorities, inserting 88
dbcUserDetailsManager, configuring 89, 90
JDBC SQL queries, determining 87
SQL scripts, updating 87
**custom UserDetailsService object**
about 58
CalendarUserDetails 61, 62
CalendarUserDetailsService 58, 59
custom user attributes, displaying 63
references, removing to UserDetailsManager 60, 61
SpringSecurityUserContext simplifications 62
UserDetailsService, configuring 60

CustomWebSecurityExpressionHandler
about 333
configuring 334
CustomWebSecurityExpressionRoot 331

# D

database credential security 18
DebugFilter
about 362
using, for debug 361
default-target-url attribute 194
deleteSession method 359
dependencies
updating 107, 108
digest 147
DispatcherServlet 28, 29
distinguished name (DN) 105, 169
domain component 105

# E

Ehcache 297
EhCacheBasedAclCache object 297
embedded LDAP
troubleshooting 110, 111
embedded LDAP integration
configuring 108
Event 50
Events.countEvents() method 387
expression-based authorization 43
external LDAP server
integrating with 131
external LDAP server reference
configuring 132

# F

Fiddler2 176
FilterChainProxy 30
FilterInvocationServiceSecurityMetadataSource 328, 329
fine-grained authorization 253
Firecookie 146
Freemarker 418

# G

GBAC. *See* Group-Based Access Control
GBAC JDBC scripts
  about 84
  group authority mappings 85
  group-based schema 85
getEvents() method 308
Google provider 207
Google Web Toolkit. *See* GWT
Gradle
  URL 417
GrantedAuthorityFromAssertion
    AttributesUserDetailsService 248
Group-based access control
  about 82, 83
  configuring 83
  GBAC JDBC scripts, utilizing 84
  JdbcUserDetailsManager, configuring 83
group-role-attribute 117
groups 82
group-search-base 117
group-search-base attribute 116
group-search-filter attribute 117
GWT
  about 365
  and Spring Roo 377
  client updates 379
  configuring 382, 383
  GwtAuthenticationEntryPoint 378, 379
  integrating 377
  method security 384
  Spring Security, configuring 383, 384
  Spring Security setup 378
GWT client updates
  about 379
  AuthRequestTransport 379, 380
  AuthRequiredEvent 380
  LoginOnAuthRequired 381
GWT INjection (GIN) 382

# H

H2 website 77
hardware authentication 14
hashing 91

Health Insurance Privacy and
    Accountability Act. *See* HIPAA
high-level authentication flow, CAS
  about 218
  actions 216
  CAS server 216
  CAS Services 216
  diagram 217
HIPAA 13
Http401EntryPoint 368
HttpServletRequest.getPrincipal() method
    262
HttpSession
  using 359, 360
HTTPS setup, Tomcat
  server certificate, generating 413-415
  Tomcat Connector, configuring 415

# I

ifAnyGranted attribute 377
ifRequired attribute 360
invalidateSessionOn PrincipalChange
    property 186

# J

jaas-api-provision attribute 399
JAAS 20
Java Authentication and Authorization
    Service. *See* JAAS
Java Development Kit. *See* JDK
Java Development Kit Downloads
  URL 417
Java EE role mapping 181
Java EE Security 20
Java Key Store (JKS) 171
Java Secure Socket Extension (JSSE) 171
Java Server Faces. *See* JSF
JBCP calendar application architecture
  about 10, 11
  data access layer 11
  diagram 10
  service layer 11
  web layer 10
JBCP Calendar architecture
  about 49

CalendarService 50, 51
CalendarUser 50
Event 50
SpringSecurityUserContext 52, 54
UserContext 51
**JBCP Calendar sample code**
  new workspace, creating 402
  sample code structure 402, 403
  samples, importing 403-405
  samples, running in Spring Tool Suite 405
  starting with 401
**JBCP LDAP users 120**
**JDBC authentication, Spring Security**
  default user schema 79
  H2 database, using 77
  H2-embedded database, configuring 77, 78
  JDBC scripts 77
  JDBC UserDetailsManager, configuring 79
  required dependencies 76
  user authorities, defining 80
  users, defining 80
**JdbcMutableAclService object 295**
**JdbcRequestConfigMappingService 326-328**
**JDK 401**
**Jim Bob Circle Pants Online Calendar 8**
**JSF**
  about 365
  AJAX supported customization 366
  custom login page, creating 371-374
  integrating with 366
  proxy-based authorization 371
  Spring Security Facelets tag library 374-377
**JSP 418**

# K

**keystorePass attribute 415**

# L

**LDAP**
  about 104, 105
  attribute name 105-107
  binding anonymously 113, 114
  binding, as user 115
  overview 103, 104
  user, searching for 114
  using, as UserDetailsService 128

**LDAP attribute names**
  userPassword 107
**LDAP attributes**
  CAS Services, authorizing 247
  mapping, to CAS attributes 246, 247
  returning, in CAS Response 246
**LDAP authentication process**
  user role membership, determining 118
**LdapAuthenticationProvider**
  configuring 133, 134
**LDAP bean configuration 132**
**LDAP password encoding 122**
**LDAP server reference**
  configuring 109
  LDAP AuthenticationProviderNext
    interface, configuring 110
**LdapShaPasswordEncoder class 93**
**LdapUserDetailsService**
  configuring 129
  configuring, for AccountController 130
**Lightweight Directory Access Protocol.** *See*
    **LDAP**
**loadUserByUsername method 62**
**logical filter names**
  migration reference 412
**login-page attribute 34, 194**
**login-processing-url attribute 194**
**logout method 159**

# M

**Maven**
  URL 417
**maven dependencies 254**
**Md4PasswordEncoderPasswordEncode
    class 93**
**MD5 147**
**Md5PasswordEncoderPassword class 93**
**method-level security**
  about 265
  annotation-based security 280
  business tier, securing 266
  layers, securing 266
  Spring MVC controllers 280
**method-level security, on Spring MVC
    controllers**
  about 280-282

class-based proxies 282
class-based proxies, limitations 282, 283
**method security**
  method parameters, incorporating 275, 276
  returned values, incorporating 277
  rules, aspect-oriented programming used 271, 272
  rules, bean decorators used 273, 274
  Spring's @Secured annotation, using 271
**MethodSecurityExpressionRoot 258**
**method security, GWT**
  about 384, 385
  authorizing, AspectJ used 386, 387
  with Spring Roo 386
**Microsoft Active Directory 131**
  integrating, via LDAP 137-139
**migrateSession attribute 349**
**mutable ACL**
  about 310
  adding, to newly created Events 311, 312
**MVC Architecture**
  URL 417
**myOpenID provider 207**

# N

never attribute 361
newSession attribute 349
new user login, SecurityContextHolder used
  SignupController, updating 57, 58
  steps 56, 57
  users, managing 55, 56

# O

object identity 287
Object Relational Mapping. *See* ORM
**OpenID**
  adding, to JBCP Calendar login screen 191
  dependencies 192, 193
  providers, list 191
  replay attacks 212
  response forgery 212
  security 212
  signing up 191
**openid4java project**
  URL 191

openid.association field 199
**OpenID authentication**
  enabling, with Spring Security 191
**OpenID authentication feature 128**
openid.claimed_id field 198
openid_identifier field 193
openid.identifier field 199
**OpenID identifiers**
  resolving 198
openid.op_endpoint field 198
**OpenID Provider**
  attributes, configuring 207
  automatic redirection 210
  conditional automatic redirection 211, 212
openid.response_nonce field 199
openid.sig field 199
**OpenID studies**
  URL 210
**OpenID support**
  configuring, in Spring Security 193
**Open Web Application Security Project.** *See* OWASP
**ORM 9, 418**
o.s.s.access.vote.AuthenticatedVoter class 324
o.s.s.access.vote.RoleVoter class 324
o.s.s.crypto.bcrypt.BCryptPasswordEncoder class 99
o.s.s.crypto.password.NoOpPasswordEncoder class 99
**OWASP 344**
**OWASP Top Ten article 151**

# P

**page-level authorization**
  conditional rendering, Spring Security tag library used 259
  configuring 264, 265
  content, rendering, controller logic used 261
**page-level authorization 258**
**password comparison**
  versus bind authentication 120
**password comparison authenticator**
  drawbacks 123, 124

password encoding configuration
  best practices 98
  new user's password, hashing 96
  PasswordEncoder awareness, creating 94
  PasswordEncoder, configuring 94
  security, checking 97
  stored password 97
  stored passwords, hashing 95, 96
path attribute 42
Payment Card Industry Data Security Standard. *See* PCI
PCI 13
persistent-based remember-me feature
  about 152
  configuring 154
  database-backed persistent, security 155
  data source, initializing 153
  expired remember-me sessions, cleaning up 156
  Series identifier 154
  SQL adding, for remember-me schema creation 153
  Token value 155
  using 153
  working 154, 155
Personally Identifiable Information. *See* PII
Person Directory 247
PGT 234
PGTIOU 234
PGT URL 234
PII 13
PlaintextPasswordEncoder class 93
postconditions 267
preAuthenticatedUserDetailsService property 186
preconditions 267
Proxy Granting Ticket. *See* PGT
Proxy Granting Ticket I Owe You. *See* PGTIOU
proxy ticket authentication, stateless services
  about 234-236
  configuring 235
  proxy tickets, authenticating 238, 240
  proxy tickets, using 237
Proxy Ticket callback URL. *See* PGT URL
Proxy Tickets (PT) 236

## Q

queryAttributeMapping property 247

## R

rainbow tables 98, 147
Read permission 304
registration process, OpenID
  implementing 200
  OpenIDAuthenticationUserDetailsService, registering 200-202
remember-me
  about 143
  authorization rules 151, 152
  dependencies 144
  Persistent-based 144
  security feature 150, 151
  Token-based 144
remember-me architecture
  about 158, 159
  custom cookie 163
  HTTP parameter names 163
  user lifecycle 159
  using 160-162
remember me option 193
remember-me schema
  created, SQL adding 153
  data source, initializing 153
remember-me session cookies
  configuration 149
replay attacks 212
request authorization
  about 319, 320
  access decision aggregation, configuring 323
  customizing 326
  decide 320
  decision types 321
  supports 320
request authorization customization
  <intercept-url> elements, removing 331
  about 326
  access control, to URLs 326
  custom expression, creating 331
  FilterInvocationServiceSecurity MetadataSource 328, 329
  JdbcRequestConfigMappingService 326-328

namespace configuration, extending 330, 331
requestee 287
requestor 287
response forgery 212
resultAttributeMapping property 247
Richfaces 367
role-based authorization 39, 40, 42
role discovery
  delegating, to UserDetailsService 135, 136
role-prefix attribute 117
roles 16

# S

salt 98
SAML 249
sample application 8-10
sample running, in Spring Tool Suite
  HTTPS, using 409-411
  previous version, removing 408, 409
  sample, shutting down 408
  sample, starting 407, 408
  Tomcat v7.0 server, creating 405-407
secure passwords
  about 91
  configuring 91, 92
secure passwords configuration
  PasswordEncoder 92, 93
  password encoding configuration 94
  rules 91
Secure Sockets Layer. *See* SSL
Security Assertion Markup Language. *See* SAML
security audit 8
SecurityContextHolder
  using, for new user login 54
SecurityContextHolder method 73
SecurityExpressionHandler configuration
  about 293
  AclAuthorizationStrategyImpl 298, 299
  AclPermissionCacheOptimizer 294, 295
  BasicLookupStrategy 296, 297
  ConsoleAuditLogger 298
  EhCacheBasedAclCache 297
  JdbcMutableAclService 295
Security Identity (SID) 287

security namespace
  used, for client certificate authentication configuration 177
security namespace style 26
security pruning 277
security trimming 277
sensitive information 19
server 405
session fixation attacks
  about 344, 345
  preventing, Spring Security used 345, 346
  simulating 346-348
session fixation protection
  configuring 343, 344
  session fixation attacks 344, 345
  session fixation attacks, preventing with Spring Security 345, 346
  session fixation attacks, simulating 346, 348
  session-fixation-protection options, comparing 349
sessions method 358
SHA 122
ShaPasswordEncoderPasswordEncoder class 93
simple ACL entry
  creating 299-301
single logout
  about 230
  clustered environment 233
  configuring 231, 232
  steps 230
Site Minder-style authentication 181
SpEL integration
  about 254
  expressions 255, 256
  WebSecurityExpressionRoot 256
SpEL logical operators 152
Spring 3.1
  using 24
Spring Beans
  used, for client certificate authentication configuring 184-187
Spring Expression Language (SpEL) 43
Spring LDAP authentication
  Apache Directory Studio, using 113
  user credentials, authenticating 112, 113
  working 111

Spring LDAP module 105
Spring MVC controllers
  method security 280
Spring Roo
  GWT 377
Spring Security
  about 21, 22, 98
  CAS 218
  certificate information, using 178
  client certificate authentication,
      configuring 176
  common issues 31, 32
  configuration, updating 99
  configuring, for HttpSession usage 360, 361
  DebugFilter, debugging 361, 362
  DefaultCalendarUserService, updating 100
  default URLs 411
  dependencies, updating 22, 23
  existing passwords, migrating 99
  goals 32, 33
  HttpSession 360
  HttpSession, using 359, 360
  JDBC authentication, using 75
  need for 20
  OpenID authentication, enabling 191
  OpenID support, configuring 193
  salted passwords 101
  sample application, importing 22
  secured application, running 31
  Spring 3.1, using 23, 24
  Spring Security 3.1, using 23, 24
  web.xml file, updating 27
  XML configuration file,
      implementing 24, 26
Spring Security 2
  migrating from 390
Spring Security 2 to Spring Security 3 class
    relocation 396-398
Spring Security 2 to Spring Security 3 login
    filter name
  changes 394
Spring Security 3
  configuration changes 391
  enhancements 390, 391
Spring Security 3.1
  built-In Active Directory support 140, 141
  updates 398, 399
  using, for security concern addressal 19
Spring Security 3.1 migration 389
Spring Security ACL
  using 316
Spring Security certificate authentication
  dual-mode authentication,
      supporting 182, 183
  unauthenticated requests,
      handling 181, 182
  working 178-181
Spring Security JIRA repository 315
Spring Security login
  customizing 33, 34
Spring Security login customization
  about 33-36
  authentication information,
      displaying 44, 45
  expression-based authorization 43
  logout, configuring 36, 37
  redirection problem 38
  role-based authorization 39-42
  user login 46, 47
Spring Security OpenID
  AX, enabling 207
Spring Security Site
  URL 417
SpringSecurityUserContext 52, 54
Spring Tool Suite 78. *See* STS
  samples, running 405
SSHA 122
SSL 166
stateless attribute 361
stateless services
  proxy ticket authentication 234
  proxy ticket authentication, configuring
      235
STS 401

# T

telephoneNumber attribute 128
throwExceptionWhenTokenRejected
    property 186
Thymeleaf 418
TLS 166
token-based remember-me
  about 144, 145

configuration directives 149, 150
configuring 145, 146
MD5 147
signature 148, 149
working 146
**token-validity-seconds attributes 149**
**Tomcat**
 HTTPS setup 413
**Transport Layer Security** *See* **TLS**
**transport-level protection 19**
**two-factor authentication 14**
**typical ACL deployment**
 about 312
 issues 316
 performance modelling 313-315
 scalability 313-315

# U

**uid attribute 139**
**UI technologies**
 Freemarker 418
 JSP 418
 Thymeleaf 418
 Velocity 418
**UnanimousBased access decision manager**
 configuring 323, 324
 expression-based request authorization 325
**UnanimousBased class 323**
**Uniform Resource Identifier (URI) 190**
**UserContext 51**
**user credentials**
 authenticating 112, 113
**UserDetails**
 additional attributes, mapping 119
 getting, from CAS assertion 245
**UserDetailsContextMapper**
 configuring 124
 implicit configuration 124
**UserDetailsManager**
 about 81
 features 81
**UserDetailsService**
 role discovery, delegating to 135, 136

**UserDetailsService method 74**
**user role membership**
 about 116
 determining 116, 117
 roles determining, with Apache Directory Studio 117, 118
**Users 83**

# V

**Velocity 418**
**Verisign's OpenID SeatBelt**
 URL 193
**void changePassword() method 81**
**void createUser() method 81**
**void deleteUser() method 81**
**void updateUser() method 81**

# W

**web.xml file, updating**
 ContextLoaderListener 27
 DispatcherServlet 28, 29
 FilterChainProxy 30
**WebInvocationPrivilegeEvaluator 263**
**WebSecurityExpressionRoot**
 about 256
 hasIpAddress, using 257
 MethodSecurityExpressionRoot 258
 WebSecurityExpressionRoot, using 256
**WebSphere integration 181**
**web.xml file, updating**
 ContextLoaderListener 27
 DispatcherServlet 28, 29
 FilterChainProxy 30
**Wireshark 176**

# X

**XSS 150, 348**

# Z

**Zytrax OpenLDAP book 106**

# Thank you for buying
# Spring Security 3.1

## About Packt Publishing

Packt, pronounced 'packed', published its first book "*Mastering phpMyAdmin for Effective MySQL Management*" in April 2004 and subsequently continued to specialize in publishing highly focused books on specific technologies and solutions.

Our books and publications share the experiences of your fellow IT professionals in adapting and customizing today's systems, applications, and frameworks. Our solution based books give you the knowledge and power to customize the software and technologies you're using to get the job done. Packt books are more specific and less general than the IT books you have seen in the past. Our unique business model allows us to bring you more focused information, giving you more of what you need to know, and less of what you don't.

Packt is a modern, yet unique publishing company, which focuses on producing quality, cutting-edge books for communities of developers, administrators, and newbies alike. For more information, please visit our website: www.packtpub.com.

## About Packt Open Source

In 2010, Packt launched two new brands, Packt Open Source and Packt Enterprise, in order to continue its focus on specialization. This book is part of the Packt Open Source brand, home to books published on software built around Open Source licences, and offering information to anybody from advanced developers to budding web designers. The Open Source brand also runs Packt's Open Source Royalty Scheme, by which Packt gives a royalty to each Open Source project about whose software a book is sold.

## Writing for Packt

We welcome all inquiries from people who are interested in authoring. Book proposals should be sent to author@packtpub.com. If your book idea is still at an early stage and you would like to discuss it first before writing a formal book proposal, contact us; one of our commissioning editors will get in touch with you.

We're not just looking for published authors; if you have strong technical skills but no writing experience, our experienced editors can help you develop a writing career, or simply get some additional reward for your expertise.

## Spring Security 3

ISBN: 978-1-84719-974-4  Paperback: 396 pages

Secure your web applications against malicious intruders with this easy to follow practical guide

1. Make your web applications impenetrable
2. Implement authentication and authorization of users
3. Integrate Spring Security 3 with common external security providers
4. Packed full with concrete, simple, and concise examples

## JSF 2.0 Cookbook

ISBN: 978-1-84719-952-2  Paperback: 396 pages

Over 100 simple but incredibly effective recipes for taking control of your JSF applications

1. Discover JSF 2.0 features through complete examples
2. Put in action important JSF frameworks, such as Apache MyFaces Core, Trinidad, Tomahawk, RichFaces Core, Sandbox and so on
3. Develop JSF projects under NetBeans/Glassfish v3 Prelude and Eclipse/JBoss AS
4. Part of Packt's Cookbook series: Each recipe is a carefully organized sequence of instructions to complete the task as efficiently as possible

Please check **www.PacktPub.com** for information on our titles

## JasperReports for Java Developers

ISBN: 978-1-90481-190-9  Paperback: 344 pages

Create, Design, Format, and Export Reports with the World's Most Popular Java Reporting Library

1. Get started with JasperReports, and develop the skills to get the most from it
2. Create, design, format, and export reports
3. Generate report data from a wide range of datasources
4. Integrate Jasper Reports with Spring, Hibernate, Java Server Faces, or Struts

## Liferay Portal Systems Development

ISBN: 978-1-84951-598-6  Paperback: 546 pages

Build dynamic, content-rich, and social systems on top of Liferay

1. Use Liferay tools (CMS, WCM, collaborative API and social API) to create your own Web sites and WAP sites with hands-on examples
2. Customize Liferay portal using JSR-286 portlets, hooks, themes, layout templates, webs plugins, and diverse portlet bridges
3. Build your own websites with kernel features such as indexing, workflow, staging, scheduling, messaging, polling, tracking, auditing, reporting and more

Please check **www.PacktPub.com** for information on our titles

CPSIA information can be obtained at www.ICGtesting.com
Printed in the USA
BVOW06s0248170913

331387BV00004B/56/P